Managing the Small Construction Business

A Hands-On Guide

second edition

A Journal of Light Construction Book

First printing: August 1992 Second printing: November 1999

Editorial Director: Steven Bliss
Production Editor: Josie Masterson-Glen
Article Editors: Sal Alfano, Clayton DeKorne, David Dobbs, Don Jackson, Marylee MacDonald, Paul Spring, Wendy Talarico

Production Manager: Theresa Emerson
Graphic Designer: Annie Clark

International Standard Book Number: 1-928580-00-9
Library of Congress Catalog Card Number: 99 075375
Printed in the United States of America

A *Journal of Light Construction* Book
The *Journal of Light Construction* is a tradename of Builderburg Group, Inc.

Builderburg Group, Inc.
932 West Main Street
Richmond, VT 05477

Introduction

"He was a crackerjack carpenter, but not much of a businessman..." How many times have we heard that epitaph recited about the owner of a failed construction business?

The reason is simple: Most small-volume contractors come up through the trades. By the time they take the big step of hanging out a shingle as an independent contractor, most have mastered the technical aspects of their craft. That's how they achieved enough success to launch a business in the first place.

Yet precious few have had sufficient experience on the business side to estimate accurately, negotiate a fair contract, keep adequate records, and deal with the myriad new relationships they must now master—with customers, employees, and subcontractors, not to mention architects, accountants, lawyers, and code officials.

So it comes as no surprise that so many builders find their progress impeded by one management snag after another, and why so few last long enough to learn on the job the business skills they need to survive.

This book is an attempt to guide the newcomer—as well as the small-volume builder who is growing his business—around many of these management pitfalls. Because no one person has all the answers, we've chosen selections from a variety of successful contractors—each writing about the aspects of the business he or she knows best.

Not every idea will apply to your business—each company faces its own market conditions and each person has his own business style. But the wealth of real-world experience boiled down in these 300-plus pages should provide any contractor with a head start in tackling the key problems he's likely to face.

Finally, our thanks to the many authors who contributed to this book. Nearly all are working contractors who have taken time out of their busy schedules to share their experience and hard-won business wisdom with the new folks coming up through the ranks. They're definitely a group worth listening to.

Steven Bliss
Editorial Director

Table of Contents

Chapter 1: Quality Control

Chapter 2: Customer Relations

Chapter 3: Personnel

Chapter 4: Subcontractors

Chapter 14: Design/Build

Chapter 15: Risk Management

Chapter 16: Conflict Resolution

Chapter 17: Diversification

Chapter 1

Quality Control

Managing for Quality Control

Build quality homes by relying on good construction details and good customer relations

Many builders believe that "quality" homes mean expensive cabinets and appliances, and lavish square footage. But quality has as much to do with how you put the parts of a building together as it does with the products you choose. We've all seen top-quality products ruined by a lousy job of installation. And we've seen low-priced products installed properly and operating satisfactorily.

As a builder in Santa Fe, N.M., I've sought to establish a reputation as a quality contractor. That has forced me to think about how to control quality on my jobs. My ultimate goal is to turn over a blemish-free building to clients, and to know that they're happy about their new home and satisfied that the building process has gone smoothly. On that final walk-through, I don't want them holding back my check, and I don't want a long punchlist.

To avoid problems, I focus on two areas. First, I pay attention to building details during both design and construction. And second, I maintain good communication with clients and tend to the little things that concern them.

Author Mike Chapman, at left, and super Andy Barbero review construction details as a house nears completion. Barbero is on site every day to assure that the subs do high-quality work.

Keeping On Top of the Details

Nothing creates more quality-control problems than poorly planned construction details. To prevent problems, we have our construction super review and critique the plans as soon as the designer finishes them. He looks for unclear details, errors, and omissions. For instance, he might see that the plan would work better if we brought the water in at another location or reversed the swing on a door.

After any further revisions, we hold a preconstruction meeting. The estimator, the designer, the construction superintendent, and the salesperson discuss the orientation on the lot, key construction details, specialty items, and specific, critical dimensions — such as the size of an alcove for an unusual piece of furniture.

After any further revisions, the super puts together a set of plans for each sub, marking notes in red pencil. The electrician's plans might be marked to highlight the exact placement of an electrical outlet or to indicate a floor outlet that needs to be roughed in before we pour the slab. Marking up each set of plans also helps the super think through the job and plan any difficult sequences.

The same subs. We build 15 to 20 custom homes a year, but unlike many companies with that volume, we do a large part of our work through subs, using the same ones on every job. We often hold open houses in houses under construction, and potential customers will say, "We want the same framer to build our house." With the same subs, we can guarantee uniform quality.

We don't deviate from our list unless the sub can't schedule us at the time we need him. This means the sub doesn't

Punch-List Pointers

Since you the builder are held responsible for the defects typically found in new homes, it's important for you to identify any problems at a predelivery walk-through. Now is the time for you and the buyer to determine who is responsible for fixing each problem. The day of the closing, or the day before, is best for this.

With pencil and master checklist in hand, go through the house room by room, checking trim, wall surfaces, ceilings, floors, paint, glass, appliances, mechanical systems, hardware, etc., finishing up in the basement or garage. Then proceed outside to examine the exterior of the house.

If possible, have the buyer sign a simple statement acknowledging that he and you have walked through the house on a particular day and identified the items that need attention. Explain that the signature represents only an acknowledgement of the walk-through, not a release for items not on the list that might require attention in the future.

Although some buyers refuse to sign, I've already accomplished what I have set out to do: to determine between us in a businesslike manner, what, if anything at this point, requires attention; to acknowledge which items are my responsibility to correct; and to educate the buyers about their responsibilities for maintenance and care. Few new home buyers are brazen enough to ask me to repair damage they've done after the inspection, such as vinyl floor covering torn when the fridge was delivered.

Some builders fear subjecting their homes to such scrutiny, viewing it only as an opportunity for the buyer to nit-pick. But don't worry, the house indeed will be scrutinized at some point in time, and the problems will have to be corrected sooner or later. It's best to do so while you are still in control of the project.

Do Your Homework

The key to a successful builder/buyer walk-through is preparation. You should do a thorough private inspection prior to the walk-through with the client. Don't allow too much time between the two inspections or new unexpected problems might crop up; but allow enough time for you to solve the problems prior to the final walk-through. Don't leave anything out, for the sooner a defect is found, the easier it is to fix it—particularly if the subs are still handy. Follow a simple, but thorough, master checklist. Don't forget to include a shakedown of all appliances and mechanical systems.

As builders, we can almost forecast the items. We've seen the same things crop up, year after year, punch list after punch list: door striker plates that don't engage, cabinet drawers that are obstructed, garage door locks out of alignment, double-hung windows stuck with paint, and always, that tub-drain toggle.

By correcting these items well prior to the closing or completion dates, things get done your way, rather than someone else's way later on. Your way is always less expensive and just as good.

Never allow a buyer to move into a house before closing. Besides the fact that the buyer could damage the home during this time, it's just bad practice. Suppose the finances don't work out, for example. It's hard to remove someone once they are in. When the customer has title to the land, of course, this is especially difficult to prevent, so protect yourself contractually as best you can.

Finally, arrange the closing or passing of title to the completed house well prior to the expiration of the purchase and sales agreement. This leaves you in a more comfortable position to postpone the delivery and closing if something requires attention at the eleventh hour. It also puts you in a better bargaining position in the event of a dispute, such as a buyer's demand to hold back money for punch-list items.

Even So...It Won't Be Perfect

Despite your best efforts, like death and taxes there always will be some punch-list items that crop up after the closing and the buyer's occupancy. Respond to the items on the list promptly. We want to avoid any unnecessary inconvenience to our buyer. In addition, we want to take corrective measures before the problem compounds — for example, a leaky toilet seal can develop into a ruined floor.

If a delay is necessary in responding to a callback, keep the buyer posted so he doesn't feel ignored. Most buyers are reasonably patient if they know they are not being given the run-around.

Any serious difference of opinion should be followed up with careful documentation and a letter. If you should ever have to go to court, the very first question asked will be, "Has there been any correspondence?"

By Richard Lind, a builder in the Wellesley, Mass., area.

have to come in with the low bid on every job. When you take the low bidder and you bring your customer to the job site, you could be embarrassed by the quality of the sub's work.

The key to getting good work from subs is to communicate with them when they begin a job and every time they arrive at the site. I want a super on site a half hour every morning and every afternoon. If the sub is going to show up at 1:00 p.m., the super will be there to go through the plans. We don't allow subs or crew foremen to solve problems without the superintendent's approval.

We also have to make sure subs remember how we want the work done. For instance, with drywall I want a three-coat job, not two coats. Without a reminder from the super, details can slip a sub's mind, particularly if he's rushing off to another job. Also, unsupervised subs may take short cuts or forget change orders.

Correcting mistakes costs time and money. If the drywall contractor leaves behind sloppy work, like a buildup of joint compound in the corners, and the painters coat the walls, someone has to come back and clean up after the drywall repair and touch up the paint.

Our superintendents do walk-throughs with the subs and provide them with a punchlist of items needing attention. The subs know they're going to get our next job if they give us good service. And we expect to get taken care of.

We'll also use payments to get a sub's attention if he's behind on service calls. Subs sometimes try to collect on jobs that aren't quite finished. The boss comes over to the office to pick up the check; maybe his crew told him they were done. But our super knows when a sub has to come back to finish up. He holds the check until the work is done completely and correctly.

The Customer Is Always Right

We place just as much emphasis on building a quality relationship with the customer as we do on building a quality house. To start this relationship on the right foot, we use a contract that clearly spells out our expectations of quality and defines how disagreements will be resolved.

Contract for quality. Customers often create problems because they're nervous about quality, but not knowledgeable about construction. This can lead to clients holding back money during payouts or until the final punchlist is complete. Haggling about payouts will cause a relationship to quickly deteriorate. If you have a qualified buyer and can get construction loans, you can avoid this problem by dealing with the bank, not the client. The bank is an objective third party that knows how to evaluate job completion.

However, if the clients are financing the job themselves, we insist that the inspection be conducted by a third party who will authorize the release of funds. This can be an appraiser or an independent construction inspector. I include in the price the cost of hiring an inspector—generally $50 each time.

Our contract is written so that our draws coincide with the start of each phase of construction rather than the end. Many contractors specify a draw at the completion of framing. However, this can create a delay in getting paid if you've substantially completed the framing, but still have kitchen soffits to fur out or a few studs to straighten. If you time your draw to the start of insulation instead of the end of framing, the customer can see when the insulation installers begin their work, and you're not in a rush to get every last bit of framing complete in order to meet Friday's payroll. Working this way reassures the customer that construction is proceeding on schedule, and helps maintain the good relationship that is so important.

Scheduled walk-throughs. We require customers to attend five walk-throughs and to sign off on the specs and plans at each stage:

1. We rough stake the home prior to excavation and have the client walk the site with us to check for proper location, orientation, and tree removal.
2. Before we begin framing, we do a "color consultation," having the client take a final look at colors for tile, paint, and cabinets. This gives us time to order all necessary items.
3. We also do a framing walk-through where we review window and door placements and electrical, TV, and telephone outlets. We also use this oppor-

Hand-crafted features, such as the rounded stucco chimney (left) and exterior scrollwork (right), require good subs and close supervision.

tunity to point out quality features the customer is not likely to recognize, such as caulked sill plates.

4. Once the drywall is hung and taped, we do a "trim" walk-through. Linen closet shelves and master closet shelving and rod heights are very important to our customers, so we mark them on the wall with the customer prior to installation.
5. During a final walk-through, the customer checks out the house completely. We prepare a detailed punchlist of items that need attention.

A key factor in quality control is having enough time to complete the house. To make sure you have enough time, you'll need to extend the completion date if there are legitimate delays. Walk-throughs are a good time to identify problems that might cause delays. On the foundation walk-through, for instance, we might say, "We lost a couple of days because of rain." Or when showing customers the framing, we'll say, "The windows didn't come in yet, and that will set us back a couple of days."

If the customer makes changes, our contract lets us add an appropriate number of days to the schedule. If these changes are made after the framing stage, we double the markup.

You really have to level with the client if you aren't going to make the move-in date. Don't wait until a week before closing to discover you're three weeks behind. Rushing to complete a house by an arbitrary date will detract from its quality.

Regular meetings. In addition to walk-throughs, we meet regularly with clients to resolve questions before they grow into problems. We keep the meetings short and precise. With difficult or worrisome clients, we schedule weekly meetings between them and our superintendent. These generally take only 10 to 15 minutes and can turn difficult clients into easy ones. The clients come with a list of questions that they're prepared to discuss, and the discussion gives us a chance to educate them about how we work.

Solving problems. When a problem arises, I call the clients and ask them to meet me at the job site. For example, on a recent job I ordered interior doors with operable transoms, but the doors showed up with fixed transoms. Although the door company had made the mistake, I knew I'd have to pull the doors after the clients moved in, which was only three weeks away.

I explained the problem and told the clients how I was going to solve it. But I didn't wait until the week before they were supposed to move in to spring this on them. Communication early on is the key.

Clients often worry more about minor details than about big ones. If you don't meet with them frequently, you may not notice these red flags. On one house, for example, we had an undersized beam. This was a serious structural problem that meant pulling the beam and replacing it. But when I called the client, he said, "Okay, but what are you going to do about the telephone outlet in the den?" That was really bugging him, because he thought I was going to forget it.

Punchlist performance. I schedule a final walk-through two days before closing and correct anything on the punchlist the next day. I like to close immediately after the job is complete. I won't sign a contract that has a retainage clause because I feel that shows a lack of trust between the client and builder, and trust is something I work very hard to maintain. If a guy wants to withhold $2,000 because of a late microwave delivery and a door that needs to be planed down, that's the last guy I want to get involved with.

We've already caught most of the problems by the time we do the final walk-through. The job super has already worked up a punchlist with the drywall sub, painter, electrician, hvac sub, and cabinet installers and has corrected any problems. The super has also checked appliances.

Items the client comes up with are usually minor and can be taken care of in a day. They typically involve finish details, such as a drawer or door that sticks, paint touch-up, missing caulk, or a carpet that's tucked up.

Warranty follow-up. If you've done a good job during construction and have finished the home as agreed, then the warranty items should be minor. We call the customer thirty days after closing to do one more walk-through and make any necessary corrections. We try to complete all the work in a one- or two-day period within two weeks after the walk-through. The work is generally scheduled with the customer the day of the walk-through.

We also pay attention to nonwarranty items that concern the customer. For instance, I had a gentleman explain to me that his toilet was too small. I was tempted to suggest that he sit down and I would take my tape out and see where the problem was. Instead, I told him we would see what was available. We found a larger one and replaced it, but at his expense. After all, he had signed the spec sheet. He appreciated the help with what he felt was a major problem, and I had a satisfied client.

Maintenance tips. Customers sometimes feel they haven't been given a quality house when little problems begin to show up after construction — drywall cracks due to wood shrinkage, for instance.

To address this problem, we supply new homeowners with information that educates them on what they can expect in the next year. We tell them that the house framing will shrink, and show them that they may get a crack between the plaster fireplace and the drywall above it. We also warn them that the beams, which come from the damp Northwest, will dry out during the first heating season, opening some joints. We ask them to let the building go through a winter and a summer and assure them that we'll be back then to take care of minor problems. Forewarned in this way, they don't get upset when small problems occur. They know we've predicted the problems, and that we'll fix them.

We also give them a three-ring binder of tips on how to take care of tile, grout, roofs, and floors. The binder also contains appliance warranties.

Quality in housing comes both from the structures you build and from the relationships you build with your clients. To succeed as builders, you must effectively manage both processes.

By Michael Chapman, president of Michael Chapman Homes in Santa Fe, N.M.

Job-Site Procedure Manuals

If budget and schedule are your destinations, a management system is your road map

An experienced tradesman is usually more productive than a guy who's just starting out. Not only does he know more about building, but he has systems for tasks he does on a regular basis. If the boss asks him to hang a door, he knows which tools he needs and can picture every step it takes to complete the job. Tradespeople who manage construction projects are in the same boat. Those who have established systems have a good shot at bringing jobs in on time and under budget. But people who manage haphazardly receive a lot of unwelcome surprises and almost never make schedule or budget.

That's why every one of our jobs is managed by a lead carpenter who swings a hammer *and* supervises subs. Our lead carpenters are able to wear both hats because we've created procedures that provide a framework for managing jobs.

Job Folder

At the beginning of every project, we give the lead carpenter a job folder containing information needed to run the job. The folder contains plans, specs, and a detailed cost estimate. It also has phone numbers for subs and suppliers, as well as for the police, fire department, and the local emergency room. We work in three different states — Ohio, Pennsylvania, and West Virginia — so having a comprehensive list of phone numbers is important.

The Lead Man Folder

Each lead carpenter also has a Lead Man Folder. Unlike job folders, these aren't linked to a specific project, but go with the lead man from job to job. The folder is actually a large binder filled with clear plastic sleeves that contain items like the company's contractor license, a copy of the change-order policy, change-order forms, message reply forms, and a weekly planner form. The binder also includes a company policy manual and a section outlining our standard construction details.

Weekly planner. Every Friday after-

Every employee turns in a separate time card for each day worked. On the front, hours are posted to job-cost work codes; the back (below) provides space to report job-site accidents.

INJURY REPORT: Did you get hurt or see someone get hurt? (PLEASE CIRCLE ONE)

Who: ____________________

Where: ____________________

When: ____________________

How: ____________________

Mileage Report

Destination	Date	Mileage

ROB BORAM CONSTRUCTION

Name____________________
Date__________

Full Name
Signature____________________

Lunch________ Start Time________ Finish Time________

DO IT RIGHT THE FIRST TIME

Total Hours				
80	Supervision			
380	Tear Out			
840	Excavation			
1140	Concrete			
1359	Foundation			
1360	Masonry			
1540	1st Floor System			
1560	1st Exterior Wall			
1565	Basement Framing			
1570	1st Interior Wall			
1600	2nd Floor System			
1610	2nd Exterior Wall			
1620	2nd Interior Wall			
1630	Roof Framing			
1670	Ceiling Framing			
1700	Rough Stairs			
1710	Decks			
2000	Insulation			
2050	Roofing			
2420	Exterior Doors			
2430	Interior Doors			
2520	Windows			
2680	Siding			
2702	Millwork			
2710	Countertops			
2790	Finish Stairs			
2810	Shelving & Rods			
2840	Cabinets			
2880	Gutters & Downspouts			
2900	Soffit & Fascia			
3130	Drywall			
3151	Ceilings			
3170	Interior Painting			
3180	Exterior Painting			
3230	Floor Covering			
3250	Interior Staining			
3260	Exterior Staining			
3310	Tile			
3380	Special Ties			
3420	Bath Accessories			
3560	Plumbing			
3760	Electrical			
3880	HVAC			
4000	Clean Up			
4020	Dump Run			
4040	Material Run			
4060	Travel/Down Time			
4140	Punchlist			

noon, the lead men turn in a completed planner form for the coming week. There's a space for each day of the week, which the carpenter fills in with a list of what he and the other people on the job plan to do that day. The simple act of completing the form ensures that some kind of plan is in place at the beginning of each week.

Time cards. Every Monday lead men are given time cards for that week. Cards are preprinted with the job, employee name, and date. There's a card for each day of the week and a carpenter working a regular week turns in five cards. The front side of the card has a list of codes for various work operations and blank spaces to record time spent on those tasks. On the back of the card is a place to record reimbursable mileage and a daily accident report.

The employee is required to fill out a section on the back of the card if he witnesses an accident that day. A comp claim is legitimate if someone hurts himself on Friday, but doesn't realize how bad it is till Saturday. What you don't want is someone filing a claim on Monday for an injury he says he got the previous week but that really happened when he was bungee jumping or working a side job over the weekend. Requiring people to report accidents on a daily basis makes it easier to separate legitimate claims from phony ones.

Time log. Lead carpenters are required to keep a log of who is working on their projects on any given day. Helpers go from project to project, so the information in the log helps to verify how many hours the helper actually worked each week. It's also a record of which carpenters and subs worked which jobs, and when.

Message reply forms. Our company does remodeling, but that doesn't mean clients are always around when we need them. At the beginning of every job we designate a particular location as a message center. Usually, it's a clipboard or bulletin board near the phone. When the lead carpenter wants to pass a message to the client, he leaves it at the message center. Likewise, the client can do the same to get in touch with the lead man. Lead men are required to write messages on a triplicate form we get from NEBS (500

ROB BORAM CONSTRUCTION

ADDENDUM TO CONTRACT PROPOSAL

CHANGE ORDER POLICY

1. The Company policy on Change Orders is that any changes will be priced according to Contractor's normal pricing policy and will also include an administrative charge of $50 to compensate the Company for time lost, scheduling changes and other administrative costs.

2. However, there will be no administrative charge for changes caused by unforeseen conditions or beyond the control of the client. These will be charged at the Company's normal pricing policy.

3. Carpenter labor will be charged at an hourly rate of:
   $28.00 per man hour

   General labor will be charged at an hourly rate of:
   $17.00 per man hour

4. All change orders must be completed in writing with signatures of both client and Contractor's representative. All change orders will be priced prior to start of work or quoted with Contractor's hourly rate. Payment is to be made in full immediately upon completion of the extra work. For changes costing over $500, a partial payment of 50% will be required in advance, with balance upon completion of work called for in the change order.

Company Representative: ____________________

Owner's Acceptance: ____________________

____

Date: ____________________

Lead carpenters use this form to write change orders on the spot for additional work valued at less than $500.

Main St., Groton, MA 01471; 800/225-6380). The client gets the original, a copy is sent to our office, and the lead man keeps one for his records. Copies are important because we want to be able to verify who said what and when they said it. It's hard for clients to claim you didn't tell them about something when you can produce dated copies of messages you sent them. Likewise, it's tough for them to say they didn't agree to something when you've got a note in their handwriting saying they did. We don't save messages so we can wave them in front of clients like Perry Mason would, but we think it's important to document communications because customers don't always remember exactly what you told them or what they told you.

Every lead man has a copy of our change-order policy in his binder. Lead carpenters are allowed to handle small change orders in the field. The lead man

ROB BORAM CONSTRUCTION
CUSTOM DESIGN • BUILDING • REMODELING

CERTIFICATE OF SUBSTANTIAL COMPLETION AND ACCEPTANCE

NAME ____________________ JOB # __________
ADDRESS ____________________ PHONE# __________
CITY __________ STATE __________ ZIP CODE __________

The Contractor considers the work on your project to be substantially complete in that it is suitable for the Owner to use for its intended purpose. The date of this certificate shall be the date of commencement of all warranties and shall be considered as approval for application for final payment as set forth in the Contract. This certificate does not relieve the Contractor from any obligation of the Contract.

Work yet to be completed	$ Value (= Value x 2)
Total	

Any additional request for service should be made in writing. If you feel there are any deficiencies, please be as specific as possible about the defects. Any claim concerning materials under warranty should be made directly to the manufacturer.

I (we) have inspected the work performed and find the job completed to our satisfaction with the exception of the items listed above as yet to be completed.

Company Representative: ____________________ Date __________
Owner: ____________________ Date __________
Owner: ____________________ Date __________

NARI

536 Charles St., Wellsburg, WV 26070 • Tel: (304) 737-1005 • Fax: (304) 737-4282

To ensure that clients cannot withhold final payment because a handful of small items are incomplete, lead carpenters list punchlist items at twice their value on this standard form.

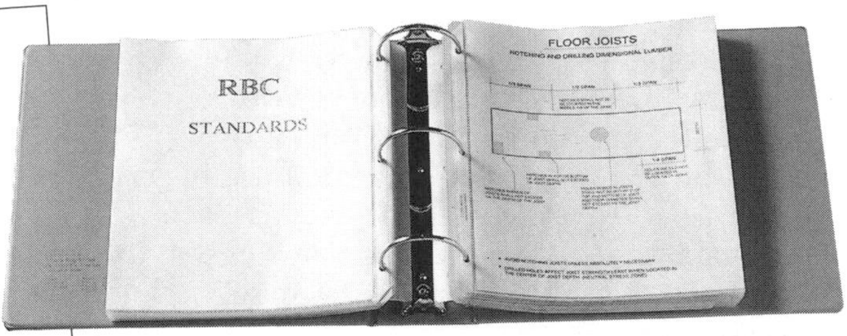

Company policies, standard forms, and construction details are carried from job to job in a three-ring binder.

estimates the cost of the change and has the client sign a change order before proceeding with the work. Processing small changes in the field helps to move the job along, but our lead guys don't have time to estimate the cost of large or complicated changes. When the cost of a change is likely to exceed $500, the lead man asks the client to call the office for the estimate. Also included in the policy sheet are the hourly rates charged for lead carpenters and helpers.

Punchlist Forms

Our company has two kinds of punchlist forms, the preclose-in punchlist form and the final punchlist form.

Preclose-in punchlist. The preclose-in form is a standard checklist of details to look for before we hang the drywall. The lead man walks the job to verify that items such as lights, receptacles, vents, and pipes are properly located in the wall. In some cases, we ask the client to accompany the lead man when he does the inspection. We tell them that if they want to add an outlet or move a vent or fixture, now's the time to do it, because after the drywall is up it will cost them a lot more to make changes.

Final punchlist. When the project reaches the point where we believe it's substantially complete, we meet with the owner and fill out the final punchlist. The job is substantially complete when the part of the building we're working on is ready to occupy. In most cases, that means it's 99.9% finished. Our contracts specify that when the job is substantially complete, we're to receive the final 10% payment less twice the value of the items on the punchlist. The client has every right to expect us to bring the project to 100% completion, but it's unreasonable for them to withhold 10% of the contract just because $75 worth of cabinet knobs are on back order.

The way we do it, we get most of what's coming to us, plus the client is protected because he's holding twice the amount needed to fix the items on the punchlist should we fail to perform.

At the preconstruction meeting, we tell clients our office will issue a certificate of substantial completion in exchange for the final payment. Throughout the job, we tell the client that the thing the lead man is working towards is the issuance of the substantial completion certificate. The certificate has no legal standing, but it's a reminder to the clients that they agreed to our payment terms before we started the job. We rarely issue the certificate, because clients usually pay up without a big fuss. It only comes up when we're having a hard time getting that last big check. In 20 years in the business, there were only two jobs where I failed to collect everything that was owed to me.

Book of Standards

As our company grew, we began to have internal conflicts about the best way to build things. Carpenters came onto jobs that were underway and complained that blocking was missing or not where they thought it should be. Since blueprints never tell you 100% of what you need to know, field guys were constantly calling me with questions like where to mount grab bars and toilet paper holders or at what height to install closet rods. One of our carpenters said we could solve this problem by creating our own set of standard construction details. Everyone agreed this was a good idea, so we began to work on it.

The first thing that went into the standards were articles I'd clipped from various trade magazines. One showed several different ways to install flashing, and another was a kitchen and bath design checklist. The checklist gave standards for the heights and depths for countertops, heights of toe kicks and backsplashes, and the distance between island and perimeter cabinets. Our lead carpenters consult the list when they're checking the kitchen designer's plans for errors and omissions. If something seems out of whack, they call the designer for an explanation.

Our construction standards contain a number of building sections lead men can refer to when they're unsure about the best way to detail something. We took some of the section drawings from trade magazines; others were generated by our designer. If the lead carpenter wants to know the best way to detail brick or stucco veneer on a wood-frame building, he can look it up in the book. When he's not sure about where to place rebar in a monolithic slab or whether or not to vent a crawlspace, he can look that up, too.

Prehung exterior door units often come with an extra-long screw to shoot through the upper hinge and into the jack stud. The screw keeps the door from sagging, so when we created our standards, we decided that every door should get a king-size screw through the upper hinge. We also specify where to shim and nail jambs and how big the gaps under doors should be.

In the past, a lot of time was wasted on calls between office and site regarding the location of bath accessories. Based on what we know of kitchen and bath industry standards, we created our own standards for locating bath accessories. For example, grab bars should be set 29 to 36 inches off the floor. Owners are free to ask for something different, but when they express no preference, we install them 32 inches above the floor. We have similar standards for the heights of shelves and clothes rods in closets. If the lead man wants to know how high to set a fixed shelf in a base cabinet, he can find that information in the standards, too.

Just because we have a set of standards doesn't mean everything we build is exactly alike. When we're deciding how to build something, we try to select details that are appropriate to the design and budget of the project. Our standards aren't so much a set of rules as they are an on-site library of good building practice.

By Rob Boram, owner of Rob Boram Construction, a remodeling company in Wellsburg, W. Va.

Chapter 2

Customer Relations

INTERVIEW

High-End Remodeling: Building on Customer Satisfaction

Quality in housing relies on good construction details and good customer relations

Many of the remodeling dollars being spent these days come from the so-called move-up or luxury market where clients expect a high degree of service and organization from their builder. California contractor Deva Rajan has just this kind of clientele and has earned a reputation for doing, as one colleague put it, "elegant business."

He concentrates on three areas of residential remodeling: complex structural repair (foundation work, hillside stabilization), high-end kitchens ($40,000 and up) and baths, and general remodeling (additions, expansions, second stories). He runs four crews, and shares the office with a full-time office manager and his son Abe, who handles both estimating and project management. His dollar volume last year was just under $1.5 million.

Rajan has spent nearly 35 years in design and construction, starting as a laborer during summers off from college. After graduate school in design at U.C. Berkeley (and summers as a carpenter) he taught for several years at the college level. In his first ten years as a contractor, he concentrated on remodeling. In the 1970s Rajan took charge of the historical restoration of a Russian fort north of San Francisco, and then remained in that area for nearly ten years doing new construction and spec building. He has since brought his company, Canyon Construction, back full circle to full-time remodeling.

JLC: *How do you find your clients? Do you advertise?*

Rajan: We stopped advertising about three years ago; we rely on referral and repeat customers completely now. But what we've done with that advertising budget is to pour it into a very thorough callback program that costs the client nothing. We go back three different times after we've completed the job: at 30 days, six months, and a year. We inspect our work, and take care of any problems the client might have without their having to call.

JLC: *Is this one of the reasons clients come to you?*

Contractor Deva Rajan, at left, succeeds at his high-end remodeling business by offering his customers an unusual degree of service. His son Abe, at right, handles estimating and project management.

Rajan: I think it's part of it. Like 98% of general contractors, we're interested in providing our clients with quality materials, good craftsmanship, and reliable subcontractors. But we also try to give them an unusual degree of service based on very thorough supervision and communication right on through to the end of the project. The teamwork approach that we use with design professionals and subs, and the care we take with estimates, scheduling, and the work itself is all part of it.

JLC: *What's your first meeting with a potential customer like?*

Rajan: In some cases we bid a project along with other contractors without even meeting the client — pretty cold stuff. But we'd like to get away from these entirely.

The second type of project comes from the clients themselves. They may have plans developed by an architect or a kitchen designer, or they may not have gotten that far yet. I take my son, who is our estimator and project manager, to the site with me to meet with the clients. We spend a lot of time just listening and asking questions about how they see the project.

JLC: *Do you suggest that they look at some of your past work?*

Rajan: We leave them a reference packet that includes ten pages of clients, at maybe 15 names per page — really stuffed. What often happens in our community is that the prospective clients will thumb through and find someone they know, and at that point you know you're way ahead.

JLC: *What's the next step?*

Rajan: We arrange for a walk-through with the subcontractors who will be key to that project. It almost always includes the plumber and electrician, but we may also ask the roofing contractor or painter, and frequently the cabinet sub. It takes about an hour, and requires the free run of the house. It gives our subs a chance to answer any questions they have: drain pipe sizes, entry service for power, things like that. At the same time, we're looking at the job for access, excavation problems, etc.

JLC: *How long will you spend preparing the estimate?*

Rajan: For a $250,000 project, the estimate will take at least a week. We'll spend five solid days doing material takeoffs and thorough labor estimates. We enter these numbers and subcontractor bids into our computer as they come in. We end up with a 12- to 15-page print-out.

JLC: *How do you present the bid?*

Rajan: We block out an hour or two with the couple — never just one of them — and go through it very thoroughly.

This is a really pivotal meeting. They already have a first impression of you, and now they are really geared up to check you out. The key thing to them is the numbers: They want to know if you're in the ball park. Assuming you are within 10% of the other bidders, the game is still wide open. We rarely get a project because we're low bidder.

JLC: *How much detail do you give the client in your estimate?*

Rajan: We literally give them everything. We use the 16 CSI codes as a format for our estimates. The first page of our bid is a summary — totals for each of the categories with our contingency, sales tax, and contractor's margin listed below that.

The second page is broken down into materials, labor, and subs. Again it's a summary page, so they can see where the costs are for each of the CSI categories. At that point we explain our markup categories: contractor's margin (10% profit, 10% overhead) and builder's contingency.

The pages that follow are detailed extensions of each one of those 16 categories. For example, category #3 is Concrete, so this page lists each sequential step in the work — form work, rebar, placement, stripping, etc. — and details the cost of materials, labor, and subcontractor. Backing that up are the labor and material takeoffs.

JLC: *You mentioned a figure for "builder's contingency;" what's that?*

Rajan: Some contractors refer to this as their risk. In remodeling, no matter how well we estimate or how much experience we have, there are always surprises waiting in the walls — pipes we can't see, more wire, less wire, whatever. But customers hate surprises; everyone hates surprises.

We take this right to the client by saying, "As seasoned builders we know that we'll run into things that we can't anticipate. We will catch any of those problems that come up and absorb them in the contingency you pay us as part of the contract."

JLC: *How do you figure the contingency?*

Rajan: We know from keeping statistics on our past jobs that our material estimates can be off by as much as 5% one way or the other. Some of this is due to price fluctuations; the rest is accounted for by waste or small mistakes in estimating. So we add a 5% contingency on materials to cover us.

On our own labor we figure 10% for discrepancies in crew performance, unpredictable field conditions, weather, and things like that. Finally, for subcontractors we add in 5%. This one puzzles some clients. But even though you get firm numbers from subs, they still manage to come up with a few extras.

JLC: *Don't clients hesitate at paying the extra cost?*

Rajan: Sure, we hear objections like "Shouldn't this be a part of your overhead or profit?" But on the whole, it's turned out to be a kind of selling point for us because clients are very afraid of surprises — afraid that they are going to be killed in extra work orders. The builder's contingency gives us a chance to say, "We won't charge you for a pipe that's discovered in the wall that we didn't see. We will charge you if you want to add another light or a larger window that's not on the drawing."

JLC: *Do they ever suggest that they keep whatever is left of the contingency money at the end of the job?*

Rajan: We hear that occasionally from clients or their architect. I explain that this arrangement would be an "owner's" contingency, which would mean that they are the risk takers, and that they would also be responsible for costs that exceed the 5%-10%-5%.

JLC: *Are there other concerns you try to deal with at this stage?*

Rajan: Clients are almost always anxious about how long the project will take or how many weeks they'll be without a kitchen. So we now give them a complete scheduling document with the estimate, but almost anything that suggests you've thought through the project in terms of its duration is a marvelous sales tool.

JLC: *If you're not relying on being low bidder, what else do you do to win the contract?*

Rajan: We're basically presenting the reasons our company is going to be better to work with. One of these is the quality of our subcontractors. We just started using actual biographies of our subs, and it's worked very well. When clients realize that you have selected the best subs there are, their confidence in your ability to build their dream grows.

This is particularly important after you leave and they begin to review the presentations of the other contractors.

JLC: *What else?*

Rajan: I think our own confidence in the numbers is very important. Being willing to talk about cost in very certain terms removes the lingering doubts in the client's mind about whether you're shooting from the hip. Because at this stage, the client is looking for little pockets of guessing, cheating, or whatever they suspect might be going on. The fact that we are disclosing the numbers — all of them — leaves little room for these thoughts.

We will even pull out a subcontract for some part of the job and then go back to our estimate to show that they are the same, right down to the dollar. It all reinforces that the numbers are real.

JLC: *But don't you often find out after all this work that the client just can't afford the work the way it's drawn?*

Rajan: Sure, the initial document almost always yields some surprises or draws some gasps. We look at the estimate as a working document that can be adjusted very easily, especially with computers. When the client says, "We didn't know that granite countertops were going to be that expensive," we explain how easily we can make substitutions. That's part of our job, as we see it — to fit the project to their budget. This puts us both — the client and the contractor — on the same side of the table. And that's so much better than the traditional adversarial position.

JLC: *Do you find a lot of resistance from architects when you close the distance between contractor and client?*

Rajan: There's a growing willingness on

the part of architects to work with builders on a shoulder-to-shoulder basis. There's still a residual element that feels responsible for protecting the client from things getting wildly out of hand, but that's probably healthy. You don't want to work with an architect who just lies down and lets you walk all over him. He's no help at all when it gets tough.

JLC: *How many meetings are usually required with a client before you end up signing a contract?*

Rajan: It varies, but for a $250,000 project we've found it takes about five meetings for everything to settle down. Maybe by the third meeting they've decided to go with us, but it will take another two meetings before everyone is really comfortable with the price and the scope of the work.

JLC: *Is it really worth all that time?*

Rajan: Sometimes it doesn't seem like it, particularly if the project doesn't materialize after all that effort. But in sticking it out, we often find other bidders dropping away, or growing impatient and showing a side that makes the client uncomfortable.

JLC: *With all of the time and attention you give to clients before they sign the contract, don't they feel abandoned once the work begins and you're not on site?*

Rajan: We handle that by trying to get everyone involved. On a larger job, we hold a preconstruction meeting with the architect, clients, subs, and foreman. One thing that's accomplished is a chance for the subs and the architect to go over quality standards with the client listening in. Painting is a good example. We use phrases like apartment grade, standard grade, or custom finish. The owner is usually eager to know the difference and that gives the painter a chance to really talk about his work.

We also ask the clients to talk about why they're remodeling, and describe their vision of the finished project. What happens at this meeting is hard to describe, but the result is that our subs and foreman end up feeling much more committed to the job.

JLC: *Isn't this also a chance for the different trades to anticipate problems and discuss scheduling?*

Rajan: Definitely. The heating guy may say "We absolutely have to get our stuff in before the plumber; get us in there first." Or the electrician may ask the cabinetmaker to leave a raceway for his wiring in an island.

We also bring a preliminary schedule to the meeting — just a bar chart based on initial impressions and our own experience of what needs to come before what. Then we talk about whether we have the durations and sequence just right.

JLC: *How do you handle the inevitable complaints and change orders as the work progresses?*

Rajan: It depends. If the client has established a good relationship with the foreman and he has the maturity to handle it, we go with it. But a lot of stuff can pass through the cracks because the foreman isn't on the job near the end when mostly subcontractor work is happening.

This is where having a project manager in the office is so critical. Because he's there from the beginning with the clients, he has established a relationship with them and knows what they want. (This also makes it pretty difficult for clients to invent stories about what they've been promised.)

In our case the project manager, Abe, is also our estimator, so he really knows the work, the crews, and the schedule, and he is in a position to resolve problems before they escalate.

JLC: *So is your role mostly sales?*

Rajan: My major part is screening projects and talking with clients; I guess you could call it sales. I also review everything: estimates, scheduling, assignment of manpower on projects, hiring, everything.

A few years ago, I thought what I had to do was step back from the business. I tried that for awhile and found that it lets you build a larger company, but you lose that essential contact with the clients. In our case, we have to deliver that; our clients come to us for that. So I've stepped back in.

JLC: *Do you think remodeling contractors are taking that direction generally?*

Rajan: I think what we're going to be seeing in the next decade is general contractors having less and less crew — carpenters, laborers, and so on — and more and more subs. This will result in larger companies, or at least loose partnerships of generals and subs which may even include things like profit sharing.

JLC: *Is that where Canyon Construction is headed?*

Rajan: We will be putting an effort into working even closer with our subs. And not just plumbers and electricians. I see us using general contractors as subs — foremen who have come up through our ranks, gotten their licenses, and come back to work with us.

It's difficult at the age of 30 to start a business from scratch. You may have complete skills as a craftsman, but to put all the elements of the business together and get good jobs is very difficult.

What we can offer a real hot general contractor, age 30, who wants to do good projects and be his own boss, is to team up with him. We'll take care of the organizational and business support (accounting, billing, all that stuff), and provide good jobs that will bring him that paycheck every week. And he gets the gravy by being able to concentrate on the work itself.

The Art of Client Management

Clients' expectations and demands will run wild—if you don't establish clear ground rules

We all know of jobs where an earnest contractor strives to produce a workmanlike job, and the client, instead of gratefully accepting his product, tries to skin him alive. Although such stories raise a builder's blood pressure, it's important that he calm down and rationally assess how things got that way. Only then can he develop strategies to avoid such trouble in the future.

Keep in mind that at the signing of the contract, the interest of the owner and contractor closely coincided. From that moment, however, those interests started to diverge — until they reached a point where mutual satisfaction was out of reach. From that point on, only one side can win — the other loses.

Even that might be acceptable if the sides were evenly matched. Unfortunately, they're not. By the time major differences emerge, the client usually possesses the completed work, control of the site, and the money. No matter how generous the payment schedule, a major portion of the contractor's profit is locked in those final draws and retainage.

What power does the contractor have? Reason? Fairness? A disputed contract and verbal commitments that no one can prove? It's no contest. The owner extracts, some would say "extorts," concessions — and the contractor often feels that he can do nothing.

It doesn't have to end that way, however. This section is based on the notion that divergent interests can be managed. Every contractor knows about project management; this is *client management*. We can define client management as "procedures that increase the chance of completing a project to the satisfaction of both parties."

A shorter definition might be: how to satisfy the client without losing your shirt. Because of the unequal strengths of the parties involved, the contractor must accomplish this by disarming potential conflicts before they arise. It has been our experience that many contractor/client problems originate in (1) unrealistic expectations, (2) the absence of ground rules, and (3) the wrong signals.

Client Expectations

For openers, take an unhurried look at the clients' point of view: Why do clients start off smiling and end up snarling? Sift through your own experiences, both good and bad. You may conclude, as we have, that a major source of some clients' distress is their unsatisfied expectations. It boils down to disappointment: What the clients see falls short of the image they were carrying in their heads.

How, you might ask, can you be responsible for the clients' imagination? The fact is, the clients' expectations are usually unrealistic. Remember that it's not easy to see the reality behind a designer's rendering. Real life is always smaller and less elegant than a pretty drawing. The real question is: What are you going to do about it?

Rather than chasing down complaints generated by disappointment, it is a lot easier to bring the expectations down to earth. How? Start by not fueling those expectations with your own words. *Don't* tell them the design is one of the nicest you've seen in years. *Don't* say, "You're going to love the way this expands your living (recreation-office-assembly-storage) area." These and dozens of other small comments tend to raise expectations. Such statements may seem harmless. Down the line, however, you will pay dearly for the expectations you excite.

Instead of building high expectations, find opportunities to prepare the clients for reality. State clearly that drawings excite the imagination and always look better – and larger – than the finished project. Meet the clients at the site after the footers are poured and show where the partitions will be. Let them visualize how the furnishings will fit. Tell them, "This is probably going to seem smaller when it is built than you visualized." Openly mention the danger of unrealistic expectations, especially if this is their first construction experience. Without disparaging their commitment or your performance, do whatever you can to wean them away from their imagination. Your credibility as a seasoned pro will be enhanced, not diminished, by down-to-earth realism.

Above all, do not promise anything! Promises increase expectations and diminish satisfaction. Even if you choose to upgrade an item out of your own pocket, do it quietly — and don't be surprised if the clients respond with even higher expectations.

In brief, to satisfy clients you must exceed their expectations. That means you must keep them reasonable. When do you start? As soon as the contract is signed.

Ground Rules

Contracts tend to tilt against the contractor. They either bind him in a straitjacket (the Standard AIA Agreement) or they leave things so loose that any question becomes a battle of wills. Both types fail to address important questions that arise time after time.

In order to avoid tedious legalistic documents, a contractor might find it useful to prepare a list of "ground rules" under which the parties agree to operate. These rules should be written to defuse the typical problems before they arise. As the contractor, you should know what those problems are going to be — the clients haven't been there yet.

The time to introduce your ground rules is after the price and specifications have been agreed to, or immediately after the contract is signed. Both the clients and contractor should initial or sign them. The rules should be written in ordinary language, and their "legality" is not too important. Most people will abide by a reasonable agreement simply because they have signed it; enforcement through the legal system is seldom feasible in any event.

If a particular ground rule is questioned, you may choose to explain the reasoning behind it, or you may simply state that "this is our company policy." One does not have to understand the basis for company policy — it just exists. If an objection arises, the rule can be negotiated and modified on the spot. (The contractor should pay attention to why the objection is raised, of course.) Of paramount importance is the clients' perception that the contractor is governed by well-established standards, not by the pressures of the moment.

Here are some examples of contract clauses which have proven useful for our company in establishing ground rules:

> *"Changes in the work specifications, including material upgrades, are subject to the contractor's written acceptance, and additional charges are payable in full at the time of the request."*

The purpose of this rule is to (1) discourage change orders, which break the rhythm of the job and severely erode profits, (2) eliminate haggling over the charges, which are always much higher than the direct labor and material costs involved, and (3) remove the clients' incentive to find credits to offset the additional charges at the end of the project.

Another major source of interruption is when the owners fail to make timely decisions, then blame the contractor for the delays. The following provision places the responsibility where it belongs:

"The owner will submit all material and color selections by ____ (date), including an alternate choice for each item. Except by prior agreement, all selections will be standard materials available from local sources."

If the selection date is not met, the contractor should notify the owners by registered letter that they are in violation of the agreement and may incur additional charges due to the stoppage of work or scheduling delays.

Every contractor should be ready to warrant his work for some period of time. With the following clause, the warranty provides powerful leverage in the event that payment is arbitrarily withheld:

"Limited Warranty. All labor and material for work covered by this contract is guaranteed against defects for a period of ___ from substantial completion or use by owner unless otherwise stated. This warranty shall not apply if final payment is not received in accordance with the terms of the agreement."

If payment is withheld, a registered letter should state, "Payment has not been received in accordance with the terms of the agreement, and you are notified that all warranties and guarantees are hereby cancelled."

The mysterious disappearance of materials and tools from the work site is always a problem, but tends to diminish with the following clause:

"Owner is responsible for the protection of work completed and all equipment and materials delivered to the site."

Anyone can make a claim. Contractors who have been subjected to excessive retainage and payment delays for real or spurious claims will recognize the utility of this provision:

"Any claim for damage by the owner will first be addressed through the owner's insurance, and under no circumstances will the existence of such a claim delay payment of monies otherwise due."

It's always better to have one individual to deal with, and frequent inspections with written acceptances are a good way to limit future problems. The following clause addresses this issue:

"The owner appoints _____ to inspect and approve work on the owner's behalf; inspections will be made in a timely manner upon the contractor's request."

Another issue that often goes unaddressed is access to the site. Including an access clause can foreclose this heavily traveled path to claims and payment delays:

"The Agreement is based on using existing access to the work area. Unless otherwise specified, no costs have been included for repairs to access areas such as driveways, walks, shrubs, trees, lawns or entries. The contractor will use normal care and procedures in moving and storing materials."

The contractor's responsibility for cleanup of the work site should be limited to a reasonable level. A surgically clean site may suit the owner, but it can be expensive to attain. Use this provision to clarify the topic of cleanup:

"Upon substantial completion the contractor will remove all construction debris and leave the premises in a broom-clean condition."

Perhaps the single most important provision of all guarantees the timely resolution of intractable problems through a swift and economical binding arbitration procedure. I use the following clause to steer conflicts toward arbitration rather than the courtroom:

"All claims or disputes arising out of this Agreement shall be decided in accordance with the rules of the American Arbitration Association, unless the parties mutually agree otherwise."

Wrong Signals

The cost of construction is intimidating to most buyers, who generally lack a clear idea of how the costs are allocated. Where so much money is involved, they suspect a lot of fat must also be present — so they probe to see if they can tap it. Initially they try to upgrade materials and request minor changes in the scope of the work. If the contractor lets them succeed, he sends the wrong signal.

A game begins — like a child testing overly permissive parents: The clients push as far as they can before meeting resistance. The further they get, the more difficult they are to stop. When the contractor finally tries to apply the brakes, he appears to be imposing arbitrary and unfair constraints.

The "deep-pockets" illusion can be corrected at the outset by the simple act of charging for every upgrade, no matter how small the amount. In fact, the smaller it is, the better. If the clients are asked to pay for a wallpaper upgrade of $1.50 per roll on a $54,000 project, they immediately perceive that money is important. Far from alienating them, this action provides assurance that the $54,000 is well spent.

Because they are paying for the project, clients sometimes get the idea that the contractor will bear all the responsibility and deliver a completed project into their waiting hands. This is another misconception that leads to a poor working relationship. Words and actions that say, "We'll take care of everything" send the wrong signal. It is unhealthy for the clients to be passive spectators on their own project. It gives them time to scrutinize every detail and bird-dog the work. Most importantly, it robs them of the chance to participate.

The best message for the contractor to send is not, "Look what a wonderful project we are going to produce for you," but rather, "Let's see how fine a project we can produce together." The clients who feel they have participated in a joint effort with the contractor are far more likely to be satisfied with the result.

It's up to the contractor to bring the clients into the project in a productive way. A good strategy is to start off with something like this: "Our construction experience has shown us that it's important for our clients to understand that we both have responsibilities in making this a successful project. One of your responsibilities is to help us get off to a good start by making the material and color selections within two weeks. We are also going to need your help in performing inspections when we need them, and in preparing for the progress payments so we can move forward without breaking stride."

Follow the clients' performance and don't be shy about reminding them when they're not following through. But also make a point of bringing them into the process by providing an occasional update on the schedule and the performance of the subs.

When materials are delivered, it's not a bad idea to look them over at the site with the clients. When questions arise, try to share the decision in a way that engenders a feeling of participation. Even if an architect is monitoring the work, it doesn't hurt to maintain a direct relationship with the owners.

On commercial work, try to establish contact with the supervisors and personnel who will occupy the new space. Show them how it's going to look. Solicit their comments. Early participation means fewer problems down the line. You will bleed off resentments and lower punch-out costs.

Tactics

The contractor/client balance of power shifts at different stages of the project. At the beginning, the contractor has considerable leverage, greater than he will enjoy later. The clients want the project badly enough to pay all that money to get it. They have finally selected the company to perform the job, have negotiated a contract, paid a deposit, and initially, have nothing to show for it. In contrast, the contractor has received a substantial payment on a promise to perform. He's in control. As the work progresses, their positions reverse: The clients possess the completed work, and control the remaining funds. The contractor is vulnerable. If there is a conflict at this point, the contractor loses.

Client management offers a way of improving the odds for a successful project. However, if the contractor intends to provide a positive working relationship, he must act early, while he has leverage. For that particular project the opportunity will not come again.

Summary

While concentrating on production and company management, contractors may overlook personal factors that are critical to a project's success. Client management can increase the chances of producing a mutually satisfactory result by using the contractor's initially strong position to (1) generate realistic expectations, (2) establish favorable ground rules, and (3) send the right signals to the clients. A variety of statements and ground rules have been included to illustrate specific points. The reader should modify the content and wording of these to fit his own situation.

By Martin King, president of Martin Churchill Associates, Inc. in Arlington, Va. After 28 years of construction and estimating experience, he now specializes in investigating and consulting on structural damage and appraising reconstruction costs.

Preconstruction Conferences

Use a preconstruction meeting with the clients to follow up the sale, review the contract and plans, and avoid any misconceptions

After too many bad experiences, we've learned that the best way to get a project straight is to hold a meeting with clients before work begins. These preconstruction conferences have saved us an incredible amount of work and confusion. They've also saved us plenty of money.

At our company, a typical job passes through two different people before work begins. The salesman works with clients to determine what they expect from a project, what it will look like, and how it will function. But once the bid is accepted, the production manager and the lead carpenter take over. Without good communication between these two and the sales rep, clients will find themselves explaining their ideas again to the production crew.

As the job progresses from an idea to working drawings and specifications, the various people involved form different perceptions. Clients may wonder how much of the information they discussed with the salesman was filtered through to production. In turn, the production manager might wonder exactly what the salesman promised.

Unless a remodeling job is small enough for our Handyman Service, where the actual craftsman is also the salesman, we hold a preconstruction conference seven to ten days after the contract is signed. Timing it this way works well for two reasons: It's a good follow-up to the sale, and it gives us a chance to measure for and order any special materials that may take several weeks for delivery.

Usually held at the job site (typically the client's home), the conference includes our sales representative, production manager, and lead craftsman, and, in the case of an insurance loss, the adjuster. If the customer is a couple, we encourage both of them to attend since this is also a good time to make sure they are in agreement about the job.

The conferences last anywhere from 45 minutes to one-and-a-half hours. This may seem like a lot of expensive time, but redoing work and, worse yet, leaving customers dissatisfied, costs much more.

Passing The Baton

The preconstruction conference provides a good opportunity for us to transfer control from the salesman to the production people. Early in the relationship, the salesman explains our company policies, and tells the client that the production manager and lead craftsman will assume control of the project once the contract has been signed. Then, at the start of the preconstruction conference, the sales rep introduces these people and lets them take over.

Because the customer expects this transition, there's no breach of confidence. At the same time, the production team can ask informed questions because they've reviewed the plans with the salesman before the meeting and have a good, basic knowledge of the project.

Getting Off on the Right Foot

by Linda Case and Walter Stoepplewerth

Among the many topics we discuss at the preconstruction conference are the following:

Storage of materials. An area about the size of a garage bay is needed for storage of finishing materials.

Dust. On an interior remodel, temporary moving or storage of the homeowner's furniture, rugs, curtains, piano, etc., must be arranged. Realistically discuss dust protection of adjoining rooms and whether a household member has an allergy to dust. Also, dust is a computer's enemy: Customers should be warned to move a computer out of the range of the inevitable dust.

Bathrooms. If a bathroom is being remodeled, there will be three or four days during which it will be unusable. Assure the customers that you'll give them adequate notice and create minimal downtime.

Kitchens. If the kitchen is being gutted and remodeled, there will be no working sink, appliances, or space for a period of time. Where should the refrigerator be temporarily relocated? Will the owner keep the removed cabinets or dispose of them?

Electrical. Discuss the routine interruptions in electric power that characterize construction jobs. This can be a real nuisance, particularly if the customer uses a computer during the day. Also, new wiring often requires opening and patching of walls. Explain that it is virtually impossible to get a perfect match on any touch-up painting and that the entire room may need to be repainted for a consistent color.

Plumbing. If you're adding or remodeling a bathroom in a home with galvanized water pipes, the contract should suggest changing all accessible piping to copper during construction. Galvanized pipes rust from the inside out and ultimately clog and rust out. When a new bathroom makes an additional demand for water, there will be a noticeable drop in pressure, and clients should know this up front.

Also explain that plumbing work may require the opening and patching of walls, and as with electrical work, this may result in mismatching paint where repairs are made.

HVAC. If the contract calls for copper-baseboard heating in a new addition but there are cast-iron radiators in the existing house, the contractor should explain that radiators work best at 140° to 150°F while baseboard heating works best at 170° to 180°F. A compromise is needed when setting the aqua-stat for the temperature in the boiler.

When a heat pump is to be installed as part of the contract, the contractor should explain that the temperature of the air at the registers will feel cool but that this is normal with a heat pump.

Missing walls. Opening up a house is just a construction problem to the remodeler, but it is a heating, air conditioning, privacy, housekeeping, and security problem to the customer. If a wall is to be removed between the existing house and a new addition, the timing is of utmost importance.

Dormers. If a dormer is being erected, requiring the doubling of 2x6 floor joists on the attic floor, nail pops or plaster damage is likely below. It's best to warn the customer to expect this problem and the likely need for repainting at the completion of the project.

Match existing. If any matching is being done, for mortaring, roof shingles, floor tiles, special molding, windows, doors, etc., inform your customers of any differences and show them samples if possible. Or send them to visit the supplier. The contract language should be pointed out. It might read: "match as closely as possible from stock materials at existing local sources of supply."

Staining. If staining a pine door is specified, the contractor should point out the different degrees of hardness of wood used for doors and explain that staining a pine door may produce a splotched effect.

Landscaping. Consider rough grading, finish grading, sodding, etc. If the customer is a gardener or landscape enthusiast, the backhoe digging a basement or footings in the existing or future yard will affect more than the actual dimensions of an addition.

One person might have an absolute fixation about no hammer marks on the trim, but be completely oblivious to whether or not the insulation is installed properly. On the other hand, another person might be extremely concerned about air leakage and energy conservation. This does not mean that the customer should set the standard of quality for a remodeler, but it is advantageous to know what areas should receive extra care and attention if the customer is to be satisfied.

By Walter W. Stoeppelwerth, a founder of HomeTech, Inc., a remodeling and home-inspection consulting firm in Bethesda, Md. Linda Case is president of Remodelers Advantage, Inc. in Silver Spring, Md.

The conference is also a good time to review the contract, specifications, and plans. It's amazing how many misconceptions can surface during this part of the meeting. For instance, the sales rep may have specified a 5-foot window on one wall, but the clients had visualized a floor-to-ceiling window. At this point, it's still easy to make this kind of change since materials haven't been ordered and work has not yet begun.

Job-Site Details

To make a project run smoothly, we've developed a list of particulars that we discuss during the preconstruction conference. These are the kinds of details that can make the job pleasant for our crew and our clients. We include the following:

- What time the work is to start and end each day. Our normal hours are 7:30 a.m. to 4:30 p.m. This is okay for the majority of our clients, but some ask that we arrive an hour later.
- How change orders are handled. We make it clear that change orders are costly and will delay the project.
- Any particulars about pets. For instance, if the cat is declawed and should not get out of the house, we need to know it.
- The dangers involved in the project. These should be explained to children who are home when their parents are not. We also ask parents to discourage their youngsters from "helping" the painter paint or the carpenter cut plywood.
- Which toilet facilities, if any, may be used by our employees and subs.
- Which telephones can be used.
- Whether smoking is permitted in the house or yard.
- The reason for lien waivers, which we supply after each progress payment and at the final payment.
- Payment schedules and procedures. We've found that customers will often send the check before we ever invoice them because we went over the payment schedule at the conference.

In addition to all of this, we make it a point to review our employee policies. For example, our employees and subs should not accept food or even coffee from our customers, and we let everybody know it. We also have a strict policy against drinking on the job, even the occasional beer offered by the client.

We also discuss our effect on the neighborhood. We explain that lawn signs are important because they help suppliers and subcontractors find the job site. Of course, this is also good advertising for us. Some clients prefer that we don't post any signs, and in some neighborhoods they may be forbidden.

We make sure to ask our clients for their permission to send a letter to their neighbors informing them of our presence in the area. In the letter, we warn the neighbors that there will be strange trucks on the street. We also ask that they report any problems, like debris flying into their prize rose gardens, to us and not to their neighbor. Once again, this is good advertising for us.

Since many of our customers are away during the day, we always designate a communication box. It's a place where notes, partial invoices, and payments can be left. This saves a lot of trouble if you need to let the customer know you won't be on the job because you're waiting on an inspection or a sub.

Finally, we discuss the phenomenon we call "remodeling fever." This is the sudden realization by the clients, which can strike at any time, that they are tired of all the inconveniences that come with a remodeling project. During the conference, we try to prepare them for what's to come, and encourage them to look beyond the disruptions to the finished product. This is especially important for those who've suffered a fire loss. They didn't ask for the remodeling to happen and they are traumatized before the project begins.

All of this information is also included in the presentation book we give to potential clients. That way they can see the kind of attention to detail we provide. In this sense, our preconstruction conferences not only help us once we've got the job, they also serve as a sales tool.

By Tom Swartz, president of J.J. Swartz Company, a 70-year-old remodeling firm with offices in Decatur and Bloomington, Ill.

Communicating with Clients

Effective communication pleases customers, wins referrals, and boosts profit

The friend who gave me my start in construction once told me that if he had to, he could build a house using only a hammer. But there's an even more remarkable construction tool available to builders, and it's one you can't get from Stanley or Bostich. It's called "effective communication."

My investment in acquiring good communication skills has returned impressive dividends. Because I communicate well, I can usually catch problems while they are small and manageable, and my customers tend to develop fewer unrealistic expectations. Surprises occur less often and jobs run more smoothly, making my life as a contractor easier.

In my experience, opportunities to establish and maintain effective communication with clients occur at seven critical points:

- early contacts
- contract signing
- preconstruction conference
- weekly site meetings
- payment collections
- punchlist procedures
- post-job checkups

Early Contacts

My first contact with a client is usually over the phone, but I'm rarely able to evaluate any proposed work without visiting the site. Site visits take time, however, so when a prospect first calls my office, I collect as much information as I can about both the job and the clients. I follow a preset list of questions on a standard form, which I use to "qualify" the caller and to help me decide whether I want to pursue the lead further. If the job sounds promising, I arrange to meet with the prospect.

During this initial face-to-face meeting (we usually meet at the prospect's home, because most of my work is remodeling), I have four major goals:

- to find out exactly what the customer wants and what he or she can afford
- to set myself apart from other contractors bidding the job
- to begin building trust
- to identify and avoid problem customers

At this stage, I use my professionalism to set myself apart from other contractors who may be bidding the job. I wear work clothes, for example, to convey the image of a "hands-on contractor," but they're clean and neat. I also watch my body language, and I try not to talk too much.

Careful listening. To find out what the prospect wants, I ask open-ended questions about the proposed work. If they want a family room addition, for example, I'll ask them how they plan to use the room and where those activities currently take place. If it's a bedroom remodel, I'll ask them what kind of furniture they plan to use or whether a proposed closet will be large enough. I want them to talk about the features and benefits they're most interested in, and if they have magazine clippings or photos to illustrate their ideas, I want to see them. Anyone can ask for a "kitchen" or a "family room," but those are imprecise descriptions that don't really help me to build what my clients want.

By allowing the homeowners to talk about their plans, I not only get a good feel for how well we will be able to work together, but I can often discover a hidden agenda that could lead to problems down the road. A proposed kitchen remodel, for instance, may be motivated by a real need for a more efficient space, but it may also spring from boredom or from a long-standing desire to build the "dream kitchen." In the first case, my work will usually meet the homeowner's needs; in either of the other situations, however, I may never be able to satisfy them and may be better off declining the work.

Budget. To evaluate the job fully and to gauge expectations, I need to ask the homeowners how much money they plan to spend. Some people will tell me; others will talk about a "range" rather than a specific number.

For those customers who refuse to budge, I won't waste my time pricing their job. If the projected budget is too low, I can begin to educate them about the real costs of construction and explore their willingness to change the scope of the project. I also like to spend some time educating the prospects on how they can get what they want. At this point, it's a matter of briefly explaining product options and design features and drawbacks. If the client already has blueprints, we may go over them and make minor modifications, discussing the advantages of tile instead of laminate, or why a light fixture should be moved. But at this first meeting, I'm careful not to overwhelm the client with details.

Building trust. Everything I do during the initial meeting, from arriving on time to listening attentively to what the homeowners have to say, contributes to building trust and confidence. I'm careful to treat their ideas with respect, and I try to defuse any awkwardness with a little humor. I've found that evening or weekend meetings are less successful, because everyone is either tired from the day's work or anxious to get to other planned activities, so I try to schedule all of my appointments for regular working hours. Early morning works best, because everyone is fresher and clients can't drag the meeting out if they're on the way to work.

Red flags. The final goal of this first meeting is to make sure that I am not selling myself to a potential problem customer. Obvious red flags are indecisiveness, fighting between spouses, and fixation on insignificant details. When I think I'm dealing with a problem customer, I politely excuse myself and recommend a competitor as I move towards the door.

I follow up all meetings or discussions with a memo to the client recapping our discussion, carefully noting any changes, conflicts, decisions, and future actions. This verifies a "meeting of the minds" and it confirms that we were communicating and not merely talking at each other.

The Contract

The contract-signing phase is what really sets the stage for the entire job. The contract must be clear on the scope of work, all specifications, and the payment schedule. Along with photos and references from past jobs, I keep standard contracts and change orders in my portfolio. I don't read every word of every document with my clients, but I

Client Deadlines & Tasks

ABC Contracting
932 West Main St.
Richmond, VT 05477
Phone 802/434-4747 • Fax 802/434-4467

Date: JAN 1 1998
Owner: JOHN & JANE DOE
Revision number: 2 Date: JAN 5 1998
Sheet number: 1 of 1
Project name: FAMILY ROOM BATH ADDITION
Project number: 3

decision	#	Flooring				Paint/color				closets/furn				elec/fixtures				plumb/fixtures				other				Notes
DATE		FAMILY ROOM	BATH			FAMILY	BATH	(OWNER TO PAINT & SUPPLY MATERIALS)		FAMILY RM (CLEANOUT)				BATH	FAMILY			BATH					MOVE SHRUBS	CLEAN BAY IN GARAGE (FOR STORAGE)		
JAN 15		X	X					*						X	X			X								CHOOSE & ORDER
JAN 19																							X	X		
PROJECT STARTS																										
JAN 20																										
JAN 30										X																MOVE EVERYTHING TO PREP FOR DEMO.
FEB 20						X	X																			CHOOSE COLOR
FEB 25						X	X																			PICK UP PAINT & PAINT ROOMS TO PREPARE FOR TRIM

Figure 1. *To keep work from grinding to a halt while homeowners decide on colors or other options, the author provides his clients with a list of tasks tied to deadlines.*

will point out the most important sections to help eliminate any gray areas.

The clients will never be more flexible than at the contract signing, and your credibility will never be as high. After all, the client picked you to build their dreams, but the stress of surprises and unexpected costs during the project will eventually take its toll. Warn them now about possible extra expenses, and your honesty will pay off later as the inevitable changes arrive.

This is also the time to present the clients with a list of any product selections and other obligations they have to take care of before work can begin. I use a simple form that lists all of the decisions they need to make tied to a specific deadline (see Figure 1). The list not only ensures that I will be able to order everything needed for the job in plenty of time, but it also makes the clients feel that they are a part of the process.

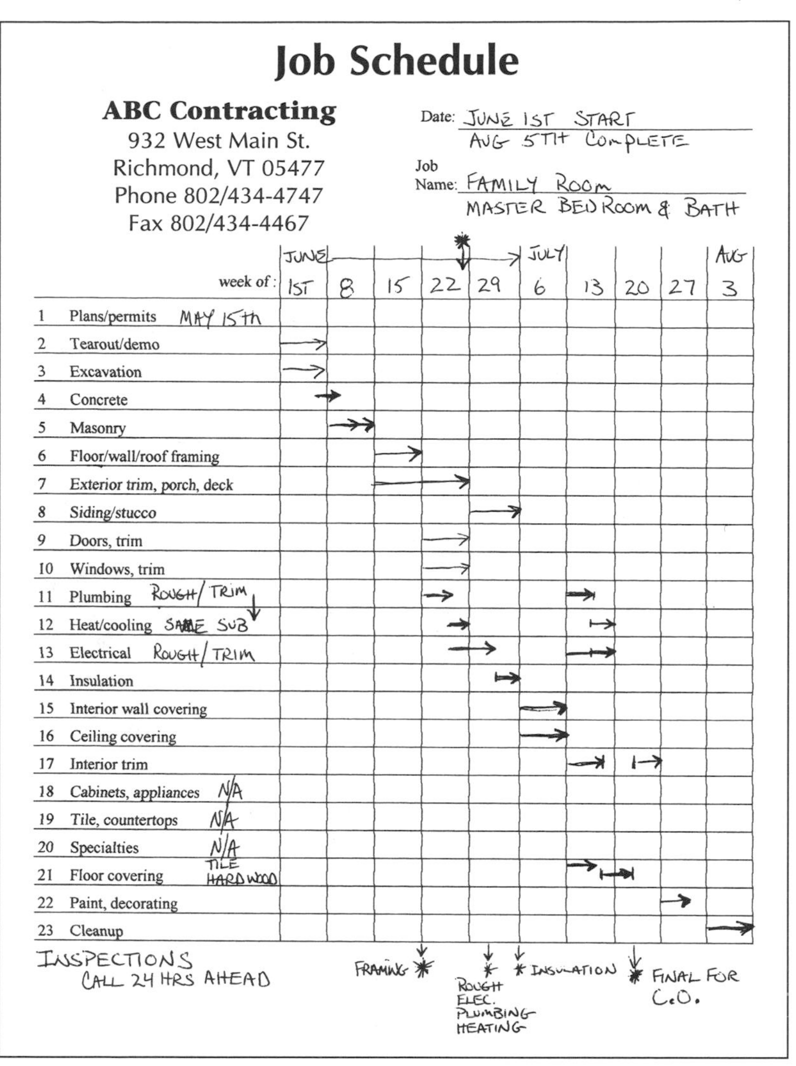

Job Schedule

ABC Contracting
932 West Main St.
Richmond, VT 05477
Phone 802/434-4747
Fax 802/434-4467

Date: JUNE 1ST START
AUG 5TH COMPLETE

Job Name: FAMILY ROOM
MASTER BED ROOM & BATH

	week of:	JUNE 1ST	8	15	22	29	JULY 6	13	20	27	AUG 3
1	Plans/permits MAY 15th										
2	Tearout/demo										
3	Excavation										
4	Concrete										
5	Masonry										
6	Floor/wall/roof framing										
7	Exterior trim, porch, deck										
8	Siding/stucco										
9	Doors, trim										
10	Windows, trim										
11	Plumbing ROUGH/TRIM										
12	Heat/cooling SAME SUB										
13	Electrical ROUGH/TRIM										
14	Insulation										
15	Interior wall covering										
16	Ceiling covering										
17	Interior trim										
18	Cabinets, appliances N/A										
19	Tile, countertops N/A										
20	Specialties N/A										
21	Floor covering TILE HARDWOOD										
22	Paint, decorating										
23	Cleanup										

INSPECTIONS
CALL 24 HRS AHEAD
FRAMING *
* ROUGH ELEC. PLUMBING HEATING
* INSULATION
* FINAL FOR C.O.

Figure 2. *The author gives all of his clients a copy of the same schedule he uses to track job progress. Extra time for possible construction delays is built in to the schedule dates, and notations serve as reminders for required inspections.*

The Preconstruction Conference

I like to schedule a meeting for about a week before beginning work. This is the last chance I'll have to prepare customers for what is coming and to eliminate potential misunderstandings. Most homeowners have difficulty visualizing the construction process, and they need to have everything explained to them. During this preconstruction conference, I go over the contract once again, but this time I have the benefit of being able to describe the work while walking through the job site. Answering questions about the project now may prevent conflicts later. I can explain, for example, that the entire living room won't be getting new drywall just because a new doorway is being created to the family room.

I also go over the schedule during this conference (Figure 2), explaining the importance of cooperative weather and the role of subs. I also explain the delays that change orders can cause, since most customers simply don't realize the way change orders can mess up the schedule. I also emphasize that any change orders must go through me, not through my employees or my subs.

Work can slow down or stop when customers freely roam the site during the workday, so I take a few moments to establish times when the owners can meet me at the site. I do mostly remodeling, so the people I work for are usually living at the job site. Even so, I ask them to limit visits to the regularly scheduled site meeting or to check in before or after working hours. A friendly but firm explanation will usually get the point across, but I've had to board up a new addition on occasion to isolate it from the rest of the house.

This preconstruction meeting is also the best time to designate a message center for written communication, and to go over any other rules for the project, such as the protocols for paging, phone calls, or change orders.

Weekly Meetings

I like to hold weekly meetings, and I impose an agenda to keep things orga-

Weekly Meeting

ABC Contracting
932 West Main St.
Richmond, VT 05477
Phone 802/434-4747
Fax 802/434-4467

Date: JAN 10th
To: JOHN & JANE DOE
From: NORM
Subject: UPDATE & CHANGES
Project name: FAM ROOM / BATH
Project number:

1) Update summary — COMMENTS:
2) Last week's accomplishments
3) Do you still want to change Jacuzzi size?
It will delay project 1 week because we would
have to move framing, outlet, and rough plumbing. — YES (JD)
4) Have paint colors for rooms been chosen? — YES BENJAMIN MOORE
5) Clean out closet this weekend. — WALL FAM RM FLAT #1AB
We are tearing out walls on Monday — TRIM FAM RM SG #1TG, BATH TRIM GLOSS 1TG
6) Plumber would like to work Saturday a.m. — BATH WALLS - WALLPAPER
Is that okay? YES (JD)
7) Dumpster is going Monday. If you have anything
to get rid of, you may toss it in dumpster this weekend.
(Nothing should be above top of container.)

Signature or initials: (NRA) (JD)

Figure 3. *An agenda keeps weekly meetings on track and provides a written record of job progress, changes to the scope of work, and homeowner decisions.*

nized and moving. The agenda should include project status (ahead of or behind schedule, and why), goals for the coming week, and a list of the questions that have arisen since the last meeting (Figure 3). I'm careful not to bog the customers down with unnecessary details, since that's the burden I was hired to bear.

Be sure to include a short question-and-answer time to clear up uncertainties. It's best to do this at the end of the meeting, since many questions get answered during the discussion of agenda items. Ask your customers to save all of their questions during the week for this time, unless something urgent comes up. Explain that unnecessary questions and interruptions during work time slow down progress and may affect the schedule and budget.

Weekly meetings also keep me in tune with the homeowners' state of mind, teaching me how to give them what they want and improve on what they don't like. Do the daily cleanups look okay? Are my guys trampling on border plants? I can't keep every client happy all of the time, but these meetings improve the odds.

Payment Collections

The way a customer pays is another form of communication that tells me a lot about the kind of job I'm doing. Cheerful payment probably means they're happy with the job, but if they write out the check grudgingly, then I suspect there's a problem.

I find that the best approach is to simply ask what's bothering them. The customer may be having a bad day that's unrelated to the job, or they might be depressed just because it's tough to let go of $10,000, no matter how good my work is. In some cases, however, there is a problem, and this becomes my opportunity to fix it. It might be something small, like the way a stack of materials blocks part of the driveway or the fact that the trim we're about to install isn't quite what they thought it would be. By tending to these concerns early, I can usually keep minor irritants from becoming major problems.

The Punch List

When the job is closing, I use a punch list to wrap things up and get the final payment. About a week before completion, I ask the clients for their list, and then add some items of my own. The punch-list process both reminds the clients of my high standards and reassures them that I will complete the job properly. I explain that I expect final payment when I've finished everything on the list; anything after that will be handled, but it will be considered warranty work.

Post-Job Relations

Finally, maintaining contact after the job is done is an effective way to get new work and good referrals. I conduct a satisfaction survey anywhere from a month to three months after the job, and do checkups at six months and twelve months. Mostly I make little repairs, like fixing nail pops or recaulking, but the cost is minimal and the payback is great.

I stay in touch with customers via phone, cards, and drop-in visits. Occasionally, I'll drive a bucket of balls or have a drink with a past client, or my wife and I will have dinner out with a husband-and-wife client, but this kind of entertaining is reserved for clients with whom I've worked well and for whom I'd enjoy working again. I typically get more than one call from clients with whom I've stayed in touch, but I get far fewer from those with whom I haven't. As a rule, I make contact at least twice a year, even if I know my customer has no future plans for remodeling. Why? Because my work will be seen by their friends and family, and I love referrals.

Communicating well makes my business run better. I get more work, make better profits, and enjoy a good reputation with satisfied clients. Like that buddy of mine, I could build a house with just one tool, but the tool I'd pick is "communication."

By Norman Allaby, a remodeling contractor from Connecticut.

Chapter 3

Personnel

Working Hard for Your Employees

Speed and quality in production depend on the people who work for you. Give them all you've got.

Trying to keep framers motivated to produce, to keep conscious of quality, and to stay committed to you for more than a few paychecks is what makes life interesting for framing contractors. Or it can be a nightmare. I carry between 40 and 50 full-time framers on my payroll these days, and over time I've discovered a few things that work, and a lot of things that don't.

Perhaps most important is realizing what service you're selling. About 70% of my company's work is custom residential framing; the balance is light commercial and multifamily. But overall, more than two-thirds of our total volume of $1.5 million is in labor-only contracts.

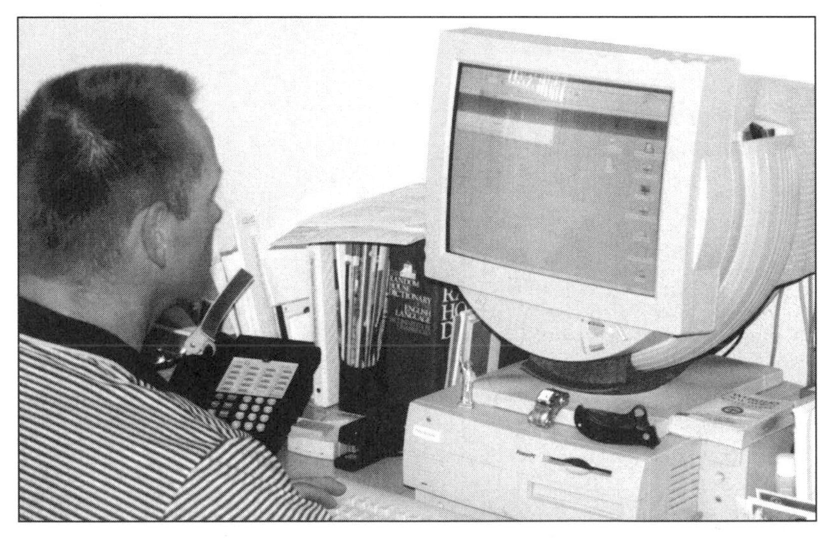

Author Mike Davis divides his time between bidding in the office (top) and visiting job sites (above).

That means our primary product is labor, and labor is nothing more than people. How my guys feel about working for me, therefore, has a lot to do with my bottom line. So I invest a lot of time and money in making my company the best place they've ever worked.

The Old School

This attitude wasn't one I saw much of when I was a framer, nor is it one I understood when I was first running my own crews. My introduction to framing was working for a piece-crew that built Motel 6 units all over the Southwest. We worked six to seven days a week and used up every hour of sunlight. We lived out of our trucks, hotels, and the occasional tool trailer. It was as rough as it sounds, but we made good money and we had a lot of fun.

Those years taught me some valuable lessons. I learned to hustle, I realized that time really is money, and I saw that no supervisor could ever hope to push an employee as hard as an employee will push himself if he's properly motivated.

Some years later, I found myself running framing crews here in Albuquerque. At first, I hired piece workers (that was the way I'd always seen it done), but I always seemed to end up on the short end of the stick. I didn't feel as though I had enough control over the work, and the quality I was getting showed that. So I switched over to hourly crews.

Although I worked hard, I wasn't sure how to motivate others to do the same without the leverage of piece work. A couple of close friends were the lead men on the crews. We were all young, and none of us had a clue about management. We basically tried to rule with peer pressure and intimidation.

I remember hiring a group of framers once, and telling them "We have purposely overhired. We don't need all of you, and so, at the end of the day the slowest man is down the road." Thinking back, it's a wonder that they didn't

Managing The Managers

Since most of the people management in our company is done by crew leaders, it's important to train them to manage effectively. And since our crew leaders are promoted from the ranks, we need to help them make the transition.

A supervisor's first duty is to supervise. This is a very difficult message to get across to a tradesperson who is used to performing physical work. Supervising means making sure that every member of the crew understands exactly what he has to do, and that he has the tools and materials needed for the job. Then, if there's any time left over, the crew leader can beat in a few nails.

To start our crew leaders thinking about how to work with people instead of with wood, we give them all copies of the book *The One Minute Manager*, by Kenneth Blanchard and Spencer Johnson (Berkley Publishing Group, New York, 1981), and we demand that they read it. Some of them aren't real keen on having to do "homework," but with lots of peer pressure, we get them to read it. Most now say that the book has helped them manage the people on their crews.

According to the authors, a manager has three responsibilities. First, a manager must communicate effectively so that workers know exactly what he wants done. Second, he must set clear production goals. Third, he must keep workers informed about where they stand.

Communicating instructions. A crew leader has to make sure he communicates his instructions very clearly. It's critical that a crew leader take the time to do this. Typically an employee doesn't want to appear stupid. When confronted, most will say they understand a job, whether they do or not. Therefore, when giving instructions, we teach our crew leaders to have a carpenter repeat the instructions in his own words. This gives the crew leaders a feel for exactly what the carpenter understands, so they can fine-tune any misunderstood points.

In one of our weekly meetings recently, a crew leader described how he instructed a carpenter to head out an opening in a TJI roof system. He showed the guy the two pieces of stock he wanted him to use, showed him how to lay it out, and left him alone to do it. Nonetheless, the carpenter botched the job and the crew leader lost his temper with the guy.

When this was discussed, everyone at the meeting agreed that it wasn't the carpenter's fault. If the crew leader had taken more time to be sure that his instructions had been understood, the problem could have been avoided.

Setting production goals. Goal setting requires that you estimate a reasonable time frame for job completion. This starts in the office. We provide each crew leader with an estimate of the worker-hours required for each job. In turn, the crew leader shares this information with his crew, so everyone has an idea of how the crew is doing. At the end of each day, they can look at how many worker-hours they've used up and see if they're ahead of schedule or behind, and whether they have to hustle to make up for lost time, or just to beat the estimate.

On an individual basis, it's up to established crew members to give new employees examples of good performance. Most of this responsibility lies with the crew leader because he's the most experienced, but we also encourage advanced carpenters to help bring less skilled guys along.

It's important to get crew members involved in policing themselves. Getting good performance when the boss is around is easy. The true measure of performance is what happens when the boss isn't around, which is most of the time.

One minute praise. The principle behind the *The One Minute Manager* is summarized by the phrase "Feedback is the breakfast of champions." You let someone know how they are doing with "one minute praisings" and "one minute reprimands." It's important to give feedback to every employee, and it's especially important when working with new employees.

A new employee is one of a crew leader's biggest challenges. The crew leader has to take special care explaining the task at hand, and then watch closely to see if the employee meets the expected goals. The idea isn't to intimidate the guy. The goal is to watch the new employee until you can catch him doing something *right*. Then let the employee know exactly what he did right and encourage him to continue.

If you're not getting the performance you want, you first have to decide whether this is an "I can't" or an "I won't" problem. If it's "I can't," then you have to redirect the person. This is just a training problem. If it's an "I won't" then you have an attitude problem and a reprimand is in order.

When reprimanding an employee, tell him what he's done wrong, but don't verbally assault or humiliate him. Call him aside and discuss the problem in a professional manner. It's important to remember that you are criticizing the person's behavior, not the person himself. Also, let him know he has value, despite his problem behavior. Finally make sure that he understands that the reprimand is over. This way you can both get back to doing your jobs and not waste time fuming. — *M.D.*

just kill me on the spot. But it was 1982, and construction in New Mexico was at a standstill. Needless to say, these techniques were less than effective. We were running about 20 to 25 men then, and we'd go through four to five hundred employees a year due to turnover.

Although construction is still pretty slow here, good framers are hard to find. If I lose a framer, I know he'll be very difficult, if not impossible, to replace. The obvious answer is "Just pay 'em better than the next guy, and you'll keep 'em," but money isn't the only thing. Last year, some of my guys were offered more money by a competitor and they turned it down.

Why? A combination of little things. There isn't any magic formula you can follow to make your employees happy. A lot of it is breaking out of your old attitudes, and treating the guys who work for you like real people. Here are some of the things I do along that line.

It Starts With the Boss

An important part of managing people is communication. I once worked for a guy who told me that the key to successful management was never to socialize with your employees — if you get too close they'll start thinking they can take advantage of you.

It's true that when you get out there and start mixing with the guys you can find yourself in some awkward situations. For instance, the new guys will always try to hit you up for a raise, but that's all part of the business. Employees need to know what's going on in a business to feel as if they're part of it. And they want to hear about it from the guy who's making the big decisions. This means getting out there, getting to know the guys on your crews, and giving them a chance to get to know you. Those of us who are tradesmen turned businessmen have a real advantage here.

Now I make a special effort to know the name of every employee, and to say hello when I'm on the job site—not as the boss to his subordinate, but as one framer to another. I don't have to fake this respect. I know they work hard, I know they're out there in the heat and the cold, and I appreciate the fact that they are choosing to work for me.

Communication

Since we have a lot of people on a lot of different job sites, the way we keep in touch with everyone is with a newsletter produced on my Macintosh computer. It gets handed out with the paychecks.

The first thing we cover in the newsletter is scheduling. We list the jobs that are under way, and jobs that are coming up. If this does nothing else, it provides the guys with a sense of job security and lets them know where they'll be going next. The newsletter also talks freely about jobs we're hoping to get, and how that fits into our plans as a company.

Another topic for every newsletter is how current projects are going. We're pretty frank — we applaud the winners and analyze the losers. We don't point fingers at individuals or crews, but if we're falling short when it comes to safety or quality, the newsletter points it out as a company problem that we all need to solve. We talk about both our strengths and our weaknesses as a company, and we ask the guys for suggestions on how we can make things more efficient.

We get some of our best ideas from our crew members. They're the ones out there doing the work, so no one should know better how to make it go more smoothly. And they appreciate that they have a say in how things are done.

While we want all of our workers to be team players, we also want to reward our top performers. Everyone has that dual need: on one hand, to be part of a winning team or a great company, but on the other, to be noticed and to stand out as someone special.

Along these lines, we talk in the newsletter about the successes of individual crew members. If someone learns something new, like how to cut stairs or figure rafter lengths, we write it up. Basically, we brag about him a little to let him know that we appreciate the effort he has made.

In addition, we have a program called "Framer of the Month." Every week the carpenters on each crew nominate the crew member they think has been working the hardest. The nominees are listed in the newsletter. At the end of each month, the framer with the most nomi-

Framing Square's bonus incentive plan doesn't reward just crew leaders—it applies to all members of the crew.

nations wins a cash bonus of fifty dollars and recognition in the newsletter.

We also recognize employees on their anniversaries with the company, and use birthdays and children's births as good excuses to joke with them in print. This helps promote a team spirit.

And speaking of teams, we play league softball as a company. We pay all the fees and buy jerseys and balls so it doesn't cost the crew members anything to play. They're not the top team in the league, but they have a great time. It's a chance to get families out there, and for all of us to socialize a little bit.

Insurance and Retirement

We have a major medical plan ($250 deductible), and anyone who has been with us for a year or more can get coverage. We pay half. For a single man, the cost of coverage is around $8 a week.

When I set the plan up, I thought it would be a big plus, but as it turned out, few of our people participate in it. Our guys range in age from about 25 to 30 — still young enough that they don't feel threatened by illness.

We also have a profit-sharing trust that contributes money towards employees' retirement in years when the company makes a profit. We started the program back in 1987, but construction has been pretty slow since then, and we've only accumulated $45,000 to date. That's not going to give any of our guys thoughts of retiring once it's divided up, but it's enough to show that we're interested in their future as well as the company's.

The Bonus Program

The latest program we've initiated is the Bonus Incentive Plan. Unlike retirement, which is a pretty distant concept for some of our guys, the bonus is based on dividing up 10% of the company's profits each month among the employees. The money goes to everyone in the company from top to bottom, not to just the crew leaders.

This system rewards the performance of the company instead of the performance of one crew or one person. This helps to build a company identity, because everyone feels they are on the same team, instead of competing against each other.

Here's how we make the split. First, we figure out how much we made for the month and come up with a pool of dollars based on 10% of the profits. Then we divide each crew member's earnings by the total payroll for the month to come up with their individual percentage. We multiply this percentage by the amount we have allocated for bonuses and come out with how much to pay each employee. It works like this:

The bonus money available for August is $2,350

Kramer Framer made $1,000 in August

Total payroll in August is $29,382.68

$1,000 divided by $29,382.68 = 3.4%

Kramer gets 3.4% of the $2,350 bonus pool

$2,350 x .034 = $79.90

By basing the bonus on an individual's wages, it reflects each worker's merit. By using total wages earned rather than hourly rate as a gauge, this system also credits the person who showed up every day. This may sound as though we're complicating the simple idea of giving a bonus for hard work, but bonuses can be tricky. Although the guys are all pals, there is a pecking order within the company and on each crew, and there are no secrets when it comes to how much everyone makes. So when it comes time to give a bonus, you don't want to cross those established lines or you can end up creating serious resentments.

Structured Meetings

While these motivational tools are important, they would be meaningless if the company wasn't well organized.

We have nine crews, each functioning as its own little company under the umbrella of the parent company. Once we have a project under contract, we schedule it and assign it to a crew leader, who takes over from there. Crew leaders order their own materials, schedule their own equipment, work directly with clients, and negotiate all change orders. They also do their own hiring and firing. The office staff is there to give any kind of support the crew leaders may need, but unless there's a problem, we stay out of their way on day-to-day affairs.

To keep all nine crews in sync with each other, we have weekly meetings every Wednesday evening. All crew leaders get paid to attend. In addition, we invite a representative who is nominated from the ranks of each crew to sit in.

After we have all the men and equipment lined up, we look at the jobs that we're bidding and negotiating, along with any payment problems, safety concerns, changes in insurance requirements, legal issues, and other general information. We also discuss financial matters. Everyone in the company participates in the bonus plan, so we all keep a watchful eye on the bottom line.

We then give the crew reps a chance to speak up. The crew rep is there to relay information back to each crew. In turn, we ask for input from them. Whether it's a production issue, a safety concern, or a policy matter, we want to know how we can do better.

We share a great deal of information with our people, far more than most companies. But we want our people involved in the decision making process, and they can't make informed decisions without the information.

Must Be Honest

These programs are expensive, but we have the happiest crews we've ever had. Our turnover rate has dropped dramatically in the past few years, and the quality of our work is up. I'm also enjoying my job more now, and that's worth something. I've even received several calls from former employees who wanted to let me know how much they enjoyed working for us and how good the newsletter made them feel. One of those framers was a guy I had fired—quite a switch from the death threats I used to get.

There is a risk in this approach, though. It doesn't work if it's not honest. If you don't believe what you're telling your crews, they'll know, and no program of perks is going to help you. If your heart's not in it, leave well enough alone — or you'll undoubtedly do yourself more harm than good.

By Michael Davis, owner of Framing Square Construction in Albuquerque, N.M.

Three Ways to Keep Good Help

Show genuine respect, offer good pay and time off, and hold on to those good employees

We all know the old saying, "Good help is hard to find," but keeping top-notch employees can be even harder. Offers from competitors, the thought of going into business for themselves, and a host of other options are a constant temptation to even the most loyal employees. Larger companies counter with benefits like health insurance, retirement accounts, stock options, and performance bonuses, but these may be too expensive for a small business.

Fortunately, I've found three other ways to retain key employees that just about any company can use. There's no magic formula, however: Unless you genuinely care about your employees, none of the following suggestions will have much value.

Acknowledgement and Respect

The work of one of our lead carpenters is so exemplary that customers go out of their way to tell us. One customer called him "an artist of woodwork;" another said he was "the god of carpentry." We call him George.

When we hear a good report about George from a customer, we make sure to tell him. Regardless of how many times I have said, "Hey, George, looks like you've gained another fan," he has yet to tire of hearing it.

We also tell George and other members of the crew what *we* think of their work. Some contractors worry that if you praise employees too often, they'll want more money, but we haven't found this to be true. Then again, we pay on the high side, and we let them know that, too.

Constructive criticism. We also refrain from screaming and yelling. If someone's work needs to be done over or changed, I figure I don't need to blast them out. Having to do the work over is punishment enough.

When critiquing the crew's work, I try to start and finish on a positive note. Even when there is a glaring mistake, I first point out something that they did well, then I give them the bad news. After discussing the problem and how to correct it, I come back to what they did well. Ending on a positive note keeps morale up, which makes for a more productive job.

Taking an employee's advice is one of the best — and most difficult — ways to show respect. When I figure a job, for example, I typically believe that I have determined the most efficient way of doing the work. Sometimes an employee will suggest a different way and, although it's tough for me to admit, it is a better way. (Sometimes it's not — that's the part I like.) If you're not taking employee ideas seriously, you may be missing out on something that could benefit your business. Whether or not you go with the suggestion, however, is not as important to the employee as the fact that you truly considered it.

Compensation

Every job requires material and labor, and both contribute to the quality and reputation we are seeking. Since we pay a premium for materials to get the best quality, why should we expect to pay any less for the labor? Of course, just paying more does not guarantee you will get better quality, but paying less almost always guarantees you will get lower quality.

We pay on the high side of competitive wages. We also pay a Christmas bonus based on a percentage of weekly pay. But we compensate employees in other ways, too.

In addition to paid vacations (one week after the first year, two weeks after the second year), we occasionally tell employees that as soon as we finish a particular task, they can take the rest of the day off with pay. It may be that we've been pushing hard to meet a deadline, or we've been doing a particularly unpleasant job, such as crawlspace work. Employees usually appreciate the gesture, even if it turns out they knock off just an hour early.

Another way we compensate employees is to split the difference between my estimate and what the job actually cost. For example, if I figured a job to take 10 hours and it takes only 6, we might split the savings with whoever worked that job.

Social compensation. We schedule three employee events throughout the year: a "pig-pickin" (an outdoor barbecue of roast pork, for readers north of the Mason-Dixon line), a weekend fishing trip, and Christmas dinner.

We invite our employees and their entire families to the cookout. One of our guys usually volunteers to cook and share his special barbecue sauce. (You probably guessed that the "god of carpentry" is also a master at preparing barbecued pig.)

Our annual fishing trip consists of a weekend in the Outer Banks of North Carolina. The cost is reasonable because we go in October, which is the off season. So far, no one's spouse has complained about not going with us, probably because we stay in fishing cabins, not the Hilton. Everybody comes back from this trip physically tired, but mentally refreshed.

Christmas dinner is for employees and their spouses. We usually hold it at one of the nicer local restaurants. It's another break in the schedule and no one has to do anything but come and enjoy.

All three of these events cost about the same, and we consider them well worth the money in boosting morale. And it gives us a chance to get to know each other outside our work routine.

Personal Time

Allowing employees time off for personal tasks is sometimes the most important thing you can do. It lets them know you understand that working is part of their life, not their *whole* life (a news flash for some of us). Granting personal time off for a doctor or dentist appointment costs us almost nothing, but it means a lot to our crew. We stay flexible and so far, none of our employees has abused this benefit.

Moonlighting. We actually encourage moonlighting, as long as it is not done to the point of exhaustion and doesn't affect job performance. We even allow employees to borrow company tools for a weekend job, provided they ask first. We haven't yet run into trouble with this arrangement; in fact, it's been beneficial. Our clients appreciate being able to hire one of the crew for a job that's too small for us to do as efficiently as one of the guys working on his own. Of course, I might feel differently if we were not as busy as we are, or if an employee left our company and took some customers with him.

Good help is hard to find. But even if you don't have the "god of carpentry" working for you, you can still treat employees with the respect they deserve. You'll find it will help them to take pride in a job well done. Isn't that what we are all looking for?

By Howard Ferree, co-owner of Halco Construction Inc., licensed general contractors specializing in remodeling, additions, and repairs in Greenville, N.C.

A Simple Profit-Sharing System

This framing contractor's bonus system motivates employees to increase productivity, and instills a positive team spirit

My company recently framed two triplexes right next to each other. While I was busy with the joists on one building, I could hear one of my employees on the other triplex yelling, "You're as slow as subfloor glue in winter! Come on, man — I want to make a bonus on this job." I had to smile, because the team spirit in that statement was a result of what I call the Simpson Sharing System — a motivational scheme I have developed over the last 16 years.

I'm a framing contractor, and my company works on everything from houses to light-commercial buildings. We do best on the 10- to 50-unit apartment jobs. I typically have eight to ten framers, but it varies widely.

When I first started doing apartments, I realized that there were two basic types of pay structures: piecework and hourly wages. I quickly learned that most pieceworkers were fast but sloppy and that most hourly workers did quality work but were slow. Since I wanted both speed and quality, I at first decided (and the crew agreed) that we would be paid for the amount of work produced each week. For each job, I deducted all overhead from the contract, leaving an amount I called the wage base. Then each week I would estimate the percentage of work we had done and multiply that percentage by the wage base. The total amount would then be divided up among the crew on the basis of their wage rate and hours worked. It was easier to make the calculations than to explain them, but there were problems with the way this arrangement played out. It was difficult to estimate accurately the percentage of work finished, and it was hard to listen to the crew's complaints about weeks when our paychecks were less than they would have been on a straight hourly basis.

Fixed Wage Plus Bonus

We worked under this system for a couple of years until I switched to what we use today. I still deduct overhead from the contract to come up with a wage base. The difference is that each framer gets paid a fixed wage rate each week plus a bonus if there is any money left over in the wage base at the end of the job. The bonus money is split based on the number of hours each person worked and his or her hourly wage. We usually make a bonus, but it doesn't always happen.

Figure 1 is the top half of an "Expense Analysis" worksheet from the last job we did. It shows the calculations I used to back out all nonlabor costs. These include any materials, office overhead, and tools (shown as "Co. @ 6%"), plus profit or return on investment (listed as "R.O.I. @ 1%"). One additional item, listed as "Lead/Office @ 1%," allows for 1/2% each for the lead man and the office help (but only if we make a bonus on the job). I subtract this total "Fixed Expense" from the job contract amount to find the "Income Base" — the total amount of money left to cover labor for the job.

Figure 2 shows the bottom of the worksheet, which is where I keep a week-

Expense Analysis

Contract Amount	27,439.00
Materials	2,387.29
Overhead ($103/week)	824.00
Co. @ 6%	1,646.34
R.O.I. @ 1%	274.39
Lead/Office @ 1%	274.39
Van	500.00
Fixed Expense	5,906.41
Income Base	21,532.59

Figure 1. *Before each job, the author backs fixed expenses out of the contract to come up with a labor-only figure, called the "Income Base."*

Running Labor Total

Date	Wage Cost	Total	Balance	Weeks Left
Railing deduct	(500.00)			
1/17/1996	863.69			
1/24/1996	2,371.85			
1/31/1996	2,051.72			
2/7/1996	3,013.78	7,801.04	13,731.55	3.77
2/14/1996	2,953.57	10,754.61	10,777.98	2.96
2/21/1996	2,813.71	13,568.32	7,964.27	2.18
2/28/1996	2,482.72	16,051.04	5,481.55	1.50
3/6/1996	1,803.69	17,854.73	3,677.86	
Extras	405.00		4,082.86	

Figure 2. *A few weeks into the job, the author begins to track labor costs on a weekly basis. The number of "Weeks Left" are used to set productivity goals.*

Balance Analysis

Framer	Total Wages	% of Base	Gross Share	Net Earnings
SS	2,849.24	0.16	651.54	573.35
GW	2,868.33	0.16	655.90	577.20
CW	2,502.05	0.14	572.15	503.49
CL	2,321.47	0.13	530.85	467.15
JW	2,492.64	0.14	569.99	501.60
TP	2,118.90	0.12	484.53	426.39
BJ	1,302.45	0.07	297.83	262.09
TM	1,399.65	0.08	320.06	281.65
Totals	**17,854.73**			**3,592.92**

Figure 3. *When a job comes in under budget, each framer earns a bonus based on his or her base wage and the amount of time spent on the job. The gross share is adjusted downward by labor burden costs.*

ly running account of the job. The second column shows the actual amount of labor money spent in each week; I record this every Thursday night when I do payroll. The third column is a cumulative total; and the fourth column shows the amount of money left in the contract (the contract amount minus the amount in the "Total" column).

The last column, called "Weeks Left," shows how many more weeks we can work on the job and still break even. (To figure the weeks left, I just figure the cost of a 40-hour week for the full crew, then divide it into the weekly running balance.) Every Friday when I hand out the checks, I tell the crew how many weeks we have left to finish the job. We talk about how many weeks we think it will actually take, then we set our goal.

I used to use a "percent complete" calculation to estimate how much money was left in the budget, but it wasn't as helpful. Not only was it difficult to estimate the progress as a percentage, but the plain fact was that even if the "percent complete" showed we were ahead of schedule, the important number was how much money we actually had left in the contract to finish the job. By translating this into weeks, I can give my crew a progress estimate that's easy to understand — and easy to use to set a goal.

Divvying Up the Loot

At the end of the job, I use a "Balance Analysis" worksheet (Figure 3) to split up any bonus that is left. Each framer's share is based on the wages that he earned on the job as a percentage of the Income Base from the Expense Analysis. The balance from the running total for the job is multiplied by this percentage to determine each framer's gross share of the savings. I then multiply the gross amount by .88 to account for deductions that cover the employer's share of social security and unemployment compensation.

Pros and Cons

Every system has its advantages and disadvantages. On the positive side, I like my sharing system for the following reasons:

- ***Work becomes a team effort.*** Everyone's bonus is dependent on everyone else's productivity, so all employees are concerned with one another's performance. And everyone looks for ways to work more efficiently.
- ***The crew and I get weekly feedback on productivity.*** This is good for both short- and long-term analysis.
- ***The system creates reward and penalty options.*** At one time, for example, poor attendance was hurting our bonuses. We discussed it as a crew and we decided that any day a framer had an unexcused absence, his bonus would be reduced. It hasn't eliminated absenteeism, but it is a fair solution to the problem.

On the downside:

- ***Booking time increases.*** It usually takes me from one to four hours to do payroll, depending on the number of jobs we have going and setup time for any new jobs. About 10 to 20 minutes of that time is spent figuring out the employer's wage cost. It takes another 15 minutes at the beginning of each job to set up the Expense Analysis, and 30 to 45 minutes at the end of the job to fill out the Balance Analysis. Plus, there's an additional 45 minutes to an hour to write the bonus checks.

- ***Books must be current.*** Especially near the end of the job, the crew is continually checking on how we're doing. This is an advantage, too, because I am continually using these figures to analyze why it takes longer to do things than I think it should.
- ***Losses.*** To stay competitive, I am always bidding tight. Since I don't allow for loss recovery in my overhead deductions, I take it out of future bonuses. It hasn't happened enough to be a problem, and I never take more than 50% of the bonus of any job.

By Scot Simpson, owner of SS Framing, who bangs nails beside his crew on framing projects in Edmonds, Wash.

The One-Man Crew

One person working alone is usually the most efficient way to build, but special management policies are needed

We have all joked about the inefficiency of the stereotypical road crew where two people are leaning on shovels while a third does all the work. But when we stop to think about it, our own practices aren't much different: There are times when too many workers on one job creates labor cost overruns, and other times when not enough workers creates a slowdown. In the remodeling business, labor mismanagement can break any budget and ultimately cause business failure. We're all looking for ways to manage our crews for maximum production, and regulating crew size is one way to do this.

Two's A Crowd

Holding the line on the labor budget often determines the success of a remodeling company. The smaller the crew size, the better your chances are of producing a quality product and making a profit. This holds true right down to a one-man crew. If a job can be physically handled by one person, productivity will be greater than when two people are doing the same job.

Ownership. The reasons for this lie more in human nature than in job skills. As a carpenter working alone on a job assumes more responsibility, the sense of "ownership" grows. This sense that the success of a job directly depends on his or her performance increases productivity. Carpenters find the challenge of ownership hard to resist because they have traditionally been considered a dispensable part of the team.

Who's in charge? When two people are assigned to a single task, one of them inevitably becomes the supervisor and the other the supervisee. When one takes time away from work to look over another person's shoulder, productivity suffers. It's reasonable for the lead carpenter to inspect the work at various intervals to ensure quality control, but that is vastly different from two people running baseboard and both of them checking to see if the miter fits. Stopping and starting to answer questions, check work, or simply talk about what you did last night wastes valuable production time. And as crew size increases, coffee breaks seem to con-

Crew Size vs. Productivity

Original crew	Cost of original crew per hour	Cost of added worker per hour	Cost of new crew per hour	Value of production per $100 spent on new crew	
				Worst case	Best case
1 Carpenter	$20	$13 (plus 1 helper)	$33	$61	$100
1 Carpenter 1 Helper	$33	$13 (plus 1 helper)	$46	$72	$100
1 Carpenter 1 Helper	$33	$20 (plus 1 carpenter)	$53	$62	$100

Figure 1. *In general, the larger the crew, the less efficient the work—particularly when you add to a crew just to keep another worker busy. The "Worst-Case" scenario assumes the added worker stands idle while the core crew works efficiently.*

sume more time, and each day's startup and cleanup take longer as well.

People skills. Carpenters, by nature, are not usually good managers. They spend years learning their craft, but almost no time at all learning how to handle people. Good carpenters can often bring out the best in themselves, but not in others. Matching tasks to people of varying abilities and motivating them to stay within the budget while still producing a quality product are skills that must be learned. Carpenters should receive some training before they are asked to manage other workers. Personality conflicts, prejudices, and bad moods complicate matters, and inexperienced managers will tend to throw up their hands and quit trying. The minute you hear your carpenters say things like "this is not in my job description," you know you're about to throw away large chunks of money from your labor budget.

Over the years, we have had people who were excellent craftsmen, but poor managers. In one case, on a large job that required three or four people, the lead carpenter didn't produce anything himself because he couldn't let the rest of the crew do their work without constantly looking over their shoulders. In another case, a lead carpenter got it exactly backwards, assigning a helper to hang a door and giving himself the job of tearing out a tile wall. But the classic example is the carpenter who left a helper to set cabinets while he took lunch orders and went to the store. This is mismanagement at its worst: $20 an hour goes shopping while $13 an hour works.

Numbers Don't Lie

Maybe some figures will help to illustrate more clearly how this affects the budget. Start with a crew of one carpenter at a cost of $20 per hour. When you add a $13-per-hour helper to the crew, you increase your labor cost by 65% to $33 per hour. Assuming that you get maximum production out of the carpenter working alone, the value of adding the helper can vary considerably (see Figure 1).

In the best of circumstances, both will produce at full capacity and you will get $33 worth of production for your $33. It is more likely, however, that at least some of the time, the helper will simply "hold the shovel" while the carpenter works. In this case, you will spend $33 for just $20 worth of production, which works out to about 61¢ on the dollar.

This means that for every production dollar you spend on the two-man crew, you will get between 61¢ and $1 worth of work — often closer to the 61¢. (In the absolute worst-case scenario, the helper works and the carpenter holds the shovel, in which case you get a mere 40¢ on your production dollar.)

The fact is that each additional person on a crew tends to lower the crew's productivity. So unless the additional person is absolutely necessary on that job, the risk to the budget is too great to keep him on. On an average job, losing $10 to $20 out of every $100 spent on labor could add up to a large sum of money.

Managing More Than One

One person can handle an enormous amount of work, including tasks that have traditionally been done by a crew of two or more. Almost all of the work on small additions, for example, can be done by one person. Even kitchen cabinets, which are almost always installed by two people, can be leveled, fitted, positioned, and screwed in place by a lone carpenter skilled in the use of jigs and temporary supports. If the countertop requires two people, send a helper, but only after the cabinets are in place.

But some portions of a job, such as installing the rafters and sheathing, require a second or third person. Whenever it is necessary for more than one person to be on the job, follow a few simple rules.

Matchmaker. Until the lead carpenter has demonstrated an ability to manage people, take responsibility yourself for matching people to specific tasks and defining each person's role. This will help the lead carpenter learn how to use individual workers effectively; it will also eliminate power struggles or the jockeying for position that often occurs when two carpenters are assigned to the same job.

Get in and get out. The second or third person should be sent to the job as close as possible to the time he is needed and taken off the job as soon as he is no longer useful. This complicates scheduling, but it can save the bottom line. Too often we leave a person on a job long after the need for him is satisfied simply because we have nowhere else for him to work. The harsh reality is that if you don't have a place for someone to work productively, you should give him a little time off.

Request forms. Finally, use a weekly request form to handle changing manpower requirements (see Figure 2). These forms should be turned in one week in advance to give office personnel time to evaluate the situation. Using forms will also force your lead carpenters to plan their manpower needs more carefully.

WEEKLY REQUEST FORM

Job________ Lead Carpenter ________ Date______

SUBCONTRACTOR SCHEDULE

	Subcontractor	Work Required	Date Wanted	Date Sched.
1.				
2.				
3.				
4.				
5.				

SPECIAL ORDER ITEMS

	Item Specs	Date Wanted	Date Sched.
1.			
2.			
3.			
4.			
5.			
6.			

INFORMATION NEEDED

1. ________
2. ________
3. ________
4. ________
5. ________
6. ________

Personnel Needed ______ When ______

What Task________

PAPER WORK NEEDED

Time Cards ______ Order Forms ____ Job Logs ______

Weekly Request ______ Hours Report____ Budget Report____

Figure 2. *The author's lead carpenters submit this form every week to keep him up-to-date on their needs for material, manpower, and information.*

Time and Space

The time frame in which a job must be completed often affects manpower scheduling. Even though one carpenter working alone will be better for your budget, time constraints may require a larger crew. Two people can complete a job faster than one, but the trick is to maintain efficiency. The best way to do this is to divide the job into smaller tasks and create several one-man crews. This gives each person ownership of a piece of the job and encourages him to work independently. For instance, while a mason lays block for the foundation, a carpenter can take care of the interior demolition. A large project can be organized by room or by individual tasks, like all door trim or all baseboard. Make lists of tasks so that each person can move quickly from one task to another without having to stop and think about what comes next. Write this list down on paper (not a scrap of 2x4) and post it on a clipboard where everyone can see it and check off tasks as they are completed.

The size of the work space also dictates crew size on many remodeling jobs. Whoever is responsible for scheduling manpower must take into account that only a certain number of people can work in one space at a time. Kitchens and baths are usually too small for more than one worker, and you waste money when you have two people working in a one-person space.

Lead Carpenter

A one-man crew works best, but only if you don't juggle your personnel too much. We solve this problem by using lead carpenters on every job. These people can have a variety of titles, but whatever you call them, they carry the job from start to finish as on-site working supervisors.

Because a lead carpenter is on the site all day every day, he acts as a go-between for office personnel and helps the company respond to the client quickly and effectively. In the traditional management approach, in which a series of different crews moves through the job, the client doesn't feel comfortable enough with any one person to discuss problems or ask questions. When this happens, clients tend to bury their concerns until later. In the meantime, small problems may grow into major points of contention.

In addition to performing a substantial amount of the actual construction, the lead carpenter is responsible for ordering material, setting the schedule, calling subs, and finishing up all punchlist details. This frees up the production manager or company owner to focus on other aspects of the business — company growth, job costs, special-order items, change orders, and customer service — instead of having to be on the job to ensure that the work is being done.

The biggest problem with this system is that as a job nears completion, the lead carpenter will become anxious to move on and will "forget" the details. The temptation is to leave punchlist items to another carpenter while the lead starts a new project. But if this is allowed to happen, the job will drag on for several weeks after it should have been completed. It's better for both morale and the budget when the lead carpenter stays on the job until all the details are finished.

Motivation

Every carpenter is different, and you must find out what motivates and challenges each person. Some carpenters are spurred by a compliment, others by fear. Approaching each person on a level that they will understand and respond to will result in greater productivity.

Responsibility. In our company, we introduced financial incentives to try to boost productivity, but it had only a marginal effect because the carpenters felt they were already working as well as they could. Since money was tight and we couldn't raise wages, we abandoned the bonus system in favor of giving the carpenters more responsibility for the jobs they were doing. The jury is still out on this plan, but it has created lots of enthusiasm and we expect to see greater profitability.

Freedom. When you give people responsibility, you must also give them the freedom to get the job done in their own way. If you micromanage, it will drive your carpenters crazy. As long as they build safely and according to plan, we allow them the freedom to use their own techniques and abilities, including problem solving. Not only does this improve morale, it also makes good use of an individual's experience to help get through the tough situations that come up regularly.

Information. For this system to work properly, however, you have to provide your lead carpenters with as much information as possible. They should have all the paperwork associated with their projects, including budget, contracts, and price lists. This also means telling them how much profit you expect the job to generate, and how you plan to earn it. This is an issue of trust, but if a person believes they've been entrusted with inside information, their production will improve. And the more they know, the easier it will be for them to make decisions that will be good for the company.

Quality control. At the same time, you have to maintain quality. Make regular checks and learn how to correct without criticizing. Use a checklist at each major step in the production process to inspect the work for conformance to the plans and specs. This will eliminate many problems down the road.

Attitude. Your enthusiasm can be catching. The way you or your field supervisor approach troublesome jobs will affect the attitude of the lead carpenters. If they are beaten down by the problems on their jobs, it will show in their work. The first rule should be "no bad-mouthing the client," no matter how hard the job becomes. I've had carpenters describe their projects as "the job from hell," and I have heard clients called worse; it has always had a bad effect on morale. An optimistic attitude will also leave its mark.

The lead carpenter concept creates a new class of carpenters who no longer feel expendable. Because they are a critical link in the success of the company, they have a more positive, optimistic outlook on the job. This leads to better productivity and improved efficiency.

By Timothy Faller, a veteran contractor and lead carpenter, and current production manager at Hopkins & Porter Construction in Potomac, Md. Faller is also the author of The Lead Carpenter Handbook, *published by* The Journal of Light Construction.

Writing a Company Manual

Putting your policies on paper improves morale and prevents misunderstandings

Did you know that, when interviewing a potential employee, you can't ask their age but you can ask their birth date? I discovered that gem of bureaucratic logic while putting together a company manual for my 20-person remodeling firm. This kind of surprise discovery is just one of the side benefits that justifies the time and effort that goes into researching and writing a manual.

Why Write a Manual?

I decided to write a manual because my company was growing. The subjective and sometimes inconsistent way I had handled policies, such as what the dress code was and whether to advance vacation time, was causing misunderstandings. I needed something that would help everyone, including me, understand the "rules," as well as the company's business philosophy. Clearly, after five years in the business, it was time to write things down.

If you're big enough to have a staffer in charge of human resources, the temptation is to have that person do the bulk of the work on your manual. You'll find, however, that the end product is likely to weigh as much as a good keeper walleye, and have a table of contents at least five pages long. Reading it will be a great cure for insomnia. I think it's best for the owner or president of the business to do at least a detailed outline of what should be included. (Once I decided it was really time to sit down and do it, I was able to sketch a rough draft in one weekend.) The end result will be shorter, plus writing it yourself will teach you a lot about your business.

What drove the writing of our manual was the need for clear and consistent policies about fringe benefits like sick leave and vacation time. Our company, like most these days, is made up of working spouses with children. When both spouses work, coordinating vacations can be a nightmare for the family, and raises several questions: Do you advance unearned vacation time to an employee whose spouse can only take vacation at a certain time? Can an employee carry over vacation to another year or take pay instead of time off? If so, how much? Do you lend some time to someone who is sick for longer than their accrued sick

Getting Started on Your Company Manual

This outline of our company manual is intended to serve as a springboard for you to start thinking about what to include in yours. If you're thorough, your manual will most likely include a lot of the same information, while differing in key areas. It depends on where you live, the size of your company, and the particulars of your business.

Whatever you decide to include, your manual will be most useful if you try to write it from the perspective of the people who will use or benefit from it. As a reality check, ask someone who is not familiar with the details of your business to critique the draft for you. Then show it to your employees. And make sure you have it reviewed by your attorney.

Introduction
This section includes our mission statement, a welcome statement, a brief company history, business references, and a statement that we're an equal opportunity employer. By its nature, a manual tends to focus on prohibitions instead of positives. The introduction is the best place to put a friendly face on your company.

Conditions of Employment
We stress the importance of giving accurate information on the job application and during job interviews. This section also includes policies on probationary status, starting and quitting times, breaks and lunch hours, and limitations on outside employment.

Compensation
This section describes how often employees are paid, when the first check is due, our overtime policy, our schedule for performance reviews, and how we handle changes in pay status. An explanation of performance reviews also belongs here.

Benefits
Included are the details of our insurance and retirement plans, holiday and vacation policies, and what company discounts are available. It's important to reserve the right to change any or all benefits without notice (provided the changes are lawful).

Conduct
This section defines what company information is confidential, stresses the need for honesty, and lays out how employees will address clients and treat their property. It also includes our dress code, the language we permit on the job, our policies on smoking, drugs, and alcohol, and our prohibition of racial, social, or sexual harassment.

Equipment, Tools & Safety
Here we list the safety equipment required on the job, the acceptable condition of the tools we use, and what employees should do in the case of injury or property damage. This is a very detailed section. It's important for personnel to know what to do in the event of an accident that causes injury or property damage. Our manual is quite specific about this, and we explain it to employees after they've read it. We also state our policy on OSHA compliance.

Administration
This section states general company philosophy, and covers any issues which don't fall under the other headings. These include what offenses will lead to termination and what conditions will be grounds for random substance abuse testing, as well as our grievance procedures.

---

leave? Spelling out the answers makes your policies clear to current and potential employees.

I believe paid time off is important. Everyone needs to get away, to spend time with the family and to get rid of the stress that comes at times to all jobs. Not too many years ago, small construction companies rarely gave paid vacations to hourly workers, and while holidays were observed, most companies didn't pay for them. With today's shortage of skilled labor, however, you need a good benefits package to lure and retain competent talent.

Assembling the Pieces

I started the writing process by looking at other companies' manuals. Some of our larger suppliers had them, as did some of the companies our employees' spouses worked for. Once I had identified what kind of tone I wanted, I asked three of my employees to list the topics they thought we should cover. Their lists were nearly identical, and included conditions of employment, compensation, benefits, conduct, tools and safety, and administration (see "Getting Started on Your Company Manual").

After settling on the list, we sought out some guidance on how to proceed. Our company is a member of the National Association of Homebuilders (NAHB), whose legal department is an invaluable source for general legal advice (though it does not act as a for-hire attorney). They warned us about some of the potential legal pitfalls we faced, especially in the areas of hiring and compensation, and let us know what you generally can and can't do (even, as I've pointed out, what questions you can ask an interviewee). The NAHB Bookstore also had some good guidelines available, as did our public library.

To supplement all of this general advice, we also asked our attorney about our state's hiring guidelines. For instance, we require potential hires to take a simple, 12-minute test that shows how well they can follow written instructions; we also have all skilled field applicants complete a construction skills profile, telling us what they know how to do. We do a background check on everyone, which includes credit, driving record, criminal history, and education verification. The requirements and procedures that go along with these checks vary from state to state.

When the manual was substantially complete, we ran it past several employees for their comments and suggestions. This improved the manual, since the employees had concerns that needed to be addressed. One of these was that the manual be manageable in size. Keep it short but clear, they said (ours is 23 pages long).

If you decide to write your manual piecemeal, don't show it to your employees until you have a complete draft. A complete draft mixes positive policies with the less palatable rules. By presenting these together, you'll get more balanced feedback. In addition, you will find that your employees bring a lot of interest and enthusiasm to the project, but may not be able to sustain it over the extended time required for a piecemeal review.

What To Cover

How many employees you have affects the issues you cover (and in how much detail) more than how much business you do. If you have eight employees, it's easy to communicate directly with all of them, so a short, basic manual may be all you need. When you have a dozen or more people, as we did when we wrote our manual, you need a lot more detail. That said, we found as we cut and rewrote our manual that we didn't need a rule for every situation. In fact, I consider the best parts to be those that help employees form judgments rather than simply giving them rules. This is so important that I'll back an employee who makes a wrong decision if the intent of the decision was to support a company policy.

For instance, we don't allow moonlighting. That doesn't mean one of our employees can't help build an addition for his parents or his church. But we want to talk about it first. Everyone understands the intent is to keep people from working a second job.

We don't let employees salvage materials on tearout either, even if the homeowner says it's okay. Salvage rights belong to the company, and are company property just as much as the new lumber. Employees who want to bring home a couple of old windows must get permission from a supervisor first. We also don't want employees to use first names with clients. The intent is to treat clients with respect and to let the client decide what his or her relationship is with the lead carpenter or project manager. If a client tells an employee to address him or her by first name, that's okay; but the client should be introduced to a third party by the appropriate title, whether it's Mr. Jones, Ms. Abraham, or Dr. Smith.

Who Gets a Copy?

Once the manual was complete, we made copies for all our employees. We asked each of them to read it, and to sign an acknowledgment that they had done so. The acknowledgements went into their permanent personnel files.

We've also found it worthwhile to show our manual to our vendors and subcontractors. Not only does this enhance our professional image among the people with whom we do business, but we consider it only fair to let them know our policies on things like smok-

Policy Excerpts

Vacation
Upon the completion of one full year of continuous, full-time employment, you will receive five (5) days paid time off. Vacation time the first twelve (12) months is not accrued and no vacation time is due to any employee until one full year (365 days) of service is completed.

Sick Pay
After six (6) months continuous full-time service, employees earn paid sick leave at the rate of five (5) days per year. Sick leave may be accumulated to a total of ten (10) days. If sick leave is taken for three or more days consecutively, the employee shall furnish a physician's explanation of the reason for absence. Earned (accrued) but unused sick leave shall not be paid upon termination.

Management may at its discretion, advance sick leave to any employees without creating a policy or obligation to do so for any other employees.

Ordering, Pickup/Return of Materials
All materials and/or equipment used for jobs are to be ordered with a job number. Suppliers are told NOT to give materials out without a job number but sometimes they forget — make sure it is on the ticket. Turn in all receipts EVERY DAY!

Salvage
Salvage of items from any job site is prohibited without the permission of your supervisor. This does not include permission of the client. Salvage rights to all materials or items removed from the job site belong to the company unless the materials and other items are to remain the property of the client.

Employee salvage is permitted and welcomed, provided it is cleared by the supervisor. Items so covered are to be removed from the job site or office immediately.

Employee Purchases and Discount
After six (6) months of continuous service, full-time employees may purchase products through the company and shall be entitled to certain discounts. All purchases shall be approved in writing by the president of WCI before placing the order. The employee will be responsible for payment (in full) upon delivery. In some cases the employee may be required to pay a deposit with the order. WCI offers no warranty for any such purchase and will not participate in any delivery or installation thereof without prior written approval by the president.

Equipment & Tools
All company-owned, portable tools and equipment for the job are to be brought back to the company each day. For any exceptions, see your supervisor. If in doubt, bring it back — Remember, you may not be going back to the same job the next morning and the tools may be needed elsewhere.

Orders from a Client
Occasionally, a client may ask you to change something from the plans or instructions you were given by the company. When this happens, make whatever notes you need to have complete instructions and inform your supervisor. If it is something the client wants done right away, explain that you are not authorized to make a change without first clearing it with the office. If the client says they will take the responsibility, it makes no difference. Apologize, but be firm and get in touch with someone. This is for your protection.

Moonlighting
If you are requested to perform duties outside your regular responsibility or asked to do work on your own time for less money or more money, politely explain that you are not allowed to do that and tell your supervisor ASAP. Do the same if a client asks you to recommend someone else.

Note: Excerpts are taken from the Weiss & Company manual and may not comply with the laws of your state. Check with an attorney. The excerpts have been used with permission and may not be reproduced without the written consent of the author.

ing and loud radios before they show up at one of our job sites.

By the way, we call our manual a "company" manual rather than an "employee" manual because the policies it contains apply not only to employees, but also to vendors and subs who interact with employees and clients.

Other Benefits

Our manual has been of extraordinary value in hiring. I ask interviewees to show up 10 minutes early, and hand them a copy of our manual to browse. It answers a lot of questions they would have asked in the interview, allowing me to focus on the questions I want to ask about them. I let good prospects take the manual home with them to show to their family. This lets the family decide together whether the company is a good fit for them, which really reduces turnover later on.

If a prospect is considering other job offers, the manual can show them why your company is a better place to work. Just the fact that you've taken the time to think through your policies and write them down can make an impression. The more organized, thoughtful, and cohesive your company is and appears to be, the more inviting it will be to someone making a career move.

At times, our manual has even served as a sales aid, since it helps reassure potential clients about our management abilities. If you decide to write a company manual, make it a good manual about a good company. I'll bet you'll discover, as we did, that it's a versatile tool.

By M.M. (Mike) Weiss, Jr., CGR, president of Weiss & Co., Inc., a design/build remodeling firm in Carmel, Ind. Weiss is national chairman of the NAHB's Certified Graduate Remodelers Board of Governors.

Getting Practical About Job-Site Safety

To prevent serious accidents, the boss must set the right tone, spell out the policies, and enforce them

As most of us know from personal experience, construction is dangerous work. That means some of the people who work for you are going to get hurt sooner or later. But how often and how badly they're injured isn't just a matter of luck; you can strongly influence the outcome by taking a realistic and consistent approach toward on-site safety.

A Few Sobering Facts

If someone gets hurt on one of your job sites because of a hazard you could have corrected, it's defined as negligence, and it can cost you everything you have in a legal judgment. If someone is killed on your job and it's defined as criminal negligence, OSHA will do everything within its considerable power to see that you go to jail for up to 18 months and pay fines up to $50,000. And it doesn't matter that you weren't there. Someone has to be held responsible, and most states protect site foremen from prosecution.

Think it can't happen to you? Try these numbers on for size. An employee sustains an on-the-job injury every 18 seconds in this country, and a workman is killed every 47 minutes. The most dangerous profession according to OSHA statistics? Construction.

But don't think you can just drive out to the job tomorrow morning and tell your foreman that you want a safe site and expect it to happen. No one cares as much about your business as you do. You've got to set the tone, spell out the standards you want enforced, and keep hammering at it.

The trick is to find that fine line between what you can do to make your job safer, and what you have to do to get the job done. You've got to tailor your safety program to fit your jobs and your people, or it won't be taken seriously at the level where it counts.

I put my greatest safety efforts into four major areas: hiring, training, drug and alcohol policies, and equipment.

Safe Hiring

Statistics tell us that 5% of all accidents are caused by unsafe conditions;

Davis warns his framers to release the nail-gun trigger between shots. In the past, one framer shattered a finger by "bounce nailing." Another had to have a 16d nail surgically removed from the ball of his ankle.

Straight Talk About Safe Tool Use

After writing $4,000 checks to your insurance carrier for workers compensation month after month, you get to the point where you see a job site not as a workplace, but as a series of accidents waiting to happen. The three biggest hazards on my sites without question are saws, nail guns, and scaffolding.

Here are the main tool safety tips my crew bosses and I give a guy on his first day and thereafter if he doesn't pay attention.

Saws. I figure the 6-inch scar on my right thigh gives me the right to talk about not getting lax with a power saw. Most carpenters know how to cut safely, but they get in a hurry. We make it clear that nobody gets fired for taking the time to set up a cut.

There are two ways most people get hurt, and both of them involve binding the saw. First, someone will try to rip a 2x4 while holding on to it with his other hand. The saw will bind and kick back, and he'll lose a finger or two. Second, someone will block up a piece of lumber on a saw horse improperly and when he tries to cut it, the saw will bind and kick back and bury itself in his leg.

To prevent saw injuries, we make the following recommendations:

- If you're cutting a large board, put a block under it and use your foot to hold it down. If you're cutting a small piece, tack it to a saw horse.
- Unplug the saw before changing blades or fishing for that 1/4-inch slice of fir that wedged itself between the blade and the guard.
- Avoid cutting nails, especially with a carbide-tipped saw blade. The nail head or carbide chunk coming your way will not only be very hot, but will be traveling at a high rate of speed.
- Always adjust the depth of the blade so it's cutting no more than 1/4-inch deeper than the material. This is easier on the saw and leaves less blade exposed.
- Make sure all saws and power cords are grounded. You don't want to get a jolt in the middle of a cut, and I don't want to have to pay the fine OSHA levies if they happen to drop by and the cords don't pass muster.
- Never operate a power saw unless you're wearing safety glasses. No ifs, ands, or buts.

Nailers and staplers. These tools are great, but they're called "guns" for a reason: Depending on the size of the compressor and how much hose is being used, these tools push between 90 and 120 pounds of pressure. I've seen a sheathing nail that missed its stud tear right through the plywood and bury itself in someone's thigh on the other side. I've also had a guy shatter the bone in his finger when he accidentally shot his hand. Here are some of the rules we have laid down to prevent these kinds of accidents:

- No one operates air equipment until everyone in the immediate area is wearing protective eye glasses.
- Don't even think about holding the safety back and shooting nails or staples into the air.
- Aim all air nailers away from you when plugging them into an air hose; they'll sometimes fire a nail when the pressure comes up inside the cylinder.
- Watch out for safeties that stick in the open position, and worn trigger mechanisms that will double fire. I've even had one gun go fully "automatic" on me.
- When nailing studs to a plate, it's important to shoot the bottom nail first, then move your hand back and shoot the upper nail. This way, if the top nail splits the plate or curls out of a knot, you won't take it in your hand.
- Don't keep the trigger depressed. This may sound a little extreme, but some of the worst injuries we've seen have come from ignoring this rule when working in tight quarters or up on a scaffolding.

Scaffolding. Scaffolding didn't used to worry me, because I kept to two basic rules: Never put an inexperienced worker out on a scaffold; and always have the person working on the scaffold build it himself.

The scaffold issue is a tough one for residential contractors. Spiking some blocks to the wall, nailing triangular jacks to them, and adding a few planks is fast, cheap, and effective. The problem is they will not stand up to the scrutiny of an insurance or OSHA inspection. (OSHA requirements are so strict I don't think I've ever seen a site-built scaffold that would pass). If someone gets hurt on one of these homemade scaffolds, the owner of the business is in a very bad spot.

Our current policy is to use tubular metal scaffolding, but you still have to make sure it's dug in level and securely anchored. And if you're going up more than one section, you must use railings. If you're running siding or sheeting off the scaffold, attach them on the three open sides. If you're working overhead, then close in all four.

—M.D.

the other 95% are caused by unsafe actions. That means that you can go out to your job and hang up nets, install big red warning signs, even pad the walls, and unsafe workers will still find a way to hurt themselves.

The first step toward changing this is extensive applicant screening, something most big companies do. You start by checking the employment references of all candidates. Then you ask about preexisting injuries and handicaps, and run a physical screen and a drug screen. This process costs a few hundred dollars per applicant and takes about a week.

Good advice? You bet, but it's not realistic for most small contractors. We've tried to find a happy medium. We used to stand there and shoot the breeze with anybody who wandered on site with nailbags looking for the foreman, which often resulted in our hiring the guys whose best skills were as talkers, not workers. Now we use a three-page, preemployment screening packet we've developed.

The first page tells prospective employees a little about our company and what we have to offer. It starts out, "We're about to ask a bunch of questions about you. So we figure that it's only fair that we answer some of the questions that you might have about us." It gives an overview of our policies, tells when payday is, and that sort of thing.

The next sheet is my pride and joy. It's a simple, 15-question quiz that we've worked up on framing. The first few questions are on materials: "How big is a 2x4?" etc. Getting these right qualifies you as a board hauler. Then the questions get into rough openings and stud heights. If you get that far, you might make a decent nail beater. From there it goes into layout, stairs, and rafter cutting. This form has saved us a ton of money by weeding out unqualified applicants.

The third and final sheet of our "hello" packet is a medical history questionnaire. It asks simple questions such as, "Have you ever been injured on a job site?" and "Is there any medical reason you can't perform the job you're applying for?" If the applicant has a bad back, he's required to tell you. If he's been hurt on every job he's worked, then you know there's a pretty good chance he'd get hurt on your job, too.

Small crews should think through risky operations, like raising this scarf-joined beam, with safety in mind. The crew leader needs to set the tone.

Training

Every new employee should go through an orientation that includes a tour of the site, an introduction to the crew, and most importantly, a review of what safety practices and equipment are expected. You may lose a few guys by insisting on this stuff — the really cool ones that would rather die than conform — but you will cut down on the most common accidents like foot and eye injuries, and saw cuts.

Never just assume that a new employee knows how to operate your equipment. You may feel a little embarrassed telling an experienced framer how to use a nail gun or operate a radial-arm saw, but there are lots of different ways of working, and many of them aren't safe.

And to really cover your butt, you should provide every employee with a written copy of your company's safety policies. Then you have them sign a document stating that they have read it, understand it, and agree to follow the procedures it outlines. We're still working on this phase; our last attempt ended up looking like the yellow pages for some major city.

Drugs And Alcohol

Everyone who gets a paycheck from us understands that we will not tolerate drugs or alcohol on our job sites. Although we can't afford to use testing as part of the hiring process, our application requires anyone who works for us to submit to a drug test if he is involved in an accident.

We use our weekly newsletter to underscore what happens to an employee if he's hurt on the job and tests positive for drugs. Here in New Mexico it voids his workers comp coverage. That means the insurance company won't pay his medical bills and he can't collect disability. We find that this is a great deterrent. Guys who are drug users won't sign the application, and guys who work for us don't use drugs because they don't want to lose their benefits if something happens.

Safely Equipped

Framers love to work in tennis shoes, shorts, and little else. That was my standard uniform when I worked in the field, and I know a few guys who'd rather be unemployed than wear anything more. But that's just too bad. They aren't paying the insurance premiums and they don't have to pay the bills if they get hurt.

We used to have a real problem with people stepping on nails. Someone would get one in the foot every week or so and it cost us a hundred bucks each time. Finally, one guy took a nail in a way that damaged some nerves. It required surgery and cost us a bundle, so now we require boots. But we try to be flexible; there are some boots that look and fit like sneakers, but have hard soles and offer the necessary protection.

On large, multistory commercial sites, Davis's framers wear hard hats. He requires boots and safety glasses on all his sites to minimize small injuries like nail punctures and sawdust in the eyes.

Another frequent problem was sawdust in the eyes. Again, this meant hundred dollar trips to the doctor's office just to get the guy's eyes washed out. But in this case we didn't wait for a disaster to occur, such as someone losing an eye to a nail. We now require safety glasses for everyone. We've made a deal with a local safety supply house to buy large quantities of good-looking safety glasses that we provide to the guys at a good price.

Then we come to every renegade framer's pet peeve: blade guards. I've heard every argument in the world against them. One of the more convincing ones is that if you use a blade guard on your saw, you get sloppy. You think it's always going to be there and then one day it sticks and you get cut. And there's the argument that you can't make angle cuts or take a quarter inch off a 2x4 with the guard on. These may be legitimate points, but the bottom line is that they are required — by OSHA, by my insurance carrier, and most importantly, by me.

Making It Work

A safety program isn't something you can just write up and distribute; it's an ongoing conversation between a contractor, his crew leaders, and the guys on site. We have two primary ways of keeping this conversation going: meetings and a company newsletter.

We use "tailgate" safety meetings when we're working a commercial site, especially if we've hired some new people. We try to keep them to 15 minutes; usually right after lunch. The idea is to get everyone thinking about safety. Although you may not have discussed saws in particular, if your guys are thinking safety, maybe they'll hesitate before making that overhead pocket cut from a shaky ladder.

We haven't found "tailgate" lectures as effective for a small residential crew where the same six guys work shoulder-to-shoulder everyday. In this situation, a

Typical Job-Site Injuries and Their Associated Medical Costs*

Injury/Event	Associated Medical Cost
Slipped on the ice, a minor sprain resulting	$195
Hit the thumb or fingers with a hammer	$350
Ladder not secured and tipped over, minor sprain resulting	$30
Slipped on job-place material, resulting in major back injury	$38,800 plus permit settlement
Slipped, concussion resulting	$9,800
Cut finger while drilling	$300
Foreign body in eye	$75
Splashed concrete into the eye while shoveling	$120
While installing door hardware, pinched finger	$265
Strained back while lifting	$300

The associated medical costs are actual costs based on the experience of one construction company in New England (1989); they may vary depending on your location and other circumstances.

dangerous move by someone on the crew is going to be met by a crew leader screaming "Don't do that!"

Getting your lead men to take responsibility for safety is a key component. We give out bonuses to the crew leaders if they bring a job in under budget, but the costs of an injury are treated as a direct job cost. If one of our guys brings in a job $1,000 under budget, but he racks up $1,000 in doctor bills because of an injury, then it's a wash and he gets coal in his stocking.

When we do have accidents, the crew leaders must fill out and submit a report at the next weekly payroll meeting. All crew leaders are present and we go over the accident in detail. We try to isolate the causes and take steps to prevent another incident. This often means having the crew leaders discuss it with their crews, and writing it up in our newsletter so the guys can also hear it from the "horse's mouth."

Safety is a serious issue. The way I see it, you either develop a workable safety policy that keeps your people healthy and limits your exposure, or you're just wasting your time waiting for bad luck to catch up with you and put you out of business.

—*Michael Davis*

Chapter 4

Subcontractors

Hiring and Handling Subs

Clear rules, fairness, and give-and-take keep subs on track and on the team

Interview

Steve Farrell is a fourth generation builder who grew up in the family remodeling business. All of the Farrell Company's $1.5 million of work last year was residential remodeling in the heart of California's upscale Silicon Valley.

Steve "runs the field" for the company, visiting each of their average four job sites daily. He keeps in constant contact with his subs and his crew — two carpenters and a helper — via the phone in his truck, and even puts on the nail belt occasionally. His father handles initial client contact and bidding, while Steve's wife takes care of the books.

Like most contractors, Farrell sees his subs as vital to his success. He works hard at maintaining clear, consistent relationships with them. Here are his thoughts on this aspect of the business.

JLC: *How important are subs to your company?*

Farrell: Their work represents about 70% of our volume, so a lot of our profit comes from the 20% we mark them up.

JLC: *Where do you use subs?*

Farrell: We do all our own foundations except for flatwork, all framing, siding, and interior trim. We'll do drywall on a small job, but everything else is subbed out. That includes the usual trades plus specialties like shower doors, security systems, special paint finishes, etc.

JLC: *Do you have just one subcontractor bid on each trade?*

Farrell: In most cases we have two. First, this allows us to compare cost and specs during the bidding process to make sure we're not forgetting anything. Second, if one of our subs gets injured or sick, we've got someone who is familiar with the job to step in. Third, since we're not the only contractor these guys work for, it means we won't have to stall a job because of scheduling problems. And fourth, it allows us to choose different skills, approaches, and temperaments for different kinds of jobs.

JLC: *Do you ever have more than two subs bidding on a single trade?*

Farrell: No, it's not fair or good business to round up fifteen guys, sign the lowest bidder — the guy who made the mistake — and then babysit him through the entire job. In fact, I'll even tell a guy if I don't have anybody bidding against him. I have an idea of what the job will run, and they know that if they nail me on a cost, I'll take it as a personal shot.

JLC: *How do you find your subs?*

Farrell: The best source is our other subs; my electrician found both my tile man and one of my plumbers.

JLC: *What do you look for?*

Farrell: We want subs that are established, but fairly small. That way our relationship is with the owner. And smaller subs are usually more responsive since we're providing them with a good part of their total business.

A few months ago we hired a big drywall firm for a monster house we were doing. Because our job represented less than 1% of their gross, they did the project on their time schedule at their level of quality.

JLC: *How do you judge things like reliability, trade skills, and attitude toward clients when interviewing subs?*

Farrell: I look for enthusiasm, for how a sub dresses, how well he carries himself, if he listens carefully, the condition of his truck.

I also want to know how he came up in the business, and even how much

Project manager Farrell, at right, reviews the coming week of framing with his carpenters, and coordinates the start dates for his subs.

education he's had. Our clients are successful, and they're used to working with people who are sharp — they demand it.

JLC: *Who are your most valuable subs?*

Farrell: The guy who does my demolition and hauling, my tile man, and my cabinetmaker are all pretty important. But the sub that makes or breaks any remodeling contractor is the painter. It's the last layer, and the one the clients always pick on. We've used the same guy for 12 years, and he's the only subcontractor with whom I have a personal as well as a professional relationship.

JLC: *Do you have your subs inspect the job prior to bidding?*

Farrell: Usually, though I don't like to drag them through a job unless I think we have a good chance of getting it.

But a walk-through can really nip problems in the bud. For instance, I can ask my plumber how he's going to get his pipes through a bearing wall, while letting him know he's going to be looking at a glulam the size of China (and I will have him shot if he gets a drill anywhere near it).

Or my electrician may find he has to upgrade a box, even though the plans don't show it. This way there are no surprises, and we can go back to the client and say, "If you choose us for your project, we aren't going to hit you with a lot of extras later on. Our price is higher, but it's because we've done our homework."

JLC: *Do you include both subs who are bidding in the walk-through?*

Farrell: This is where it gets tricky. Usually only one guy goes out, but if we discover a problem that's not on the plans, I'll tell the other sub who's bidding. If I don't, I'm essentially sticking the guy who didn't come out with the financial consequences.

The sub that was on the inspection can say, "Hey, I killed my time coming out and you gave all the information to the other guy." That's a hard point to argue, but I'll give him the job if he's within 5%.

JLC: *Do you get written bids?*

Farrell: I ask them to phone in a number, but then back it up with a "scope of work" description so I'm covered later on when we get into the job.

JLC: *Do you award the contract based solely on price?*

Farrell: I start with price. If there's a big difference between the two bids, I call up the guy with the lower number and ask him if he feels comfortable with it. If he says yes, I tell him I'm going to hold him to that number even if he comes crying to me midway through the job. But I'll also give him a chance to refigure it if he feels at all hesitant.

If the difference between the two bids is minor, 5% or less, and the guy with the lower figure is sounding wishy-washy, I'll just go with the higher guy. But I also try to match the job with the sub.

JLC: *Once the client has signed, do you hold preconstruction meetings?*

Farrell: Yes, but they're not long and drawn out. I just introduce three or four of my primary subs — electrician, plumber, painter, and sometimes my tile man — to the homeowners. This increases the clients' confidence level once the job starts because it's no longer a bunch of strangers walking into their house.

JLC: *How do you let your subs know when they're going to start?*

Farrell: After my bid has been accepted I sit down and draw up a schedule. I use a relatively simple bar chart and go over it with the homeowner. Then I call up each subcontractor and let him know exactly when he's starting.

JLC: *What about changes?*

Farrell: They're a fact of life. When I see a change coming up, I'll call my subs and inform them. I'm in contact with my major subs every day, and they can always reach me in my truck.

JLC: *Do you intentionally overlap your subs?*

Farrell: Yes. Everybody has an effect on the next guy and I overlap them slightly so they're communicating. For instance, I run my sheet-metal sub through while my carpenters are still on the job, to straighten out any problems.

JLC: *Is the sheet-metal sub the first to rough in?*

Farrell: No, my plumber is always first. Getting his pipes around everything is tough. The sheet-metal guy is next; he also needs a break. The electrician is last, because his material is a lot more flexible. Worst case, he's going to use an extra 100 feet of Romex and complain a little more because he's last in.

JLC: *What about the order of finish?*

Farrell: That's just as critical. For instance, you don't want your hardwood flooring sub in there while the painter is driving the humidity through the roof; and you want the cabinets sealed before the tilesetter turns the wood black with mortar.

I let my painter finish inside, then while he works outdoors, my electrician and plumber trim out. After that, the flooring sub can come in, followed by a final touch-up tour by the painter.

JLC: *Sounds great in theory, but aren't there conflicts?*

Farrell: Sure. If I have subs growling at each other, I'll just say to one of them, "Hey, this isn't working, come back next Tuesday when the other guy won't be in your face."

And sometimes you just need to turn the site over to one guy to get him out of there. Drywall is a good example. It's messy and dusty and nobody likes being there while it's happening. I tell the homeowner to visit relatives, and give my drywall sub whatever he needs to get him the hell out of there. If the other guys don't have anything to do during that time, I'll get them started on one of my other jobs.

JLC: *But subs have scheduling problems too, and can't always start when they promised.*

Farrell: True. They often get loaded with extras on the job before yours. When this comes up, I can usually give them slack on the front end, but I set an absolute finish date. If they're going to have trouble meeting that, we figure out a schedule of weekend work, or I help out by picking up material, etc.

Sometimes they're just tight financially, and are trying to finish up their current job so they can buy materials for my job. In that case, I'll give them a check ahead of time. But when I do, I expect them there the next day.

JLC: *Does your lead carpenter handle problems with subs when you're not on site?*

Farrell: No, I try to take that load off my guys. They'll make other decisions on their own work — frame, finish, whatever — but typically not with the subs.

I'm on every job at least once a day. If it's critical, I'll get all my other jobs out of the way early, and spend the rest of the day on one site. The subs know that, and they know the decisions all have to be made by me, because I'm the only guy who is carrying all the relevant information in his head.

JLC: *Any problems with homeowners asking your subs for changes?*

Farrell: It's the same deal. All of this stuff has to funnel through me or it just doesn't work. If the homeowner requests something and the sub goes ahead, he just did that work for free. The sub's contract is with me, not the homeowner. I'm flexible on a lot of stuff, but not this.

JLC: *How do you handle change orders?*

Farrell: When the client asks for a change, I go to my sub immediately and get a rough guesstimate, right on the spot. Then I'll double it and go back to the homeowner to get a "go" or "no go."

This does two things. First, it's fast, so that change orders don't end up shutting down the job. Second, if we do the work, I bill the client for actual costs plus mark-up, and we end up as "good guys" when we come in below the estimate. With all the stories homeowners hear about remodelers hosing their clients on extras, this is more important than you might think.

JLC: *What about the gray area between a change order produced by hidden conditions, and an item the sub missed when he bid the job?*

Farrell: If my electrician comes to me and says he's going to have to put in a new service box and didn't bid it, I might split it with him if I'm doing okay on the job to that point. Technically, it's not my problem, but by giving a little I end up with a happier sub and a little leverage with the guy that I didn't have before.

However, I don't do this often; I expect these guys to be professionals and know their trade.

JLC: *How about conflicts between trades about who does certain tasks?*

Farrell: The trick is to pick these up right away — before bidding — and circle them on the plans. Where I see it most often is between the plumber and the hvac or sheet-metal sub over venting. The way I handle it, bath fans are provided and hooked up by the electrician, but ducted by the hvac sub. My plumber usually vents his own water heater, and provides roof jacks for his vent pipes.

And I don't let anyone but my plumber run gas lines, even to the furnace. He also hooks up all appliances — another area where I don't want mistakes.

JLC: *How do you proceed when you find a problem with a sub's work?*

Farrell: I tell the tradesman on the job so he can correct it without having to look bad in front of his boss. But I expect him to turn to it right away, not finish what he's doing and come back. That way he's not making the correction a separate project, and the problem is less likely to mushroom.

JLC: *What if he shrugs it off or argues the point?*

Farrell: I tell him to pack it up and I call his boss. I'm real demanding — these guys are always one bad job away from not working for us again and they know it. It's important to have a little leverage with these guys, but I also know I can never abuse it. I've got to be clear in communicating what I want, and absolutely consistent and fair in how I deal with them.

JLC: *How about callbacks?*

Farrell: Ideally, I do a walk-through before the subs leave, but if not, I'm still holding that final payment. Since I do all the scheduling and okay every invoice before it's paid, it won't slip past me.

JLC: *Have you been "liened" by subs very often?*

Farrell: Never. We pay our subs as soon as we're square on the work and they've invoiced us. In fact, most of our guys don't even send the pro forma, pre-lien notices to the homeowner because they trust us. However, I never object if they do; we all need to protect ourselves by getting things down on paper. But I do remind the guys who sent notices to issue a lien release the day they get my payment; you can't do just the paperwork that's advantageous to you.

JLC: *Do you do anything special to reward your subs? Christmas parties, bonuses?*

Farrell: Not really. We provide them with a steady source of good work and we keep our word. That's a lot. If we throw a big Christmas party and invite our subs, it'll cost us $1,000 and they'll remember it for about four months. But if we offer them a solid business relationship where the rules are consistent and there's some give and take, they'll remember that for a lot longer.

Success With Subs

Find the best, communicate clearly, and pay them what they're worth

Home builders are presented with many more operational and management dilemmas than most other business owners. The builder often has little control over his toughest problems. On-again, off-again market conditions, diminishing land supply, and increasingly stringent environmental regulations all require that the builder think more in terms of survival than profit. The old saying "When you're up to your tail in alligators, you almost forget you set out to drain the swamp," couldn't be more appropriate.

Builders do, however, have control over the way they operate their businesses. Chief among their management decisions is the selection of subcontractors. Maintaining healthy, businesslike relationships with subs certainly increases (if it doesn't guarantee) the likelihood of business success.

Finding Good Subcontractors

Successful working relationships rarely "just happen." They almost always result from a well-thought-out approach.

For starters, find the best subcontractors you can. They can be hard to find at times, since many subs do quite well by word-of-mouth, and therefore don't bother to advertise. But you can find pretty good leads from other builders (especially if you are involved in a local home builders association), from other subcontractors (in another field), from suppliers to the sub's specific trade (plumbing supply firms, for example), and from the bulletin boards at your general building supply house. And

What I Look For in K&B Subs

My philosophy is to locate good subs and work with them exclusively; my tile setter has been with me for over ten years. I couldn't and wouldn't ask the sub whom I used only when he was the lowest bidder to do the things I ask my regular subs to do. It may cost more to do business this way, but the level of service is much higher.

The Right Stuff

Although most of us are looking for the perfect sub, we'll settle for quite a bit less. Here's a list of the qualities I look for in order of their importance:

Technically competent. Most of my jobs are high-end, and my clients demand top-notch work so I need to trust that my subs' work will be consistently good.

In some of the trades such as plumbing and electrical, it's fairly easy to judge. But in a trade like tile setting, you get into subjective areas: Is this the best layout for tile of this size on this countertop? Will the grout still look good five years from now?

I have become a better judge of who is "good" with experience. For example, my hardwood flooring contractor is expensive. However, he has been in the business for years. He has seen most problems before, and often has an esoteric tool or technique that can fix a problem without ripping out the first attempt. Having him available to solve problems is well worth the cost.

Caring. We can usually find competent people, but if they don't go the extra step, it doesn't work for me. I want my sub to take care of things that need fixing. For instance, if my plumbing sub sees copper attached directly to galvanized, I want him to replace it with a dielectric union without even asking.

Reliable. I've got to be able to count on these guys to turn in a bid, show up on time, and finish when they say they will. You can't maintain a schedule if your subs don't.

I know a cabinetmaker whom I really enjoy working with because of the quality of his product and his sense of humor, but who routinely gives me bids late or not at all. I now ask him to bid only when his work is specified by the customer.

Clean and neat. If you're going to succeed in the kitchen and bath remodeling business, you'd better be clean, neat, and careful. You can't have a glazier who routinely scratches the tub or the ceiling when installing full-height doors. Nor should there be metal filings on the floor when he leaves.

These guys should also look professional and consider the impact they are having on the customer. For instance, most of my customers don't smoke, and I don't smoke. So I look for employees who don't smoke, and I apply the same yardsticks to subs.

Available. Accessibility and availability are the next most important criteria. I stopped dealing with one painter because he never returned my calls — even to get a bid. Given a choice, I prefer to deal with a sub big enough to have an office with a secretary who can relay a message during the day to someone who can make a decision.

Another advantage of dealing with a larger company is that they are better able to get someone to the job when we need them. We are willing to give up the choice of which tradesman actually does the job for this flexibility. This sometimes means that the quality varies. But if you have a sub who stands behind his work — and you're one of his larger accounts — he'll come in and make any necessary corrections.

Good client skills. Next, we come to the "gorilla factor." We want our employees and our sub's employees to be pleasant and courteous. Although they don't work directly for the client, about 50% of our work—one-half the impression the client is left with—is subbed out.

Interested in the long term. I want to work with a sub who wants to form a relationship. This means there will be give and take. If my sub clearly makes a mistake, I expect him to cover it. Usually, the fault is not clear, and we agree to split the cost.

Priced right. I purposely placed price last. I do have a price pain threshold, but it is relatively high. If someone is above the threshold, I rely on the traits I mentioned above.

By Lynn Comeskey, a remodeling contractor who specializes in kitchens and baths. His firm, Mac & Lou Construction, is based in Palo Alto, Calif.

don't forget the local coffee shop at 6:30 in the morning. Sometimes I think that coffee shops survive exclusively on the construction business. In fact, if you want a good indicator of how the market is in your area, check out how the local coffee shop is doing.

Get an Early Start

Allow sufficient lead time to line up the subs. The time needed will depend on the specific trade, the market and economic conditions, and the weather. Getting an early start will help you to avoid unnecessary delays, higher "rush" charges, and promises made under pressure that can't be kept.

Check Them Out

There is absolutely no excuse for not checking out a subcontractor that you haven't worked with before. Secrets are a rare commodity in the building community and bad news travels fast. But in this instance, it's a blessing. A few well-placed phone calls can tell you a great deal about a subcontractor: his performance, credit rating, and call-back reliability, for example. Is the sub accessible? Are phone calls returned? Few things can be more damaging to the relationship between a builder and home buyer than the failure of a subcontractor to respond to complaints promptly. The question is rarely one of competence in the trade, but more of how a sub runs his business. You can generally get a pretty good idea from other builders a sub has worked for, as most people are familiar with the standards of their peers. Since consistency seems to be part of human nature, it's reasonable to expect your relationship with a particular sub would be similar to what others have experienced with him. So a little effort to check around up-front can save time, expense, and a lot of heartache later on.

Keep It Clear and Simple

When soliciting bids for a job, be accurate, open, and above board with the job description, so that the sub will know exactly what he is bidding on and so there is no question as to what your specifications are. This puts all bidders on a level playing field and enables you to make apples-to-apples comparisons when reviewing bids. Don't hesitate to ask for suggestions on where to cut costs if the specifications are flexible, as they might very well be on a spec house. Let the sub perform his job the way he usually does, unless it compromises the specs: It will generally cost less. This situation typically occurs in the bidding process for mechanical installations, where savings can result from using the equipment the subcontractor usually installs, as long as there is no reduction in quality.

Most people in business are honest and well intentioned and disputes generally result from communication breakdowns and inadequate direction. Communicate clearly so that the sub can figure the costs for the job. Be careful to avoid coming across in such a complicated manner that the sub is frightened away or pads his price to protect himself. Items that are clearly understood before a job begins rarely present problems later on.

When you agree on the contract price, make sure your contract includes a payment schedule. The timing and amount of progress payments should be predetermined, based on work completed. Avoid a per-diem payout, except perhaps with specialty work where the time required to do the work is unknown but there is a definite beginning and end to the task.

In addition to clear job descriptions and specifications, subs need to know when they are expected to start, and you need to know how long it will take them to perform the job. Make sure, as much as you can, that the sub has sufficient crew available to do the job, so that your schedule is maintained.

Schedule the various trades realistically so that the job is ready for them when you said it would be, and do whatever you have to in order to meet your commitment. For instance, if through no fault of yours, temporary electric service has not been connected, provide a generator for the interim. This not only keeps the job moving, but sends an unmistakable message of your determination to meet the schedule, and establishes your dependability in the building community. Assuming no work interference, schedule several subs with their respective trades on the site simultaneously; it not only keeps the job moving,

SUBCONTRACTOR AGREEMENT (CONTRACTOR/SUBCONTRACTOR)

Agreement made between the Contractor: ______________________

____

____

and the Subcontractor: ______________________

____

____

1. General project description: ______________________

____

____

2. The specific work of this Agreement shall consist of: ______________________

____

____

and shall be in accordance with the specifications, drawings, or as reasonably inferable from either or both, and other contract documents.

3. The work shall begin no later than ______________________
and be completed no later than ______________________
subject to adjustments as provided in the General Conditions of the Construction Agreement.

4. The Contractor shall pay the Subcontractor the sum of ______________________
______________________ Dollars ($ ____________),
for the work under this Agreement, subject to additions and deductions as stipulated in the General Conditions.

5. The Contractor shall make progress payments to the Subcontractor according to the following schedule:

Completed Work	Amount to be Paid*
Total	

* An amount equal to ten (10) percent of the payment shall be retained by the Contractor in accordance with Section 9 of the General Conditions.

SUBCONTRACTOR AGREEMENT (CONT'D)

Final payment shall be made when the work has been completed and the Agreement fully performed to the Contractor's satisfaction.

6. The Subcontractor agrees to be bound by the construction documents as follows:

   a. The Construction Agreement is the executed agreement between the Owner and the Contractor dated ______________________ .

   b. The General Conditions of the Construction Agreement executed and dated

   c. The Specifications contained in the Project Manual and dated ____________________ .

   d. The Drawings as follows: ____ .

   e. Other documents as follows:

7. Other provisions:

This agreement entered into this __________ day of ______________ , 19 ____ .

____
Signature of Contractor

____
Signature of Subcontractor

____
Printed Name

____
Printed Name

but livens the pace, as one person works alongside another, rather than alone.

Require subs to visit the job well in advance of the start of their work, to make their needs known (when relevant) to the prior trades. This usually involves them with the framer. We have all witnessed at one time or another a "scene" that took place when a justifiably irate framer was asked to open up (and later replace) a door frame in order to place a bulky fiberglass tub unit, or to widen the bay between two floor joists, after the fact, to accommodate a warm-air duct. Had the framer been alerted early on, the disruption could have been avoided. Any requirements for cleanup imposed by the builder should be agreed upon, as well as conditions the sub requires of the builder, such as equipment to be provided, job access, or heat in season.

It is good practice to meet with all subs at the site when their work begins to review the game plan and layout of the work. As the work progresses, make frequent inspections to keep on top of things. Be available throughout the job, so that if unforeseen problems or emergencies arise, you will be there to make a decision. By keeping an eye on the work and making frequent inspections, errors often can be nipped in the bud.

After the foundation is in, the first major sub on the job will be the framer. Since trade schedules tend to overlap on the job, the first subcontractor's performance will set the stage and establish the pace, appearance, and discipline for all that follow. Anything less than good performance will necessarily carry on to the next trade. So make it your business to start out on the right foot.

Contracts and Other Paperwork

Your contractual arrangements with your sub, whether written or oral (so common, unfortunately, in residential building) should be the result of an informed business management decision. It should be established beyond the shadow of a doubt that you are, indeed, dealing on a builder/subcontractor basis and not on an employer/ employee basis that could make you liable for F.I.C.A. taxes, workers comp coverage, and the like. Have legal counsel hold your hand while preparing the form that the relationship will take. The subcontractor agreement should be simple, but specific. Each trade has different requirements (see Sample Contract, previous page).

Don't expect your lawyer to know the intricacies of a specific trade: You will have to let the lawyer know what you want included in three major areas. First, you will want to define the scope of the work. If you are contracting with a framer, you will need to state that he will be responsible for the framing from the top of the foundation up, and to the point of installing the mechanicals. Second, you will need to make clear who is responsible for supplying the materials. For instance, plumbers normally provide their own materials, whereas the builder usually supplies the concrete for the foundation, and the wood for the frame. Finally, you will need to determine who is responsible for coordinating municipal permitting and inspections. The builder usually organizes these items for the frame, but the hvac sub will usually coordinate the fire chief's inspection and permits himself, for example.

It's good practice to sit down from time to time with your lawyer and insurance advisor to review overall business direction and strategy, as well as any liability exposure. Make sure you include a discussion of subcontractor involvement with your company.

Every state in the union has a workers compensation statute, and although the laws vary a bit from state to state, the statutes typically require that all employees be covered by workers compensation insurance. Accordingly, every employer — including subcontractors — must provide coverage for his employees. If a sub fails to do so, the builder becomes liable in the event of a claim for injuries received on the job by a sub or his employees. In addition, the builder's insurance company will raise his premium to cover the sub's work. No subcontractor works on my job unless he has first provided me with a certificate issued by his insurance carrier stating the workers comp coverage. A prudent builder (even one without employees) will carry his own workers comp policy as back-up protection.

Builders should also familiarize themselves with the federal "right to know" law, as it applies to hazardous substances in common usage on building sites, as well as any similar state laws. And anyone running a business today should be well aware of the obligations under Occupational Safety and Health Administration (OSHA) regulations, not only to provide safe working conditions, but also to limit liability. In view of ever-increasing regulations (and unfortunately, a society ever-ready to sue), it's important to document your compliance with these rules by keeping good records — copies of correspondence, a daily log, lots and lots of snapshots, and anything else that might tend to support your position if called upon. All too often, when a problem or a serious accident gets a lot of publicity in an area, the agencies are prone to make sweeps of the territory looking for scalps.

Finally, but perhaps most significant: When you negotiate your contract, allow your subs to make a profit on the job. This is not just being a "good guy" — it's simply good business judgement. It is totally unrealistic to expect good performance, including callback dependability, unless the job has been profitable for the subcontractor. There are exceptions to every rule, but it is unreasonable to think that you wouldn't have to eventually pay some price for low bids. A contract is good only if all parties to the agreement are happy.

When Things Go Wrong

In spite of your best planning efforts and investigation, there will be occasions when your relationship with your subcontractor sours and has to come to an end. End the marriage with a handshake and no hard feelings. This is not inconsistent with your displeasure, for whatever reason, but a decent and businesslike way to react. And you just never know when your paths will cross again. Let them go with a kiss.

There will be times, too, when you feel you are the only one making a contribution to the marriage, such as cooperation, prompt payments, having the job ready — and you don't seem to be getting the same in return. Don't be a glutton for punishment; do what has to be done, part company, and find another sub that meets your criteria. However, if it seems to be a recurring problem, it's a clear indication that you're doing something wrong. Take stock of your methods and make the corrections you need to get back on track.

Subs Are a Goldmine

Besides their obvious function, subs can be a tremendous source of information and ideas. Most subs, like builders, really enjoy their work and are eager to talk about it, given the chance. Seize the opportunity and pick their brains; find out as much as you can about their trade, product, or system. Also, subs who travel from builder to builder can be an enormous source of fresh ideas carried over from job to job: little tips learned on another job that can make your project go a bit easier, or some new and cost-saving approach that you might benefit from. And, of course, rely on the sub's experience in his own trade to help you get an optimum installation or layout. In contract work, it's not unusual for customers to provide blueprints of overdesigned (and pricey) mechanical installations. Your hvac sub can help you avoid doing a disservice to that customer, who is ultimately paying the bill.

In their travels from development to development, subs often glean other useful tidbits, such as what is "hot" and what is not. They can tell you what price ranges are currently selling, and what buyers seem to be looking for or are willing to forego in making choices based on price. They often know where lots may be available, or where there is a brick-box apartment building for sale that is ripe for conversion or rehab. They can tell you what town is talking moritoria, so that you might hustle with your permit applications.

These extras make good working relationships with your subs even more appealing. But of course the bottom line is that you want your job to go smoothly, and your customers to be happy. A healthy relationship with your subs can go a long way towards doing just that.

By Richard Lind, a builder in the Wellesley, Mass. area and a longtime member of the Builders Association of Greater Boston (BAGB).

Sub or Employee?

The law is gray, but the risks are clear if you hire "subs" who are really employees

Most people think of small builders and remodelers as general contractors who maintain crews of carpenters and only sub out special trades. Many firms, however, now subcontract major portions of their work. Often this includes tasks traditionally performed by employees, such as framing and finish carpentry. At one extreme are firms that even sub out the job management to a construction-management firm, which in turn manages the other subs. With the persistent and growing shortage of skilled labor, this reliance on "non-traditional" subs has spread from sophisticated companies to more conventional firms that also maintain a core crew. But in many cases, the legal and tax status of such subcontractor relationships lies in a gray area.

Are Your Subs Legitimate?

Consider a journeyman-level carpenter who becomes a sub on his way towards going out on his own. He stays with his old crew. Few things change. He takes home a better paycheck (one without withholdings) and he feels more independent. And you, the hiring contractor, go along willingly. Why shouldn't you? You hang on to your skilled labor without the burden of payroll taxes and workers compensation insurance.

But if you maintain the subcontractor relationship in name only, you face considerable risks. The courts, in the event of a lawsuit, or the IRS, in an audit, will always investigate this working relationship. If they reclassify a worker, you could be liable for third-party claims — claims made against you by someone injured by the subcontractor's actions — or claims made by a sub who injures himself. Moreover, you can be assessed for back payroll taxes including both halves of social security, unemployment taxes, federal income tax withholding, and penalties.

There are ways to legally change the status of a worker from employee to sub. But you have to actually change the way you do business with the person.

Insurance Matters

Since insurance companies routinely audit their clients, the insurance risks of hiring subcontractors are the most apparent. Most business liability coverage designates only the owner and employees as "insured." Such a policy probably will not cover third-party claims unless you have additional coverage, such as contingent liability, to cover your subs. Thus, in its annual audit, your insurance company will request a certificate of insurance to show that each subcontractor you hire carries his own liability insurance. Without this piece of paper, your insurance costs will be raised to cover the risk.

A subcontract agreement is only marginally helpful in sorting out liability claims. Standard forms specify that the subcontractor is responsible for workers compensation, public liability insurance, and all income taxes and unemployment compensation. This establishes a record of your mutual intention. But a court of law often looks at a contract as just another piece of paper. It is not certain evidence that a contractor and sub have an independent business relationship. The plaintiff's attorney may try to make a case that a contractor actually functions as an employer and the "agreement" is but empty words.

In the event of an insurance claim or a lawsuit, a subcontractor's status will be examined to see how it conforms with the following common-law guidelines:

1. The extent of control, which, by the agreement, the contractor may exercise over the details of the sub's work;
2. Whether or not the sub is engaged in a distinct occupation or business;
3. The sub's occupation and whether it is one traditionally done without supervision or direction by the contractor;
4. The skills required for the work;
5. Whether the contractor or sub supplies the tools needed to perform the job;
6. The length of time the person is employed;
7. The method of payment — whether by time or by the job;
8. Whether the work performed is part of the contractor's regular business;
9. The intent of the parties in entering the relationship;
10. Whether the contractor is an established entity.

The first determinate — commonly called "the right to control" — is the most important. In a 1976 appellate court decision, the judge wrote (concerning liability for a construction site accident) "all of these factors are of varying importance in determining the type of relationship involved, and, with the exception of the element of control, not all elements need be present." This is a clear affirmation that you can legally work with nontraditional subs, even though factors #3 and #8 seem to exclude this.

This ruling has given rise to a common-law definition of employee and subcontractor. An employee is someone you direct step-by-step through the job, and you are an employer if you have control over the specific task you are hiring a worker for. An independent sub is someone you turn loose on the job after showing him what needs to done. When you subcontract out work in this way, you hand the right to control the job over to the sub. A sub must be free to negotiate when he performs the job and to choose the tools and techniques he deems best. And since the definitions are based on a worker's approach to a specific *job*, it requires paying and billing a worker out *by the job*.

Tax Concerns

In years past, the IRS had a strong incentive to classify a worker as an employee, simply because an employee used to earn more money for the Treasury than a subcontractor. Perhaps because the IRS felt it has not been able to adequately track down all the subcontractor earnings and has been losing money by this scheme, it recently increased the self-employment tax contribution. An independent subcontractor now is required to pay 15.3% of his wages to Social Security, as required by SECA (Self Employed Contributions Act). This equals the total tax contribution acquired from an employee, which includes both the employee's withholding and an employer's contribution, as required by FICA (Federal Insurance Contribution Act).

General contractors are required to file Form 1099-MISC for all nonincorporated subcontractors who are paid $600 or more each year. This enables the IRS to track the earnings of self-employed workers.

According to John Wyckoff, a business consultant from South Burlington, Vt. who specializes in counseling building professionals, a contractor should require two things of every subcontractor who walks onto the job site. First, you need verification that a subcontractor is incorporated. If the subcontractor

IRS Subcontractor Guidelines

1. Is the individual providing services (the sub) required to comply with instruction on when, where, and how the work is to be done?
2. Is the individual provided with training to enable him or her to perform the job in a particular manner?
3. Are the services performed by the individual a part of the contractor's business operations?
4. Must the services be rendered personally?
5. Does the contractor hire, supervise, or pay assistants to help the individual performing under the contract?
6. Is the relationship between the parties a continuing one?
7. Who sets the hours of work for the worker?
8. Is the individual required to devote full time to the party for whom the services are performed?
9. Does the individual perform work on another's business premises?
10. Who directs the sequence in which the work must be done?
11. Are regular oral or written reports required?
12. What is the method of payment — hourly, weekly, commission, or by the job?
13. Are business or traveling expenses reimbursed?
14. Who furnishes the tools and materials necessary for the provision of services?
15. Does the individual have significant investment in the tools or facilities used to perform his services?
16. Can the individual providing services realize a profit or loss?
17. Can the individual providing services work for a number of firms at the same time?
18. Does the individual make his or her services available to the general public?
19. Can the individual be dismissed for reasons other than nonperformance of contract specifications?
20. Can the individual providing services terminate his or her relationship at any time without incurring a liability for failure to complete a job?

is not incorporated, he should supply an employer identification number to facilitate filing Form 1099. In some cases this may be a social security number. And second, a certificate of insurance is needed to verify that the sub has liability insurance.

This will set the stage for establishing a true contractor-sub relationship. But if you are audited, you may be required to prove that you actually work as contractor and sub rather than as employer and employee.

The IRS Training Manuals 8463 and 3142-01 list 20 factors used to determine whether an individual is an independent contractor or an employee. (See "IRS Subcontractor Guidelines.") These questions have been compiled to cover all industries. Some of the questions, such as #4, #11, and #13 often are not relevant to the building trades. Others, like #7, #9, and part of #14 are invariably gray areas. Setting the hours of work is often a mutual agreement based on a project's schedule. The business premises—a job site—are common to the principal and his subs. And often a contractor will supply all the materials from the concrete to the shingles, even though jobbers will install them.

Factor #6 looks gray, too, because general contractors often have continuing relationships with their subcontractors. But, according to Wyckoff, the rule is specific. A "continuing relationship" is interpreted as a steady, rather than a repeated, relationship. For example, a contractor might always hire the same plumber. But the plumber also works for other contractors. Similarly, a finish carpenter can work repeatedly for the same contractor. If he works for only one, however, he is, without dispute, that contractor's employee.

Wyckoff asserts that a few other factors are key to establishing a true contractor-sub relationship with nontraditional subs in the building trades:

- *Skills and independence.* Above all else, a subcontractor should have the necessary skills to perform the work on his own. If a worker receives training or supervision from the contractor, he is considered an employee. Similarly, a subcontractor must hire his own helpers. He cannot use a contractor's helper on a routine basis.
- *Risk of profit or loss.* Often this factor

can validate a subcontract agreement. It confirms that a sub operates a distinct business.

- *Furnishing tools.* The larger a worker's investment in tools, the more likely he is considered to operate an independent business.
- *The method of payment.* An independent subcontractor should be paid by the job.

There are no rules on how many factors a worker must conform with to be classified as an independent contractor. A contractor should set things up to conform with as many conditions as possible. He then has a fighting chance in the world of lawsuits and tax audits.

By Clayton DeKorne, a former editor at The Journal of Light Construction.

Subs and Workers Comp: Avoiding Hidden Costs

To help control your comp premiums, get a certificate of insurance from every sub before the work begins

Workers comp costs have skyrocketed in recent years. Since premiums for this type of insurance are based on total payroll, builders everywhere are reducing the number of workers they employ directly in favor of using more subcontractors.

The tax consequences of hiring a sub whom the IRS considers to be your employee are well known — you may end up paying the sub's federal withholding and social security taxes. But hiring a sub who does not carry his own workers comp insurance can be just as costly. Yet many builders who use subcontractors often end up paying workers comp premiums as if the subcontractors were employees. This usually happens during the insurance company's annual payroll audit.

Certificates of Insurance

Workers comp premiums are calculated as a percentage of payroll that is based on an elaborate formula. At the start of each policy year, the insurance company estimates the next year's payroll, and applies the rate from the workers comp formula to come up with your premium. Then, at the end of each policy year, an auditor reviews your account to see if your actual payroll was higher or lower than estimated. If your payroll was higher, you are billed for the difference in premium; if lower, you get a rebate.

Auditors treat subs as if they were employees when the builder has paid for work done by a sub, but cannot provide a certificate of insurance showing the dates and amounts of the sub's own workers comp coverage (see sample certificate, next page). If you don't have a certificate of insurance for a sub — or if you have the wrong one — here's what will happen.

First, your premium will go up because the auditor will increase your total payroll for the current year — as well as the estimated payroll for next year — by the amount you paid to the subcontractor. Strictly speaking, only the labor portion of payments made to an uninsured subcontractor are subject to workers comp premiums. But unless you can produce an invoice or other record that breaks down the sub's costs into labor and material, you will have no way to convince the auditor to add less than the total amount.

Second, since the workers comp formula matches premium amounts to the type of work performed — the so-called manual rate — you may pay more for the sub than for regular employees. If the sub is a roofer, for example, you could pay 10% to 20% more than the rate for general carpentry.

As if all this weren't bad enough, your general liability insurance premium will go up because it's also based on payroll. And the additional liability premium will also be based on the manual rate for the kind of work the uninsured sub does.

Exempt Subs

In many states, a sole proprietor is exempt from workers comp requirements and won't have a certificate of insurance. You can still keep them off

ACORD. CERTIFICATE OF INSURANCE

ISSUE DATE (MM/DD/YY)

PRODUCER
Smith Insurance Agency
Main Street
Richmond, VT 05477

CODE SUB-CODE

INSURED
Jones Construction
2 Park Street
Richmond, VT 05477

THIS CERTIFICATE IS ISSUED AS A MATTER OF INFORMATION ONLY AND CONFERS NO RIGHTS UPON THE CERTIFICATE HOLDER. THIS CERTIFICATE DOES NOT AMEND, EXTEND OR ALTER THE COVERAGE AFFORDED BY THE POLICIES BELOW

COMPANIES AFFORDING COVERAGE

COMPANY LETTER A ABC Insurance Company
COMPANY LETTER B
COMPANY LETTER C
COMPANY LETTER D
COMPANY LETTER E

COVERAGES

THIS IS TO CERTIFY THAT THE POLICIES OF INSURANCE LISTED BELOW HAVE BEEN ISSUED TO THE INSURED NAMED ABOVE FOR THE POLICY PERIOD INDICATED, NOTWITHSTANDING ANY REQUIREMENT, TERM OR CONDITION OF ANY CONTRACT OR OTHER DOCUMENT WITH RESPECT TO WHICH THIS CERTIFICATE MAY BE ISSUED OR MAY PERTAIN, THE INSURANCE AFFORDED BY THE POLICIES DESCRIBED HEREIN IS SUBJECT TO ALL THE TERMS, EXCLUSIONS AND CONDITIONS OF SUCH POLICIES. LIMITS SHOWN MAY HAVE BEEN REDUCED BY PAID CLAIMS.

CO LTR	TYPE OF INSURANCE	POLICY NUMBER	POLICY EFFECTIVE DATE (MM/DD/YY)	POLICY EXPIRATION DATE (MM/DD/YY)	ALL LIMITS IN THOUSANDS	
A	GENERAL LIABILITY X COMMERCIAL GENERAL LIABILITY CLAIMS MADE X OCCUR. OWNER'S & CONTRACTOR'S PROT.	X99999999	1/1/98	1/1/99	GENERAL AGGREGATE	$600,000
					PRODUCTS-COMP/OPS AGGREGATE	$600,000
					PERSONAL & ADVERTISING INJURY	$600,000
					EACH OCCURRENCE	$600,000
					FIRE DAMAGE (Any one fire)	$ 50,000
					MEDICAL EXPENSE (Any one person)	$ 5,000
	AUTOMOBILE LIABILITY ANY AUTO ALL OWNED AUTOS SCHEDULED AUTOS HIRED AUTOS NON-OWNED AUTOS GARAGE LIABILITY				COMBINED SINGLE LIMIT	$
					BODILY INJURY (Per person)	$
					BODILY INJURY (Per accident)	$
					PROPERTY DAMAGE	$
	EXCESS LIABILITY OTHER THAN UMBRELLA FORM				EACH OCCURRENCE $	AGGREGATE $
A	WORKER'S COMPENSATION AND EMPLOYERS' LIABILITY	X9999999999	1/1/98	1/1/99	STATUTORY	
					$ 100,000	(EACH ACCIDENT)
					$ 500,000	(DISEASE—POLICY LIMIT)
					$ 100,000	(DISEASE—EACH EMPLOYEE)
	OTHER					

DESCRIPTION OF OPERATIONS/LOCATIONS/VEHICLES/RESTRICTIONS/SPECIAL ITEMS

CERTIFICATE HOLDER

CANCELLATION

SHOULD ANY OF THE ABOVE DESCRIBED POLICIES BE CANCELLED BEFORE THE EXPIRATION DATE THEREOF, THE ISSUING COMPANY WILL ENDEAVOR TO MAIL 10 DAYS WRITTEN NOTICE TO THE CERTIFICATE HOLDER NAMED TO THE LEFT, BUT FAILURE TO MAIL SUCH NOTICE SHALL IMPOSE NO OBLIGATION OR LIABILITY OF ANY KIND UPON THE COMPANY, ITS AGENTS OR REPRESENTATIVES.

AUTHORIZED REPRESENTATIVE

ACORD 25-S (3/88)

Before work starts, obtain a certificate of insurance from each subcontractor. The top half of the form names the subcontractor, his insurance agent, and the insurance company providing coverage. The workers comp section at the bottom of the form shows the dates and amounts of the sub's coverage (circled).

your workers comp payroll, but you'll have to prove they meet IRS criteria for exemption. Among other factors, the IRS requires that the sub is self-directed on the site, that he performs the same kind of work for other contractors, that he works with his own tools, and that he supplies his own materials.

Some auditors will accept a printed invoice bearing the sub's company name and logo as proof of exemption. Others may require a trade name registration form or other document that shows the sub has registered with the state.

Uninsured subs. When an uninsured sub doesn't meet the exemption criteria, some builders carry the cost of covering the sub under their own workers comp policy. They estimate how much their own insurance company will charge to cover the uninsured sub and deduct that amount from the sub's bill. While this may appear to solve the problem, it actually compounds it.

For one thing, while you may be able to estimate the amount to withhold from the sub's bill to cover the current year, the insurance company will include this year's payments to the sub in the estimate of your next year's premium. This is the case even if you have no plans to use the uninsured sub in the coming year. As always, the manual rate may be higher, depending on the kind of work the sub performs, and the calculations will probably be based on the total amount you paid the sub, not just the labor portion.

The real danger in accepting liability for an uninsured sub, however, is that it leaves you vulnerable to claims if the sub is injured. Strictly speaking, you are liable only for injuries that occur on your job. But if a roofer develops a bad back, for example, he could claim that the ailment started while he was lifting shingles or tiles onto the roof of one of your jobs. The same is true of repetitive motion injuries, like carpal tunnel syndrome. The sub could make a case that his injury started or was compounded by work done on one of your jobs. Unless you can prove otherwise, you are liable for medical costs and wage reimbursements, both of which will raise your workers comp premiums.

Remember, too, that when you accept liability for a sub, you also accept liability for the sub's employees. A sole proprietor may not have employees when you subcontract the work to him, but if he falls behind schedule, he may hire help. Without a certificate of insurance, it will be hard to prove that the sub's employees are not your own.

Get Proof Early

The best time to ask a sub for his certificate of insurance is before work begins, but you should at least be sure to get one before you make final payment. Once the job is over and the sub is paid, your chances of getting a certificate in time for your annual audit are slim. And even though you can make adjustments after the audit, it's much easier to prevent being charged for a sub in the first place than it is to have charges rebated later.

Read the certificate. When you do receive a certificate of insurance from a sub, don't just file it away — read it. The workers compensation section near the bottom of the sample form lists the "Policy Effective Date" and the "Policy Expiration Date." These dates must include the calendar dates when he performed his work for you. It's especially important to check this information if, instead of an original, the sub gives you a photocopy of his certificate, which may apply to a prior year.

Also check to see that the amounts of coverage match or exceed your coverage. The series of numbers — 100/500/100 — on the right hand side of the workers compensation section of the sample form corresponds to thousands of dollars of coverage for each accident, the total policy limit, and the limit per employee, respectively. Injuries to a sub or one of his employees are covered to the limits of the sub's workers comp policy. If medical treatment and wage reimbursements exceed those limits, however, his insurance company will look for higher limits on your policy to make up the difference. The excess costs will then be charged against your workers comp record.

By Sal Alfano, a former builder from East Calais, Vt., and the editor of The Journal of Light Construction.

Contracting Without a Crew

Employee-free doesn't mean hassle-free: A solid schedule and good lines of communication are crucial when you sub it all out

Running a construction company using only subcontractors has allowed me to streamline and simplify my building and remodeling business. Using subs leaves all the employee headaches for someone else. But a "sub it all out" operation is not for everyone: Organization is the key element. Since your subs are your company, you have to organize them as well or better than you would employees. But if you use sound business practices, you'll have no trouble making a smooth transition. Here's how I do it.

Use Good Subs

It is imperative to use trustworthy subs, and awarding contracts is an exacting part of running an all-subs job. Responsibilities may vary from job to job, but a subcontractor must faithfully live up to his word, the contract, and your expectations of him. If the sub fails in any of these areas, your job is in for trouble. For this reason, I always try to use subs that have proved themselves on previous projects. Sometimes this means paying more money in the short run, but in the long run it saves money by avoiding miscommunication, shoddy workmanship, and no-shows that throw off the entire job. With proven subs, I'm able to work out problems quicker and with greater satisfaction. Using unknown subs is like playing Russian roulette.

Finding a new sub. There are times when it is impossible to hire tried-and-true subs. In these instances, I have had relatively good luck using subs recommended by associates in the trades. I don't trust a single recommendation, however; I always require at least two more references. Don't skimp on a couple of phone calls now or you could be making a lot of those "why aren't you on the job?" calls later.

Schedule First

I create the schedule for a sub-only project before estimating the job. This gives me my first chance to catch those "who does what" gray areas of subcontractor responsibility, and to factor them into the bid.

I don't expect subs to do the initial bidding for me, so I prepare the preliminary bids. As a result, I can turn an estimate around quickly and eliminate the hassles of dealing with many different bidders. Of course, there are specialty projects or estimating items where I have no choice but to involve a sub. For simple problems like the capacity of a boiler or an electrical panel, this may mean a phone call or a faxed sketch. For the most complex estimates, I meet the subs on site for an inspection.

Formula pricing. In order to prepare a bid accurately enough to get the job and make a profit, you must know what your subs charge. Most subcontractors have simple formulas for figuring jobs. I've asked my subs for their "rules of thumb" and use them in my estimates. But I'm careful not to abuse these formulas. I'm always on the lookout for extras or problems that are not included, and I don't hesitate to consult with the sub if there's any detail I don't understand. After I find out how much the sub's portion will cost (including their profit and overhead), I add my overhead and profit. My bid also covers my wages for the hours I spent estimating and managing the project — you must get paid for your time. When I put all the costs together, I've got my bid.

Awarding the Contract

As soon as I know I have the job, I begin contacting subs for firm bids and contracts. I always ask about the sub's work load and schedule before getting a bid. Since I rely on the same dependable subs, I will often call only one, and never more than three. It's a balancing act: If you don't reward a sub with enough jobs, you may lose his loyalty. Since I know the pricing schedules of my subcontractors, I'm comfortable awarding a contract with only one bid. And I get priority because my subs know that when I call them, they have a good chance of getting the work.

Avoiding no-man's-land. Although

many builders still do business with a handshake, it's wise to use detailed contracts — even with good subs. This is more to avoid tasks slipping through the cracks than to force performance.

Good contracts leave nothing to chance. I try for an airtight contract that spells out all requirements and expectations. Any "no-man's-land" of responsibility noted in my preliminary scheduling is spelled out in my sub's contract. For example, the electrician's contract specifies that the electrician, not the hvac company, will be installing the bathroom venting. Some of the decisions as to who does what will be based on local customs, while others may be strictly arbitrary. In any case, they must be nailed down.

Trash and cleanup are everyone's responsibility, so these items are mentioned in every contract. All subs are required to take out everything they bring in. Even so, I sub out site cleanup on a regular basis, and keep trash cans and a dumpster on the site.

Subcontractor insurance. I require every subcontractor to have his insurance agency send me proof of coverage. Many states have minimum requirements on liability and workers comp insurance. Make sure the subs meet all the requirements or you may end up liable. A sub's insurance dates must cover the job time frame; the amounts of coverage must equal or exceed the G.C.'s policy. In my experience, many subs do not carry the type or amount of insurance they should. Check with your insurance agent to be sure that if an uninsured sub has a mishap, you have protection.

There have been numerous articles written about the IRS and what constitutes subcontractors and employees (see "Sub or Employee?" in this chapter). Workers comp insurance is one of the IRS tests, but if you are subbing it all out, make sure that you and Uncle Sam agree on what a "subcontractor" is.

Managing the Job

Customer relations are completely different when you sub everything out. Good communication between all the players is paramount, and the subs must be fully aware of your role in the project. I make it very clear to the subs (and their employees) that any and all questions are to be directed only to me. They know they can reach me via my pager or leave a message on my answering machine.

Most homeowners do not realize how much a contractor does for them beyond the job site. And they are inclined to feel that you are not earning your keep if your subs are constantly asking them how they want this, or where they want that. Worse, if clients begin telling the subs what to do and where to do it, they may wonder why they hired you. Customer relations will go sour if the G.C. is ever perceived to be out of the loop.

Planning and scheduling. Planning and accurate scheduling are essential in an all-sub operation. I start the job with the original estimating schedule and update it as needed. For me, the critical path method (CPM) is the most comprehensive. Most important, it accurately displays which subs can work concurrently and which ones can't. It also keeps me from expecting the same sub to be at two different jobs at the same time.

My schedules are very detailed. In addition to the major tasks, I list material order dates, calls for inspections, and calls to subs. When I complete the schedule, I call all the subs and have them pencil in the expected dates for their work. Once they know my schedule, slight adjustments are easier to deal with. I call subs weekly to keep them posted regarding their expected start date.

On-the-go communication. Your subs must always be able to contact you. To keep the communication immediate, consider using pagers, car phones, and even a portable fax machine in your truck. I leave a fax machine on every job. Very often, a faxed sketch or detail saves a special trip to the site. A fax on site pays for itself quickly.

Keys to the job. To give subs access to the job, we use a combination lock-box similar to those used by realtors. There is only one key for the job, and the subs get the combination to the box. With this method there are no hidden keys, or keys in the hands of the wrong people.

Each job also gets a portable "office in a box" (see photo, next page). I use a plywood box with a fold-down front that sits on a pair of sawhorses in some out-of-the-way place. The "office" contains

The "office in a box" contains the basic tools needed to maintain communication between contractor, clients, and subs, as well as other job-site essentials such as first-aid supplies and a fire extinguisher.

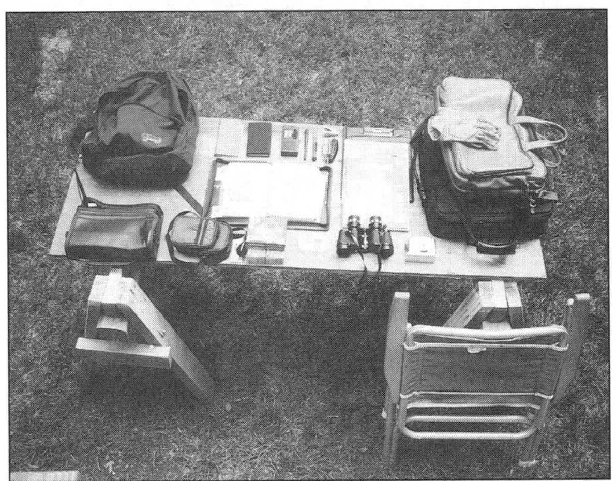

The author visits every job site every day, carrying with him a mobile kit of necessities, including a laptop, cellular phone, calculator, tape measure, camera, binoculars, and an assortment of desk supplies.

pencils, paper, portable phone, and a fax machine (which doubles as a copier). There's also a set of plans, and a bulletin board for exchanging messages with subs, suppliers, and homeowners. To secure the office, the box is padlocked and the key placed in the lock-box with the job key.

Quality Control

The best defense against poor-quality work is committing yourself to using good subs. But, in addition, you must visit the job site at least once a day. I carry a kit of "necessities" to each of these visits (see photo at bottom left). On each visit, I have a list of things to accomplish, including vendor's questions, messages from subs, and changes made by the homeowner or designer.

I try to talk to every sub on the project during each visit. Each day, I do a visual inspection of the work in progress, because the sooner a problem is discovered the easier it is to remedy. Also, making a daily inspection shows the subs (and owners) that I care about the job and about them.

Materials and supplies. Since subs typically get better discounts than GCs, my subcontractors normally supply their own day-to-day material needs, as well as specialty items. This makes them responsible for any problems with the merchandise. It also saves countless hours of shopping around, and passes one more IRS test for subs.

Material warranties are one of those gray areas that you need to bring up with subs. Make clear who is responsible for materials at each stage of construction. Do the same for customer-supplied materials.

By Norman R. Allaby, owner of Coppermine Construction in Bethel, Conn.

Site Rules for Subs

Educate your employees and subs to obtain high quality conduct, safety, and customer relations

A bustling job site is like a hive of bees, with one important difference: Bees know instinctively what their jobs are; humans, on the other hand, need to be taught what to do and what's expected of them. There's no shame in that. In fact, it shows that our actions are not a product of base instinct, but rather a creation of free will.

That being the case, however, I don't want everyone else's free will running roughshod over our project schedules, our profits, or our reputation. In the past, we've had our fair share of employees and subcontractors who didn't show up on the job when they were scheduled, who showed little concern for leaving debris on the job site, or who damaged a client's property. One client made a point of telling us that he had overheard some pretty offensive language from the crew, and a female client mentioned to me, woman to woman, that one male worker in particular made her feel

This one-page list of rules is mailed to each sub prior to the start of work. A copy is also posted prominently at each site.

Site Rules

1. No one is permitted to work on the site without proof of current insurance coverage, a completed W-9 form, and Independent Contractor Statement (when necessary). No payments will be issued before receipt of all required forms, including Stipulation Against Liens when required.
2. You must sign in daily at the job site. If you have several workers on the site, assign one person to sign in, but please indicate how many workers are on the site.
3. Profanity, unprofessional behavior, and unkempt appearances will NOT be tolerated.
4. Everyone is required to use personal protection devices (PPDs) as required by the work being performed. Each job site is stocked with a small supply of safety eyewear, ear plugs, and dust masks. (Safety eyewear must be returned in usable condition or you will be billed for it).
5. If you suffer a work-related injury, report it to your employer AND to our project supervisor immediately.
6. All materials and tools must be kept in a safe and orderly fashion. If your work area or work habits become a hazard to you and/or others, you will be directed to clean up your work area immediately and/or correct your method of working. If you think someone is creating a safety hazard, report it to the supervisor immediately.
7. There normally is minimal storage space available on the job site for tools and materials. Do NOT bring more than necessary to the job site.
8. You are responsible for removing and placing in storage all fixtures relevant to your portion of the project, and to protect them from damage.
9. Smoking is NOT permitted in or near the job site. Smoking is allowed in designated areas only, and all butts will be disposed of in butt cans. Grounds cleanup will be done either on your own time at your own expense or at our expense chargeable to you at $35/hr.
10. Trash containers will be provided for proper disposal of food debris. Grounds cleanup will be done either on your own time at your own expense or at our expense chargeable to you at $35/hr.
11. Clean up and remove all your construction debris on a daily basis. If we must remove your construction debris, you will be charged the dump fees plus our labor at $35/hr. Check with the job supervisor to find out if a dumpster is available for your use.
12. Everyone is responsible for protecting the homeowner's property as well as the work of other trades. Any damage should be reported immediately to the supervisor.
13. Please take all necessary precautions to protect any landscaping around the property. If you think certain plantings may get damaged, report it to the supervisor so that he can make arrangements to protect or remove the plantings.
14. Phone and fax facilities are available for your use. If you use them, you must fill out the required information on our posted phone/fax log sheet. You will be charged for any toll calls placed by you or your employees.

uncomfortable because of his long, unkempt hair and rough appearance.

Nowadays, we educate our employees from the day they're hired about our expectations for work performance, safety, personal conduct, and customer relations. Our Employee Manual spells out exactly what we will not tolerate.

Educating subs. But what about our subs and their employees? Contractors work hard to make sure everyone on the job is working from the same set of drawings, but rarely do anything to make sure everyone is working to the same set of professional standards.

Our solution is to provide our subs with a one-page list of Site Rules (at right) that spells out exactly what we expect from them. We mail a copy of our Site Rules along with a cover letter to the office of each new subcontractor prior to job start. We also post a copy of these rules at each larger job site, and hand out copies to any new workers on the project.

Tough love. Because we vigorously defend our reputation, we deal swiftly with infractions. For small goof-ups, we give our subs a second chance. For example, say someone smacks his thumb with a hammer, and blood and cuss words go flying. If the client is home and overhears the commotion, the offender tenders his apologies immediately.

We do not, however, tolerate intentional or blatant infractions of the rules. If someone blatantly ignores safety issues or habitually uses foul language — or worse yet, directs profanity at a client — that person is sent off the job site, immediately and permanently, with no chances for apologies.

The Reasons Behind the Rules

Every item in the Site Rules list is there for a reason. Aside from those that address administrative issues (Rules 1 and 2), all of the rules are based on just three basic themes: respect for others and their property; safety; and keeping the project on schedule.

Rule 3, for example, recognizes that elderly people and women tend to feel uncomfortable when rough-looking men are working inside their homes. We want our clients to feel comfortable and safe around our workers. Rule 4 makes it clear that safety equipment is to be used to prevent injuries, not simply to cover our backside should the OSHA agent show up on site. An injury-free project runs on schedule, which translates into profit. Rule 5 ensures that we are made aware of every accident so that our job supervisor can follow up with a brief phone call to the injured person's employer (the subcontractor). We ask if the employee is okay and if the sub needs any more information about the incident, and we find out if the injury will affect the sub's schedule.

All of our Site Rules show concern for others while at the same time enabling us to continually monitor and control our schedule. And that's important to our bottom line, since our slim profit margins will disappear altogether if a job falls behind schedule.

Site Storage

Rules 6 and 7 both deal with material and equipment storage problems. An uncluttered site is not only safer for all concerned, it makes a good impression on our clients. Rule 7 also recognizes that it costs money to move materials from one spot to another each time a new trade needs to get into a particular area to work.

Rule 8 applies to almost any project, but especially to the type of restoration and renovation we do. Our projects often require the temporary removal of historic or otherwise valuable fixtures (lighting fixtures, Victorian-era tubs and lavs, fireplace surrounds, moldings, and so on). If the sub's contract requires that he remove, refurbish, and re-install an item, then we want the sub to be responsible for that item every step of the way. If something's lost or damaged, we know who to call.

Clean Up and Trash Disposal

Rule 9 forbids smoking because of something Gary experienced years ago while working for another contractor. An employee had a habit of laying his smoldering cigarette on the edge of the nearest flat surface between puffs. Inevitably, he forgot about it once and left a burn mark in a countertop. The contractor had to replace the whole thing at considerable cost in time and money.

We also have a reputation for sparkling clean work sites at job completion, including the grounds outside the house. There's nothing that ticks us off more than having to police the grounds for cigarette or cigar butts, lunch wrappers, and foam coffee cups. Rule 10 shifts the costs, which are not accounted for in our project estimate or our schedule, to the subs.

The same is true of Rule 11. With waste disposal fees climbing yearly, we can't afford to be saddled with additional costs caused by inconsiderate subs who leave their debris all over the place. If we're running a large project, we provide a dumpster for all trades to use, but subs still must pick up after themselves daily. If we're running a small project, each trade is responsible for its own debris removal. In fact, on small jobs we don't include the cost of trash removal in our proposal. So if we're forced to clean up a sub's debris and pay to remove it, we'll blow our estimate. And because we'll have to schedule workers to do the clean up, we'll blow our schedule.

Property Damage

We treat each client's home as though it were our own, and we understand the value of each trade's hard work. We don't tolerate others who show little concern for either. Rule 12 makes it clear that we expect subs to respect one another's work as well as our client's property.

Rule 13 recognizes that renovation and restoration work usually entails working around old, established trees and shrubs. We want our subs to show as much concern for our clients' property as we do. When necessary, we'll even bring in an arborist or nurseryman to temporarily move plantings that would otherwise be damaged.

Phones and Faxes

Our supervisors rely on phones and faxes to keep the work progressing on our larger job sites. By providing these services to our subs as well, we help their portion of the project move along quickly and efficiently, too. Rule #14 helps us to control the cost, and ensures that we have a paper trail of our communications, should disputes or misunderstandings arise.

By Denise David Baer, co-owner of Restore 'N' More, a remodeling and restoration company in Lancaster, Pa.

Chapter 5

Estimating

Estimating for Profit in Remodeling

To produce a profit, identify and compensate for unexpected costs in your estimates

I prefer to open estimating seminars with two questions:

Question 1: *"What is the most profit you can possibly make on a $15,000 remodeling job?"*

Answers usually start at $3,000 and peak at $8,000 with a lot of haggling. Of course, even if your labor and materials were free, and you were the world's most efficient company, you could not exceed a profit of $15,000.

Question 2 is easier: *"What is the most money you can lose on a $15,000 job?"*

Every contractor knows that answer: There is no limit on how much you can lose. A single project can consume six months worth of profits...and more.

That paradox is the reason why good estimates are so important. Profit is limited but losses are not.

The goal of estimating is to produce an appropriate profit, so the consideration of profit is an appropriate place to start a discussion of construction estimating.

Profits Are Produced, Losses Occur

We produce profits consciously, by taking specific actions. The production of profit requires experience, foresight, and planning — things that minimize uncertainty and risk.

Losses flow from everything else. Losses require no conscious effort, and are simply the monetary expression of Murphy's law.

Unless an estimate contains a conspicuous omission, we tend to blame losses on production factors. That's where the costs appear that can overwhelm profits. When we do lose money, we scrutinize the production area for ways to prevent similar losses in the future. Profitable jobs seldom receive the same scrutiny, even though they usually include unexpected costs as well. Whether the job was profitable or not, however, unexpected costs always eat into profits.

This section will examine some factors that contribute to unexpected costs and will show how a good estimator manages them. It is the estimator's job to identify areas of uncertainty, and to compensate for them.

By identifying areas of uncertainty in your remodeling estimates, you can anticipate the unexpected — and charge for it.

Closed and Open Costs

One set of problems arises from the way that estimates are prepared. A typical estimate lists the material and labor costs, along with subcontractor quotes. The unit material and labor costs are multiplied by the quantities required. To the sum of these costs are added factors for supervision, contingencies, overhead, and profit. This orderly array is really a mixed bag of both predictable costs and highly variable costs.

The material costs are predictable and easy to find. You look at recent invoices, call suppliers, or send them a material takeoff and let them quote you a price. If you track job costs you may transfer material prices from other projects. Except for outright estimator error, there is no reason for variation between estimated and actual material costs. Similarly, if the specs are right, a firm quote by a responsible sub should match his billing.

These precisely defined costs can be termed closed costs. They stay put, and don't start to grow as soon as you look the other way. Closed costs are easy to calculate, and tend to get more emphasis than they deserve. If estimating were just a matter of listing closed costs, contractors would rack up profits with unwavering regularity. The fact that they don't means that there must be another kind of cost.

We can call these other costs open costs. Unrecognized open costs are a major reason why year after year, some contractors have so little to show for their efforts.

For contractors, the principle open costs are labor, supervision, overhead, and sales costs. Two other open costs that can be significant are financing and insurance. Open costs are time-sensitive. The longer it takes to perform a procedure, the higher its overhead, supervision, and other costs become.

A successful estimator looks at all the variables that may affect open costs and provides for them in his estimate. His provisions may take the form of either higher prices for specific categories or of limiting clauses in the contract document. One way or another, the estimator uses informed judgment to provide for open costs.

Labor

Even though pricing manuals and data bases show standard unit costs for labor, it is a mistake to plug labor into an estimate as a closed cost. Published unit-labor costs are usually based on large quantities and ideal site conditions. They also assume specific levels of skill, equipment availability, and supervision that may not apply to the company and project at hand. There is no procedure so simple that production costs cannot increase from two to ten times because of difficult conditions, incompetence, or other unforeseen problems. As a major component of cost, labor requires the estimator's close scrutiny. Some of the variables affecting labor cost are:

Project duration. Mobilization and setup, as well as closedown and cleanup, are part of most operations, and their time is distributed over the total quantity of work performed. Small quantities bear a greater portion of this labor "overhead," and will exhibit a higher unit cost. In addition, small or divided work units deprive tradesmen of time to develop efficient work rhythms. The result will be an unexpectedly high production cost.

Unfamiliar materials. New materials come on line all the time, and architects love to spec them. The anticipated cost advantage of a new material will not materialize until installers learn how to handle it and understand the manufacturer's storage, preparation, and installation standards. First time around, someone has to pay for this training — the estimator's job is to be sure it's the buyer.

Complex or unorthodox design. The possible impact of complex or unorthodox design on performance time is devastating. Standard production rates go out the window when drawings must be scrutinized at every step and when work is delayed while questions are answered. And unorthodox designs almost invite mistakes. This in turn means tearing out completed work, ordering more material, paying additional labor, and rearranging the work schedule.

When confronted by an unorthodox project, the estimator should review the plans with experienced superintendents and tradesmen, as well as with manufacturers' reps. Such consultations help educate the estimator about new construction techniques that can lead to more competitive quotes. They also may help him to see unforeseen complications. Either way, the project benefits.

Incomplete plans or specs. Whenever the estimator encounters an ambiguity in the specs, he has two choices. He can sidestep the issue or he can meet it head-on by asking for a time-consuming clarification. Facing problems head-on is difficult, but sidestepping them means that they will have to be resolved later, probably at the worst possible moment, by personnel who may be unskilled in negotiations.

An example of this is the customer who can't decide on cabinetry, appliances, and other materials. It's tempting to sidestep such choices by including "allowances" for them in the estimate. But such allowances guarantee that decisions will be postponed until the last possible moment. At that point, however, selections may complicate or delay other work underway, or conflict with work already completed. Leaving these questions unresolved may make it easier to get the contract signed, but they are time-bombs waiting to blast holes in your profit. Smart estimators avoid them.

Supervision

On-site supervision frequently becomes an unexpected open cost. Some contractors don't show it at all. Others include it as a percentage of the total job price. But we have not found a relationship between the job price and the amount of supervision required. Jobs that use many trades, unorthodox design elements, or an extended production period are supervisor-intensive. Other projects may be large and simple, requiring little supervision. In other words, the price of a job may or may not reflect the amount of supervision required.

A more accurate way to estimate supervision cost is to project the actual quantity of superintendent days required, based on the length of the project, and charge them out at a superintendent's rate. Site mobilization and punch-out also involve supervision costs, which the estimator should evaluate and include as specific items.

The important fact to notice is that anything prolonging the project also increases supervisory cost. This hidden multiplier effect can make delays extremely costly.

Overhead

Overhead is office rent, telephone, utilities, the secretary, the boss's salary, the estimator's salary, the company's cars, trucks, and insurance: everything that's not a direct project cost. Estimators should not treat overhead lightly. The goal is to have all costs covered by year's end, leaving profits intact. For this to play out, all costs not covered as estimate line-items must be included in overhead.

Overhead is especially high in smaller businesses. For many contractors, insufficient overhead allocation is a chronic drain on profits. Some contractors add an arbitrary overhead factor gleaned from a pricing manual. If you enjoy groping in the dark, that's one way to do it. Others look at last year's sales and divide their total overhead expense by that number. This provides a factor that expresses overhead as a function of sales. Multiply that factor by the price of the job and you will find an overhead allowance for that job.

Even this is haphazard, however, because overhead is really a time-sensitive open cost. Each of us has 260 days a year to cover our overhead. How much overhead a project uses depends on the length of time it runs, not its dollar amount.

The result of calculating overhead as a function of job cost is to earn an unexpected profit on one project (the excess overhead allowance), then spend that profit to cover the inadequate overhead allowances of other jobs. Successful business owners believe in retaining the profit they make, not using it to subsidize other work.

Estimator Accuracy

The profit margin of a given company is based on decisions made by the management and sales departments. Whether management decides on a 23% profit factor or a 2.3% profit factor, it has no effect on the accuracy of the estimate.

An estimate that yielded an additional 20% profit would probably be considered a superb estimate by most standards, and one that lost 20% would be a disaster. However, from the professional estimator's point of view, both estimates were equally inaccurate, and a conscientious estimator would analyze both to see where he went wrong. Success for the estimator is a zero difference between estimated and actual costs.

Tying It Together

The purpose of a business is to earn and retain a profit for the owner. Activity not directed to that end is not business — it's a charitable endeavor, a hobby, or something else.

Again, the construction estimator's job is to anticipate the costs of a project as accurately as possible so that the business can earn an appropriate profit. To simplify this process he splits the project into its component parts and assigns costs to each part. Some of these costs are precisely known, closed costs. Others are variable open costs.

We have found that a major cause of lost profit lies in the estimator's failure to provide for unexpected open costs. In order to avoid this failure, the estimator must first recognize all the variables in a project. Then he must evaluate their probable effect, and express that effect in estimated dollars.

Because many costs — overhead, labor, and supervision in particular — vary with the length of the project, they should be estimated as open costs in order to produce a consistent and predictable profit.

By Martin King, president of Martin Churchill Associates, Inc. in Arlington, Va. After more than 28 years of construction and estimating experience, King now specializes in consulting on structural damage and appraising reconstruction costs.

Remodeler's Estimating Checklist

This list of trouble spots will help you to avoid omissions and oversights in your estimates

Missing one or more major details on an estimate can quickly eat up your profit. To prevent omissions, you can spend long hours analyzing the plans, but it may not be worth the time if you are one of five bidders. To help me attend to all details without getting bogged down by them, I've developed a checklist of items that I use to logically work through an estimate. Some items on the list don't apply to every job, but it's important to get into the habit of looking at everything.

The organization of the list roughly follows the order of construction, and is similar to the way estimating books and software are organized. Through a process of trial and error, I've tailored the list to fit my area, the local building codes, and my subcontractors. It hasn't been easy, but taking notes during each job helps prevent mishaps on the next estimate.

Plans and Permits

Each building department in the area has its own way of calculating permit fees, which are loosely based on the total cost of the project. On large projects I guess high and place that number in the allowance column. On smaller projects, I try to be more accurate and include the cost in the base price.

Water, sewer, and sidewalk upgrades can be costly and are often required with larger-scale remodels, but may not be indicated on the plans. I always check with the building department to see if they will require these upgrades.

Demolition

Tearing out old work to make way for new work needs to be priced carefully or you'll bust your budget before the job begins.

Slab thickness can make a big difference. More than once, a slab I assumed was 4 inches thick turned out to be twice that — and it took twice as long to break out and produced twice as much rubble. When I can't determine the thickness before doing the estimate, I specify that the price assumes a 4-inch-thick slab and that demolishing a thicker slab will be billed as an extra.

Concrete reinforced with wire mesh and rebar can also take two to three times longer to break out than regular concrete.

Multilayer roofing — wood shingles, for example, with two layers of compo-

Removing mortar-base tile takes more time than stripping tile from drywall.

sition shingle on top — will take almost twice as long to tear off as a single-layer roof. Disposal costs will also be higher. The only way to be sure is to inspect the site.

Tipping fees and container rental can cost $60 or more per day and over $500 to empty. Hauling our own debris to the dump isn't any cheaper. For estimating purposes, I include the cost of a disposal box because it's easier than calculating the time for laborers to haul trash to the dump.

Asbestos removal requires a special license in California. If there's asbestos on the job, I get a price from an asbestos contractor for removing the visible asbestos. I also specify that if concealed asbestos is discovered during demolition, it will be removed at additional cost.

Stumps, landscaping, and sprinklers may need to be moved to make way for construction.

Restricted access may prevent you from pulling a truck up close to remove debris or deliver materials.

Mortar-base tile floors and walls can take five times longer to remove than tile on drywall.

Skilled carpenters may have to perform some demolition, such as salvaging window and door casings and breaking out stucco near an electric meter.

Excavation and Foundation

Accurately calculating volume is the critical factor in estimating earth work. This is especially true on sloped sites, which usually require removing more dirt to make room for the new foundation. If the grade is high enough, you might also need to build retaining walls.

Deep piers are becoming more common in areas with poor soil conditions, and need to be handled case by case. If access is limited and a rig can't drive up to the location, add the expense of a special crane auger.

Hand excavating under an existing building is also very costly. The loose dirt also has to be dragged by bucket to a truck or disposal box.

Sewer line trench depth can be deceiving unless you take a peek in the crawlspace to check the elevation of the existing pipes. A pipe that is already underground at the house will be several feet deeper at the street than one that is above grade under the house. Count on between 1/16-inch and 1/4-inch fall per foot.

Doweling into an existing foundation always adds cost.

Surface prep at joints between existing and new concrete may require hand work with a rotary hammer, adding to labor costs.

Waterproofing may be needed for areas exposed to the weather following demolition.

Sawing concrete — either a slab or a stem wall foundation — almost always

Figure on extra labor to bolt shear walls to the foundation.

requires an outside contractor with a diamond blade.

Reinforcing bars required in both directions can bump up the cost of the foundation.

Tall stem walls require extensive bracing.

Special flashings where concrete meets wood — especially if it involves hot-mopping or kerfing a slab — can be expensive, and may require getting a price from a subcontractor.

Framing

On many bids, I spend over half my time analyzing the framing, which often makes up 25% or more of the total cost of the job. Because remodels have many costly complications that you won't find on the plans, I always schedule a walk-through of the site. Here's a list of what we look for.

Bolting ledgers to concrete requires more labor than a standard platform framing system.

Two-by-six and 2x8 decking on the roof and floor take about five times longer to install than plywood, and the materials are more expensive.

Long joist spans require multiple rows of blocking, which take almost as much time to install as the joists themselves.

Second-floor beams sometimes require custom-made templates for bearing plates, and extra labor to fit the beams to the hardware.

An out-of-level floor is difficult to match without running strings and using the transit, both of which add to labor costs.

Custom-cutting studs is more expensive than using precuts.

Balloon framing is more difficult to lay out, and the tall balloon-framed walls are awkward to handle, particularly on cramped sites. The same is true of gable-end walls.

Rough-cut stud walls may need furring strips to match the new construction.

A chopped-up floor plan, or one with lots of corners and 45-degree angles, always takes more time to lay out and build than an open plan with square corners.

Tall wood-framed chimneys are awkward to frame and difficult to lift into place, especially on a second story.

CAROLYN BATES

Roofs with hips and valleys are more expensive to frame and finish than gable roofs.

Shear walls are labor intensive, especially interior shear walls that need to be bolted to the foundation and tied in to the roof framing.

Steep roof slopes (7/12 or more) require ropes and scaffolds for nailing on the sheathing.

Hips and valleys use more material and labor than gable roofs.

Large roof beams are expensive to purchase and transport, and require lots of labor to lift into place. You may need a crane as well.

Deep soffits and one-of-a-kind eaves details are more expensive than standard details.

Venting a cathedral ceiling adds material and labor to maintain a continuous air space, and often requires more expensive rigid insulation.

Fly rafters, whether simple or complex, sometimes are forgotten in the estimate.

Exterior Finish

Estimating stucco is easy — we use a square-foot price — except for special projections or coving. But estimating wood siding is complex.

Matching existing siding often entails extra cost for special milling. On the labor side, weaving the new siding at a transition to the existing takes much

CAROLYN BATES

Tall windows and complex window walls are much costlier to install than standard units.

more time than applying field pieces.

Matching trim details is often more costly than it first appears. Sometimes, for example, we will need to build a redwood sill for an aluminum window to make it match the existing windows.

Siding gable walls takes longer, especially with horizontal siding, because of the long angle cuts.

Windows

Retrofitting windows takes more time than installing windows in new construction because of time-consuming details like modifying casings to cover gaps in existing drywall. I ask my window supplier to look over the plans to make sure everything will fit, and to make sure every bedroom window meets egress requirements.

Special windows. In my experience, almost any size window can be installed in a new rough opening in 30 minutes, though there are a few exceptions. Allow extra time for tall stairwell windows (over 8 feet) or second-story windows with only ladder or scaffold access. I always get a price on glass block windows from our tile subcontractor.

Matching trim. Be sure to examine both the exterior and interior wood trim details required to match the existing. On the interior, wide stain-grade casings can cost several times more than stock beveled casings.

New openings. Cutting or changing a rough opening in an existing wall may require new headers. Also, plumbing and wiring in the wall may have to be rerouted.

Skylight framing and flashing can be costly. Skylights in an attic roof almost always need a flared shaft, which is more expensive to frame than a skylight in a cathedral ceiling. I trust the roofer to correctly flash a standard curbed skylight, but with a highly engineered skylight, such as a Velux, I price the time of a skilled carpenter to make sure it is done properly.

Doors

Most prehung doors — both interior and exterior — take less than an hour to install, assuming the rough opening is correct. Sliding glass doors, French doors, and pocket doors are exceptions, and need two to three hours to install properly. Double pocket doors are the worst, and can easily take all day.

Stain-grade doors and trim are more expensive than paint grade.

Fire doors are much more expensive to purchase and install than standard doors.

Front entrance doors are usually more expensive than other exterior doors. If we're unsure, we include an allowance price.

Locksets and other door hardware are often not specified, so it's easy to forget to include their cost. We use an allowance of $250 for an entry latch and deadbolt, and $20 for each interior door.

Plumbing

Examining the existing plumbing materials is critical when estimating the cost of new plumbing work. Copper is the easiest material to work with, while galvanized pipe requires special connectors and may be old and failing at the joints. For DWV systems, cast-iron pipe with packed lead joints is more difficult to cut in place and is susceptible to rust damage. ABS pipe is much easier to work with.

Second-floor waste lines for new fixtures sometimes interfere with existing floor joists. We always trace the path of the upstairs waste line and add some time to deal with working the framing around the plumbing.

Difficult venting situations, like sinks under windows or in an island, are costly, as are vents in cathedral ceilings or ceilings without an attic.

A new water heater location may require moving the existing hot water line, and instant water heaters may need recirculating pumps.

Appliance and fixture allowances are easy to overlook.

Electrical

With few exceptions, electrical work is predictable. Homes with 2x tongue-and-groove decking systems, however, often make it slow and cumbersome to run Romex: It requires more drilling and more material when you have to pull wire long distances through walls or under floors rather than across a ceiling.

Knob-and-tube wiring is usually cheaper to replace than to trace and tie into.

Recessed can lights may conflict with existing framing.

Fishing wire through existing finish walls is more expensive than wiring in new construction.

A meter upgrade required to boost available amperage is a big-ticket item that is often not indicated on the plans.

Mechanical

To estimate mechanical work, the most important factor is the condition of existing systems.

Planning ductwork runs for forced-air furnaces — both supply runs and cold return ducts — can take a lot of head scratching and framing modification.

Existing ducts held together with brittle duct tape will probably have to be replaced.

Range hoods and downdraft cooktops can take a long time to rough in, especially if the ductwork has to snake through a wall.

Bath fans in 2x roof decking sometimes need a curb to enclose the duct.

Existing gas lines often need to be replaced with new 3/4-inch pipe back to the gas meter. And don't forget to check the supply lines for a gas fireplace log starter.

Insulation

My insulation subcontractor checks the plans against code for wall, floor, and ceiling insulation requirements, but I like to double-check. A cathedral ceiling is the most difficult to estimate because of the expense of buying and installing rigid insulation.

Sound insulation around bathrooms, bedrooms, and between the first and second floors is easy to forget while estimating.

Insulating wide joist bays, such as in a deck-and-girder floor system, makes suspending fiberglass blankets very difficult.

Interior Wall Finishes

For larger drywall jobs, I always have a subcontractor look at the plans to give me a price, but I also like to have them visit the site, especially if the floor plan is all chopped up. On smaller jobs, wall finishes can be a real profit eater if you don't learn to keep your eyes open for the following:

Adding smooth-surfaced walls to a room with textured walls requires floating a new layer of mud over everything — it's almost impossible to get a smooth finish on a painted textured wall by sanding alone.

Rounded corners are more expensive to tape.

Taping skylight shafts costs $150 to $200 extra for each shaft.

Twenty-four-inch-on-center framing may need 5/8-inch drywall to reduce waviness.

Garage walls require fire code drywall.

Cabinets and Countertops

If there is one area that needs an allowance, this is it. Plans rarely contain enough cabinet details to accurately estimate, so I make up my own specifications. For high-end work, I get a quote from a cabinetmaker. For more economical kitchens, I price manufactured cabinets at home-improvement warehouses. I always include extra time to install these cabinets because they usually have to be modified to fit, and parts are often missing. I also allow extra time to install special accessories, like pantry storage systems.

A built-in soffit over wall cabinets is easy to overlook.

CAROLYN BATES

To blend patched hardwood flooring, you may need to sand and refinish the whole room.

Countertops — tile, plastic laminate, and solid surfacing — vary greatly in price.

Backsplash height and material makes a big difference in the cost of installation.

Toe-kick trim may need to be custom milled.

Floor Covering

I usually plan on replacing 25% to 50% more hardwood than would ordinarily be required. As an alternative, I plan on refinishing the entire room. Refinishing everything is also the best way — although not the cheapest — to blend new and old flooring.

Hardwood species can make a difference in price — white oak is more expensive, for example, than red oak.

Borders and inlays are labor intensive.

Coved linoleum requires a larger sheet and better craftsmanship to install properly.

Painting

Painting can make up as much as 10% of the total cost of the job — and it doesn't pay to cut corners.

More than two colors — whether it's on the interior or exterior — increase costs because of all the cutting-in that needs to be done.

Prepainted gutters are cheaper than painting raw metal.

Preprimed siding is cheaper than back-priming raw wood.

Painting closet shelves is easy to forget when you're doing the estimate.

Repainting an entire wall or ceiling is usually necessary if any part of it needs painting. Sometimes an entire room needs repainting.

Special trims, moldings, and baseboards — especially in more than one color — can add cost to the painting estimate.

By Art Prindle, a contractor based in East Palo Alto, Calif.

Estimating Rules of Thumb

These pricing shortcuts will improve estimating speed without sacrificing accuracy

Ask two estimators to take off and price a specific item on a plan, and most times the takeoffs will be different. Both may be correct and even usable, but every estimator has tricks and shortcuts that affect the way the estimate comes out. After 18 years of estimating residential jobs, here are some of the methods that work for me.

Different Levels of Accuracy

The estimates I do are for pricing construction, not for materials purchase. Therefore, I don't get too hung up on what's called neat, or precise, estimating. If you're estimating $150-per-square-foot granite for a countertop, you need to be as precise as you can. But if you're calculating the concrete for a foundation footing that will be poured on less than perfectly level ground, and the estimate is for the bank loan, then you can use what I refer to as "regular" or what some estimators call "quick" estimating.

There are times to estimate quickly and times to do it neatly, but you should be consistent so your historical data can be used for job-costing and to adjust future estimates.

A word about waste. I've never understood why some estimators go to the nth degree in precision when doing a takeoff and then add in a seemingly arbitrary percentage to cover waste and errors. For "quick" estimating, I try to incorporate the waste factor directly into the initial number, rather than do several calculations. For example, when figuring drywall square footage, the amount of board taken up by windows and doors usually covers the waste. (I say "usually" because if you've got a 16x7-foot garage door or an entire window wall, you'll have to subtract square footage to avoid too much waste.)

Efficient Estimating

I try to work as efficiently as possibly when I estimate. I gather up the plans, a couple of sharp pencils, a scale, an electronic ruler, and a calculator. I go to a room with a large table, shut the door, and don't answer the phone. Occasionally, I may call out to check with a subcontractor on a detail or construction method, but that's it.

I keep the paperwork organized and simple. Each task gets a separate sheet of paper from a legal pad. I write with pencil because it can be easily erased. I know I'll need to make revisions, and a clean takeoff sheet lets me quickly see how I arrived at certain amounts when I look at it weeks later.

Notice that I haven't mentioned the computer — yet. Only when I've finished estimating, when I've made all my calls to suppliers and subs, and when I've clearly marked all my totals, do I return to my desk and enter all the data at once into a spreadsheet template on my computer. It's fun to see the bottom line change as you enter data during a takeoff, but for me it's not worth the effort it takes to change gears from pad and paper to computer. Delaying computer entry to the very end when I have all accurate numbers saves a lot of time.

Concrete Foundations

We usually sub out concrete on a per-yard basis, so the trick I use to calculate yardage is to imagine the concrete foundation wall as a concrete slab standing on edge: The thickness of the slab equals the width of the wall. The wall height is easily taken from the plans and the wall length is the total of all the foundation sides.

Coverage of One Cu. Yd. Concrete

Thickness	Square Feet
18"	18
12"	27
11"	29 1/2
10"	32
9"	36
8"	40
7"	46
6"	54
5"	65
4"	81
3 1/2"	93
3"	108
2 1/2"	130
2"	162
1 1/2"	216
1"	324

Find the thickness of the wall or footing in the first column to determine the number of square feet (second column) covered by one cubic yard of concrete.

For example, a simple 8-inch-thick rectangular foundation wall measuring 25x40 feet has a total length of 130 linear feet. If the wall is 8 feet high, then the total square footage of the wall is 130 x 8 = 1,040 square feet. According to the concrete estimating chart I use (above), one cubic yard of concrete will cover 40 square feet of an 8-inch-thick slab. So I just divide 1,040 square feet by 40 square feet per yard to arrive at 26 cubic yards of concrete for the wall.

If there are lots of windows and doors, you may want to take out the square footage for them and then add in a waste factor. In simple basements, I leave in the footage from the windows to cover the waste.

Since the concrete table calculates yardage on slabs up to 18 inches thick, footings can be calculated the same way as walls.

Framing

Most framing subcontractors bid their labor by the square foot of finished living space, and contract on either a "turnkey" (one price for everything) or labor-only basis. On a turnkey job, the framing contractor will take off and purchase all of the lumber, exterior trim, and even the trusses. But if you are subcontracting only for framing labor, then you'll need a lumber takeoff. This can be done in house, by a lumberyard, or by your framing contractor (probably for a fee, since he won't be handling and marking up the lumber). Completing an accurate lumber takeoff is beyond the scope of this section, but I'll offer a few tips for quick estimating.

Wall plates. I order plate material at least four and sometimes five times the total length of all walls. Walls need three plates running the length of each wall section. On walls that run in the same direction as the trusses or joists, an additional plate is needed for drywall backing at the ceiling. More will be needed to cover waste, miscellaneous backing, and continuous fire blocking for walls over 8 feet high.

Studs. Typically, wall studs are 16 inches on-center. It follows then that the number of studs per foot should be about 12/16, or three-fourths, the total wall length. But with braces, trimmers, corners, partition channels, and cripples, you'll have to adjust upward.

I use one stud for each linear foot of wall, but your own experience may suggest a different factor. I know one framing subcontractor who uses 1.25 studs for each foot of wall length.

Subfloor. I've seen subflooring taken off many different ways. One lumberyard simply divides the square footage of the floor by 32 and uses that value for the number of plywood sheets. Another squares off any jogs or cantilevers from the entire outside perimeter to form one large rectangle, then takes that square footage and divides by 32.

These are both adequate "quick" approaches, but in the case of plywood, neither approach is "neat" enough for me. This is one area where I typically use a more careful approach: I roll out the prints and pencil in the plywood sheets, drawing parallel lines every 4 feet to scale, then breaking the sheets every 8 feet, allowing for staggered joints. I then count up full and half sheets to get a total. I add in one or two extra sheets for miscuts and bad pieces to make sure there's always enough to cover the floor. If the two extra sheets aren't used on that floor, they'll be used during framing pickup or on the second floor.

Roof Slope Adjustment Factors

Roof Slope	Adjustment Factor
1 in 12	1.003
2 in 12	1.014
3 in 12	1.031
4 in 12	1.054
5 in 12	1.083
6 in 12	1.118
7 in 12	1.158
8 in 12	1.202
9 in 12	1.250
10 in 12	1.302
11 in 12	1.357
12 in 12	1.414

First calculate the horizontal area covered by the roof (including overhangs), then multiply by the correct adjustment factor to arrive at roof coverage area.

Roofing

There are two main things to consider when estimating roofing: the adjustment of the coverage area due to the roof pitch — the steeper the roof the greater the increase — and the waste factor.

Adjustment factor. The table above gives adjustment factors for different roof pitches. For example, if the horizontal area under the roof is 2,000 square feet and the roof pitch is 5/12, then the actual area to be covered equals 2,000 multiplied by the adjustment factor, 1.083, or 2,166 square feet. The adjustment factors work for all types of roofs, whether straight gable, hip, or a combination.

When measuring the area to be

roofed, don't forget about eaves and gable overhangs. The roof actually begins and ends at the overhangs. Remember also that most shake and shingle roofs need a starter course, so be sure to add that to the estimate.

Waste factor. Because waste factors vary widely by roofing type, it's wise to check with roofing contractors in your area to determine what they consider to be an accurate waste factor for each roofing type. The roofer who coached me adds anywhere from 5% to 13% for waste, depending on shingle type.

Using the example above, a waste factor of 13% applied to the adjusted 2,166 square feet of roof gives 2,448 square feet or 24.5 squares of material needed to cover that 2,000-square-foot area.

Exterior Masonry

A rule of thumb for modular brick veneer is "3 bricks equals 8 inches." That means 3 bricks will cover 8x8 inches, or 64 square inches, which translates to 6.75 bricks per square foot. But I use 7 bricks per square foot when calculating a brick count. Using the whole number 7 is easier on the arithmetic and also covers some of the waste.

Omissions. Don't rely solely on elevations when doing a brick or masonry takeoff. Check both the foundation and engineering plans for information on stepped-down brick ledges and buried courses. Similarly, by not checking the end elevations and sections through the building, it is easy to miss courses that extend up to the underside of a sloped soffit.

Insulation

Insulation is estimated by the square foot of floor, wall, or ceiling. If the outside walls are 140 linear feet and the walls are 8 feet high, then you'll need 1,120 (140 x 8) square feet of the specified insulation. Since there is very little waste in insulation, I take the time to subtract the window and door areas from the total. Remember also to add in the rim joist, or box sill, insulation to the total.

For the ceiling, the area to be insulated is the same as the finished floor area. To arrive at a cost, multiply the totals by installed prices you obtain from your favorite insulation contractor.

Drywall

I first learned to do drywall takeoffs by adding wall areas and ceiling areas and dividing that total by 48 to get the number of 4x12 sheets of drywall.

Board formula. Later, an old drywaller who probably invented gypsum gave me a "board" formula that I still use. Multiply the square footage of the finished area of the house by 4.5 for the house total. If the garage is full-finish, multiply its square footage by 2.25 and then add the result to the house amount. Divide by 48 to get number of sheets. For partially rocked garages, adjust the 2.25 number downward.

Quick ratio. No matter which method you use, sheet takeoff or board formula, the ratio of drywall board feet to finished square feet, including garage, should be between 3.0 and 3.5. This ratio may begin to fail on houses with large rooms, as there are not as many walls to cover when the rooms are large. But the ratio is a good check on your calculations.

Painting

Most painters bid by the square foot. I've received many painting bids over the phone by simply describing the interior (for example, doors and woodwork all painted or all stained) and the exterior of the house (stucco, hardboard siding, or brick) to the painting contractor and getting his square-foot price on that type of house.

If you are hiring a labor-only painter, you will need to know how many gallons it takes to cover everything. If you've done your drywall takeoff, you've already got the area you need to cover. Multiply it by 2, or 3 if you'll be requiring more than one coat. Check the coverage rates for the type and brand of paint and simply divide to get the number of gallons. As a rule, I don't trust the coverage rates on the can. I always use two-thirds to three-fourths of what the container says a gallon will cover.

Mechanicals

Plumbing, heating, and electrical costs are best estimated from historical unit costs. But the estimator needs to be aware that unit costs are average costs and therefore very sensitive to fixture quality and quantity.

Plumbing. I've tried to force a square-foot price onto plumbing quotes with little success. It's best to have a plumber bid the job turnkey, but in a pinch a "price per trap" works. Every plumbing fixture needs at least one trap, while the kitchen sink needs two because of the dishwasher. The washer hookup counts as one and the floor drain in the basement floor also counts as one.

To use historical data to determine a price per trap, you need only divide the total plumbing cost for the house by number of traps. The more houses you figure this way, the better your unit price will be.

Heating. In the southern and western parts of the country, where I work, the heating load is determined by the cooling load. Each region has a ratio that is either implied or dictated by the local building officials. The ratio states how many square feet can be "conditioned" per ton of cooling. If the ratio is 600 feet per ton and the price per ton of cooling is $750, then the heating/cooling costs for an 1,800-square-foot house is 1,800/600 x $750, or $2,250.

Electrical. Electrical costs can also be estimated by the square foot, although you probably won't find many electrical contractors willing to tell you their unit costs. In fact, heating and electrical costs are usually very close unless special conditions prevail, such as lots of recessed lights, jetted tubs or spas, or an oversized electrical panel. As with plumbing, your own analysis will tell you what square-foot prices work in your area.

By Allen Matz, a former residential builder with 18 years of experience in both the field and office. Matz is currently a purchaser for a Denver, Colorado home builder.

Unit-Price Estimating

Pricing by the square foot or linear foot speeds takeoff without sacrificing accuracy

Estimating makes or breaks a builder. A reputation for good craftsmanship may get you in the door, but your price gets you the job. The hours spent estimating are especially dear to small companies where the owner does a little bit of everything. After working all day on the site and meeting with clients in the late afternoon, many small builders spend the evening working up prices. But after all this hard work, even a good estimator lands only about 25% of the jobs he prices; time spent estimating the others is wasted. That's why every builder dreams of finding a faster way to estimate costs without compromising accuracy.

Everybody has their own way of estimating, but most systems fall into one of three categories: stick-by-stick, square foot, or unit pricing. Stick-by-stick estimating yields the most accurate price because every piece of lumber and every sheet of plywood in the building is counted individually. This method also gives you a complete bill of materials at the estimating stage, so you're ahead of the game when you sign the job. But stick-by-stick estimating is slow and tedious. While you may be able to justify the effort on negotiated projects, it's risky for competitive bids because so much time is wasted if you don't get the job.

Square-foot pricing is much faster, but it's also less accurate. This method uses square feet of floor area to arrive at a price for the whole job. At $65 per square foot, for example, the cost of a 1,600-square-foot ranch house would be $104,000. The drawback of square-foot pricing is that it doesn't account for unusual detailing or factors like oddly shaped structures. A long, narrow two-story building will not cost the same to build as a square one-story building of the same total square footage. Square-foot prices are useful when you need to give a ballpark figure to an owner, but I wouldn't want to sign a contract based on this kind of estimate.

Between these two extremes is unit-price estimating, which is both fast enough and accurate enough for most projects. It takes some time to develop a good unit-price estimating system, but in the long run, it's worth the effort.

What Is Unit Pricing?

Unit-price estimating combines elements from stick-by-stick estimating

Item Price Lists

	Framing Lumber					
	Spruce		Fir		Treated	
Size	each	per lf	each	per lf	each	per lf
2x3 8'	$1.43	$.18	$10.00	$1.25	–	–
2x4 8'	3.40	.19	13.20	1.65	$4.28	$.54
10'	4.38	.44	16.50	1.65	5.36	.54
12'	5.26	.44	19.80	1.65	6.42	.54
14'	6.15	.44	23.10	1.65	7.49	.54
16'	7.01	.44	26.40	1.65	8.55	.54

	Plywood					
Type	1/4"	3/8"	1/2"	5/8"	3/4"	other
2-4-1	–	–	–	–	–	$35.20
AA	–	–	–	–	$37.58	–
AC	$15.54	$18.79	$22.97	$27.61	31.78	–
CDX	–	12.32	15.23	18.82	22.85	–
Lauan	16.90	–	–	–	–	–
MDO	–	–	43.38	–	57.48	–
TG	–	–	–	13.78	23.07	–

Figure 1. *A price list for framing lumber (left) should include all standard sizes and several species. Plywood (right) can be listed according to grade, species, and thickness.*

and square-foot estimating. Unit-price estimating accounts for all of the individual items that go into constructing a building, but instead of being counted one by one, components are grouped together into assemblies so you can take off quantities for the whole group at the same time.

Most builders already use unit pricing for parts of their estimates. If you figure the cost of roofing by the square, for example, you're using a unit price. A price of, say, $100 per square for roofing includes the cost of the roofing, underlayment, flashing, caulk, nails, and labor. The takeoff unit is a square — 100 square feet of roof area. If the roof requires 14 squares of roofing, the total price would be $1,400 (14 squares x $100 per square).

Most price books, such as those published by R.S. Means, Craftsman, and Hometech, contain unit prices. They break the job down into component parts, like exterior walls, floor systems, and roofing, and give a price for each component based on a common unit of measure, such as square feet or linear feet. Price books usually show you the cost of the material and labor separately, as well as an installed cost.

One problem with price books, however, is that they assume ideal conditions and typical construction. The price book may assume, for example, that the subfloor is 5/8-inch tongue and groove, glued and hand-nailed. But you may need to estimate the cost of 3/4-inch subflooring, glued and air-nailed. In this case, your material costs will be higher than those in the book, and your labor costs will be lower. The regional multipliers most price books provide to allow for geographic differences won't adjust for these kinds of variations. What you need is a unit price book based on material costs in your area and on the productivity rate of your own crews.

Item Prices

A unit-price estimating system requires you to keep track of prices for individual items as well as for items grouped into assemblies.

Make a list. Since material prices change several times a year, you need to keep track of individual items, like two-by stock, plywood, and siding. Most price books use the format established by the Construction Specifications Institute (CSI). This system divides a structure into 16 major divisions, such as rough carpentry, thermal and moisture protection, and doors and windows. Whether you use the CSI format as is, modify it to suit the kind of work you do, or devise your own system, you need to establish a list of materials and prices that is well organized, easy to change, and allows you to find what you need quickly.

Before I began using electronic estimating software, which stores item prices in a database, I kept lists of prices in a three-ring binder (Figure 1). I orga-

Using Unit Prices

The more assemblies you have, the faster you will be able to complete an estimate. But assemblies work best when you can easily remember what's included and what's not. Otherwise, you may accidentally omit the cost of some materials from your estimate, or count some costs twice. For example, because the number of corners in a building varies, it is easier and less confusing to exclude from a wall assembly the studs needed to provide corner nailers. You may also want to omit nails from your assemblies in favor of calculating a single lump sum quantity for each type of nail you will need.

Start with assemblies for elements of construction — such as floor systems, roof systems, windows, and doors — that remain the same from job to job. To price items deliberately left out of an assembly, you will need to estimate portions of the building twice — once using the assembly, and a second time to pick up the omitted materials. Work through the sample takeoff below to see how this works. — *S.A.*

Sample Takeoff

1. **Choose an assembly** that matches the specs on the drawing for 2x12s @ 16" o.c. with 3/4" tongue-and-groove decking.

2. **Calculate the unit price from the total floor area to be framed.** To keep the numbers straight, calculate the two full-length sections separately from the stairwell section.

Full-length framing:
28.5' x 24' = 684 sq. ft.
684 sq. ft. x $3.71 per sq. ft. = $2,537.64
Stairwell framing:
3.5' x 12' = 42 sq. ft.
42 sq. ft. x $3.71 per sq. ft. = $155.82
Total floor area $2,693.46

3. **Add material not included in the assembly.** The doubled joists and headers at the stairwell are not covered by the assembly, and neither are any joist hangers. Calculate the cost of these items separately, omitting costs for incidental items, such as nails.

4 joists 2x12-12' @ $19.99 ea.= $79.96
2 headers 2x12-8' @ $13.33 ea.= 26.66
4 sgl. jst. hngrs. @ .56 ea. = 2.24
4 dbl. jst. hngrs. @ $1.09 ea. = 4.36
Tax (5%) 5.55
Labor: 1 hr. @ $20/hr. = 20.00
Total at stairwell $138.77

4. **Add the estimated totals** together to get the total price for the floor system:

Total floor area $2,693.46
Total at stairwell 138.77
Total Floor System $2,832.23

Framing Plan

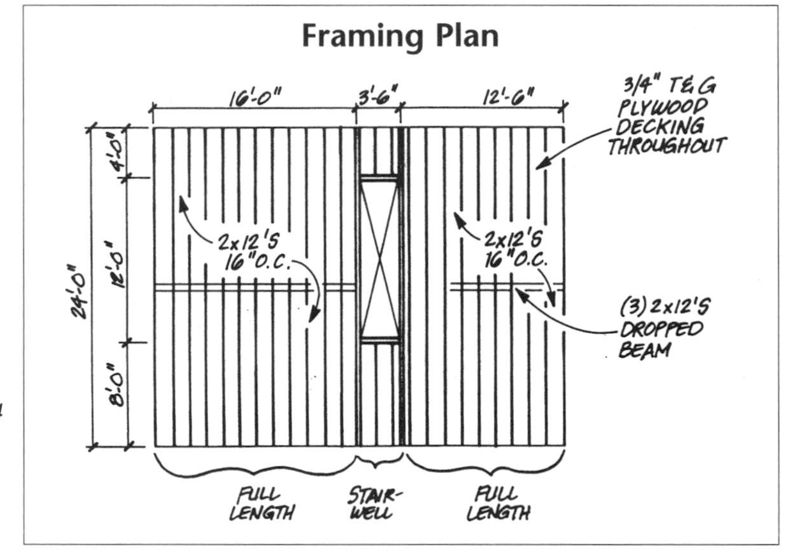

FLOOR ASSEMBLY X SF — **2x12 @ 16" o.c., 3/4" TG**

Description	Type	Qty	Unit	Price Per Unit	Total Price
Joists	2x12-12'	10.0	ea	$19.99	$199.90
Rim joists	2x12-12'	2.0	ea	19.99	39.98
Glue	PL400	2.0	qt	4.45	8.90
Decking	3/4" TG	4.5	ea	23.07	103.82
Nails, decking	8d Paslode	.1	bx	35.75	3.58
Subtotal					$356.18
Tax (5%)					$ 17.81
Total Materials					**$373.99**
Labor *(crew of 2)*	Framing	2.5	hr		
	Decking	1.5	hr		
Total Labor		4.0	hr	$40.00	**$160.00**
Total Price for 144 sq. ft. of floor					**$533.99**
Price per square foot ($533.99 ÷ 144 sf)					**$ 3.71**

nized the list into sections that roughly followed the logical order of construction. Once or twice a year, I called my local suppliers to update the prices. At other times, I used my monthly material invoices to update pricing. When I didn't have time to update my price book regularly, I called suppliers to check current prices before I made the final calculations for each estimate.

Assemblies. Once you have an itemized list of materials, you can begin to group them together into assemblies. Start with six or seven assemblies for phases of construction that you know well. Your initial list of assemblies might include the following:

- Floor system
- Roof system
- Exterior walls
- Interior partitions
- Windows

Next you need to choose the takeoff unit you will use to estimate the work of each assembly. The determining factor in choosing a takeoff unit is whether or not the portion of the building described by the assembly varies in one or two dimensions. A takeoff unit of linear feet, for example, is convenient for an exterior wall assembly if most of the exterior walls you build are the same height — say, 8 feet tall. In this case, the only variable is the wall's length, so you need only to determine how long the wall is to find the price (Figure 2). Some projects, on the other hand, will have walls that vary in two dimensions — length and height — and are better suited to a takeoff unit of square feet. Another option is to create separate assemblies for each wall height, using linear feet as the takeoff unit for all of them.

Calculating Prices

One easy way to determine the price per unit for an assembly is to work up a stick-by-stick price for a typical section of work and divide the total cost by the number of takeoff units. Using the example of an exterior wall assembly, you could estimate the cost of a 10-foot

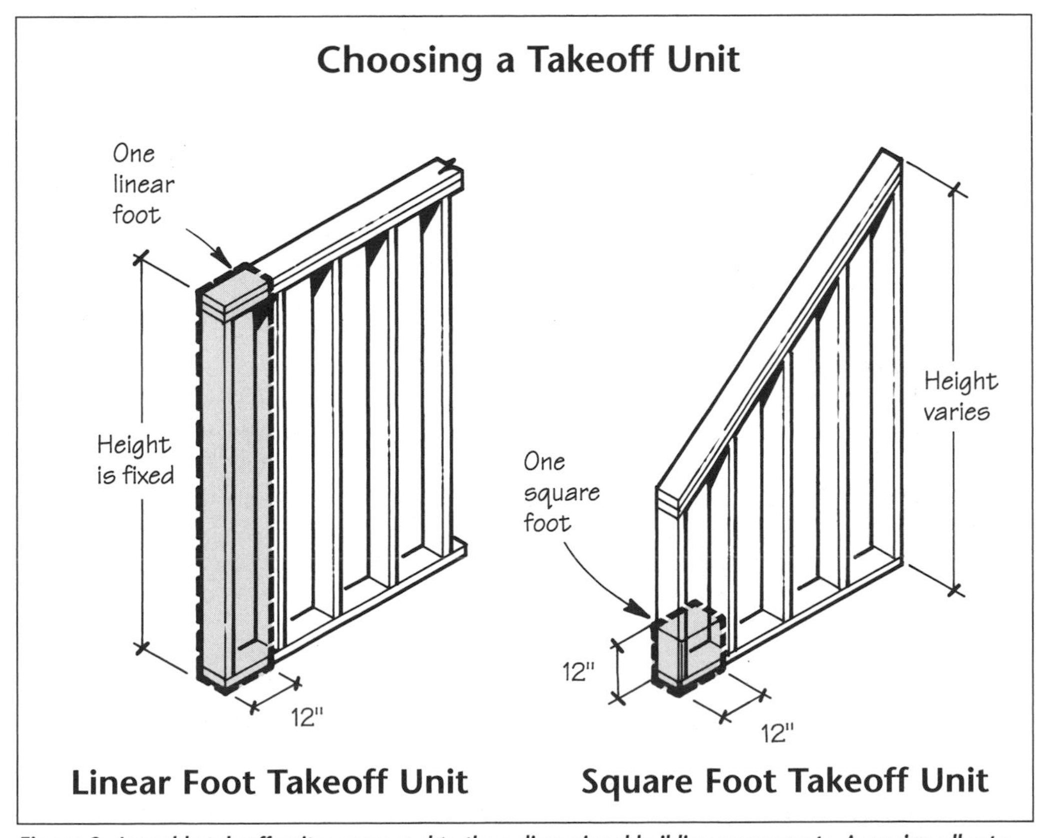

Figure 2. *Assembly takeoff units correspond to three-dimensional building components. Assuming all exterior walls are built out of 2x6s, the takeoff unit can be linear feet (left) for walls of the same height, and square feet (right) for walls of different heights.*

Figure 3. *To find the unit price of an exterior wall assembly, first do a stick-by-stick estimate for a typical section of work, then divide the total cost by the number of takeoff units. If the wall in this example had a takeoff unit of square feet (instead of linear feet, as shown), the unit price would be $3.32 per square foot ($265.74 ÷ 80 square feet).*

Sample Wall Assembly

EXTERIOR WALL ASSEMBLY				2x6 @ 24" o.c.	
Description	**Type**	**Qty**	**Unit**	**Price Per Unit**	**Total Price**
Plates	2x6-10'	3.00	ea	$ 6.09	$ 18.27
Studs	2x6-8'	6.00	ea	3.92	23.52
Sheathing	1/2" CDX	2.50	ea	19.23	48.08
Housewrap	Tyvek	90.00	sf	.09	8.10
Insulation	R-19 FG	80.00	sf	.25	20.00
Vapor barrier	Tu-Tuff	90.00	sf	.06	5.40
Drywall	1/2"	80.00	sf	.55	44.00
Subtotal					$167.37
Tax (5%)					$ 8.37
Total Materials					**$175.74**
Labor (crew of 2)					
	Framing	1.00	hr		
	Sheathing	.50	hr		
	Housewrap	.25	hr		
	Insul/VB	.50	hr		
	Drywall	sub			
Total Labor		2.25	hr	$40.00	**$ 90.00**
Total Price for 10-foot length of wall					**$265.74**
Price per linear foot ($265.74 ÷ 10 sf)					**$ 26.57**

length of wall, then divide by 10 to get the price per linear foot (Figure 3).

Having a complete list of materials and labor for each assembly helps to avoid omissions and overlap in your assemblies. And when prices change, an itemized list makes it easy to adjust individual line items to recalculate the assembly unit price. Using a drawing (Figure 4) while developing an assembly price will also help you to visualize material quantities.

Pricing Labor

Unit prices are most useful when they include labor prices. By tracking labor according to the assemblies you want to price, you can develop an historical record of labor costs. Then you can use an average from all jobs to establish a labor price using takeoff units from each assembly.

In the case of an exterior wall assembly, for example, you will need to track the time it takes to install all of the materials included in the assembly. But instead of using a 10-foot section of wall, as you did for material prices, use an average of the total labor for all exterior wall assemblies on several jobs. This will help to level labor costs and reduce the effect of specific conditions that might skew the labor costs on a particular job.

To break out labor costs, you have to keep track of what your crews are doing and how long it takes them to do it. I used a timesheet that listed all the phases of construction I wanted to track. When my field crew filled out their timesheets each day, they recorded the hours they worked as well as the number code of the type of work they were doing. At the end of each phase of a job, I used this breakdown to calculate labor prices for my assemblies.

For example, if a crew of three spends 8 hours framing 120 linear feet of exterior wall, the total cost of the labor divided by 120 is the unit price for labor per linear foot. Follow the same procedure for each item in the assembly — sheathing, housewrap, insulation, and vapor barrier — and add them together to get the unit labor price for the whole assembly.

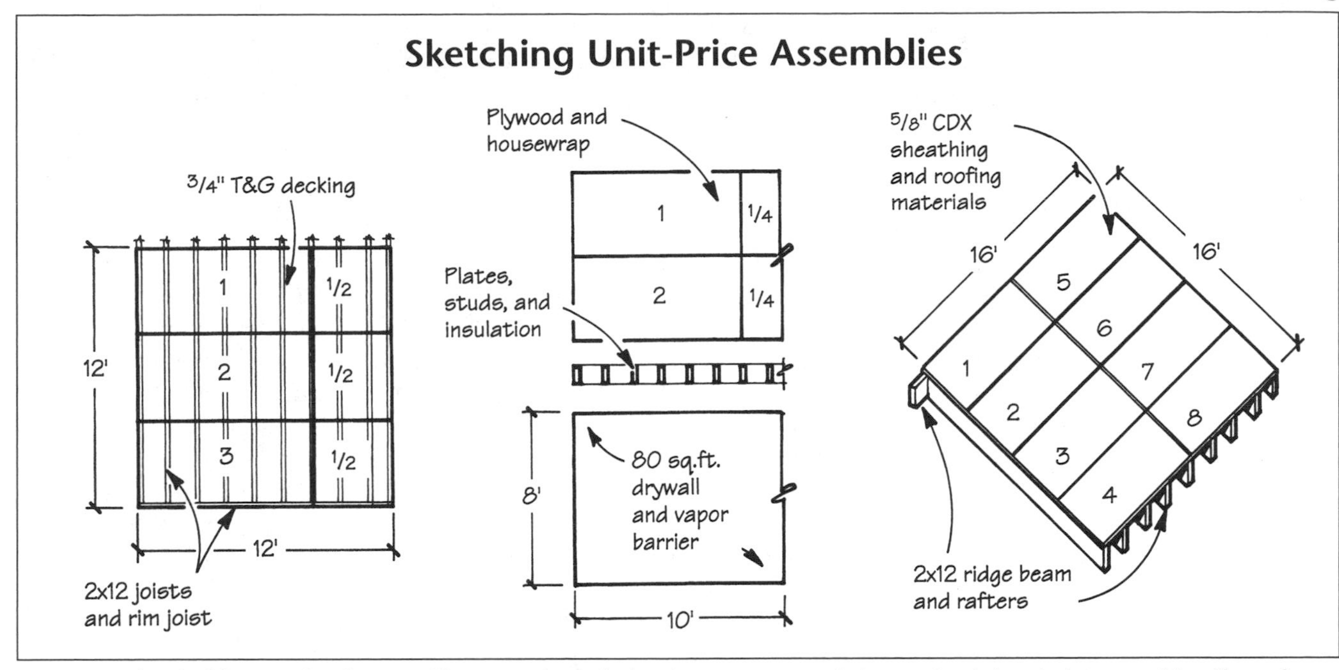

Figure 4. ***When building a unit-price assembly, use a schematic drawing to prevent omissions and to help calculate quantities. Shown here (left to right) are sketches for a floor system, exterior wall, and roof system.***

Refining Unit Prices

Developing a unit price history improves accuracy and helps dilute the compromises you have to make when creating assemblies. For example, two skilled carpenters working together may frame the exterior walls of a building faster than one skilled carpenter working with a helper. But the labor cost for the skilled crew may still be higher because they work for higher wages. Taking an average over several jobs tends to level out these differences.

You can also refine your unit pricing system to account for different crews or special job conditions by building a set of alternate assemblies. An exterior wall framed on 16-inch centers, for example, uses more studs than one framed on 24-inch centers. Depending on how accurate you want your pricing to be, you can develop three exterior wall assemblies — one for 16-inch centers, one for 24-inch centers, and one that assumes one stud per foot.

Subassemblies. You can also incorporate subassemblies into your system. In the exterior wall example, the price for drywall is a subassembly. The line item price of 55¢ per square foot includes the drywall, tape, screws, and joint compound, as well as the labor to install the boards and finish the joints. If you use subcontractors for this kind of work, they can usually supply you with unit prices that you can plug into your assemblies.

Exclusions. It's also important to keep track of what is not included in your assemblies. An exterior wall assembly with studs on 16-inch or 24-inch centers won't cover the cost of three-stud corners. I recommend leaving corner studs out of your assembly and figuring them separately because the number of corners you need to frame will vary from estimate to estimate.

Odd angles, high ceilings, extra flashing, layered trim, and a host of other details will all affect your final price. In general, it's best to leave nonstandard items out of your assemblies and figure their cost separately.

— Sal Alfano

Pricing for Small Jobs

Use over-the-phone estimates to streamline your estimating and sales of small jobs

For years our small jobs endured the same sales and administrative routine as our larger jobs. Whether we were installing a $100 screen door or doing a $20,000 kitchen remodel, we met with the customer, wrote up the estimate, issued a contract, and went through the scheduling process. Over and over, we found that the time and money we spent on estimating small jobs was eating up our profit. In many cases we were even losing money.

As a result of this learning process, we launched our Handyman Service, a new division of our company designed to handle small jobs and make them profitable. We defined small jobs as anything that could be completed by one person in a day or two. We didn't set a strict dollar volume since costs are greatly affected by materials, but the majority of these jobs fall in the $100 to $300 range. Few are higher than $2,000.

Creating this service entailed finding new ways to streamline our sales and estimating process. We realized that many of our calls were for the same sorts of small jobs, such as patching drywall, repairing or cleaning gutters, trimming interior doors, or recaulking windows. Developing a manual with standardized prices for these typical jobs would keep us from reestimating them every time they came in. It would also let us give customers an estimate during our first contact, usually over the phone. Finally, having a price book would mean that anyone, with a little bit of training, could give an accurate price.

The ability to quote a price quickly and then stick to it tells our customers we are experienced and gives them confidence in us. By comparison, pricing on time and materials, something we still have to do occasionally on some small jobs, means warning the customer that the price is approximate. It also practically guarantees an argument when costs run significantly higher than the initial quote.

Giving a price up front is also an instant qualifier. We no longer find ourselves running out on sales calls only to find that the customers are just "shopping" and can have their nephew do the work for $20.

Some remodelers might argue that paying a sales call in person, even on a $200 job, is a great opportunity to get to know a client. This may be true if your company is young or if business is slow. But last year we did about 1,500 small jobs that earned our company $550,000, or 25% of our total sales. With this kind of volume, we can't afford to send a salesman out to each site.

Creating A Database

The first step in this process was to choose software. We decided to go with a program called First Choice (Spinnaker Software Corp., 201 Broadway, Cambridge, MA 02139; 617/494-1200), but similar software, such as Dbase (Borland International, 1800 Green Hills Rd., Scotts Valley, CA 95066; 408/438-5300) or Lotus (Lotus Development Corp., 61 Medford St., Somerville, MA 02143; 800/872-3387), would work just as well. In some cases, an estimating program that lets you combine the tasks involved in a small job might do the trick. Timberline's Precision Estimating Plus (Timberline Software Corp., 9600 S.W. Nimbus, Beaverton, OR 97005; 503/644-8155) is a good example.

After choosing our software, we reviewed the most recent two years of files and pulled all the invoices on jobs that totaled less than $2,000 and didn't involve subs. This gave us about 1,000 invoices to work from.

We were then ready to start inputting data. We established three fields on which to sort our data. We called the first field "Type." This gives the general nature of the work, such as "Carpentry," "Painting," or "Plumbing." We called the second field "Classification," which further focuses the job. If the type is "Carpentry," for example, the classification might be "Exterior Doors." The next field is "Phase." In this example, the phase would be "Install storm door."

We also created a series of fields to help us analyze job costs. Our database

Handyman Price List

Classification	Phase	Description	Price	Clarify
Deadbolt	Install	Install single cylinder deadbolts — deadbolt to be Schlage #G120	$ 98.50	
Ext. Door	Install	Install exterior metal door	$ 325.00	
	Weather Strip	Furnish and install weatherstripping around the door	$ 75.00	
	Screen	Replace screen door and jamb	$ 450.00	Ea. $225.00
	Lockset	Install lockset using Schlage #3 finish	$ 98.00	
	Closure	Repair rear door closer	$ 89.00	
	Break-in	Repair sprung door due to break-in	$ 75.00	(no parts)
	Threshold	Furnish and install a new aluminum threshold	$ 115.00	
	Cut Off	Trim bottom of front door, put in high rug threshold to fit the door opening	$ 105.00	
	Adjust	Put longer woodscrews in hinges so service door will close properly	$ 55.00	
	Install	Install a new exterior door unit — labor only — pre-hung or slab only	$ 185.00	
Garage Door	Repair	Repair overhead garage door cable	$ 95.00	(labor only)
	Opener	Install garage-door-opener hardware	$ 175.00	(no parts)
Int. Door	Cut Off	Cut off doors to clear carpet	$ 55.00	1st door
	Cut Off	Cut off doors to clear carpet	$ 45.00	Ea. additional door
Show/Doors	Install	Inst. shower doors	$ 140.00	(no parts)

The author's Handyman Price List makes it possible for his small-job salesmen to give accurate telephone quotes. Specific descriptions of completed work make it possible for the salesman to compare the job being quoted with similar jobs done previously. The book is updated regularly and is accessible in the company's computer database.

originally included labor hours, labor costs, material costs, and what we charged for the job. This information gave us a job history and helped us set our handyman prices. To avoid confusion, we erased all this information once we came up with our price.

In our last field, called "Description," we input as much detailed information as possible about each type of job. For example, under "Install storm door" we might write, "Remove existing aluminum storm door, install new 3'-0"x6'-8" Larson storm door (number 273-55) supplied by customer with three standard hinges, latchset, and door closer (all of which come with the door)."

As we've refined our database, we've shortened our descriptions enough that they can be read quickly. But we've left enough information that the salesman can make sure the job that's being quoted is close to the one described in the book.

Finally we've printed out copies of the database for our small jobs salesman, who gives about 95% of the phone quotes, as well as for our office staff. Copies also go to our handymen, who may use the book to give a quote to a customer while they're in the field. The current version is about 20 pages long and includes 164 items. We use a three-ring notebook with tab indexes to make the book easy to use. Our staff can also access the database on the computer by entering key words, prices, or any other information.

Setting Prices

While inputting all this information is fairly straightforward, things get complicated when it's time to sort through it all on the computer and decide which jobs to keep in the database and how to price them. My first step was to eliminate all the jobs that were unique or unusual, such as getting squirrels out of the attic or hanging a tie rack on someone's closet door. Next I consolidated similar jobs. For instance, we had dozens of different descriptions of gutter repairs. I consolidated these into four jobs: maintenance, repair, and cleaning (one-story house or two-story house).

As a rule we mark up labor and materials 100% to achieve a 50% gross margin on small jobs. But this varies from job to job. It's not unusual for our book to have two different prices for each line item: one that we charge for installing the materials and one that we charge for both installing and supplying the materials. If we're not supplying the materials, we may raise the price to cover us in case we damage the materials and have to replace them. This extra also helps compensate for the fact that we're not making anything on materials.

For example, we allow three hours of labor to install a storm door even though the job is likely to take only two-and-a-half hours or less. Our cost per hour is $18, including taxes and insurance. With a 100% markup, that's $36 an hour, times three hours, for a total cost of $108. If we're supplying the door, we can get only about a 40% markup on it. We've found that it's hard to go higher than this on big ticket items since people generally know what these items cost and prefer to buy them directly. Our charge to install the door we supply is $348. That includes $90 for two-and-a-half hours labor, $10 for disposing of the old door, and $248 for the new storm door.

We also charge more for jobs that are done under adverse conditions. Anyone who's worked in an attic in the Midwest on a steamy day in July knows that it takes more time to get the job done. The same goes for a moldy, muddy crawlspace in the middle of a rainy April.

In some cases I've substituted a unit of measurement to cost by. For example, we charge $50 for every 8 feet of soffit we install on a one-story house. This includes all of our labor and materials. (In this case we mark up our materials by 100%.) We also use a combination of unit pricing and flat rate charges for some jobs. To fill hairline cracks in brick veneer, we charge $185 for 200 square feet. We then charge another 60¢ for each additional square foot.

The problem with developing a price book is that once it's done, you have to start updating it. We try to adjust our prices once every quarter, based on changes in overhead, material costs, and other factors. We also add new jobs as our experience and our services grow.

Using The Book

There are a few tricks to using a price book correctly. When pricing over the phone, it's imperative that our salesman ask the customer to be very specific in describing the job so that he can visualize the work. If someone calls asking us to come out and replace some missing roof shingles, we need to find out whether the roof is leaking. If so, we'll probably need to add in the cost of patching some drywall and doing some touch-up painting. We'll also find out how many shingles are missing (people can answer this more easily than if you ask how many square feet of shingles are gone), the shingle color, whether the roof is steep, and whether any gutters need to be repaired.

Next we give them a price range for the job, between $100 and $150 to replace fewer than 20 shingles, for instance. A range gives us some room for error, since our handyman may get to the site and discover the shingles that the customer said were green are actually gray. Having some cushion in the price means the handyman can run to our supplier and pick up the correct color. It also means we can often give a bill that's lower than the price we quoted, something all customers appreciate.

If we get out there and discover the price will be significantly higher, we call the clients and explain the difference. But if we'll lose only a few dollars, we go ahead and do the job anyway. It's easier, and probably less expensive, than going to all the trouble of rescheduling.

Our price book is meant to serve as a guide, not a bible. As we've gained more expertise in pricing jobs over the phone, we've learned when to follow the book and when to send a handyman over to look at the job first. Servicing your customers well sometimes means being flexible.

By Tom Swartz, president of J.J. Swartz Company, a 77-year-old remodeling firm with offices in Decatur and Bloomington, Ill.

Chapter 6

Bidding Strategies

Pricing for Profit

Five strategies for winning jobs *and* making a reasonable profit

Many contractors consider estimating and pricing to be the same thing, yet the two are entirely different. A job's price should be shaped not just by the estimated cost, but by your assessment of the customer, the market, and most importantly, by your own need to make a reasonable profit. Until you recognize these differences and master the "art" of smart, profit-driven pricing, you will not be able to make money consistently.

Unfortunately, few contractors understand the several different pricing strategies available. Big corporations have full-time employees who figure out what price a widget must carry to increase market share, generate the largest net profit, and beat the competition. This is not always the lowest price, and the cost of producing the widget is often a secondary factor. Contractors need to do the same thing when pricing their work.

A Lesson in Pricing

To survive in business, you must not merely cover your costs, you must make a profit. Profit provides a return on the money invested in the company, generates funds for further investment, and provides a cushion to absorb bad markets, sudden expenses, or unexpected opportunities. To fail to provide for profit is to subvert all business logic, and to leave you, your employees, and your suppliers at needless risk.

I learned the hard way that the lowest price isn't always the best price — even from the customer's point of view. About 14 years ago, when I was just starting out, I prepared an estimate in my usual way for a nice remodeling job, and submitted a bid of $72,000, including a 5% profit. After learning that the other two bids came in at more than $112,000, I went to meet the customer, expecting good news. Instead, the customer told me he simply couldn't believe I could do the work for that price, so he was going to go with one of the other contractors at the higher price.

When I got home, I did a postmortem on the dead proposal with my partner, who is also my brother, to see what went

MOIRA NORTH

wrong. We discovered that in our eagerness to come in with a low but realistic price, we had neglected some important factors. We found out, for example, that the owner was president of a Fortune 500 subsidiary division, who personally earned in one year what our whole company did — about $250,000. We also learned that rather than being called in from left field to place a bid, we had been heartily recommended by the already-retained kitchen designer. The other two bidding contractors — both old-line, upscale remodelers with great reputations and extensive work experience, as well as the highest hourly rates in the county — had also been invited to bid the job.

When we drove through the neighborhood in the daytime (our previous visits had been at night because the owner always worked late — another vital fact I ignored), we realized that the house was in an exclusive and expensive neighborhood flanking a golf course. The kitchen designer told us that the job's lead "designer," who had introduced himself simply as a friend of the owner, was in fact a senior partner in the largest architectural firm in Connecticut. Finally, the kitchen designer (who turned out to be from another prestigious firm that had won national design awards) explained that the client's last remodeling job had run into many problems, and that he was worried far less about the job's cost than about running into hidden problems and delays.

None of this had anything to do with our ability to do the job at any given price. Yet it could have affected the way I treated the scope of the job. Instead of considering the owner's expectations about price, quality, and service, I priced the job based on my idea of what was involved and what the costs might be. As a result, my low bid cost me a chance to do a high-profile, high-quality job that might have led to others.

The lesson was valuable. I learned — in a way that stuck — the importance of knowing what my clients want and of learning about their personalities, their values, and their positions in the community and at work. I also learned the importance of evaluating what the presence on the job of other building professionals — architects, kitchen and bath specialists, interior designers — implied about the owner's values and expectations. Simply put, I discovered strategic pricing.

Choosing the Right Pricing Strategy

After this expensive lesson, I read a lot about pricing strategies, and thought about ways to generate a price that balanced the possibility of getting the job with the certainty of making a profit. I came to see that the challenge in pricing lies not just in winning jobs, but in winning jobs that will make money.

Winning such contracts requires choosing one of the following five pricing strategies for each job:

- cost-based pricing
- competition-based pricing
- cover pricing
- demand-based pricing
- novel-product pricing

If used properly, the first three — cost-based, competition-based, and cover pricing — should generate a reasonable, if often modest, profit on almost every job — what I call "profit satisfaction." The last two, demand-based and novel-product pricing, can generate more profit than usual on some jobs while still satisfying the customer. In fact, because they can achieve maximum profit, you should never fail to use them when they are called for.

I will focus here exclusively on fixed-price jobs. "Cost Plus" and "Time and Materials" pricing techniques tend to focus attention on a job's price rather than on its quality.

Cost-Based Pricing

This is the most common pricing strategy. Usually, the price is the result of adding gross profit (overhead plus a target net profit) to estimated costs. When contractors use reasonable "markups" or "margins," cost-based pricing satisfies reasonable profit goals. Unfortunately, many contractors don't include enough of a gross profit margin above the direct job costs, either because they don't know what their overhead is or because they don't recognize the need to make a profit on every job. Along with poor estimating, such inadequate margins are the main reason many contractors fail to make money.

Target pricing. This is a second type of cost-based pricing, in which you know (or guess) the budget allowed for the job, then figure out whether you can do the job for that amount. If you can, you bid right at or below the budget, knowing you can make a profit; if you can't, you don't bid the job. This strategy can also yield consistent (if modest) profits, but only if you don't succumb to the temptation to price too low.

By either method, successful cost-based pricing requires accurate historical job-cost records and an accurate estimating system. It also requires that you understand and control your overhead. Finally, it requires that you write proposals that leave no ambiguities or voids in the scope of work. If you do all this, you can steadily win jobs that satisfy a reasonable profit demand, even in slow markets. The downside is that even if your estimates are dead accurate, cost-based pricing is not a good tool for winning potentially high-profit jobs.

Competition-Based Pricing

This strategy sets prices primarily in relation to competitors — either the competition in general, or other contractors bidding on a given job. A competitor in your area, for instance, may heavily advertise a certain price for a product or service that is essentially the same as yours. You will have difficulty selling

Profit and Probability

The best price for a job isn't necessarily the price most likely to win the job, nor is it always the price that will produce the most profit. A low price will win a lot of jobs, but at very little profit, if any. A high price will produce good profit, but has little chance of winning the job. The best price is somewhere between the two — a price in which the net profit margin is both adequate and has the highest probability of winning the job.

Don't guess at the probability of winning a job: Figure it out from your bidding history. First, count the number of past jobs you won at various net profit margins (1%, 5%, 10% net profit, and so on). For each net profit margin, divide the number of jobs won by the total number of bids — that's the probability of winning the job at that profit margin. For example, if you win one out of every three jobs you price at 5% net profit, the probability of winning the job at 5% net profit is 33% (1÷3).

I win about 81% of the jobs I bid at 1% net profit, about 30% at 6.3% profit, and about 10% at 12% profit. Which net profit margin makes for the best price? I use the following formula to test the probability of winning a job at various net profit margins:

Net profit x Probability of winning job = Effective profit

Using the formula to compare various prices (see table at left), I can see that my best price is one with a net profit of 6.3%. If I bid that way consistently, I know I'll lose two out of three bids, but the ones I get will yield good profits.

— *B.H.*

Finding Effective Profit

Bid Price	Planned Net Profit	Probability of Winning	Effective Profit
$ 9,000	$ –400 (–4.3%)	.99	$–396
$ 9,500	$ 100 (1%)	.81	$ 81
$10,000	$ 600 (6.3%)	.30	$ 180
$10,500	$1,100 (12%)	.10	$ 110
$11,000	$1,600 (17%)	.02	$ 32

Note: *The chart assumes a job for which the estimated cost — without net profit — is $9,400. Effective profit for each bid price in column one is calculated by multiplying the Planned Net Profit by the Probability of Winning. The best price — $10,000 — is the one with the highest effective profit.*

your product for more than that advertised price unless you can somehow distinguish your product.

Sealed-bid pricing is another form of competition-based pricing. You don't know your competitor's bid, of course, but your own bid price will be based largely on your guess about what your competitor's will be, leavened, I hope, by a realistic assessment of how much you can do the job for.

Competition-based pricing can yield profits if you resist the temptation to underbid contractors who don't offer your level of quality and service, or who themselves fail to use adequate margins. Good competition-based pricing requires knowing your competition well — their work load, their ability to do the job, their lead time, and any ties they have to the owner. You must also know those things about yourself, for this pricing method will devastate the contractor who does not know or cannot control his own costs and merely reacts to other contractors' prices. Never lower your price unless you can make up the difference by getting cost concessions from your subs or suppliers.

Cover Pricing

Cover pricing, also known as "courtesy bid" or "cover-your-ass" pricing, is a defensive strategy used to guarantee a profit. Its use is limited to jobs you don't really want or which you know have high potential for trouble, as when a customer gives you bad vibes, the job requires too much travel, or you don't have time to do the work but it's for the friend of a good customer. Cover pricing may also be useful when you can't give an accurate price because there isn't enough time to get firm quotes from your subs and suppliers.

The goal of cover pricing is not to gouge the customer, but to add enough money to the price — say, an extra 10% to 15% — so that if you indeed win the job, you'll either make some extra profit or have enough margin to absorb any problems.

Additional Work Required When You Drop Your Price

This chart shows how cutting your price increases the total volume of work you must do to earn the same net profit. For example, if you cut your selling price 10% and your present gross profit margin is 25%, the chart shows that you will need to sell 67% more work to earn the same gross profit margin as you would have earned at full price.

Price Cut	Present Gross Profit							
	5%	10%	15%	20%	25%	30%	35%	40%
1%	25%	11%	7%	5%	4%	3%	3%	3%
2%	67	25	15	11	9	7	6	5
3%	150	43	25	18	14	11	9	8
4%	400	67	36	25	19	15	13	11
5%	—	100	50	33	25	20	17	14
6%	—	150	67	43	32	25	21	18
7%	—	233	88	54	39	30	25	21
8%	—	400	114	67	47	36	30	25
9%	—	1,000	150	82	56	43	35	29
10%	—	—	200	100	67	50	40	33
11%	—	—	275	122	79	58	46	38
12%	—	—	400	150	92	67	52	43
13%	—	—	650	186	108	77	59	48
14%	—	—	1,400	233	127	88	67	54
15%	—	—	—	300	150	100	75	60

Demand-Based Pricing

This strategy, common to markets in which demand is high, is based on what the market will bear. It aims explicitly at achieving maximum profit. Demand-based pricing sounds mercenary, but in reality it is an opportunity to make up for the jobs in which for some reason you made less profit than you expected.

Demand-based pricing works best in strong or growing markets. I believe that in such markets you should raise prices across the board for all jobs — at a rate of, say, one percent a month, until your rate of closing deals begins to drop.

Demand-based pricing is probably the best way to achieve maximum profits, but you must be certain your market is strong, and you must know a lot about the particular job you're seeking. This includes knowing the owners' expectations about quality and service, their priorities, their social and economic standing, and the roles of other professionals working on the job — all of the factors I failed to consider in my bungled Fortune 500 job.

But demand-based pricing is more than simply pricing high on country-club jobs; you can also gain maximum profit if you accurately assess the desires and expectations of a young middle-class family adding a room or remodeling a kitchen. Don't gouge the customer, but charge a price commensurate with their desire to have you do a particular job at a particular level of quality.

To determine how much net profit to seek with this method, you must also know a lot about your own company — the average gross profit per job, the number of promising sales leads, and, most important, your rate of closing sales at different net profit margins (see "Profit and Probability," page 106). Armed with this knowledge, you can bid intelligently at higher prices.

Novel-Product Pricing

If you can offer a unique or distinctive product or service, you're in a position to use novel-product pricing. Ideally, a novel product is a patented product, service, or franchise that only you can offer, but it can also be something for which you've staked out a territory. If you're the only contractor who knows how to build floating staircases or cantilevered decks, or if you've got the only plaster-and-paint crew in the area who can produce that trendy Mediterranean look, you can name your price to the customers who want those products. The novelty usually lasts only so long, however, as other contractors make an effort to learn the needed skill, or, in the case of a patented product, the patent runs out. For that reason you should try to achieve maximum profit during the time you exclusively offer the distinctive product or service, while maintaining quality in your other work to build a strong general reputation.

Putting It All Together

With these strategies in mind, you should be able to intelligently price any job. But we all fail to do so at times, either because we don't know our costs, or because we lose our nerve and price too low. So as final inspiration, I offer this multiple-choice quiz, with answers based on the actual alternatives that flash through most of our minds when we sit down to bid a job.

Question: Which of the following is the best pricing strategy for a given job?

A) **Bid within the customer's stated budget figure.** *A huge mistake unless your own costs and gross profit margin allow it.*

B) **Drop your gross profit target to get this job.** *An even bigger mistake. When you get the urge to do this, look at the chart on the previous page. Climbing back from a low-profit or no-profit job is like trying to raise a grade-point average in school — if you get one bad grade, it takes a lot of good ones to make up for it.*

C) **Bid the "going price," regardless of your cost.** *Fine if the going price allows room for your gross profit; trouble if it doesn't.*

D) **Use a rational pricing strategy that will ensure a reasonable profit — and still get enough jobs.** *Enough said.*

Obviously, my quiz is rigged, but pricing intelligently is more than an academic exercise; it's the difference between struggling and prospering. The contractor who learns not to price down, and who understands that not every job is worth winning, is the one who will keep working and enjoy doing it. The others are doomed to struggle.

By Bob Hanbury, a partner in House of Hanbury, a remodeling firm in Newington, Conn.

Working Cost-Plus

A well-crafted cost-plus contract protects the interests of both the contractor and the customer

As most builders understand it, cost-plus construction is a recipe for disaster. How can you sell a job, they ask, without putting a limit on the total cost? And why would anyone in a competitive business like construction want to come right out and tell his clients what his materials really cost and how much he really pays employees?

In my 20 years as a builder, I used cost-plus contracts for about half my work, and I'll admit that it's more complicated than working with a fixed price. After all, a fixed price contract rewards you with large profits if you buy right and perform efficiently, and the owner isn't looking over your shoulder every step of the way. Most owners are happy with fixed price contracts, too, because they know what the project will cost before construction begins. And since owners usually hire the low bidder, they don't care how much money the builder pockets as long as the work is up to snuff and completed on time.

Still, there are good reasons to work

with a cost-plus contract at least some of the time. For one thing, a fixed price is impractical on jobs that have a lot of unknowns or that require new materials and unfamiliar methods. The same is true on "fast track" jobs where the owner needs to start construction before plans and specs are complete. Under these circumstances, a cost-plus contract reduces both your risk and the need to pad your price to cover contingencies.

But the strongest reason to work cost-plus is that it helps to establish trust and good communication between you and your clients, and gives you a tool you can use to break out of the competitive bidding wars and into negotiated projects. On top of that, a cost-plus contract forces you to develop good record-keeping habits. Properly administrating a cost-plus contract amounts to doing job-cost accounting every time you requisition for payment. If you're already doing job-cost analysis regularly, the transition to cost-plus work will be easy. If you're not job-costing, cost-plus work may motivate you to start.

What Is Cost-Plus?

Most of the complaints about cost-plus work are the result of misunderstanding or wrongheadedness. In the first place, working cost-plus does not necessarily mean that there's no cost estimate or that the contract is open-ended. I always worked with a guaranteed maximum cost, sometimes referred to as an "upset price." The basic idea is for the owner to reimburse the builder for the actual costs of construction, plus a fee (for administration and a fair net profit), up to the amount of the guaranteed maximum cost. Cost overruns are borne by the builder. These provisions take care of the owner's worries about limiting the total cost of the job, but still leave room to save money.

Nonbelievers are only partly right when they complain that cost-plus contracts don't give builders a way to cover overhead. While it's true that the cost-plus format prevents builders from charging owners for general overhead expenses, it does permit reimbursement of specific overhead expenses that are directly related to the job covered by the contract. Obviously, success in cost-plus work depends on how the contract itself is structured, and on the procedures you use to administrate it.

Reimbursable Costs

The single most distinguishing feature of a cost-plus contract is the need to document in detail the costs of construction. Because you get paid for only those expenses you can prove, it's necessary to keep accurate and timely records of your direct costs (materials, labor, and subcontractors) as well as job-related indirect costs. Cost-plus contract language should be very specific about what is and what is not reimbursable (see Figure 1, next page). Using a detailed estimate during contract negotiations helps to explain the costs of construction and prevent misunderstandings later.

Materials and equipment. Direct costs for materials and equipment that become a part of the building are reimbursable dollar-for-dollar, including delivery charges. However, you should also be reimbursed for materials and equipment that are not a permanent part of the building, but are consumed during construction. Temporary bracing and poly used to protect stored materials or work-in-place are good examples. Also include charges for tool sharpening, as well as the cost of blades, bits, and small hand tools like cold chisels and shovels, that are broken or dulled beyond usefulness during the ordinary performance of the work.

Rental charges for machinery, equipment, and special tools (like pneumatic hammer drills) are also reimbursable, including transportation costs to and from the site. In fact, you can charge a rental fee for some of your own equipment. For example, the cost of pipe staging that you own, which on a fixed price job would be figured into your overhead, can be billed as a reimbursable expense on a cost-plus job, as long as the rate is competitive and reflects the value of the equipment. Temporary heating and lighting equipment are other good examples.

One problem is figuring out how to handle the several types of contractor discounts offered by vendors. If you receive a cash advance from the owner to secure a cash discount on a specific purchase, the discount ought to be passed through to the owner. In general,

Costs To Be Reimbursed

The term Cost of the Work shall include costs set forth below incurred in the proper performance of the Work and paid by the Contractor.

1. Wages paid for labor in the direct employ of the Contractor in the performance of the Work, including welfare, unemployment compensation, social security, and other benefits.
2. Cost of all materials, supplies, and equipment incorporated in the Work, including costs of transportation thereof. All discounts for cash or prompt payment to vendors shall accrue to the Contractor.
3. Payments made by the contractor to Subcontractors for Work performed pursuant to subcontracts under this Agreement.
4. Cost of all materials, supplies, equipment, temporary facilities, and hand tools not owned by workers, which are consumed in the performance of the Work.
5. Reasonable rental costs of all necessary machinery and equipment, exclusive of hand tools, used at the site of the Work, whether rented from the Contractor or others.
6. Cost of premiums for all bonds and insurance, permit fees, and sales, use, or similar taxes related to the Work.
7. Cost of removal of all debris.
8. Costs incurred due to an emergency affecting the safety of persons or property.
9. Minor expenses, such as long-distance telephone calls, telephone service at the site, and petty cash items in connection with the Work.

Figure 1. ***To avoid misunderstandings, a cost-plus contract should specify both reimbursable and nonreimbursable costs. A good model for cost-plus contracts is AIA document A111, available from the American Institute of Architects, 1735 New York Ave. NW, Washington, DC 20006; 202/626-7300.***

however, do not pass on discounts based on total monthly volume from all jobs, or discounts based on prompt payment.

Subcontracts. Subcontractor costs are also fully reimbursable, including materials, labor, and the sub's gross profit. You may not, however, add your gross profit on top. But you can recover the costs of direct supervision of subs in your estimate and billing for labor. Treat discounts as you would for materials and equipment.

On fixed price contracts, which are almost always awarded to the low bidder, the owner's concern is that the quality of a low-priced sub's work will not be up to snuff. In a cost-plus contract, however, the opposite is often true: Because actual costs are reimbursed, the owner may be concerned that your subcontractors' prices are too high and that the same quality can be had for less money. I was able to counter these objections because: (1) I had established long-term relationships with good subcontractors who priced their work fairly; and (2) I explained to my clients that, even when my subs' prices were comparatively high, they represented a good value. Subs who use high-quality materials where they have a choice and who are good at solving problems will find ways to save money in the long run.

Labor. All wages for your employees are reimbursable, including labor burden. In other words, the hourly rate you charge for employees should include federal and state taxes, health insurance, vacation and sick pay, and general liability and workers comp. It's a good idea to include in the contract an hourly labor rate schedule for each employee who will be working on the job, either by name or by job classification (Figure 2). Include language that allows you to add to this list after construction has begun.

To avoid clock-watching by the owner, explain your normal work schedule, including daily start and finish times, and coffee break policy. Also explain that some billable time is spent each day setting up, cleaning up, and standing around reading plans and solving problems.

Indirect costs. Some expenses that are considered to be overhead in a fixed price contract can be billed directly to a cost-plus job, providing they relate only to that job. Transportation costs fall into this category, including mileage for company vehicles used to commute to the site. Telephone service at the site is reimbursable as well, including long-distance phone calls that pertain directly to the job.

On very large commercial and industrial cost-plus projects, the contract distinguishes between a builder's home and field offices, and only field office expenses are reimbursable. For small builders, however, the home office and the field office are the same, and your contract should allow you to be reimbursed for legitimate office expenses. Usually this includes billing for time spent preparing requisitions for payment, for photocopies of invoices, and for long-distance phone calls directly related to the job. Be sure to include estimates for these costs in the guaranteed maximum cost.

Nonreimbursable Costs

A cost-plus contract should specifically exclude expenses for which the owner is not obligated to reimburse you. The most obvious nonreimbursable expenses are costs that exceed the guaranteed maximum cost. Capital expenses, such as interest on borrowed money, are also excluded, as are costs incurred due to your negligence or the negligence of your employees and subs. This applies to defective work and costs associated with the exchange or return of materials and equipment that were incorrectly ordered or delivered.

The Fee

The "plus" part of cost-plus is the fee. It compensates the builder for his skill in coordinating all phases of construction, and indirectly reimburses the time spent estimating and negotiating the project. The fee also rewards the risk of taking on these responsibilities by providing for a fair net profit. The fee is usually expressed as a percentage, which when added to the estimated reimbursable costs of construction, establishes the guaranteed maximum cost.

Fifty-fifty split. One objection to cost-plus work — often raised by the owner — is that there is no incentive for the builder to try to save money. In fact, there's a disincentive: If the builder is paid a fee on top of his costs, then he makes more money as costs go higher because the fee increases proportionately. This is true up to the amount of the guaranteed maximum cost, and even a little beyond. Setting a fixed fee — an unchanging dollar amount — solves the problem for the owner, but is unfair for the builder if change orders increase the value of the work substantially.

A better solution is to split the difference between actual costs and the guaranteed maximum cost at the end of the job, with half the savings going to the builder and half to the owner. This gives the builder an incentive to save money because half of the savings goes straight into his pocket as profit.

Retainage. There is less need for retainage with a cost-plus contract because the billing process gives the owner detailed information about the progress and cost of the job. If the owner insists on retainage, however, the easiest way to track it is to withhold a portion of the fee from each payment. For example, I usually agreed to have 30% of the fee withheld from each payment until the total retainage reached a specific dollar amount, like $3,000. In any case, all retainage should be paid in full with the final payment.

Labor Rate Schedule

The following rates will be charged for the employees listed. New employees will be added at a rate based on their gross hourly wage plus 30% burden.

Name	Rate/Hr.
S. Allen	$25
D. Pruitt	$25
W. Roberts	$20
E. Bertrand	$18
M. Clarke	$15

Figure 2. ***A labor rate schedule lists the rates you will charge for each employee who will work on the project. Make sure the contract allows you to add to the list after construction has begun.***

Applying For Payment

In cost-plus work, the owner pays for the actual costs of construction, so it's important to establish a billing system that gauges the progress of the work. I used three interrelated forms for each billing. The numbers on the Application for Payment (Figure 3, page 114) are taken from the detailed cost information provided on the Construction Cost Itemization sheet, to which are attached copies of invoices and statements, and the Progress Summary sheet, which compares budgeted to actual costs (see "Tracking the Cost of the Work," next page). Depending on the size and duration of the project, preparing these documents can take from a few hours to an entire day each time you apply for payment. Be sure to include this time in your estimate and to bill for it as a cost of construction. I prepared an application for payment once

Tracking the Cost of the Work

Over the years, I developed a system that tracks change orders, current expenses, and past payments, and that gauges job progress by comparing actual costs to estimated costs. All of this information appears on a single form, called a progress summary sheet, which I submit with every application for payment, accompanied by supporting detail. Because of all the calculations involved, I set it up on a computer spreadsheet, but it can also be prepared and maintained by hand.

My progress summary sheet is organized into three sections: estimated costs (columns A, B, C, and D), actual costs (columns E, F, and G), and projected costs (columns H, I, and J). Its purpose is to document expenses and to predict cost overruns and savings. How you use it depends on the level of detail you and your client decide is necessary. You can easily scale down or expand the version presented here to meet your needs. — *S.A.*

Estimated Costs

Column A is a list of construction cost categories. I loosely follow CSI format, but you can organize the schedule room-by-room, by interior and exterior work, or by some other scheme that makes sense.

Column B is a breakdown of the dollar value of each cost category. You can combine material and subcontractor costs together into one category, making sure to include a category, such as the line labeled "General," for indirect costs like permits, fees, and other miscellaneous expenses.

Create separate categories for all labor costs and for the fee. This is easier than distributing these costs throughout all categories. The same is true for allowances. Here, the "A" on line 10 denotes an allowance for structural work.

Column C shows the estimated cost of change order work. To keep the numbers in this column straight, break out change order estimates into three parts — materials and subs, labor, and the fee — and distribute them to the appropriate categories.

Column D holds the sum of the scheduled value plus the value of change orders (B + C). The total of column D shows the revised guaranteed maximum cost. Changing the scheduled value is necessary to accurately reflect the change in the scope of the work, and to allow the 50/50 split to work properly.

Actual Costs

Column E holds the amount previously billed for expenses in each cost category.

Column F shows the amount currently payable in each category. The total of column F equals the total *itemized costs* currently billed.

Column G (the sum of E and F) shows the expenses to date for each category. Every time you prepare an application for payment, you must update column E by transferring into it the number in column G.

To help keep the numbers straight in columns E, F, and G, prepare a construction cost itemization sheet (opposite page). For each cost category, list every invoice for materials and subcontractors, and transfer the subtotals to column F.

Projected Costs

Column H is an estimate of the percent complete for each cost category — your best guess of how far along each phase of construction has progressed. When determining this percentage, include work-in-place, as well as materials — like windows — that have been delivered to the site but are not yet installed.

Column I. To get the value for Column I, multiply the revised scheduled value by the percent complete and subtract the result from the revised value: D – (DxH). This shows how much money is required to finish the work of each cost category based on the percent complete estimate.

Column J. In this column, subtract the total expenses from the revised value (D – G) to determine how much money is available to complete the work of each cost category. When compared to column I, the number in Column J shows whether you are ahead of or behind your estimated cost.

Progress Summary

Job: Sandage Residence **Application No. Three** **8 Feb 99**

A		B	C	D	E	F	G	H	I	J
	Cost Category	Sched. Cost	Cost of Change Orders	Revised Sched. Cost	Previous Billing	Current Billing	Total Billed To Date	Percent Complete	Required To Complete	Available To Complete
1	General	$ 1,100		$ 1,100	$ 850	$ 146	$ 996	90%	$ 110	$ 104
2	Framing	4,100	$ 615	4,715	2,357	(17)	2,339	100%	0	2,376
3	Drywall	9,100	1,365	10,465	8,392	1,717	10,109	100%	0	356
4	Doors/Windows	4,500	675	5,175	3,175	638	3,813	90%	517	1,362
5	Trim	2,000	300	2,300	511	1,165	1,676	65%	805	624
6	Painting	5,600	840	6,440		3,413	3,413	50%	3,220	3,027
7	Flooring	6,650		6,650						6,650
8	Heating	7,600		7,600	7,003		7,003	99%	76	597
9	Electrical	4,350		4,350	2,071	1,457	3,528	80%	870	822
10	(A) Structural	440	66	506	477		477	100%	0	29
11	subtotal	45,440	3,861	49,301	24,834	8,520	33,354		5,599	15,947
12	Labor	13,626	1,043	14,669	7,831	4,993	12,823	95%	733	1,846
13	subtotal	59,066	4,904	63,970	32,665	13,513	46,177		6,332	17,793
14	Fee (12%)	7,088	588	7,676	3,920	1,622	5,541		760	2,135
15	**Totals**	**$ 66,154**	**$ 5,492**	**$ 71,646**	**$ 36,584**	**$ 15,135**	**$ 51,719**		**$ 7,092**	**$ 19,928**

Construction Cost Itemization

Job: Sandage Residence **Application No. Three** **8 Feb 99**

Cost Category	Amount	Vendor	Inv. No.	Notes	Category Total
General	$ 146.44	Mitchell's	12392	trash	$ 146.44
Framing	(16.92)	White Lmbr	M47378	CREDIT	(16.92)
Drywall	40.53	Sloan's	12592	mud	
	1,676.00	Dennis	12292	sub	1,716.53
Doors &	335.23	White Lmbr	M47522	window	
Windows	302.99	White Lmbr	M47523	window	638.22
Trim	764.16	Dix Hardwds	A12292	hardwood	
	401.31	White Lmbr	M48009	moldings	1,165.47
Painting	3,413.08	Aldey	20292	sub	3,413.08
Elect.	314.12	M. Stone	11292	sub	
	629.23	M. Stone	11992	sub	
	513.44	M. Stone	12892	sub	1,456.79
			Total Material & Subs		**$ 8,519.61**

Application For Payment

To: William Sandage		**Application No.:**	Three
19 Baldwin Terrace		**Period From:**	01 Jan 99
Richmond, Vt. 05477		**To:**	05 Feb 99
		Contract Date:	07 Nov 98

The undersigned Contractor certifies that to the best of his knowledge, information, and belief, the Work covered by this Application for Payment has been completed in accordance with the Contract Documents, that all amounts have been paid by him for Work for which previous Applications were made and payments received from the Owner, and that current payment shown herein is now due.

Guaranteed Maximum Cost	$66,154
Net Change by Change Order	5,492
Revised Guaranteed Maximum Cost	71,646
Total Itemized Costs	46,177
Fee (12%)	5,541
Retainage (Fee x .3)	1,662
Total Earned Less Retainage	50,056
Less Previous Payments	(35,408)
Current Payment Due	**$14,648**

Contractor____________________ Date ____________

Figure 3. ***The application for payment provides the financial history of the job at a glance.***

a month, timed to meet my vendors' "net 10" discount schedule. You may want to bill more frequently.

Analysis. The progress summary sheet can cause some confusion. It's important for your clients to understand that they are liable for the current payment even if the summary sheet shows or predicts cost overruns in one or more categories. This can happen inadvertently, for example, when costs are put in the wrong category. I once mistakenly distributed expenses for interior painting to a category labeled "Interior Finish" instead of to a separate category for painting, which was also listed. At the end of the job, the "Interior Painting" category was empty, while the "Interior Finish" category showed a cost overrun. It took quite a bit of explaining to convince the owner that I didn't owe him a rebate for painting work that, according to my own summary sheet, had never been done. You can avoid this kind of confusion by using clearly defined categories and taking care to be consistent when you distribute expenses.

Of course, the owners have a legitimate interest in protecting their investment if the majority of categories on the Progress Summary sheet show a cost overrun. More often, however, overruns in one category are balanced by savings in another. And in any case, the guaranteed maximum cost functions to protect the owner from overpaying for the work.

—Sal Alfano

Controlling Costs with Allowances

Don't guess at the price of incomplete product specs or unknown site conditions: Put them on allowance

Have you ever signed a contract for what feels like a good price, then watched helplessly during the job as your costs rose far above what you projected? Your early optimism turned to frustration and despair as profits drifted uncontrollably away.

This familiar, disheartening scenario points up the fact that every job includes some unpredictable costs that can easily grow out of control. Like a puzzle, some parts of the jobs can be fitted into place easily, while others remain a mystery until work has progressed. Reducing risk and gaining control in the game of contracting often depends on being able to identify and separate out from the whole as many pieces of the puzzle as possible.

One of the most powerful control tools for builders is the allowance price. Like other parts of construction contracts — sections covering change orders, hidden conditions, and exclusions — allowances provide for a high degree of control over seemingly uncontrollable aspects of a project.

An allowance is an approximate or "best guess" amount that covers the cost of a designated item of work. Allowances are included in the cost of the job provi-

Contract Sum and Allowances

3.1 The Owner shall pay Hartman-Baldwin in current funds for the performance of the Work, subject to additions and deletions by Change Order as provided in the Contract Documents, the lump sum of:

Four Hundred Forty-Five Thousand Six Hundred Eighty-Three and 00/100 dollars ($445,683.00)

3.2 Quotations herein, unless otherwise stated, are for immediate acceptance and subject to change.

3.3 The Contract Sum includes the following Allowances:

Category	Amount
Plumbing Fixtures	$ 1,500
Ceramic Tile	$ 3,300
Carpet	$ 5,000
Resilient Flooring	$ 900
Light Fixtures (chosen by Owner)	$ 6,000

Figure 1. ***Include a list of allowances and prices in your contract, and explain to clients how the actual cost to construct allowance items will affect the total price of the work.***

sionally; after completion of construction, the total price for the job is adjusted to reflect any difference between the allowance price and the actual cost of all allowance items. The beauty of the allowance is that it partially releases the contractor from the pressure of having to predict the future and guess at unknowns.

Identify Allowance Items

Every time you bid a job, you should make a special effort to identify possible allowance items. The extreme case is a time-and-materials contract; even on jobs worth hundreds of thousands of dollars, T&M work is nothing more than an allowance for the whole job. While this may be unpalatable to most clients, there are usually a few items or portions of work in every job that are either not clearly specified or about which some information is unknown. The key is to identify these issues in the contract stage, before the job begins, not during the job or after it's finished.

Using allowances as a part of a fixed-price contract gives both parties the benefit of T&M pricing for some items. The client is assured of cost containment for most of the work; the contractor, while pinning down all known costs, is able to isolate questionable work into an allowance.

Only the politics of your relationship with your client limits the number of allowances on a job, and almost any item is a candidate. We tend to have some standard ones, such as hardware, lighting, and carpet choices. Often, the client has not made these and other material choices before the job starts. Instead of trying to guess the cost of their eventual selection — or including an unrealistically high number to cover every possible choice — we put those items into an allowance.

Remodeling jobs are especially notorious for incomplete or unclear work specifications that can't be resolved before construction begins. Sometimes, for instance, the framing is standard except for one area, such as where new joists must meet old in an existing attic, or where reframing an existing floor may require dealing with concealed rot. An allowance is usually the best way to handle these kinds of problems.

Setting the price. How we decide on what price to use depends on the nature of the allowance. Tile, for example, is almost always put on allowance in our contracts: We usually know the extent of the tile work, but the client rarely chooses a particular tile before work starts. Since tile costs can vary from less than $2 per square foot to more than $20, we use a price for a middle-of-the-road product that matches the quality expectations for the rest of the job. For tile, this

Daily Field Report

Job Name McFARLAND #____ Day WED Date JUN 5
Weather: norm rain windy hot smog Safety Meeting: Y N subject ____

LABOR

name	work performed	hours	cost code	w/c code	total
SWEENEY	ALLOWANCE	1.5	1000.02		
		8.5	6100.01		10.0
HUDSON		1.5	1000.04		
		8.6	6100.01		10.0
LOWRY	Allowance	1.0	1000.04		
		2.0	1000.05		
		7.0	6100.01		10.0

subcontractors	man-hours	subcontractors	man-hours
JONES ELECTRIC	10.0		
ALLOWANCE	3.5		

MATERIALS

chg	cash	chk #	supplier	$ amount	invoice #	cost code	del/PU		remarks
✓			POWELL'S	14.79	22696	5700.02		✓	
			CLARK	114.96	95588	6100.02	✓		

MISC

deliveries; rubbish bins, special dump; inspections; owners; visitors; accidents; shop

Figure 2. *To track allowances in the field, the author uses a time sheet that breaks out allowance work into separate categories. The job foreman fills out the form every day, noting the amount of labor, material, and subcontractor time devoted to allowance items.*

is usually $8 to $10 per square foot; for carpet, we usually allow $25 per square yard installed. We follow the same rule for appliances: We price good-quality equipment, but not the most expensive.

It's a little harder to arrive at an accurate allowance price when more than a product selection is at stake. If we're pricing the remodel of an old office building, for example, the existing acoustic ceiling and wall paneling may obscure the condition of the drywall and plaster behind. The walls may require extensive patching and possibly a skim coat, both of which would raise the cost. In this case, our solution would be to use an allowance for the drywall work, setting the allowance price as close as possible to what the actual costs might be. This means either closely estimating the drywall work we're sure of, then adding a cushion for the unknowns, or including a fixed price for standard drywall work in the base bid and using the allowance only for any required patching and skim work.

What's included? The allowance prices we show to the owner typically do not include overhead and profit, which are part of the base price for the job. This reduces confusion when clients are shopping for products, like tile or carpet, for which they have an allowance: The vendor's quote is the price they will pay.

Unfortunately, if the owner decides to spend more than the allowance price, we're stuck with the margin we've

Shopping List

Item	Room	Allowance	Selection
Plumbing Fixtures			
Basin Fittings	Bath #1	$150	
	Bath #2	$150	
	Bath #2	$150	
Shower Fittings	Bath #2	$200	
Finishes			
Carpet – 1st Floor	Living Room	$25/sq. yd.	
	Bathrooms	$20/sq. yd.	
Carpet – 2nd Floor	All Rooms	$20/sq. yd.	
	Except Baths		
Ceramic Tile	Bath #1	$8/sq. ft.	
	Entry	$10/sq. ft.	
Resilient Flooring	Laundry	$16/sq. yd.	
	Bath #2	$20/sq. yd.	

Figure 3. ***A shopping list given to clients at the start of the job serves both as a budget and as a reminder for decisions that need to be made about allowance items.***

included in the base price. For instance, if we allow $2,000 for light fixtures, our base price includes our margin based on that price. But if the client decides to buy a couple of expensive chandeliers and ends up spending $4,000, we don't double our margin.

We're currently trying to include contract language to provide for a 10-and-10 margin — 10% overhead plus 10% profit — on all allowances. In the case of the light fixtures, we would then receive $400 on $2,000 worth of lighting, and twice as much on $4,000 worth. Unfortunately, this type of pricing scheme is sometimes difficult for owners to swallow. If we can't convince the owner that the higher margin is necessary to cover our increased liability, we forgo the additional charges in favor of preserving the relationship.

Be accurate. We use middle-of-the-road pricing for most allowances. Lowballing allowances sometimes helps to win the job, but only when you know your client has more money to spend (and won't mind spending it). On the other hand, an allowance that's too high to begin with may cause you to lose the job, or may require you to make other types of cuts to get the price down. With product allowances, the fairest approach is to choose an allowance price that will cover what the client is likely to buy.

When the allowance covers framing or finishes or other types of work, it's relatively easy to explain that while you could give a fixed bid for everything, the price would have to be very high to cover every contingency. Most clients understand the fairness of the allowance approach: I can't remember a single time when a client has argued to have a fixed price placed on an item that we recommended should be an allowance.

Contract language. To link allowance prices to the cost of the work, and to avoid misunderstandings later, we include a list of allowances in the section of our contract that deals with the total cost of the job (see Figure 1, page 115). This also gives us an opportunity while reviewing the contract with the client to answer questions about what the allowances are for and how the costs will be tracked.

Keeping Track

It's important to have a good way to track the costs of each allowance. Product allowances are easiest to document: With an allowance for appliances, for example, simply compare the total cost of the selected appliances with the allowance amount. For other types of allowances, however, labor and subcon-

Change Order

☐ Owner	Change Order #: 6
☐ Contractor	
☐ Architect	Project: Alcott Residence
☐ Field	
☐ Other	Contract For: Alcott Residence

The following are changes to the contract:

Breakdown of Net Allowances from Statement #8

Description	Allowance	Over/(Under)
Plumbing Fixtures	$1,500	$(616.25)
Ceramic Tile	3,300	(700.00)
Carpet	5,000	(284.79)
Resilient Flooring	900	49.52
Light Fixtures	6,000	881.00
Net Total of Allowances		$(670.52)
Total This Change Order		$(670.52)

Original contract sum $445,683.00
Net change by previous change orders 14,532.81
Contract sum prior to this change order 460,215.81
Contract sum will be decreased by this change order .... (670.52)
New contract sum including this change order $459,545.29
Contract time will be increased by (0) days
New date of substantial completion is: unchanged

Owner Date Hartman-Baldwin Date

Figure 4. ***At the end of the job, material receipts, subcontractor invoices, and other supporting documentation are attached to a single change order that summarizes all allowance costs. In the sample above, the change order reduced the total contract price, since several allowance items were completed under budget.***

tractors will need to be tracked as well. We use a time sheet filled out daily by each job foreman (Figure 2). The sheet contains a cost category for each individual allowance in that job's contract, including subcontractors, who are also asked to break out costs for allowance items. We use this information to keep a running total for each allowance in the contract. This helps us keep tabs on expenses as the job progresses and also provides a paper trail for each allowance at the end of the job.

We also help the owner track allowances by preparing a detailed "shopping list" at the beginning of the job (Figure 3). If electrical fixtures are on allowance, for example, we include the total allowance price, plus a breakdown of the specific fixtures needed — two dining room wall sconces, one exterior entry lamp, and so on. The shopping list not only reminds owners which items need to be selected, but keeps the budget in front of them. If they exceed the allowance price, it comes as no surprise.

Billing for allowances. Since the original allowance price list is included in the total price for the job, we get paid for allowances as a part of each scheduled draw. At the end of the job, we present to the client a single change order that summarizes allowance activity (Figure 4). We list all allowances, showing both the original allowance price and the difference in what was actually spent, as well as the net total change to the contract. We include all supporting documentation, such as receipts, labor charges, and any profit and overhead charges.

By Devon Hartman, a partner in Hartman-Baldwin, a design-build firm in Claremont, Calif.

Farewell to Competitive Bidding

Competitive bidding wastes time and discourages teamwork. Here's a better way.

I hate competitive bids. I hate them because I have to put in a lot of time and I don't always get the job. Instead of wasting time, I'd rather spend it on almost anything other than estimating a project.

I also don't do well with competitive bids because the process focuses everyone's attention on the one area where my company doesn't look so good: initial price. We charge a lot for what we do, and if the focus is on initial price, we're going to be at a real disadvantage.

Bidding isn't all bad, though. I would have missed the chance to work for some gracious clients and talented architects had I not submitted and won competitive bids. In fact, most novice contractors get all of their early jobs because they are the low bidder. It's hard to break into the market any other way, and like all novice contractors, I got a lot of work and experience because I was so cheap. But in the past ten years, my priorities, both as a businessman and as a father and husband, have dramatically changed the way I want to spend my time.

So a while back, when the market was strong, I decided to reward myself for all the work I'd put into developing a top-notch crew and an exceptional client base. My reward was to stop bidding, except very selectively. Eventually, all of the lessons I learned from being extremely selective about where I bid convinced me to stop bidding altogether. Here is why and how I did it.

The Rules of Bidding

Over the years, I have deduced the following set of "rules" that clients use to determine the accuracy and fairness of bids. These rules apply to any collection of three or more bids, for any project, at any time:

1. The high bid is always inaccurate and unfair, no matter what.
2. The low bid is always more accurate than the high bid, unless it's lower than the client's budget by a greater margin than the high bid is higher than the client's budget, in which case it's less accurate, but more fair.
3. The accuracy and fairness of any bids in the middle depend on where they fall in relation to the high and low bids and to the client's budget. For instance, if the low bid is right near the client's budget, a middle bid that is close to the high bid and way over the budget is neither accurate nor fair. However, if a middle bid is much lower than the high bid and very close to the client's budget, then it is both very accurate and very fair.

The fascinating thing about these rules is how they apply absolute meaning to relative data. When a contractor's bid is high compared with one group of competitors, the bid is by definition wrong. But compared with an entirely different set of competitors, the exact same bid becomes, as if by magic, both accurate and fair. Or "more reasonable," in the parlance of clients.

The assumption underlying all of these rules is that the plans and specs are so clear and unambiguous that any randomly selected, reasonably competent contractor will be able to do the job exactly as envisioned. It follows from this assumption as well that any over-budget bids are not due to different interpretations of the plans and specs —which are, after all, perfectly clear — but are the result of the bidder's sloppy estimating, high overhead, and inefficient construction practices.

The fact is, however, that the more thought and research that goes into a bid, the higher it becomes. When proofreading an estimate, for instance, contractors will more often find omissions they need to add than waste and inefficiency they can safely take out (unless, of course, they really need the job, in which case they can find all sorts of waste and inefficiency to take out). In the grand irony of bidding, then, estimates that are slapdash and carelessly prepared tend to be "more reasonable;" estimates that are thoughtful and carefully researched tend to be "less reasonable."

Anecdotal Evidence

Everyone has a story about a bid, and here's mine. I once participated in a sealed-bid competition with two other companies for a moderately large residential remodel. When we opened the bids in the client's dining room, I was somewhere around $180,000 and one other bidder was somewhere around $165,000. The "winning" bidder had already turned white as a ghost by the time his bid of $119,000 was opened. I thought he was going to lose his lunch when one of the clients, in an attempt to be helpful, said, "That seems very reasonable."

Although the best possible outcome would have been to win the bid by a just a little bit, I was the happiest contractor in the room because I had received the second best possible outcome, which was to lose by a whopping margin. Next comes losing by a little bit. But the absolute worst outcome was to get the job by a whopping margin.

But is this any way to run a construction company?

Cost Benefit

Bidding experiences like the one just described might have been enough to convince me eventually to stop participating in bidding competitions. But the real reason I stopped bidding was a moment of revelation I had during a meeting of ten remodeling contractors gathered together for intensive peer review of our businesses. I was standing before this jury of my peers, each of whom had a copy of my marketing data, reporting confidently that architects were a good source of work for my company, and that I was, therefore, cultivating those relationships diligently.

At one point, a remodeler in the group said something like this: "You got 30 leads from architects, but only 2 jobs. You got about 60 leads from past-client referrals, and 40 jobs. Why are you schmoozing architects and not past clients?" The truth of his insight was as hard to avoid as the blinding light on the road to Damascus: Architects were a great source of bids but a bad source of jobs.

Let me be clear that I have a profound respect for the difference a good design professional can bring to a project. While I have often regretted not bringing an architect into a project, I have never regretted using a good architect to help us through a tricky design or detailing issue. Yet many architects and their clients believe that bidding is essential, that the best way to choose a builder is to dangle a project in front of three or four of them and see who wants it most desperately. Although the bid process does not eliminate the possibility of good teamwork, it does nothing at all to cultivate or encourage good teamwork. On the other hand, the alternative — a good architect and a good builder working together with a client from the beginning toward a common goal — can make an unbeatable team.

Try telling this to a client: "I'm looking at four jobs right now for that time slot. They're all good jobs, so I'll be picking the one that will make me the most money." How interested will that client be in you or your services? But we builders are supposed to be interested and committed when a client says: "I'm talking to four builders. They're all good companies, so I'll hire the one who gives me the best price."

While more and more clients are aware that they can't just hire the low bidder, few do much research about which contractors to ask for proposals. Who can blame them, when we contractors play along? A free proposal is like an ante in poker: It's the minimum required to get into the game.

Contractors tell me, "If I stop bidding, I won't have any work." This fear sure weighed heavily on me, and long postponed my decision to stop bidding. But consider how much work comes your way without your having to bid for it. Sure, you may not get "the big jobs" that way, but the big jobs are often better for the ego than the bottom line. I'll bet your most profitable jobs were negotiated, not bid.

Sales Fright

I don't like being a salesperson — I don't even like the word. I want people to hire me because I'm a nice, honest guy and because I do good work. If I try to talk people into hiring me and fail, that's a real blow to my self-esteem. In this sense, bidding is completely safe. If I get the job, it means I offered a good price because I'm fair and fast; if I don't get hired, it's not because I don't do good work and am not a nice guy — it's because some back-of-the-pickup, low-bid bubba undercut me by a few thousand dollars. There's no way an honest, quality builder like me can compete against that.

I think competitive bidding means we don't have to be good salespeople — in fact, we don't even have to call ourselves salespeople. I hear so often from contractors (including myself): "I like meeting people; it's one of the best parts of my job. But I hate sales, and I hate estimating even more."

There's a connection between those statements. It's true that we like to meet new people; we like to be invited into someone's living room to talk about a project and to be listened to as an expert. We usually establish a strong rapport and often go away thinking, "I'm the one they want to hire." But after we do the estimate and realize how much the thing is going to cost, we start thinking: "Boy, they're not going to like me quite so much after they see this price."

At that point, we have two choices: We can stick the proposal through the mail slot and run away, as if we've just egged their house, or we can try to sell the job.

Sell It — Don't Bid it

Choosing not to bid means choosing to develop your sales skills. This may require sophisticated training and penetrating self-appraisal — it's not for the faint of heart. I have benefited tremendously by working with Fred Huyghue of the SSIM Group (617/237-6900), who has taught me more clearly than anyone (other than my clients) that integrity, openness, and a commitment to service need to anchor any serious, sustainable sales effort. I have also realized that a salesperson has the most credibility with prospective clients when telling them something they don't want to hear. A contractor is supposed to slip on his own drool at the opportunity to bid a big project. If you tell the prospect you won't do that, you will, ironically, have more credibility — and more of the prospect's attention — than the four or five other contractors who are panting into the phone.

Apples to Apples?

In remodeling, as a builder friend once told me, "We're building the prototype and the finished product all at the same time." There's no such thing as an "apples to apples" comparison of bids when you're offering such a unique combination of services and highly customized products. Services are notoriously hard to sell because their value is not understood until after the services have been delivered. So whenever a prospective client uses the phrase "apples to apples" in an initial conversation, I make sure I explore at length just what they mean by that. Or I start walking backwards out the door.

Clients are mostly good, fair, reasonable people. If you explain to them that you play by different rules, and that you do it in the interests of better service, you will have their attention. They will not run away scared or laugh in your face. If they do, they are probably not qualified prospects anyway.

Value, Not Price

How you get work depends on how you are perceived in the marketplace. Do people come to you for a bid, or do they come to you to do the work? If you're perceived mostly as a bidder, then yes, you may have trouble getting work if you stop bidding. But it's not preordained that a builder has to be seen exclusively, or even predominantly, as a bidder. If you want to get out of the bid arena, you need to make sure your marketing maximizes the number of leads that come your way that are to do the work rather than to do a bid.

How? In my case, I used the insight of that builder friend I mentioned earlier and started marketing to past clients. I stopped spending money on Yellow Pages ads, newsletters, and door-hangers, and put it into free, unsolicited warranty work for my past clients.

Of course, you still have to change the way you respond to inquiries. When a prospective client calls to ask you for a bid, tell them, "I'm sorry, but my company policy is not to provide bids." They will either hang up on you (although that has not yet happened to me), or they will ask you to explain how you do business. This second result, if handled well, gives you a wide-open opportunity to shift the client's focus from "Who's giving me the best price?"

to "What are my needs and which contractor is best equipped to meet them?" Now you have a chance to discover early on — usually within an hour or two of conversation if there's going to be a good fit between you and the prospective client. If there isn't, you can part company amicably, having lost little and gained time for other activities or more promising clients.

If there is a good fit, you can talk some more. If nothing gets in the way of a win-win agreement, then the job is yours as long as you continue to identify and satisfy the client's needs, and they reciprocate with a commensurate financial commitment. Make no mistake, however: Clients who work with me exclusively don't often get the "best price," but they always get the best value we can ever offer. They benefit from our full attention throughout the process.

Competitive bidding discourages such relationships because of the uncertainty of the outcome. I remember a John Wayne movie from years ago in which a kid eagerly asks John Wayne what his horse's name is. In his gruffest voice, Wayne responds: "You don't name something you might have to eat one day." I haven't worked this analogy out to the point of knowing who the horse is — the client or the contractor — but the moral is the same regardless: It's hard to make a commitment when there's no guaranteed relationship.

What Refusing to Bid Does *Not* Mean

Refusing to bid doesn't mean you get a free ride. In fact, refusing to bid does not necessarily result in positive consequences. Here is a list of things that will *not* automatically occur:

You cannot charge whatever you want. In fact, you will have to be even more focused on value than before. You may also have to be a lot more open about where the money goes, but your clients will be more comfortable with what they pay for your services.

The sales cycle will not be shorter. To the contrary, you will spend more time at each step of the process for each lead you choose to pursue. But you will be spreading this effort over many fewer prospects, so the net effect will be a time savings.

Clients can still talk to other contractors. Instead of discouraging clients from interviewing a number of contractors, you should encourage them to focus on the relationship until they find a good fit. If your goal is outstanding client service, you have to understand that you cannot possibly be the best choice for every client. Be prepared, as part of your service, to offer referrals to other contractors who might be a better match.

It is not guaranteed you'll get the job. The job, however, will be yours to lose. If you don't get the work, it's probably because you failed to ask enough leading questions, or you mishandled the process to the point of losing the client's trust. Occasionally, you'll lose a job because a client takes advantage of you. Usually, the warning signals will have been there from very early on and you will have chosen to ignore them.

Time Well Spent

The time I used to spend on putting together a bid was of service to the client only if I got the job. So 80% of the time, my effort benefited absolutely no one. The exceptions were cases when, in the course of putting together my losing bid, I offered new ideas about how to approach a problem or raised warnings about troubling products or details in the plans or specs. But this sort of free consulting was not a very good strategy for making a living from my knowledge and expertise in a demanding field.

Since I've stopped bidding, the time I devote to turning a lead into a contract is spent exclusively on activities that will be of real service to the client. I identify the client's needs and budget, and devise a plan that enables those two sometimes conflicting priorities to converge gracefully. I am able to profit by managing the process to everyone's benefit. Alternatively, I spend time determining that I am not a good choice for the project. This process also benefits the client by saving them time and by helping them think about what would constitute a good fit.

With a no-bid policy, I get a lot of work with very little traditional marketing. I don't need many leads, just enough really good leads. I don't waste resources bringing in four or five times as many prospects than I need to meet my revenue and gross profit goals. Most important, I can focus my marketing efforts on serving past clients, who are without exception the single biggest and best source of any good contractor's leads.

By Paul Eldrenkamp, president of Byggmeister Associates Inc., in Newton, Mass.

Chapter 7

Contracts

A Plain-Language Construction Contract

A simplified contract can protect you from pitfalls on small jobs

"Get it in writing" is a pretty good rule of business. For a variety of reasons, however, contractors often ignore this adage. The job is too small, or you know the client; or, maybe you think it's not worth the time or money to pay an attorney to draft a proper contract. But informal documents, verbal agreements, and handshakes can break down and lead to conflicts or courtroom battles.

A written contract that anticipates potential areas of conflict helps prevent later misunderstandings. On smaller jobs, the contract needn't be pages thick with dense legal lingo. A simple, "plain-language" contract will serve just as well. In fact, the clearer the terms are, the more likely it is that you and your client are starting out with a common set of expectations.

For this purpose, we've developed a sample "plain-language" contract ("Sample Construction Contract," opposite page). With minor changes, the sample contract can be used for new or existing construction. The contract is designed for use in Illinois, where we practice construction law. Go over the suggestions in this article with an attorney licensed in your own state: Each state's construction laws are a little different.

The Construction Contract

In any project beyond handyman dollars, you'll want your contract to have a general description of the work, right in the body of the contract, even if plans are attached. The payment terms should be clear. The insurance provisions and completion dates should be clear as well.

1. General. The contract must provide an accurate written description of the work, with plans, specifications, and a visual representation of the work to be done. The specifications should describe the quality of the materials (for example, 1/2-inch, CDX ply sheathing; 3-tab fiberglass shingles). Drawings should be clear. Simple drawings are better than none because they reduce possible misunderstandings.

If you are using a third party's documents, such as an architect's plans, you have a duty to look them over carefully when you bid. The courts frequently side with the owner if you err in your bid.

Be sure to have adequate language regarding change orders and extras, and simple language alerting the owner to unforeseen conditions.

2. Price. The price should be crystal clear and set out on the very first page of the document.

3. Starting and completion. For new construction, you should spell out starting and target completion dates, along with permitted reasons for delay. Contractors can still get owners to sign contracts without dates, but this frequently cuts two ways. The owners say X was a reasonable date, and the contractor says X plus 30. Since the law presumes a "reasonable time" where no precise time is set out, failing to use dates only invites litigation, unless there truly is an understanding that the project may proceed at its own pace.

Small companies frequently don't have as much experience scheduling and coordinating jobs as they do with the construction itself. But even a small company can meet completion dates by agreeing only to realistic time frames, making sure the crew size is adequate, making allowances for weather delays, and most important, communicating with the owners about the many legitimate reasons for delays. Owners will usually accept that a rough-in plumbing inspection is holding things up, if they are told. Owners also have to accept responsibility if they cause delays by not making materials' choices on time.

Related to completion-date terms are penalty clauses, usually in dollars per day, for late completion, and bonus/incentive clauses, also in dollars per day, for early completion. While these are primarily used in bigger projects, they are often asked about by owners anxious to establish a move-in date.

If possible, avoid penalty clauses,

Sample Construction Contract

This contract, dated________________, is by and between the following owner and contractor:

Owner:________________________ Property address ____

City, State, Zip ____

Telephones (days) ____________(eves)____________ Mailing address (if different) ____________________

Contractor: ____________________________ Representative: ______________________________________

Street ____________________________ City, State, Zip ________________________ Telephone ________________

1. GENERAL

This contract is for the following work and materials to be performed by the contractor on the property address above. This project is for new construction. (Strike if not applicable.) The project is generally described as follows:

____

____

The contract consists of this document, any plans or specifications or exhibits referenced herein, and the General Conditions following the signature page. (Identify here any plans or drawings, with enough specificity to show which attachments are included in the contract.) Change orders and modifications shall be in writing and shall become part of this contract.

2. PRICE

The total price for the work agreed upon is $____________. Payment terms are set out below in Paragraph 6.

3. STARTING AND COMPLETION PROVISIONS

The work will begin on ____________, and will be completed, absent unusual circumstance on ____________. *(Optional)* Owner agrees that if the work is completed earlier than the above date, a bonus of $________ per day will be paid. A penalty of $__________ per day will be deducted from the final payment for each day beyond the completion date that the work remains incomplete.

4. PERMITS AND APPLICABLE CODES; COMPLIANCE WITH LOCAL LAW

A. All work to be done under this contract will be in accordance with the building codes presently in force in the City of ________________, ______________ County, State. Contractor shall obtain all necessary permits and pay all required permit and plan fees from the contract sum.Unless otherwise agreed, all plan and permit fees shall be paid by Contractor from the down payment paid by Owner.

B. Contractor shall at all times comply with the laws of this state regarding mechanic's liens.

5. SPECIFIC REQUIREMENTS FOR MATERIALS AND WORKMANSHIP

A. This contract will be completed by Contractor in a good and workmanlike manner, using good quality materials. The parties agree upon the following materials specifications and work description, together with any plans or specifications incorporated herein:

windows ____________________________ wall construction ________________________________

roof detail ____________________________ cabinets ________________________________

fixtures ____________________________ other as applicable ________________________________

B. If applicable, the contract price includes the following allowances:

kitchen cabinets ________________________

bathroom tub, toilet, and vanity ____________

other as applicable ____________________

6. PAYMENT

A. Timely payment by Owner of all sums due under this contract is of the essence to this contract. The parties agree to the following schedule of payments:

1. Initial payment: ____________________________

2. Progress payments:

	stage of work	date expected	amount
a.	____________	____________	____________
b.	____________	____________	____________
c.	____________	____________	____________

Contractor shall provide Owner with his own waiver or cumulative subcontractors' waivers equal to the amount paid for any progress payment.

B. Contractor may cease operations if any progress payment is not made by Owner as required herein, and proceed to collect any balance due with any legal remedy. Alternatively, Contractor may continue operations, as set forth in the attached General Conditions.

7. SIGNATURE
Attached hereto are General Conditions governing the rights and obligations of the parties to this contract. The parties are further subject to the laws of this state governing contracts and mechanics' liens.

IN WITNESS WHEREOF, we have hereunto set out hands and seals this ___________ day of _________, 1999.

______________________________	______________________________
Owner	Contractor

GENERAL CONDITIONS

These General Conditions are part of the contract between ______________________________ ("Owner") and______________________________ ("Contractor") for work at ______________________________ ______________________________, (dated) ______________________________.

1. CONTRACTOR'S DUTIES — GENERAL

A. To direct and control the work contracted for in accordance with the terms of this contract and all applicable codes, laws, and regulations, and as the building permits, if any, issued for this project require.

B. To inspect the site, examine the plans and specifications, if any, and supervise all of Contractor's employees, and to direct the work of all subcontractors selected by Contractor.

C. To maintain the work site in a safe and clean condition, to the extent consistent with the contract.

D. To advise Owner promptly if concealed conditions are ascertained which require additional or different work, and to proceed in such event in accordance with this agreement.

E. To provide locked storage for any equipment, tools, or other property used in the performance of this contract, unless otherwise agreed upon in writing.

2. OWNER'S DUTIES — GENERAL

A. To provide adequate utilities for the work agreed upon.

B. To advise Contractor of any condition of the property which affects Contractor's ability to perform.

C. To provide secure storage areas for materials delivered to the work site.

D. To execute in a timely manner all permit applications and other documents necessary for the work to proceed.

E. To perform no work on the project without a written agreement with Contractor.

F. To avoid interfering with workers.

G. To make no agreements with any tradesperson, subcontractor, or Contractor's employee outside the scope of this contract without the written consent of Contractor.

H. Owner shall be entitled to make periodic inspections of the work site when accompanied by a representative of Contractor, provided such inspections do not interfere with the work and can, in the sole judgment of Contractor, be made safely. Any other entry onto the construction site shall be at Owner's risk.

I. Owner shall notify his insurance agent of the execution of this Agreement and obtain any necessary Riders to his current coverage or any locally customary forms of coverage, such as Builder's Risk, to cover Owner's interests and liabilities during the construction process.

3. CLOSING (new construction/with sale only)

This transaction shall close within 10 days of the contractor's notification to the purchaser that the property is ready for occupancy. The closing shall take place at a location agreed to by the parties or at the office of the title company. The parties agree that the home shall be ready for occupancy at such time as a Certificate of Occupancy is issued by the appropriate government agency.

As to those minor finish matters which may not be completed at closing, a pre-closing inspection shall take place and any such unfinished matters noted. Contractor shall complete any such items within _____ days of closing: as to such matters, Owner's agreement to close does not constitute acceptance of such unfinished work which has been identified.

4. DEED (new construction/with sale only)

The Contractor shall deliver his stamped Warranty or Trustee's Deed conveying the subject property to the Purchaser. This Deed shall be subject only to real estate taxes for the current year that are not yet due and owing, easements and restrictions of record, building and zoning laws, highways, and rights of way.

5. TITLE INSURANCE (new construction/with sale only)

At least three business days prior to closing, Contractor shall deliver to Purchaser, at Contractor's expense, a commitment for ALTA Extended Coverage Owners Title Insurance Policy in an amount covering the total purchase price of the property, including extras, but excluding any personal property. Said commitment may be subject to matters to which the conveyance will be subject.

6. MATERIAL SUBSTITUTION

Contractor reserves the right to substitute other materials, products and/or labor, of similar, equal or superior quality, utility, or color. Contractor reserves the right to make alterations to the heating and/or cooling system, provided any such substitution or alteration has comparable durability and performance characteristics. In the event of the substitution of any appliance or heating equipment, the warranty terms of the substituted materials shall be equal to those originally specified unless Owner otherwise agrees in writing.

7. DELAY

Contractor shall not be responsible for delays caused by events beyond the control of Contractor, including but not limited to: strikes, war, acts of God, riots, governmental regulations and restrictions. Delays caused by Owner's failure to make allowance materials' selections or caused by the performance by Contractor of extras or necessary work (as described in Paragraph 9) shall likewise be excusable delays.

8. INSURANCE

Contractor agrees to maintain all necessary forms of insurance to protect Owner from liability for any occurrence arising from the performance of this contract. Contractor agrees that he shall cover his own employees for worker's compensation and carry general liability, and that all forms of insurance carried hereunder shall be with reputable companies licensed to do business in this state.

Owner agrees to carry full coverage on the subject property covering Owner's risk of loss during the construction period, together with all special forms required by reason of the performance of this contract. Specifically, Owner shall contact Owner's insurance agent and secure any necessary Builder's Risk coverage prior to the commencement of the work.

9. HIDDEN, CONCEALED and UNFORESEEABLE CONDITIONS

The parties agree that in the event Contractor discovers a condition requiring an extra cost that they shall proceed as follows: Contractor shall notify Owner verbally at once to expedite agreement as to the charge to correct or cure such condition, and provide a written estimate as soon as practicable. The parties must agree to such extra charges, or agree to a resolution method, or this contract may be canceled by either of them.

For purposes of this section, a "hidden, concealed and unforeseeable condition" shall mean a condition not readily observable to a prudent contractor inspecting the subject property for the purpose of performing this contract.

10. EXTRAS

Any extra work or materials desired by Owner shall be agreed upon in writing and such extras shall become a part of this contract. Unless otherwise agreed, extras shall be paid for as performed. Failure of Owner to sign an extras order shall not preclude recovery for same by Contractor, and acceptance of said extra work or materials shall be presumed, unless there is written notice to the contrary. Contractor shall advise Owner at the time of agreement on an extra as to any additional time required to perform this contract.

11. SUBCONTRACTORS

A. Contractor shall select subcontractors as required to complete this contract. Owner acknowledges that various portions of the work will be done by subcontractors. Any subcontractor selected by Contractor shall have all requisite licenses for the work to be done by such subcontractor, and Contractor shall issue subcontracts in writing whose specifications are consistent with this agreement.

B. It shall be the duty of Contractor to use reasonable care in the selection of subcontractors. Absent objectionable performance by any subcontractor, the selection of subcontractors shall be with the contractor exclusively. Contractor shall require all subcontractors to have such types of insurance in force as are required to hold harmless and indemnify Owner from any claim for injuries or property damage by any agent or employee of any subcontractor.

C. Contractor shall pay subcontractors on a timely basis and obtain from subcontractors any necessary documentation required to release their lien rights, if any, as the work proceeds.

D. Contractor shall exercise reasonable care in the selection of materials used by subcontractors, but shall not be responsible for later discovered materials' defects or damages from installation methods, not reasonably ascertainable at the time of installation.

12. ARBITRATION

This contract shall (not) be subject to binding arbitration by the ______________________________.
Such arbitration shall be (non) binding on the parties hereto.

13. TERMINATION and CANCELLATION

Contractor may terminate and cancel this contract if any payment called for hereunder is not received as scheduled, provided that notice is given to Owner as provided below. Upon such termination, Contractor shall have all remedies provided by law, including such lien rights as then apply. Owner may terminate this contract upon the following conditions:

A. Failure of Contractor, or his subcontractors, to pursue the work contracted for, absent excusable delay, as provided in Paragraph 7 above, for a continuous period of ____ days, without a written agreement permitting same, which may be satisfied by a simple notation to this agreement.

B. Failure of Contractor to rectify any condition regarding which building code enforcement authority has issued a citation or violation notice, within ____ days' notice of such violation, unless Owner and Contractor otherwise agree.

C. Any other failure to perform this contract required by the terms of this contract.

D. No termination shall be effective unless 10 days notice of Owner's intent are given as provided below, during which time the default may be cured by Contractor.

14. WARRANTIES

A. The work of Contractor, including materials and labor, shall be guaranteed for a period of ____ years, during which period Contractor shall at his own expense correct any defect arising from his work unless Paragraph 11(D) of these General Conditions applies. This provision is in lieu of all other warranties, express or implied, and Owner has no action at law or in equity against Contractor after said date.

B. Any and all warranties for appliances or mechanical systems shall be delivered to Owner when Contractor's final payment is received.

C. Notwithstanding any manufacturer's warranty of any component, appliance, or system, no action may be brought against Contractor on this contract, for the performance of the work, except as provided above.

15. NOTICES

Notices may be sent to either party at the addresses shown above, or mailed by certified or registered mail. Any mailed notice shall be deemed given as of the date of mailing.

16. SEVERABILITY

If any portion of this agreement is found invalid or unenforceable by any court, the remaining provisions shall remain in force between the parties.

17. ENTIRE AGREEMENT

This contract consists of the documents defined above, and constitutes the entire agreement of the parties. It can be modified only by a written document.

IN WITNESS WHEREOF, we have hereunto set out hands and seals this __________ day of ________, 1999.

______________________________ ______________________________

Owner Contractor

since they create an area of dispute, and few of us want to admit fault in a late completion case. You might try leaving in a bonus/incentive clause only for early completion: it will probably be received well by owners who have heard their share of construction horror stories.

*4. **Permits and codes;*** compliance with local law. A clause reflecting the laws of your state in this regard may be required by statute and is always appropriate. Obviously you have to do work according to codes. Some states, such as Illinois, still give unpaid material suppliers and subs the right to place a lien on property and be paid, even if the general contractor has been paid. It also is a sign of professionalism and invites a discussion with the owners about how the payouts they make will be applied. You should review not only the building codes, but the lien laws as well, in order to protect yourself and prevent possible problems.

5. Specific requirements for materials and workmanship. We have put enough space in the sample form to provide specific details. This makes the form more flexible, since not every project calls for separate specifications. Also, many owners can describe in a few words what they want, based on work they've seen on a nearby project. Even when the particulars are repeated on a plan or spec sheet, a few extra words are better than a misunderstanding.

Allowance provisions are common in new home construction. Fixed dollar allowances permit the owner to select appliances, colors, carpet, or light fixtures. Allowances work well unless they are unrealistically low. Large developers usually limit the buyer to a fixed number of choices.

6. Payment. Owners expect to make a reasonable down payment, often as much as 25% of the project's total price. In at least one state, consumer laws limit front money by law to 25%. You must know any such law in your area and incorporate its terms in your documents.

Most owners will willingly sign a contract with payments keyed to developments they can see, such as a portion after excavation and foundation work, a portion after framing, etc. But problems often arise when the owners refuse to make a final payout, based on a minor punch list. Key your entitlement to the last payment to a Certificate of Occupancy, or some other objective standard, rather than to the owner's satisfaction.

A key phrase in this section is "time is of the essence." This time-tested legal phrase permits the contractor to stop work without being in default if the payment due is not made when due.

7. Signature. Sometimes work starts without a signed contract. Since your rights under your local lien laws may be limited to the "reasonable value" of the work unless there is a contract with the value agreed upon, an unsigned contract is worthless.

General Conditions

The second part of most construction contracts is called the "General Conditions." These are the things that stay the same from job to job. As in the main body of the contract, there may be differences from state to state. You can have the "General Conditions" reduced to illegible "fine print," but that is a mistake. Go over these provisions with your client.

1. Contractor's duties. This section spells out who is going to be responsible for what. Two of the most important points are D) to notify the owners about unforeseen conditions and E) to provide locked storage. You don't want the owners to worry about their child getting into your tools.

2. Owners' duties. The model contract contains self-explanatory owners' duties. While the owners may be under the impression that they have no obligations beyond the payment of the construction bill, this is incorrect. Owners are involved in selection of materials, negotiation of extras, and final approval of the project.

Owners today frequently want to participate in construction. This often sounds okay until you consider your liability. Formalize any arrangement about client labor, in writing. Any claims against you should be expressly waived by the owners.

3. Closing (new construction only). You are entitled to close on a spec house as soon as you finish construction and receive a certificate of occupancy. If a "perfect home" standard is specified, you may never get agreement that the house is perfect. Most owners, however, will sign a clause that they are obligated to close when the building inspector says the structure is habitable.

4. Deed (new construction only). If you are developing and selling new homes, your local title insurance company or escrow service probably handles the legal work on the deed. Select a deed clause that is customary in your area.

5. Title insurance (new construction only). Any sale requires title insurance acceptable to the buyer's lender. Most title insurers are members of the American Land Title Association and use a standard title insurance policy. Loans are often resold to investors who want to see a standard title insurance, not an abstract. If you build spec houses, you will get a builder's rate from your local title company and a great deal of valuable assistance processing lien waivers and releases.

6. Material substitution. The "substitution clause" allows a contractor to substitute materials that are in substantial conformance with the materials set forth in the contract. That way, if you get a price break from a supplier of a comparable brand, you can switch.

Be careful, however, about switching brands of major components on an owner without notice. If an architect has specified a particular Lennox air conditioning unit and you think Carrier is better, the prudent course of action is to get the buyer's consent, regardless of equivalency.

7. Delay. The "acts of God clause" protects you from liability for acts or events that are beyond your control. These include war, riot, lightning, earthquake, tornado, strikes, and the like.

Owners must be conscious that extras and changes will cause delays, as will their failure to select materials on schedule. Some General Conditions expressly include "owner-originated" delays.

8. Insurance. Insurance is a hot topic among contractors. It costs too much and covers too little. Buy whatever you need for the work you do. Not paying for insurance is the world's worst idea for saving money.

You need to remind owners to get "builder's risk" or owners' risk policies. These cover losses to buildings undergoing substantial improvements. If a fire burns down the building, and the owner hasn't insured the cost of improvements, the owner may not be able to pay for your work.

9. Hidden, concealed, and unforeseeable conditions. These clauses alert the owner to necessary cost increases if concealed conditions require the owner to spend more money than the original contract called for. Common remodeling surprises include asbestos, radon, structural defects, and lead plumbing. Owners justifiably react with alarm when told that the new bathroom will cost $1,000 more because the contractor has found (now that the walls are open) that there's no vent stack. You'll have a particularly tough time persuading an adamant owner that you're getting a raw deal if you don't have this provision in the contract. Once the walls are open, try to figure out what's reasonable, and put the resolution in writing.

Remember that the owner thinks you are the expert and should have known what was behind the walls. Take the time to educate the owner up front about this important clause.

10. Extras. Most contractors want extras paid for in cash, when ordered. Problems can arise when owners change their minds after giving verbal approval. But stick by your guns on any extras. It's best to get all orders in writing, and get paid before you order.

11. Subcontractors. Contractors need to develop written subcontract forms to maintain orderly scheduling and improve the efficiency of their subs. Too many subcontracts are verbal, and on some smaller jobs, the subs don't see the prime contract and may not have all the information they need to perform their subcontracts properly.

Do not allow owners to pay subs directly, or you may lose control of your job. Be prompt about your payments, however. In those states where subs can file liens, the owner can be directly affected by your failure to pay your subs as required.

12. Arbitration. Arbitration sounds good, but don't agree to it unless you find that it really works in your area. You and the owner can select a dispute resolution mechanism and put it in your contract. However, many contractors feel that the "Better Business Bureau" type of arbitration may be partial to owners. Sometimes the courts provide a more equitable decision.

13. Termination and cancellation. The courts interpret termination and cancellation clauses on a case-by-case basis. The contractor should have a right to stop work if a payment is not made within a specified grace period, and owners have rights when contractors don't show up for days at a time. The law also excuses performance when property is destroyed.

It is hard to draft a clause that adequately compensates a contractor for the owner's default; if the owner isn't paying, chances are the dispute is headed for court. Problems also arise when the owner has reason to fire the contractor, such as for not showing up. It's hard to determine the fair value of the work in place, especially when a second contractor cannot finish the work for the unpaid balance. A contractor would not, however, be in default if the job site flooded.

14. Warranties. By all means use something in writing, or you may find that your state law dictates an implied warranty far longer than you thought. New home contractors often have warranty provisions separate from their contracts. We suggest that you give a reasonable warranty on materials and labor for one year.Thereafter there should be no warranty or a limited warranty. Such limited warranty should indicate that the contractor is not responsible for any labor costs to replace defective materials. Further, the contractor should not give any warranty for materials greater than that given by the manufacturer. Many new materials are installed by small contractors who can least afford the labor costs of replacing them if the materials prove inadequate through no fault of the contractor. If you have doubts about a novel building product, remember that you are on the hook unless an architect specified it.

15. Notices. There should be a notice clause so that it is clear whenever you have properly notified the owner. Sometimes a notice of termination of the contract is not effective because it can't be properly delivered.

16. Severability. These clauses protect you from having an entire contract declared invalid, just because one part of it is invalid. If a lawyer in your state says to use this clause, do so.

17. Entire agreement. These clauses protect you from having some scrap of paper "incorporated" into your contract by a court. Additional provisions to a contract should be formal enough to be recognized as part of the original contract.

Conclusions

A good contract is something like a good car; no single model captures all the good features. Not every clause in our model contract applies to every project, nor does every project require every clause.

Analyze your contracts and contract procedures just as carefully as you do your business plan and your hands-on work. Develop your own forms to eliminate future problems. Bear in mind that each year contractors' lawyers lose cases they should win because the contract is not as clear as it could be, the attached plans and specifications are vague, or the contractor fails to document a change order or an understanding between himself and the owner with a cover letter. While there seems to be too much paper in the world, the one piece you need to win a case is often missing due to a lack of attention to the most basic aspect of contracting — the contract between the parties.

By Thomas O'Brien and Paul Barbahen, partners in the law firm of O'Brien and Barbahen, in Chicago, Ill., which specializes in construction law.

Getting Paid for Changes

Be clear about what constitutes a billable change order *before* the contract is signed

Recently, a builder consulted me about an owner who refused to pay overhead and profit charges on change orders and allowance work. The owner argued that the extra work was merely an "upgrade" to work that the builder already expected to do, and did not warrant payment beyond additional labor and material charges.

Is there such a thing as an upgrade that is not subject to the builder's charges for overhead and profit? The short answer is "No," but it depends on what you have agreed to in your contract. In fixed-price construction agreements, all additional work or deviations from the scope of the work should be written up as change orders and should carry overhead and profit charges.

To avoid misunderstandings about what constitutes a change order and how changes may be billed, address the issue *before* the contract is signed and work begins. The simplest way to do this is to include appropriate language in your construction contract. If you don't, you won't have much of a case with the owner, the arbitrator, or the judge. Whoever you end up arguing with, you'll soon regret your failure to include simple contract language that deals with change orders.

Changes or Deviations in the Scope of the Work

A. **Additional Work.** During the course of the project, owner may order additional work, which will be written up as Change Orders. The net cost of these changes will be determined by the contractor, including contractor's profit and overhead at the rate of 20%.

B. **Additional Work on Allowance.** If the actual cost of any "allowance" work identified in the contract exceeds the allowance line item amount in the contract above, this increase in work and cost will also be subject to contractor's profit and overhead at the rate of 20%.

C. **Deductive Change Orders.** Contractor's profit and overhead, and any supervisory labor (as stated in this contract) will not be credited back to owner with any deductive Change Orders or with any credits related to allowance work.

D. **Payment of Change Orders.** Payment for each Change Order is due upon completion of change order work and submittal of invoice by contractor for this additional work.

Figure 1. *These four clauses from the author's construction contract preserve the contractor's right to be paid fully for extra work, including overhead and profit. They also prevent having to refund overhead and profit charges when the original scope of work is reduced.*

Legal Road Map

Devoting a section of your construction contract to change orders creates a legal "road map" you can follow if you run into an owner who makes unreasonable demands. I include change order provisions in a section called *Changes or Deviations in the Scope of the Work* (see Figure 1). Each is designed to preserve my right to be paid fully for extra work, including my overhead and profit, and also to prevent my having to refund overhead and profit charges when the original scope of work is reduced.

But it's not enough simply to include the proper language in your contract — you may still have to explain the change order provisions to your client. When that happens, it helps to have a consistent line of reasoning to back you up.

Who determines cost? Some owners are uncomfortable having the contractor determine the cost of change orders. They feel they are at the contractor's mercy without any way to prevent being overcharged for the extra work they request. I insist, however, on having the last word on the cost of change orders because I am in the best position to know what the extra work will entail. If the owners think my quote is too high, I sometimes give them a breakdown of costs to show them how I arrived at the price. But if they still do not agree, I make sure my contract allows me to refuse to perform the extra work. Otherwise, I am at their mercy, without any way to prevent losing money on work that was not a part of my original contract.

Allowances. When I list allowances in a contract, the price I attach to each item includes only the cost of labor, material, and subcontractors; overhead and profit is figured into my base price. So when my clients see an allowance of $500 for floor tile, for example, they know that it represents an installed price, and that they can spend the entire $500 and still remain within the allowance.

When the allowance price is exceeded, however, I treat the difference between the scheduled allowance price and the actual cost of the allowance work as a change order. I am entitled to additional overhead and profit charges because I am taking responsibility for work of greater value.

Deductions. One of the most difficult concepts for owners to understand is why overhead and profit is not refunded when work is deleted from the original contract. When asked, I explain that by the time the owner deletes a particular portion of the work, much of my overhead is already spent on estimating costs, mobilizing equipment and labor, and coordinating subcontractors. And even though the deleted work is not performed, I still have to spend administrative time rescheduling the job to accommodate the deletion, adjusting subcontracts, and writing up the deductive change order.

Get it in writing. While it helps to have the proper language in your contract, and to review the contract with your clients, you must also follow through on the paperwork. Always put change orders in writing (even if there is no change in the contract amount) and get them signed by the owner prior to starting the change order work (Figure 2). If this is impossible, communicate by telephone with the owner, and make a written note that details the owner's authorization to perform the change order work. Then immediately provide the owner with a written change order.

CHANGE ORDER

ALPHA DESIGN
& CONSTRUCTION
P.O. Box 93
EAST CALAIS, VERMONT 05650
(802) 456-7429

TO: HAROLD WALSH — CHANGE ORDER NO. 4
ADDRESS: 123 PLEASANT LANE, RICHMOND, VT 05477 — DATE 6/8/99 — PHONE 434-4747
JOB NAME AND LOCATION: WALSH ADDITION, BEAR CREEK ROAD — JOB NUMBER 94012 — DATE OF EXISTING CONTRACT 4/21/99

1. ADD VELUX TPS-304 SKYLIGHT (W/L FLASHING) TO M. Bid. ON SOUTH ROOF PLANE.
CENTER OPENING SIDE-TO-SIDE; SILL @ 40" FROM T.O.F.F.
– MATERIALS $475.–
– LABOR 325–
– SUB (TAPE + PAINT) 30–
$830–
– OVERHEAD/PROFIT (20%) 166–
$996–

Note: This revision becomes part of, and in conformance with, the existing contract.

WE AGREE hereby to make changes as specified above, at this price ➡ $ 996 —

Date 6/8/99 — PREVIOUS CONTRACT AMOUNT $47,200 —
(Authorized Signature) — REVISED CONTRACT TOTAL $48,196 —

ACCEPTED: The above prices and specifications of this Change Order are satisfactory and are hereby accepted. All work to be performed under same terms and conditions as specified in original contract unless otherwise stipulated.

Figure 2. *Using pre-printed change order forms is a good way to ensure you get written approval for extra work. Keep a pad of forms on site so you can take care of changes on the spot.*

Finally, be sure to consult an attorney familiar with construction law and with your business before making changes to your construction contract.

By Gary Ransone, a working general contractor and a practicing attorney specializing in construction law near Santa Cruz, Calif.

A Change Order Policy That Works

Good documentation and accurate pricing of changes make for a sound change order policy

My change order policy, like many of my construction management systems, evolved over a period of several years. One by one, as I recognized problems with existing procedures, I took steps to improve them. The change order policy I use today ensures that all changes are clearly documented and paid for in advance.

But it wasn't always that way. Before I overhauled my policy, I usually proceeded with change order work based on estimated costs and a verbal agreement. I hardly ever submitted a change order till the end of the job. In fact, I sometimes batched together thousands of dollars worth of accumulated change orders and submitted them along with the request for final payment. Most clients paid, but they weren't happy about it. I never got burned by a client, but I often burned myself. If I'd batched, say, $10,000 worth of changes at the end of the job, I would realize there was no way I could slap a bill for that much extra money on my client. Instead, I'd cut the charges in half and take a loss because I was embarrassed about the whole thing.

I'm sure every builder has the same kinds of difficulties, which have to do with proper documentation, accurate pricing, adequate contract language, and timely billing.

Proper documentation. The first remedial step I took was to improve documentation of changes. I started using a triplicate form from NEBS (New England Business Service; 800/225-6380) called an Additional Work Authorization. The form looks a lot like an invoice, with room for a brief description of the additional work and for prices. Since the job foreman is in the best position to deal with changes, I made sure my lead carpenters were armed with forms. The forms were usually filled out at the same time the change order work was being done — not perfect, but better than waiting until the end of the job.

Accurate pricing. Once everyone was in the habit of documenting changes in a timely fashion, I focused on how to price them. Even though the forms had helped me and the lead carpenters to include prices with change orders, the pricing scheme was not profit oriented. It was "good guy" pricing, which amounted to simply passing through the extra work at invoice cost. If a plumber billed $100 for a faucet, for example, that's how much the client was charged.

Not only did this strategy — or lack of a strategy — fail to cover our general overhead, it cost the company money because change order prices didn't

Change Order Pricing Formula

Procedure. Homeowner may be assessed a nonrefundable $50 processing fee from Byggmeister for every request by Homeowner to determine the feasibility and to provide an estimate of costs of any change in the scope of the construction project. If Byggmeister determines that the change order request requires work to be performed within 24 hours, then Byggmeister will prepare a written change order agreement with a detailed description of the changed or additional work to be performed, the adjusted date of completion, if applicable, and the adjusted payment schedule, if applicable. The costs for the change order agreement to be performed within 24 hours will be assessed by adding the invoice cost of any subcontractors used, plus the invoice cost of any materials used, plus $35 per hour for work performed by Byggmeister, plus 21% of the preceding total to cover overhead costs.

Figure 1. *This contract language establishes a formula for calculating the cost of urgent changes for which there is no time to prepare a complete cost estimate in advance. Other language in the author's contract provides for fully priced change orders when time allows.*

Byggmeister, Inc.
123 Maple St.
Newton, MA 02159
617-555-1212

Change Order Authorization Form

Project name: PETERS
Change order number # 2

Description of change in work	Job phase	Labor hours	Hourly rate	Labor total	Subcontract costs	Material costs	Profit & overhead	Item total
Re-roof house	09	2	35	70	3,900	—	833.70	4,803.70
(see attached specs)								
Add Velux VS-106	06	8	35	280	150	291.27	151.47	872.74
(see attached sketch)								

Notes:

Subtotal change orders: 5,676.44
Administrative fee: ~~$50.00~~ waived

Total this change order: 5,676.44

Payment due date: on signing

Contract substantial completion date changed to: 5/27/95

Paul F. Eldrenkamp 3/17/95
Contractor signature date

Kim Peters 3/17/95
Owner signature date

Figure 2. ***This change order form is an Excel spreadsheet which the author has printed as a three-part form that lead carpenters keep with them on site. It has a column for every element in the contract formula for pricing extra work, and ensures that important elements, such as labor, profit, and overhead are not omitted. The $50 administration fee, which is usually waived, discourages owners from shopping for prices for change orders that have little chance of being built.***

include the expense of estimating the change and preparing the documentation. This approach also did nothing to discourage change orders. Because it cost nothing to explore possible changes, clients requested prices for all kinds of extra work that ultimately was never approved. In some ways it was a misguided effort at service-minded customer relations: I didn't want to be perceived as a builder who gouged on price.

Another problem was that sometimes changes had to be made immediately or the job would come to a standstill. This seldom left enough time to prepare a formal change order with accurate prices.

Pricing formula. The solution to both problems was to add a clause to our contract that included a formula for calculating and marking up change order costs (see Figure 1). I tried to come up with a formula that was fair, yet generated positive cash flow. The formula charges a flat $35 per hour for labor, plus invoice cost for subs and materials, then adds 17% gross profit to the total.

To make sure we weren't losing on changes, we also made a special effort to include labor in the change wherever it applied. For example, most subcontractor changes require some labor by the GC. It might be only 15 or 20 minutes to prepare an opening for a plumber or electrician, but it should be included in the cost of the change. Additionally, the labor rate in the formula is about 10% higher than our burdened cost for labor. If I underestimate administrative or construction time for a change, this slightly higher rate helps to cover my shortfall.

I also added a $50 administrative fee to defray the cost of pricing out a potential change order. I consider the fee optional — in fact, I waive it most of the time — but it is designed to discourage the owner from shopping for alternatives. It reminds the owner that there is some cost involved in estimating a change, even if the actual work is never approved for construction.

Custom forms. Having the pricing clause in the contract, however, didn't mean we always followed that policy. Some lead carpenters forgot to use the contract formula; others were not always comfortable with it. Either way, some changes were still being passed through at cost, and there was nothing on the blank NEBS form to indicate otherwise.

To give carpenters a better administrative tool, I created a form in Excel and had it printed in a three-part form (Figure 2). It includes a column for each element of the formula, including labor and gross profit. With the custom form, lead carpenters were able to write changes completely in the field, including takeoff and pricing, providing cost information was available from subs and suppliers. And although I still write some change orders directly in Excel in the office, these change orders are consistent with those written in the field.

In practice, however, lead carpenters often work together with me to prepare the change. It depends on how urgent the extra work is. Because the contract includes a change order pricing formula, we have the option of simply describing the work on the form, then figuring the price according to the formula. This is very useful when a change has to be done quickly. Although I rarely ask an owner to sign a blank change order, I like to have the right to do so.

Collecting up front. The crowning touch of this change order system is that clients pay for changes up front. Instead of waiting for the next scheduled draw or batching change orders with the final payment, standard practice now is to collect for changes at the next weekly meeting with the owner. My clients have never questioned this policy, partly because I prepare them for it early on when I explain our contract. I also schedule other regular contract payments at the start of a new phase of work instead at the end of a phase. Since clients are already accustomed to paying in advance for other parts of the work, they feel comfortable doing so for changes as well. But if I ever am questioned about asking for change order payments up front, I'll simply explain that I believe payment is due at the time I incur the obligation to do the work.

Besides, it's good to get into a routine of asking a client to pay something at each weekly meeting. If they're suddenly reluctant to pull out the checkbook, it's a red flag that something is wrong.

—Paul Eldrenkamp

Time Is of the Essence

Understand the ramifications of completion date language in your contracts

Contractors should treat a contract that contains the phrase "time is of the essence" as if it were a package from the Unabomber: Examine it with great care and suspicion, because it might blow up in your face.

In a contract with a "time is of the essence" clause, the completion date is so important to the customer's needs that if the contract is not completed on time, the work is practically worthless and the customer does not have to pay for it. "Time is of the essence" language means that the contractor's failure to finish on time is so damaging to the customer that the contractor might as well not have bothered starting.

For example, every year our company erects a display booth for a local florist. The booth is part of a state fair that only lasts a few days, so unless we complete our work on time, the booth has no value to the florist. Under these circumstances, a "time is of the essence" clause would ensure that the florist did not have to pay for a booth he could no longer use.

There is a difference, however, between a contract that contains completion dates and one that includes a "time is of the essence" clause. To say that the customer does not have to pay for a contract for which some or most of the work has been performed is unfair to the contractor. Even when the contractor does not finish on schedule, usually some value has been added to the customer's property. So as a rule, building contracts with completion dates — even those with penalty clauses for not meeting those dates — are not considered "time is of the essence" contracts. The customer still has to pay something for the work that has been completed.

Liquidated Damages

There are plenty of building projects, however, in which the completion date is particularly important to the customer. In a commercial job, for example, your client may have an advertising campaign planned around the new building or the improvements being made to the old building. Obviously, your client does not want its customers stepping over construction debris at the grand opening. Similarly, insurance companies that are paying to house burned-out or flooded-out customers at a local motel are concerned about when the remodeler will finish the repairs. And a homeowner who has sold the old house and is waiting for a new house to be finished will consider the completion date very critical.

Fortunately, most of these problems can be adequately addressed by a "liquidated damages" clause in the building contract. A liquidated damages clause says that the contractor will be assessed a penalty for each day the work remains unfinished beyond the specified completion date. The dollar amount of liquidated damages is usually agreed to in advance and stipulated in the contract.

This arrangement is fair to both the contractor and the client. It recognizes the inconvenience and financial loss to the customer, while at the same time acknowledging that the contractor's work has increased the property's value. The customer still pays for this increased value, offset by the actual damages caused by the delay.

No Cake and Eat It, Too

Some customers want contracts with both a liquidated damages clause and a "time is of the essence" clause. You have my permission to sneer at them. A liquidated damages clause, which spells out how much will be deducted from the contractor's fee if the work isn't completed on schedule, is the logical opposite of a "time is of the essence" clause, for which the remedy is no payment at all.

I know of lawsuits in which the courts ruled in favor of a liquidated damages clause, even though the contract language also included a "time is of the essence" clause. The reasoning is that where the parties have agreed to liquidated damages as an offset against the contract price, the contractor obviously had not intended to agree to forfeit all rights to payment if the work was not finished on schedule. In fact, "time is of the essence" clauses are looked at with suspicion by the courts, which are aware of the potential for abuse and for the unjust enrichment of certain customers. Typically, "time is of the essence" clauses are not enforced where there have been change orders, where the delay was actually caused by the customer, or where the customer has, for practical purposes, waived the finish date.

But be careful. In the absence of such mitigating circumstances, if you have knowingly and voluntarily signed a contract with specific language that says meeting the completion date is the essence of the contract, then you'd better finish on time. If you don't, then head for cover; your contract is about to explode.

By Quenda Behler Story, a partner with her husband in a remodeling company in Okemos, Mich., and a member of the National Association of Women in Construction. Behler Story has practiced and taught law for 23 years.

Who Pays for Job Surprises?

A differing-site-conditions clause can help you avoid paying for unforseen problems

Renovation contracts pose a unique problem for a building contractor: In bidding, a contractor cannot tell precisely what hidden conditions may increase the job's cost. But it is possible to ensure that you get compensated for such unexpected work. The best vehicle for this is the inclusion of a *differing site conditions* clause in the contract.

This clause allows the contractor to recover costs if he or she encounters either of two conditions while performing the work. The most common condition, called the "Type I differing site condition," is a latent physical site condition that differs materially from the conditions indicated in the contract documents. The second condition, called the "Type II differing site condition," is an unusual and unknown physical site condition that differs from those generally recognized as inherent in the type of work specified in the contract.

Despite careful planning, unexpected — and costly — problems can appear after a wall is opened up.

A case that came before the General Services Board of Contract Appeals some years ago, *Alart Plumbing Company, Inc.*, GSBCA Nos. 6487, 6690, 6923, 7123 84-1, BCA Para. 17229 (1984), illustrates how a differing-site-conditions clause can protect a renovation contractor. In the Alart case, the contractor agreed to install a sprinkler system in an existing government building. This called for a main feedline to be installed in a crawlspace above the ceiling.

The drawings indicated the height of the crawlspace above the ceiling, but gave no indication of what, if anything, was in the crawlspace. The contract documents also contained the following clause:

> *"The drawings indicate the general arrangement of piping and the location of the sprinkler heads, but are not intended to establish or show actual or relative elevation of piping with respect to other piping structure or ducts, nor are the drawings intended to find exact locations of cross mains and branch lines. The drawings are not intended to relieve the contractor of any responsibility for avoiding conflicts or obstructions or installing the number of sprinklers and supply piping thereto as are required."*

The contractor visited the site to inspect the work before bidding, but did not look into the crawlspace because doing so would have required him to cut at least one access hole in a wall or ceiling. The contractor determined from the drawings that one worker could place the main feedline in the crawlspace by moving through it from one end to the other.

Unfortunately, when the contractor started work, he found that the crawlspace contained a series of beams blocking access to the space. The beams prevented a worker from entering the space and running the feedline as planned, so the contractor had to employ a much more costly method of running the lines. Alart sought recovery under the differing site-conditions clause, alleging that the contract documents failed to depict the true conditions of the area above the crawlspace. Despite the government's arguments to the contrary, the General Services Board found that the contractor was entitled to recovery and awarded him the additional costs.

The government's prime defense was that the drawings were silent on what, if anything, was in the crawlspace. Remember that the Type I clause applies when site conditions differ from those "indicated in the contract." Thus the government argued that because the plans were silent about what was in the crawlspace, the Type I clause could not be used.

But the board ruled that this silence indicated that nothing in the crawlspace would preclude the contractor from working as planned. The board also noted that the specifications and drawings "bristled with all sorts of details." Notes were contained on all drawings that alerted the contractor to many local conditions. They even gave the exact height of the crawlspace. Given such exhaustive contract information, the board found that the government's silence about what was in the crawlspace "was as good as a warranty that nothing was there."

The government, however, argued that if the contractor had performed a reasonable site investigation, he would have known that the beams existed. The board rejected this defense, stating that because the building was in use during the prebid inspection, it would have been "unimaginable" for the contractor to have poked holes in the ceiling.

The purpose of a differing-site-conditions clause is to avoid inflating a bid to account for contingencies that may or may not arise. By giving the contractor a means to recover the actual costs of such contingencies, owners benefit from lower, and more realistic, bids. Without such a clause in the contract, renovation contractors should include sufficient contingency factors in their bids to allow for the unexpected.

A further point to remember is that even with a differing-site-conditions clause, a contractor on a renovation project is charged with reasonably inspecting the site and determining the actual conditions. While what constitutes a reasonable site investigation will depend on the facts of a given case, courts look very carefully at the extent of the contractor's site investigation before awarding any recovery based on a differing-site-conditions clause.

By Michael C. Loulakis and Jeffrey G. Gilmore, lawyers with the firm of Wickwire, Gavin & Gibbs, P.C., specializing in construction and public-contract law.

Chapter 8

Office Administration

Let's Get Organized: A Builder's Guide

Use this strategic checklist to speed through routine tasks and prioritize your paperwork

Have you ever been so busy making money that you didn't have time to stop to collect it? Administrative tasks like billing clients need to be done routinely, not randomly whenever you can find the time. You need a system that *makes* time for routine tasks and helps you focus on getting your day-to-day work done.

Most builders make several false starts before either giving up entirely or finding something that works but is far from perfect. The first strategy many builders try is to schedule routine tasks for a particular day of the week. Friday might be a good day to do the billing because you can review the outcome of the week's work. And billing on Friday also lets you end the week on a positive note.

But how will you remember to do the billing when Friday rolls around? You could write it on your calendar or on Friday's To-Do List, but you'd have to rewrite it the *next* Friday and the Friday after that. In fact, you'd have to write "Do billing" 52 times a year. If you schedule all of your routine tasks this way, you'll be too busy writing reminders to get any of the actual work done.

Routine Tasks

Daily Activities	M	T	W	Th	F
Sort contents of In Box					
Deposit all checks					
Back up data files					
Visit job sites					

Weekly Activities	M	T	W	Th	F
Collect time sheets	x				
A.M. meeting with lead carpenters	x				
Enter week's payroll		x			
Do filing		x			
Balance checkbook			x		
Send labor hours to payroll service			x		
Enter cash receipts				x	
Enter client billings				x	
Add new Change Orders to job files					x
Code & enter invoices and manual checks					x
Reconcile supplier statements with invoices					x

Figure 1. *Develop a checklist for routine tasks. This ensures that nothing is forgotten, and spreads the work load evenly throughout the week.*

Making a Routine Checklist

The solution is to make and use a routine checklist. Your list may differ from the sample shown, but you can adapt it to your own needs. Here are ten steps you should follow to develop a routine checklist that works.

1. On a piece of lined or graph paper, create a rough form similar to the one in Figure 1, including a grid with a box for each day of the week. Label the top half of the form "Daily Activities" and the bottom half "Weekly Activities."
2. List all of the things you need to do every day under "Daily Activities." Don't worry about the order for now, just list the tasks as they come to mind.
3. List all weekly tasks under "Weekly Activities."
4. Beginning with activities that must be done on a certain day, mark the appropriate box in the days-of-the-week grid. A good example of this kind of task is reporting labor hours to your payroll service.
5. Next, look for tasks that are related to the ones you just assigned, and if it makes sense to do them on the same day, or on the day before or after, mark them accordingly. For example, you need to collect and summarize your employees' time sheets before you can report your labor hours to the payroll service. Assign the remaining tasks to days that appear to have the lightest work load.
6. Now estimate the amount of time (rounded to the nearest quarter hour) it will take to complete each task, and write it down next to the activity name.

It Ain't Over Till It's Over

Most of the information that comes across your desk falls into one of two categories: *active* or *pending*. Active information demands that you — and only you — do something. You may need to make a phone call, write a letter, or send a fax, but the point is that the ball is in your court.

Pending information is slightly different. It still requires action, but the ball is in someone else's court. This means, however, that you must follow up to ensure that the necessary action is taken.

To see how this works, let's say you're looking over your schedule and you realize you need to get your plumbing sub to the site on a particular day next week. The note you make to "Call plumber" is active — you have to make the call. You phone at noon, hoping to catch the plumber in his office eating lunch. He's not there, however, so you leave a message on his answering machine.

Most builders make the mistake of believing that because they made the call to the plumber, they're done. They wrongly assume that the plumber will respond appropriately and reasonably soon. But he may be struggling with his own time-management problems, and returning your call may not be at the top of his list of things to do. Worse still, he may never get your message, or he may lose it or ignore it.

To get your work done, it isn't enough to track your own responsibilities. You must also monitor the actions — and inactions — of others who supply you with necessary goods, services, and information. When you called your plumber and left him a message, you weren't "done" with that particular task: The task simply changed from active to pending. You still need to follow up with a second call, and maybe a third. In fact, most of the information you deal with daily switches back and forth several times between active and pending status. Before you cross something off your list, make sure that you are done with it and that it is done with you.

— *C.N.*

7. For each day of the week, calculate the total number of hours allotted to routine tasks (daily and weekly tasks combined).
8. Look for days that have been overbooked or underbooked. Remember to allow time each day for non-routine tasks, emergencies, and special projects. And don't forget lunch.
9. Balance the time spent each day of the week by making adjustments to those weekly activity assignments that are most flexible.
10. Transfer everything from your rough form to a master form (Figure 1). A hand-written or typed form will do, but using a word processor or spreadsheet will make it easier to modify the form later.

Using the checklist. As you begin to use the checklist, watch for items you overlooked when you originally developed the list. Also pay attention to any changes you want to make in the way the checklist is laid out. You may prefer, for example, to have your weekly activities listed by day — Monday's activities listed first, then Tuesday's, and so on. When you're sure the arrangement of activities works, generate a fresh master copy.

Of course, developing a checklist doesn't guarantee that you'll use it regularly. To help you get into the habit of consulting your checklist, keep it on a clipboard or tack it to the wall near your desk where you can easily see it. Using the checklist will take some effort initially, but once you grow accustomed to following the system, you'll spend more time doing things and less time thinking about what to do next. The checklist also comes in handy when you need to write a job description for office staff, and it will help you keep tabs on people in the office when you need to spend time in the field.

The Paper Processor

Routine tasks are only a part of your total work load. You also need to perform special tasks, like filling out a credit application, mailing a tax return to your accountant, and reading a trade newsletter. The papers associated with these tasks often lie around a builder's office in piles, clogging valuable work space, simply because there's no assigned place to put them.

The Paper Processor solves the problem. The Processor is a system of sorting,

Figure 2. *Set up the Paper Processor near your primary work area using standard office supplies like wall files and stacking trays.*

storing, and handling every piece of paperwork that flows into your office. Eventually, you'll use specific office supplies, like wire baskets and desk trays, to hold the paper, but you'll get a better idea of what you need if you set up a temporary Paper Processor first.

Sorting the pile. The first step is to take care of the paper backlog. Start by using sticky notes, index cards, or small scraps of paper to make five labels: *Read Later, Action, Follow-Up, Transfer, and Store.* On either the floor or a table top, clear enough space to make five separate stacks of paper. Arrange the labels across the cleared area, allowing room to stack papers side by side or in rows. Also make sure there's a large trash can or box within easy reach.

Starting with your desk top, sort your scattered papers into stacks corresponding to the five categories you've labeled. Most builders need help developing this skill (if they were already good at it, they wouldn't have a big pile of disorganized papers in the first place). Try this technique: Pick up and read one piece of paper at a time. Ask yourself, "Do I really need to keep this?" If the answer is "No," toss it. If you decide to keep it, ask yourself, "What needs to be done with this next?" and put it in the appropriate stack. Above all, don't lay the paper down again without identifying which pile it belongs to.

So what goes in which pile? Here are some guidelines to help you decide.

- ***Read Later.*** Newsletters, magazines, and reports.
- ***Action.*** Any item that requires *you* to take some action. (Unpaid bills do not go here; you should have a separate system for them.)
- ***Follow-Up.*** Any item that requires you to make sure *someone else* takes action.
- ***Transfer.*** Items to pass along or delegate to someone else.
- ***Store.*** Items to be filed in your general filing system. Try to reduce this pile by immediately filing as many papers as possible.

After sorting the papers from your desk, sort all of the other piles of paper that have sprouted in your office. When everything is in the temporary stacks, you're ready to set up the permanent version of the Paper Processor.

In addition to containers for the five categories you used for sorting, you'll need a sixth for *Incoming* papers. You can use any combination of wall files, stacking trays, manila folders, and hanging files (Figure 2). Choose containers that match both the size of the temporary piles you just sorted and the kind of space available in the office. Wall files take up wall space, stacking trays occupy desk tops or table tops, hanging files and manila folders require a rack or frame and a horizontal surface to put them on. Also make sure the containers you choose will accept labels.

Work Flow

Once you get the accumulated piles of papers under control, you can begin to use the Paper Processor on a regular basis. How often you check the contents of each container depends on both the kind and quantity of information it holds.

Incoming. Most people call this the In Box. It temporarily stores new items, like the day's unopened mail, until you have a chance to sort through them. Empty the Incoming container at least once daily. If you don't, it will have twice as much stuff in it tomorrow, and soon it will come to symbolize all of the decisions you've been putting off.

Read Later. You will quickly outgrow your container unless you take the following steps to reduce the amount of material you put in this category:

- Add reading to your Routine Checklist, picking a time that is relatively free from distractions.
- Try not to place entire magazines,

newsletters, or newspapers into your Read Later slot. Instead, scan the Table of Contents and detach only the articles that interest you.
- Be realistic about how much you can read. Reduce your subscriptions to those that provide information you can't afford to miss.

Action. The papers stored here, along with those in the Follow-Up slot, will receive most of your attention. Your system must allow for the fact that some action items are more critical than others (see "It Ain't Over," page 145). Rank papers in order of priority, keeping the most pressing ones in the front or on top of your Action slot. If necessary, create subcategories such as one for date-specific items. An item is date-specific if it requires action on a particular day or if it contains information about an event happening on that day. For example, a letter requiring a response on or before May 31 is date-specific, as is a flyer containing details and directions for a half-day seminar on June 15. Highlight the key dates on the documents themselves, and place them in sequence by date. Include a reminder on your Routine Checklist to check the Date-Specific section of the Action box every day.

If less important items start to pile up in the back or on the bottom of your Action box, review each one, asking yourself, "Is this something I want to do someday?" If so, store it for now in your general filing system, where you can easily retrieve it in the future. If not, throw it away, move on, and don't look back.

Follow-Up. Some pending items require closer scrutiny than others. Again, place the most pressing ones in the front of your container or use subcategories. Remember that many of the papers in the Follow-Up slot started out in the Action slot, and depending on the outcome, they may make the trip between these two slots several more times.

Transfer. Create a folder for each person with whom you regularly communicate or share information. For example, when you jot down a question for your accountant or get a piece of paper to pass along to her, place it inside her folder. Next time you see her, talk with her, or assemble a packet to mail to her, all of the information will be in one place.

Store. Whenever possible, prevent buildup of the proverbial "To File" pile by filing papers immediately. If your general filing system is well-designed, it takes just a few seconds to store passive documents like supplier catalogs and letters. If you need to start a new folder or establish a new heading, keep the item temporarily in the Store container. Remind yourself to file its contents weekly by including it on your Routine Checklist.

By Cheryl Norris, who operates Order Out of Chaos, a Washington, D.C., consulting business specializing in office organization.

Office Basics for Field Carpenters

Tips on teaching carpenters to take paperwork seriously

Carpenters enjoy the smell of a freshly cut pine board, and they like stepping back to see the progress after eight hours of framing. But most carpenters don't enjoy paperwork. In fact, when given the opportunity to "move up" to supervisor, many carpenters decline, just to avoid paperwork.

The perspective in the office is different. In my case, I realized just how inefficient and inaccurate our on-site information-gathering process was. It was clear that our carpenters and foremen needed training in field-office basics so that the home office could count on steady, accurate data. Here's how we educate field carpenters to generate the valuable information needed by the home office.

The Right People

From the outset, I make sure that new employees are in harmony with our thinking about staying organized and doing paperwork. And because paperwork gets even more important as you climb the management ladder, I'm careful to find out if production carpenters

All employees in the author's company receive a planner as part of their training. Filled with addresses, phone lists, time cards, and job data sheets, as well as daily and monthly calendars, the planners keep all job-related information in one place.

really want to move up to lead carpenter and site manager positions. If a person has a resistant attitude toward organization and record-keeping, I seriously question his or her management intentions.

The Reason for Paperwork

Even motivated people need good reasons for what may seem to be mindless paperwork. People who haven't run a construction company probably don't understand a concept like job-costing, let alone why it's so important. As an owner, it's your responsibility to help them see the "big picture," as well as teach them the fundamentals.

My company's most important teaching example (and one I have repeated dozens of times) uses our time card with labor codes (see Figure 1, opposite page). I explain that in a typical remodeling job, 90% of cost overruns are labor. Without good feedback from the time cards, our estimators will never know what is really happening out on the job site. It's the job of carpenters on site to accurately transmit the labor costs to the office. The same is true of the daily job log and change orders. In every case, I try to explain to field carpenters the connection between good information and getting more jobs — which translates to more work and job security for them.

Crawl before you walk. Often our new employees are afraid that they will be overwhelmed with paperwork, so we start them off gradually. We furnish them a small spiral notebook with a pen, and encourage them to write topic headings on the tops of four pages: materials list, questions for the boss, questions for the client, and phone calls to make. This becomes the basis of their "system." It takes the fear out of list-making and gets the information off the drywall scrap.

Four kinds of information. To simplify the paperwork and make sure the information makes its way from the field to the office, I've devised four broad categories:

- Personal-time and paper management
- Ongoing and always-around paperwork
- Short-term, project-oriented paperwork
- Long-term, ongoing paperwork

Personal-Time and Paper Management

Have you ever watched someone follow the project manager around with a 2x4, taking notes as they talked about punchlist items? When it comes to retrieving information, the fewer places you have to look, the more likely you are to find it. We quickly teach our field personnel that the place to store and retrieve information is in their Personal Planner (available from Franklin Quest Co., 2200 W. Parkway Blvd., Salt Lake City, UT 84119; 800/877-1814) or Day-Timer (Day-Timers Inc., One Day-Timer Plaza, Allentown, PA 18195; 800/253-7601).

The daily picture and the big picture. Our company requires all of our carpenters to learn, maintain, and use a planner. They use the planner to keep track of notes and lists, things to do, and people to call, as well as "personal" items.

We don't just issue a planner and expect them to "get it." We teach them to organize their information into general (big picture) tasks and daily (specific) tasks. Whenever a task comes to mind, whether it concerns ordering material or calling an inspector, they are taught to quickly flip open the calendar and write it down on the day they need to do it — or maybe a day ahead of time — and then forget about it; it'll show up when they do their nightly check for the next day's activities.

Long-term personal planning. In

addition to the everyday short-term personal items, we encourage planning months or even years in advance, by filling out calendar entries for company meeting dates, fishing trips, and seminars they want to attend. It can't be stressed enough: The best part about the planner is that if it's used consistently, users will be able to find things, work in a proactive fashion, and, most important, never forget.

Planners are available in 8½x11-inch and 5½x8½-inch formats. Our superintendents are happy with the latter, but they are encouraged to customize them with tabs, notes, special forms, and other items to help them work more effectively. As an example, we punched holes in our time cards so they fit in each employee's planner. We also supply employees with "planner-ready" cut sheets of common construction details, such as web-hole details for I-joists.

In addition to our own coaching, classes are available to help workers learn how to use planning systems. We send them to one-day seminars — the couple of hundred bucks in time and money goes a long way to help our field personnel better manage their paperwork.

SYLVESTRE CONSTRUCTION

NAME ______

WEEK ENDING ______ TOTAL HOURS ______

REG. HOURS ______ OFFICE HOURS ______

O.T. HOURS ______ HOLIDAY HOURS ______

JOB					JOB NO.		
CODE	TASK	MON	TUE	WED	THU	FRI	+
10	SUPERVISION						
20	PRELIM/DEMO						
30	FRAMING						
40	EXT. FINISH						
50	ROOFING						
60	INSULATION						
70	SHEETROCK						
80	INT. FINISH						
90	CLEAN UP						
100	EXTRA						
SUBTOTAL							
JOB					JOB N		

Figure 1. *Sylvestre Construction has its time cards printed on card stock, sized and punched to fit in an employee's planner. Carpenters are taught the importance of filling in time cards accurately and sending them back to the office on time.*

Ongoing and Always-Around Paperwork

The ongoing and always-around papers include the weekly time cards, daily job logs, weather reports, employee information, and other special items. This material is used often, so we put it together in a "weekly file." Depending on a job's size, the file can be a manila folder, expandable folder, plastic crate, or a set of file cabinets. What's important is that there's a place for the paper. Managers are taught to "close out" the file every Friday and review it every Monday.

Time cards. The most important piece of ongoing paper, and the one that connects the field staff to the office, is the time card. From the carpenters' view, it's also the most time-consuming and boring task they are required to do. "Why do we need these codes?" and "This is just extra paperwork" are typical comments from new employees who haven't yet gotten the message that the success of our remodeling company depends on the accuracy of the information found on time cards.

It's my job to make sure employees realize that properly coded time cards enable the office staff to compare estimated costs to actual costs, and that this information helps not only for current jobs but for future jobs, too. The field employee must understand that information analysis is extremely important to making a profit. Without good data from time cards, estimators will keep on thinking that it takes 8 hours to frame an addition instead of the 12 hours actually spent.

Field personnel must also understand that we need information in a timely manner so we can make changes or adjustments, sometimes during the job, to keep the labor costs in line as well as to modify future estimates.

Garbage in, garbage out. At times our system has proved to be too complicated for our own good. At one time we had over 70 codes on our time card. It's only a slight exaggeration to say it took 40 hours to complete the time card. We have since consolidated these into 10 categories — enough to give the office the detail it needs, yet keeping it simple

Time-Card Tasks

#10 Supervision
Phone calls to office
P.M. job-site meetings
Work with subs
Time spent setting up task
Organizing job site
Ordering material
Putting together materials lists
Talks with client

#20 Prelim/demo
Temporary walls
Temporary doors
Footings
Backfill
Fence removal
Demolition
Transfer to dumpsters
Removals: plaster
siding
flooring
Move lumber

#30 Framing
Floors/sheathing
Walls, exterior & interior
Modify openings
Soffits
Roof framing
Roof sheathing
Rough stairs

#40 Exterior finish
Soffits, rough & finish
Install windows
Install doors
Siding
Exterior trim
Garage door trim
Decks

#50 Roofing
Roof felt
Ice & water membrane
Roofing
Flashing

#60 Insulation
Insulation
Vapor barriers
Foam windows
Install air chutes
Foundation insulation

#70 Drywall
Install wallboard

#80 Interior finish
Interior trim: windows
doors
base
Cabinets
Countertops
Stairwork

#90 Cleanup
Daily cleanup
Weekly cleanup
Straighten lumber piles

#100 Miscellaneous
Work not on contract

Figure 2. *Too much information can be just as confusing as too little. The author's time-card codes evolved from over 70 codes to the 10 shown.*

enough for the field staff to fill out quickly (Figure 2).

Time-card procedures. New employees are given an employee manual, which contains a section devoted to time-card procedures. We also spend time during their introductory meeting reviewing the importance of time cards (and all information flowing in from the field) and how to fill them out.

Each carpenter is responsible for his or her own time card, which is due in the office Tuesday morning (we provide stamped, addressed envelopes). The intent is for employees to fill in their cards after work Friday, then drop them into the mail on the way home from work. In the real world this doesn't always happen, but they are still responsible for getting them to the office on time.

Change orders. Our change orders are written in the office and sent out to the field. We use a preprinted change-order form that signals to the owner that this is standard operating procedure. Often, it's the field carpenter who gets the change order signed and sends it back to the office for processing. We teach our carpenters that until it is back in the office, the change order is not considered complete.

Short-Term Paperwork

Short-term, project-oriented paperwork is more satisfying to deal with — once you complete a project you can turn it in. This category includes anything related to a specific project, including contracts, building permits, change orders, job invoices, shop drawings, and lumberyard bills. This information needs to be on the job site, protected and well organized.

The easiest way to organize project-specific material on a small job is to have a single manila folder labeled with the job name. The paperwork for larger jobs is broken into several categories. We put the contract and change orders in one file, and have one file each for lumberyard invoices and office memos. Very

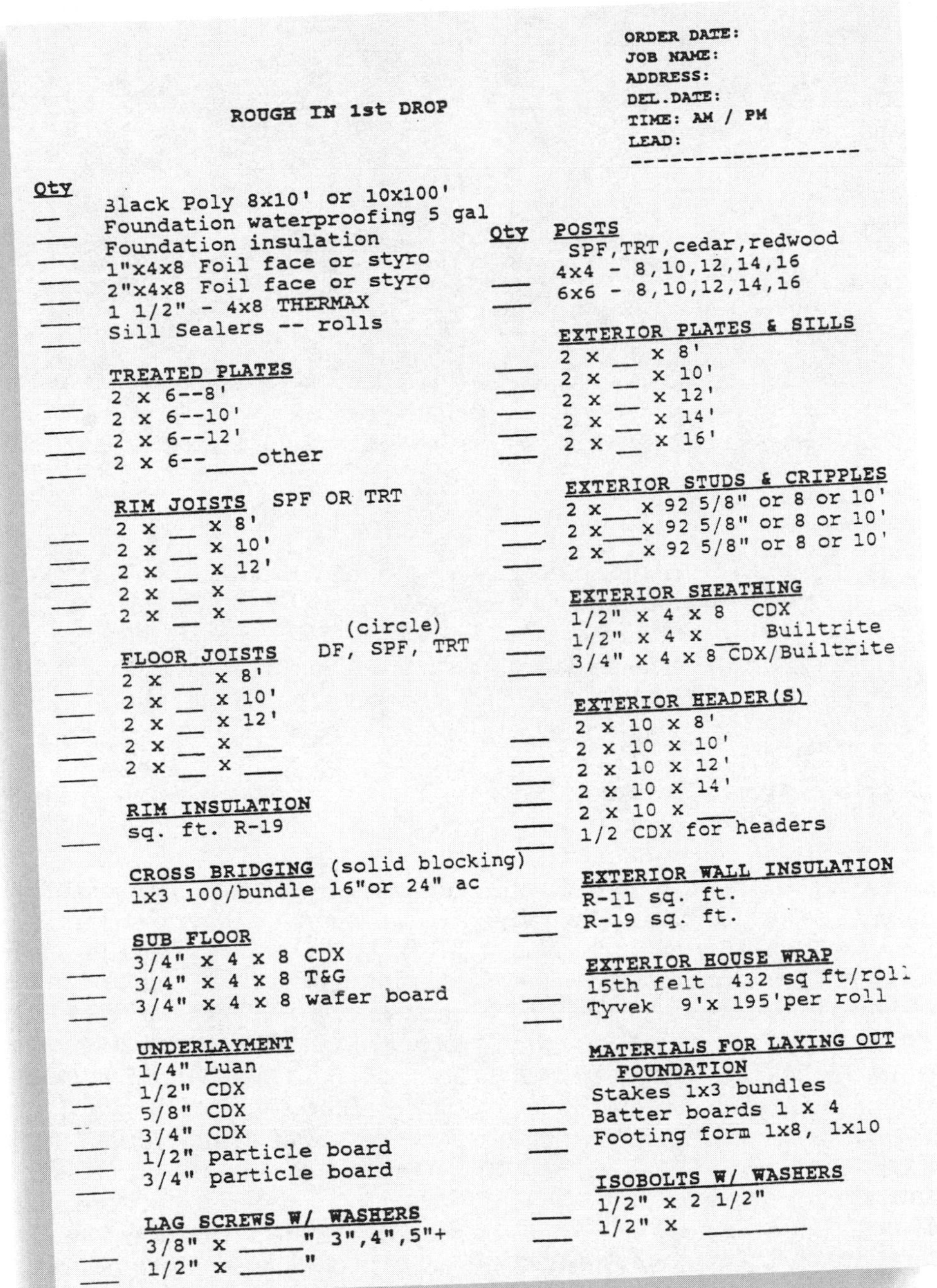

ORDER DATE:
JOB NAME:
ADDRESS:
DEL.DATE:
TIME: AM / PM
LEAD:

ROUGH IN 1st DROP

Qty
Black Poly 8x10' or 10x100'
Foundation waterproofing 5 gal
Foundation insulation
1"x4x8 Foil face or styro
2"x4x8 Foil face or styro
1 1/2" - 4x8 THERMAX
Sill Sealers -- rolls

TREATED PLATES
2 x 6--8'
2 x 6--10'
2 x 6--12'
2 x 6--____other

RIM JOISTS SPF OR TRT
2 x __ x 8'
2 x __ x 10'
2 x __ x 12'
2 x __ x ___
2 x __ x ___

FLOOR JOISTS (circle) DF, SPF, TRT
2 x __ x 8'
2 x __ x 10'
2 x __ x 12'
2 x __ x ___
2 x __ x ___

RIM INSULATION
sq. ft. R-19

CROSS BRIDGING (solid blocking)
1x3 100/bundle 16"or 24" ac

SUB FLOOR
3/4" x 4 x 8 CDX
3/4" x 4 x 8 T&G
3/4" x 4 x 8 wafer board

UNDERLAYMENT
1/4" Luan
1/2" CDX
5/8" CDX
3/4" CDX
1/2" particle board
3/4" particle board

LAG SCREWS W/ WASHERS
3/8" x _____" 3",4",5"+
1/2" x _____"

Qty POSTS
SPF,TRT,cedar,redwood
4x4 - 8,10,12,14,16
6x6 - 8,10,12,14,16

EXTERIOR PLATES & SILLS
2 x __ x 8'
2 x __ x 10'
2 x __ x 12'
2 x __ x 14'
2 x __ x 16'

EXTERIOR STUDS & CRIPPLES
2 x___x 92 5/8" or 8 or 10'
2 x___x 92 5/8" or 8 or 10'
2 x___x 92 5/8" or 8 or 10'

EXTERIOR SHEATHING
1/2" x 4 x 8 CDX
1/2" x 4 x __ Builtrite
3/4" x 4 x 8 CDX/Builtrite

EXTERIOR HEADER(S)
2 x 10 x 8'
2 x 10 x 10'
2 x 10 x 12'
2 x 10 x 14'
2 x 10 x ___
1/2 CDX for headers

EXTERIOR WALL INSULATION
R-11 sq. ft.
R-19 sq. ft.

EXTERIOR HOUSE WRAP
15th felt 432 sq ft/roll
Tyvek 9'x 195'per roll

MATERIALS FOR LAYING OUT FOUNDATION
Stakes 1x3 bundles
Batter boards 1 x 4
Footing form 1x8, 1x10

ISOBOLTS W/ WASHERS
1/2" x 2 1/2"
1/2" x ______

Figure 3. *Preprinted materials lists that live in the planner speed up the takeoff process and help to make estimating understandable to everyone on the crew.*

short (one- or two-day) jobs still need a folder, because sorting information as it comes in is much faster than having to recreate it in the office.

I prefer folders with a large folding staple on top. You can keep papers in chronological order, and they don't fall out (you'll need a two-hole punch, however). Pocket folders in three-ring binders also work. This eliminates the hole punch, and you can stuff papers quickly into the file, but the papers are less orderly and need to be sorted often.

Long-Term, Ongoing Paperwork

Because phone numbers and addresses for suppliers, subcontractors, and emergencies are reference material that field workers constantly use, we create a company reference list. We update it regularly, print it on card stock, punch holes in it, and make it part of each employee's planner system.

At each job, we also stock preprinted, prepunched pads for lumber, door, and window takeoffs, as well as to-do schedules and materials orders (Figure 3). We've

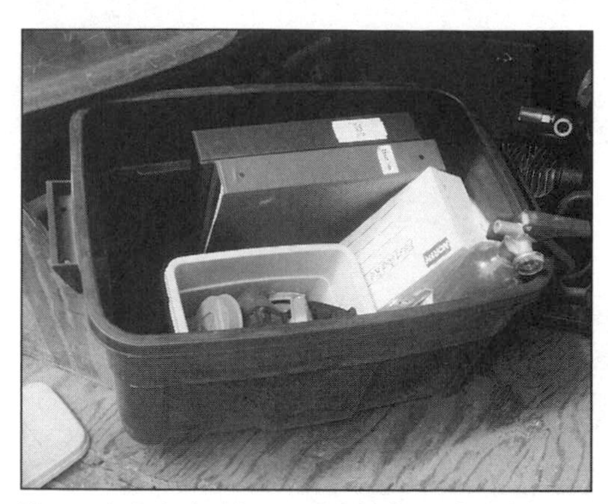

Figure 4. *Polyvinyl boxes with tight-sealing lids make good containers for job records (left). The Auto Office Seat Desk from Rubbermaid retails for $90, and turns the passenger seat into a transportable desk (right).*

formatted the order pads and lumber schedules to fit in the planners (the more of these forms you can get into the planner, the better). Finally, there are safety books like OSHA and HAZCOM that are required on the job site at all times.

What System Works for You?

It would appear that a carpenter has a ton of paper to organize and manage. How are you going to keep this material organized? The first step is to distinguish short-term, job-related paper from documents you will need for the long term. Short-term, job-related paper goes in job-labeled manila folders. Long-term paper, such as permits or job specs, will go in a file folder or, on large jobs, a file cabinet. This system will help you "file, then find" the information.

If you have a lot of small projects going on at the same time, an expanding-paper file is a good idea. This will accommodate the manila file folders (the ones you have divided up for each of your jobs), and can expand to hold more files and thus more jobs.

Transporting the Paper

Unfortunately, paper usually moves from the job site to the office in a pickup truck, where it tends to get lost or mixed up with fast-food wrappers and gas receipts. Some kind of container (other than jacket pockets) for transporting job records is a must. I know that "briefcases" have a bad connotation among carpenters, but over-the-shoulder models are becoming popular. The Duluth Trading Company (P.O. Box 7007, St. Paul, MN 55107; 800/505-8888) offers one that is designed for contractors. In any case, workers need something that will hold all the job paperwork and be in one spot that can be easily moved from site to site.

For the long-term and project-specific paperwork, we store our hanging file folders in PVC containers with handles on top. Rubbermaid (1427 William Blount Dr., Maryville, TN 37801; 800/827-5055) makes storage bins with tight-fitting tops that effectively protect and transport field-office materials from job site to job site (Figure 4). Rubbermaid also makes the Auto Office Seat Desk, a transportable office that fastens to the passenger seat of a car or truck.

When organizing the interior of any of these containers, use different-colored pocket folders with tabs. Label the folders with bold markers, both on the tab and on the side of the folder.

Keeping paperwork in order may seem like an overwhelming task, but if you take it one step at a time, it's manageable. Spend some time thinking about the paperwork items that you deal with and design a system that you feel comfortable with. Finally, make sure you and your crew are on the "same page" when it comes to the daily chore of organizing paperwork.

By John Sylvestre, owner of Sylvestre Construction, a design-build firm based in Minneapolis, Minn.

A Billing System for Builders

Spend less time chasing your money and more time earning it by using a single form to track progress payments and change orders

It's been said that you have to spend money to make money. But you can't spend money until you've collected it, and timely collection requires good communication between bookkeeping and production. If you do both in your company, you have less of a problem than companies in which one person runs the jobs while another bills for them. But in both cases, the left hand has to know what the right hand is doing.

To collect money from clients, many builders use a draw schedule based on progress payments, such as "down payment," "start of work," and "start of roof." With only one job on the boards, you're not likely to forget to collect each draw at the appropriate time. But if you've got several jobs going at once, it can get a little crazy keeping track of who owes how much and when payment is due. What you need is a system that tells you at a glance which jobs should be billed, and that conveniently tracks amounts paid and amounts owing.

Job Income Journal

First, create a place to store all of your billing information. I recommend a three-ring binder, which I call the "billing binder." Choose a binder color — like green — that represents money to you, and fill it with five dividers (called "ring binder indexes"), labeled *Signed, Started, Punchlist, Completed, and Past Due*. Insert the dividers into the binder in the order listed to represent the chronological stages of the job.

To keep billing simple, use a form I call the Job Income Journal (see Figure 1, next page). The form gives you a snapshot of the entire job's financial picture — including change orders — on one piece of paper. It will help you keep your billing straight, and you can give a copy of the form to your clients at any time to update them on the current status of their project.

Client information. The top portion of the Job Income Journal holds client information, including the job number and the client's name, address, and home and work phone numbers. Besides identifying the form, all of this information will be handy when it's time to send the bill.

Draw schedule. The rest of the form is taken up by two sets of rows and columns. The upper set holds information about the draw schedule. On the left are the descriptions and amounts of progress payments as defined in the original contract. The rows and columns to the right are used to track billing dates, payments made, and unpaid balances. The bottom row — labeled "Draw Subtotals" — shows a financial summary of scheduled payments.

Change orders. Jobs often have change orders that modify the original contract amount. The lower set of rows and columns on the Job Income Journal is designed to prevent these extra dollars from slipping through the cracks. Be sure to get an agreement in writing for all extra work, then record the description, amounts, and dates on the form. The summary in the bottom row lets you see the status of change order payments at a glance.

Job summary. At the very bottom of the Job Income Journal is a single row of numbers representing the combined amounts for draws and change orders.

Making Progress

Cash flow is the lifeblood of any business. Collecting money should be part of. If handling receivables is just one of the things you do, the Job Income Journal will speed the billing process. In a larger company, it helps the production and bookkeeping departments run through all jobs in relatively short order.

If you don't use an electronic spreadsheet, you can create the form on paper. Because you will need to revise the subtotals each time you receive a payment or add another change order, I suggest you fill out the form in pencil.

Ready, set, collect. Regardless of whether billing is a one- or two-person task, the process is the same. Starting at the front of the billing binder, review

Billing History at a Glance

When payments come in, record the "Date Received." By comparing the actual billing date to the date payment was received, you can spot slow-paying clients and take measures to expedite collection.

Record the "Amount Received" and fill in the "Remaining Balance" for each draw. Full payment will leave a balance of zero. Add the balance due from partial payments to the next scheduled draw.

Fill in the "Actual Bill Date" at the time you prepare the statement. Comparing projected versus actual bill dates can help you pinpoint job delays.

The "Projected Bill Date" is taken from the job schedule and is the date you expect to bill for each draw. You can use the numbers in this column to look ahead to see when your money is coming in.

The first two columns hold the description and amounts of each scheduled draw as established in the original contract.

To check your math, make sure that the following formula works for your subtotals: Draw Amount – Amount Received = Remaining Balance.

The total of column two should equal the original contract price.

Check your math for change order subtotals: Change Order Amount – Amount Received = Remaining Balance.

The last line of the form summarizes combined totals for both draw and change order amounts. When the job is completed and all payments have been received, the "Remaining Balance" total will be zero. At any time, your math check for "Job Totals" is: (Draw Amounts + Change Order Amounts) – Amounts Received = Remaining Balance.

Job Income Journal

Client Name: Sam & Sarah Smith   Job Number: 9321

Street: 555 Main Street

City, State, Zip: Anywhere, VA 55555

Work Phone 1: (703) 555-1492   Home Phone: (703) 555-1954

Work Phone 2: (703) 555-1776

Draw Schedule

Draw Description	Draw Amnt.		Proj. Bill Date	Act. Bill Date	Date Rec'd.	Amount Rec'd.	Remain. Balance
Down Payment	5,500		12/8	12/8	12/8	5,500	0
Start of Work	9,190		12/10	12/11	12/13	9,000	190
Start of Roof Framing	17,700		12/17				17,100
Substantial Compl.	4,000		1/3				4,000
Screening & Guttering	300		3/15				300
Draw Sub-Totals	36,690					14,500	22,190

Change Orders

C.O. Description		C.O. Amnt.	Proj. Bill Date	Act. Bill Date	Date Rec'd.	Amount Rec'd.	Remain. Balance
Upgrade Light Fixt.		350	12/17				350
C.O. Sub-Totals		350				0	350
Job Totals	36,690	350				14,500	22,540

Form designed by C. Norris

Figure 1. *The Job Income Journal provides a complete billing history on a single sheet of paper. The top half of the form holds information about scheduled payments, while the bottom half tracks change orders.*

one Job Income Journal at a time to see if the next scheduled draw is due. If so, prepare an invoice or statement for the draw amount and record the date in the column labeled "Actual Bill Date." Store a copy of the statement in the job file.

Also check the lower portion of the form for any change orders that haven't been billed. Include these amounts in the statement and fill in the "Actual Bill Date" column. Keep copies of the change orders in the job file.

If the job has progressed to a different stage, move the Job Income Journal to the appropriate section in the binder (Figure 2). Review each form in this manner until you reach the back of the binder.

When a job is going smoothly, the Job Income Journal will be stored behind the "Started" index most of the time. But if the journal lingers in the "Punchlist" section, it's a signal that something is holding up the work — and your money with it.

Recording payments. As each payment comes in, fill in the last three columns in the draw schedule section — and the change order section, if appropriate. Full payment will leave a "Remaining Balance" of zero; for partial payments, record the balance still due. When you prepare the next statement, add any remaining balances from previous billings to the totals due for scheduled draws and outstanding change orders.

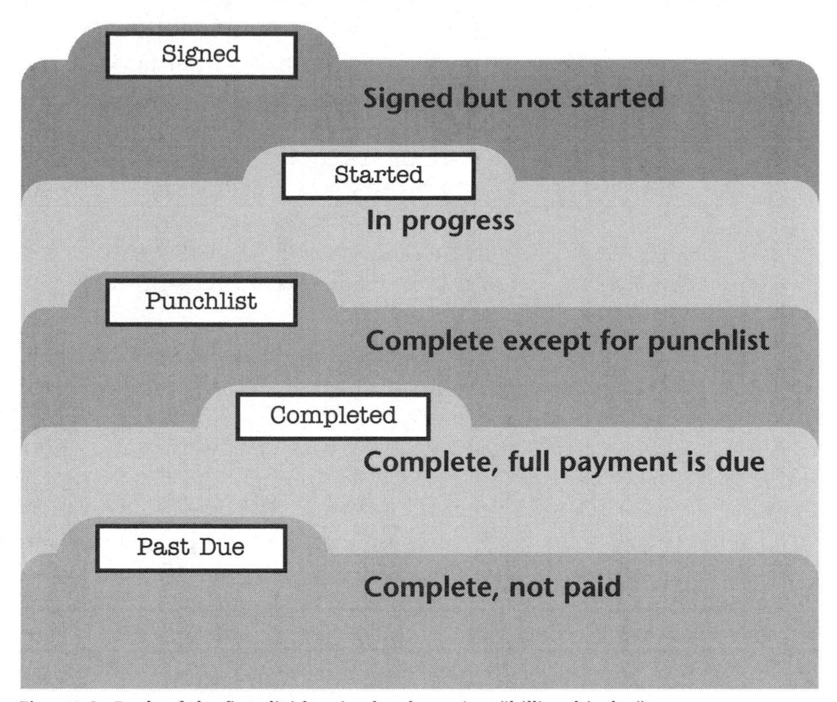

Figure 2. *Each of the five dividers in the three-ring "billing binder" represents a stage of construction. As a job progresses, the Job Income Journal moves from one divider to the next.*

A Billing System For Subcontractors

The Job Income Journal works great for a general contractor who works on larger jobs and bills from a draw schedule based on progress. But what about plumbers, roofers, electricians, and other specialty subs who turn over a high number of smaller jobs that get billed upon completion? They need a different system.

The billing system I recommend for subtrades uses multipart proposal or work-order forms. A three-part form is ideal — one part for the client, one for the job file, and one working copy. The working copy will help you remember to schedule the work, complete the work, bill for the work, and collect the money.

To set up the system, first create four "compartments." These could be four stacking trays, four manila folders, or four wall files, depending on your needs and personal preference.

Next, identify each compartment with one of the following labels: To Schedule, To Complete, To Bill, and To Collect. Arrange and keep them in that order. If you use stacking trays, for example, the one on top would be "To Schedule," the next one down would be "To Complete," and so on.

To determine which of these four compartments should hold the working copy of each proposal or work order, use the following criteria:

- ***To Schedule:*** You've gotten the go-ahead to do the work, but you haven't scheduled the job yet.
- ***To Complete:*** The work's been scheduled, but the job either hasn't been started or is still in process.
- ***To Bill:*** The job's finished, but hasn't been billed.
- ***To Collect:*** The job's been billed, but payment hasn't been received.

As a job progresses through each one of these four stages, move the working copy from compartment to compartment. Once a week, take the contents of the "To Bill" compartment and prepare an invoice or statement.

Then check the "To Collect" compartment. Use the dates of the statements and invoices stored here to determine which jobs have not been paid according to the agreed upon terms. Prepare a reminder notice for those that are overdue.

Finally, put the new invoices and statements, as well as the reminder notices, into the "To Collect" compartment. Add the most recent paperwork to the bottom or back of the compartment. That way, the oldest invoices will be on top or in front, where they command your attention. You can also insert a divider, like a manila folder, to isolate past-due invoices and statements.

Repeat this whole process every week. Once you've collected your money, you can discard the working copy of the proposal. Or, if you prefer, you can mark it with payment information (date paid, check number, etc.) and store it inside the job file. Some people attach working copies to their respective deposit receipts, storing them as part of their financial records.

Now go out and spend some money. After all, you not only earned it, you collected it.

—Cheryl Norris

Chapter 9

Keeping Your Books

Overhead, Markup, and Profit

To make a profit, track your expenses accurately and calculate the correct markup

Ask the average small builder on the street what his net profit is and you might hear something like, "Well, I made $70,000 dollars last year." But, in fact, that number is probably what's left over after paying for materials, labor, and subcontractors. What most builders forget is that the cost of doing business still has to come out of that money. In other words, they forget about their overhead.

But even builders who know what their overhead is often confuse it with the markup they apply to get the final selling price for the jobs they estimate. To know the difference between overhead and markup, you have to understand the relationship between three basic concepts: *gross income, direct costs,* and *indirect costs.*

Cost Categories

Totaling up the dollar amounts for each of these three categories is the first step. You don't have to be a CPA to track these numbers. If you know how to keep a checkbook, you have what it takes to compile the figures you need. But this is precisely where most people fall down. They don't have a bookkeeping system that accurately records their company's expenses, nor the discipline to add up everything at the end of each year and look at the important relationships between income and expenses.

One advantage I have is that my remodeling business is small enough ($300,000 per year) that I can keep an eye on all expenses. But my system for recording costs will also work for companies larger and smaller than mine. The basic idea is to set up specific cost categories and make sure that each expenditure or income transaction is recorded only once, in the proper category.

Gross Income

For small builders like me, income is simple. Most of the money flowing into my business comes from contracts, interest on my checking account, or discounts earned from vendors (Figure 1). The total amount from these and all other sources is called *gross income.*

Direct Costs

Expenses are a bit more complicated and cause the most confusion. There are two kinds of expenses — *direct costs* and *indirect costs* — and you have to keep track of them separately to determine your overhead.

Direct costs are the most obvious. I think of direct costs as *any expense I would not incur if I did not do a specific job.* I keep track of five general categories of direct costs: permit fees, Home Owners Warranty (HOW) premiums, subcontractors, labor, and materials (Figure 2, next page).

Labor includes more than just hourly wages. I also add up all the costs I would not incur if I did *not* have field employees. This includes social security tax, federal and state unemployment taxes, and all fringe benefits, like health insurance, vacation pay, and holidays. I also count workers compensation premiums as direct costs because they are linked directly to total payroll. I lump all these labor costs together for the purposes of job costing and calculating my overhead, but I keep them separate for tax purposes.

Gross Income

Amount	Source
$281,865	Contract Income
3,135	Interest Income
$285,000	Gross Income

Figure 1. *Gross income is your total income from all sources. If you have more than one kind of business interest—say new construction, remodeling, and a handyman division—you might want to track income and overhead for each separately.*

Where the Money Goes

Indirect Costs (Overhead)

Amount	Percent Gross Income	Category
$1,995	.7%	Advertising
1,425	.5	Dues & Subscriptions
1,425	.5	Education
2,850	1.0	General Liability Insurance
600	.2	Legal & Professional
5,700	2.0	Medical Insurance
11,400	4.0	Office Rent
31,350	11.0	Office Salaries
5,700	2.0	Office Supplies
5,700	2.0	Part-Time Office Help
710	.2	Repairs & Maintenance
400	.1	Shop Expenses
2,850	1.0	Small Tools
2,850	1.0	Taxes & Licenses
1,995	.7	Telephone
1,425	.5	Travel & Entertainment
1,425	.5	Trash Removal
7,695	2.7	Truck Expenses
2,850	1.0	Utilities
855	.3	Work Clothes
$91,200	32.0%	Total Indirect Costs

Net Profit

Amount	Percent Gross Income
$10,545	3.7%

Annual Gross Income

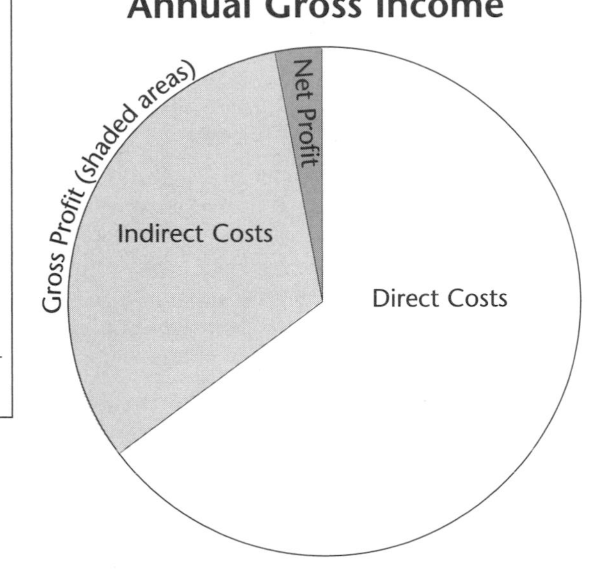

Direct Costs

Amount	Percent Gross Income	Category
$ 570	.2%	Permit Fees
285	.1	HOW Premiums
68,400	24.0	Materials
57,000	20.0	Labor
57,000	20.0	Subcontractors
$183,255	64.3%	Total Direct Costs

Figure 2. *Your gross receipts fall into one of three categories: direct costs, indirect costs, and profit. Direct costs follow this rule: If you have an expense only because you're doing a particular job, it's a direct cost. Indirect costs, often called overhead, are expenses you incur just by being in business. What's left after all these expenses are accounted for is net profit — what you get to keep or reinvest in the business.*

The formulas are as follows: Gross income – direct costs = gross profit

Gross profit – indirect costs = net profit

Figuring Your Markup

To cover this overhead	Mark up direct costs this much	Markup for every $10,000 of direct costs
26%	35%	$3,500
27%	37%	$3,700
28%	39%	$3,900
29%	41%	$4,100
30%	43%	$4,300
31%	45%	$4,500
32%	47%	$4,700
33%	50%	$5,000

Note: For other numbers, use the formula:

$$\left(\frac{1}{1-\text{Overhead}}\right) - 1 = \text{Markup}$$

For example: $$\left(\frac{1}{1-.34}\right) - 1 = .52$$

Figure 3. *Overhead and markup are often confused. To recover a given percentage of overhead, you must charge a larger percentage of markup.*

Indirect Costs

When you subtract direct costs from gross income, you are left with gross profit. Unfortunately, this is the number many builders quote when asked how much money they made last year. But gross profit doesn't go into your pocket. It includes expenses that represent the cost of doing business in general but that don't specifically apply to this or that job. These are called indirect costs.

Many of the indirect cost categories I use are self-explanatory and will work for almost any small builder or remodeler. The basic rule I follow to determine my indirect costs is just the opposite of the one I follow for direct costs: A cost is indirect if I incur it whether or not I do any remodeling.

For example, my own salary and the hourly labor costs of my part-time secretary are indirect costs because we work strictly in the office. If I swung a hammer part of the time or did direct field supervision, that portion of my time would be counted as a direct cost to the job. But my secretary and I work only in the office, and we work whether or not anyone is working in the field. It's true that we might not be employed very long if there were no remodeling jobs at all. But the point is that these personnel costs are not incurred by a specific project — the Jones or Smith job — but by the fact that Criner Construction exists as a business entity.

I treat general liability insurance premiums the same way because they're based on gross receipts and not tied to a single job. The same is true for office rent and utility bills, telephone charges, advertising, and all the rest.

A couple of indirect cost categories I use may seem puzzling, but they work for me because of the way I run my business. For example, I consider small tools an indirect cost because I supply all hand and power tools to my two full-time field employees. The tools are not consumed during the course of any single job, and the purchase price and maintenance costs are expenses I incur over a long period of time.

I also supply my field employees with company vehicles, and for the same reasons, their operating and maintenance expenses are indirect costs. The purchase price for large capital expenditures like this should be amortized over the expected life of the equipment. Otherwise it will throw your numbers out of whack. For example, if you pay $12,000 cash for a new vehicle and include the total amount as an overhead expense in just one year, your indirect costs will be inflated for that year. Unless you expect to buy a new truck every year, you should divide the $12,000 by the expected useful life of the truck — say five years, at $2,400 each year.

Keeping Track

Once your cost categories are set up, it's important to make sure that no money is spent without being recorded. I have one checkbook and it never leaves the office. I have credit accounts with all my vendors, and I give every employee a charge card. This ensures that I have a canceled check, vendor invoice, or charge card receipt for every expense. On the rare occasions when a credit card isn't acceptable, I reimburse employees by separate check for out-of-pocket expenses and log it into the proper cost category.

Once in a while I may have to run out with a check to pay for something in person. But I don't mind doing it because it's easier than losing track of the accounting.

Everything begins with estimating and job costing because you can't calculate your overhead without knowing what your direct costs are. When I do an estimate, I group the direct costs into 25 categories, such as "carpentry," "roofing," and "insulation." As the job progresses, I use the same 25 categories for job costing. I don't use a purchase order system, but whenever someone orders material, they include a job name and direct cost category. A load of framing lumber, for example, will be designated for the "Smith Job" in the "carpentry" category. If more than one category is required, they break it down right on the invoice. We try to keep invoices separate for different jobs. My field employees keep their hours daily and break them down the same way. All invoices that don't have anything to do with a particular job are recorded as indirect costs.

Stay Up-To-Date

At a minimum, you should update your record totals at the end of each fiscal year. But because the numbers in each category serve as budget figures for the coming year's expenditures, a monthly tally is better. Knowing what you spent last year on health insurance, for example, will give you something to compare this year's premium to. If the cost goes up, you can adjust your overhead to cover it.

I like to keep current with my books two or three times each week, so I always know where my business stands. It helps me to foresee problems, and it gives me time to react to them. Builders who don't keep track like this don't find out they're broke until it's too late.

Keeping good records also lets me pick and choose my jobs without the fear of not making enough money. I know that I have to make my overhead on every single job. And because I know what I need to make to cover my overhead, I can choose jobs that consistently provide that amount.

Good records also tell me which kinds of jobs my company is best equipped to do. We look for jobs where we can produce a superb product and get a good profit. If we can't be competitive on a job, we'll pass it up.

Overhead vs. Markup

Once you've made sure that all of your income and expenses are accounted for and distributed to the proper cost categories, you have all the numbers you need to find your gross income and direct and indirect costs. Now you can calculate overhead and markup.

Let's take overhead first. At the end of the year, when you total all of your indirect costs, you get a dollar amount that represents your overhead for the year. This is the amount you need to earn over and above your direct costs to cover the cost of doing business.

But the dollar amount for overhead isn't very useful when you're preparing an estimate. If you divide it into an average monthly amount and apply it to every job you estimate that month, you won't be competitive on small jobs and you'll be underpriced on larger jobs.

Because builders need to include indirect costs in every estimate, no matter how big or small, overhead is usually expressed as a percentage. Overhead is the ratio of indirect costs to gross income. Using the totals from Figures 1 and 2, the calculation looks like this:

$$\frac{\textbf{\$91,200}\ \textit{(Indirect Costs)}}{\textbf{\$285,000}\ \textit{(Gross Income)}} = 32\%\ \textit{(Overhead)}$$

The most common mistake people make is to confuse overhead with markup. When they estimate a job, they figure the total cost for materials, labor, and subcontractors — the direct costs. Then, if they know that their overhead is 32%, they multiply their direct costs by 32% to get their markup. For example, if they estimate the direct costs for a job at $10,000, they add 32% of this or $3,200 and quote the price to the owner as $13,200.

That's just plain wrong. You lose money very quickly that way, and here's why. In the example, if your estimate is correct, you'll spend $10,000 for materials, labor, and subcontractors (direct costs), and have $3,200 left over to cover your indirect costs. Divide this by your gross income for the job ($13,200) and you get an overhead percentage for the job of only about 24%. That leaves you 8% short of the 32% you need.

Instead, after you've estimated your direct costs, you need to multiply them by your markup to find the amount to add for overhead. Markup is always expressed as a percentage of direct costs. The mathematical problem you need to solve is this: What percentage of direct costs, when added to direct costs, will cover your overhead? In the example used a moment ago, the markup should have been 47% ($4,700), which makes the selling price $14,700. The $4,700 is 32% of the selling price (the gross income for this job), and will just cover indirect costs:

$$\frac{\$4{,}700 \ (\textit{Indirect Costs})}{\$14{,}700 \ (\textit{Gross Income})} = 32\% \ (\textit{Overhead})$$

Figure 3 (page 160) lists the percentage by which direct costs must be marked up to break even at various overhead percentages.

Profit

These calculations establish your break-even price — the selling price at which all of your costs (direct and indirect) are covered, with nothing left over. But every business needs to accumulate some wealth to cover down times and finance capital expenditures, like new equipment. So you should include net profit in your markup. Net profit is what's left after direct and indirect costs are subtracted from gross income. My net profit is usually about 4% of gross receipts, which adds a little over 6% to my markup. In the example, a 47% markup covers overhead, and an additional 6% markup ($600) takes care of profit:

$10,000	*(Direct Costs)*
x .53	*(Markup)*
$ 5,300	*(Overhead & Profit)*

The selling price for this job, therefore, should be $15,300.

Common Mistakes

Most builders don't take a salary; they just draw from their checking account when they need to pay their bills. But not paying yourself is the biggest mistake you can make. All of the things you do in the office or after hours are necessary to the success of your company and should be accounted for as an indirect cost. Just because you're not banging nails doesn't mean your hours are less productive or less costly, in terms of overhead, than those of people in the field.

I bid everything on a fixed price because it means I never have to explain my overhead to clients. The minute you do that, you've lost the job because they will never believe you. They just can't fathom it, and no amount of explanation will change that. The best thing to do is bid your price and stick with it.

By Robert Criner, president of Criner Construction Company Inc. of Yorktown, Va.

The Mistake of Markup

I recently attended a business seminar in which a roomful of builders discussed various ways to "mark up" direct costs to arrive at a selling price. The seminar speaker explained that he uses a divisor to arrive at his selling price. For example, take a job where the total estimated direct cost (material, labor, and subcontractors) is, say, $10,000. To add an additional 20% gross profit, this builder divides by .8. The selling price would then be $12,500 ($10,000÷.8).

A number of builders in the room spoke up, saying that this was the same as multiplying by 1.2. At first glance, this makes sense: Multiplying by 1.2 marks up costs by 20%, right? Wrong. Multiplying by 1.2 is not the same as dividing by .8.

In the ensuing debate, it was obvious that about half the people in the room were calculating the selling price for estimates in a way that guaranteed they would lose money on every job. In the sample estimate mentioned above, multiplying $10,000 in direct costs by 1.2 yields a selling price of $12,000 — $500 less than the method that uses a divisor. On larger jobs, the difference is greater: If direct costs are $100,000, the two selling prices are $5,000 apart; on a $500,000 job, the difference is $25,000. Builders can't afford to throw away that kind of money. What's going on here?

Gross Profit, Not Markup

The term "markup" is responsible for some of the confusion. In fact, most of us are familiar with markup because of its opposite — "markdown." When an item in a retail store is on sale, it is usually marked down a certain percentage. To arrive at the "sale" price, shoppers simply multiply the tagged price by the percentage, and subtract. For example, when an item normally selling for $100 is marked down 10%, it sells for $90.

It's a mistake, however, to assume that markup is simply the reverse of markdown. To get our $90 on-sale item back up to list price, we cannot simply add 10%. If we do, we get $99, not $100. Yet this is exactly what many builders do when tallying estimates.

Forget markup. If you want to consistently price your jobs to cover all of your expenses, abandon the concept of markup and start thinking in terms of gross profit. Gross profit is a dollar amount equal to the sum of overhead plus profit.

Overhead for a small construction company typically includes the salaries of the owner and any office help, plus all the costs of running the business that are not directly related to construction. These costs include office rent and utilities, office supplies, insurance, and vehicle expenses, among others.

Profit is the amount of money earned after all expenses — both direct costs and overhead — have been paid. Profit is not simply the amount of money left over at the end of the year — it's a specific dollar amount representing, among other things, the return on your capital investment, as well as compensation for the risks you take in your business. Ideally, profit should be 10% of total sales, but many construction companies earn closer to 5%.

Typical Overhead & Profit

$ 30,000	owner's salary
2,000	phone, utilities
500	office supplies
1,000	tools, repairs
1,000	liability insurance
+ 2,000	vehicle expenses
$ 36,500	**Total General Overhead**
+12,500	Profit (5% of total sales)
$ 49,000	**Gross Profit**

Gross profit is the sum of overhead, such as your salary and the costs of running an office, plus profit. Use last year's bookkeeping records to estimate gross profit for the coming season.

If you don't know what your overhead and profit amounts are, use last year's records to find out. A simplified schedule of overhead and profit for a typical small construction company ($250,000 in total sales) is shown in the table below.

Gross profit percentage. One of your business goals should be to earn the required gross profit on every job. To do this, however, you can't just divide the total dollar amount of gross profit by the number of jobs, and add the result to direct costs. If you did, you would overbid small jobs and lose your shirt on big jobs.

The easiest and safest way to include gross profit in every estimate is to convert gross profit dollars into a percentage. To do this, divide gross profit by total sales:

$$\frac{\$49{,}000 \text{ (Gross Profit)}}{\$250{,}000 \text{ (Total Sales)}} = 19.6\% \text{ (Gross Profit)}$$

You'll need to estimate what your total sales will be for the year, but this number usually doesn't fluctuate much. If you did $250,000 worth of work last year, you'll probably do at least that much work this year. If you anticipate more or less work, recalculate the gross profit percentage based on a higher or lower sales figure.

Find the Selling Price

Once you know the direct costs of a job and the gross profit percentage you need to earn, it's easy to come up with the selling price. First, subtract the decimal value of the gross profit percentage from 1:

$$1 - .196 = .804$$

Now use this divisor to figure the correct selling price:

$$\frac{\$201{,}000}{.804} = \$250{,}000 \text{ Selling Price}$$

You can do everything right when preparing an estimate — take off materials down to the last stud, plug in firm quotes from subs, and figure labor costs to the man-hour. But if you use the wrong formula to cover gross profit, you'll lose money every time. To avoid this costly mistake, make one simple change in your process — using a divisor instead of a multiplier — and cover all your costs on every job.

By Sal Alfano, a former residential contractor in East Calais, Vt., and editor of The Journal of Light Construction.

Double-Entry Accounting Basics

Do debits and credits scare the daylights out of you? Master these basic accounting principles and overcome your fear of figures.

Many small contractors think of accounting as a necessary evil. If financial records weren't required for tax purposes, they would bid the whole process good riddance. Call me a bean-counter, but I take the opposite view. I'm a remodeler in the Chicago area, and I spend most of my time selling and administrating the jobs my field crews are working on. For me, the financial end of the business is its heart and soul. I work hard and have a lot invested in my company's success. I've learned from experience that if I don't keep an eye on my money, no one else will.

I don't mean to say that other builders don't want to make money — they do. But as soon as an accountant-type starts talking about equity, debits, credits, assets, and liabilities, they're lost. Faced with this bewildering terminology, contractors who have spent years in the field perfecting their craftsmanship tend to give up on trying to understand the principles that make an accounting system work.

Don't make that mistake. Account ing isn't that difficult to understand. In fact, it's a lot easier than laying out rafters or designing a room addition. But there is a lot to learn, and I can't cover it all in this section. I can, however, introduce basic principles of accounting, and show you how standard financial reports are put together.

Checkbook Accounting

Most builders start out using their checkbook to keep track of their company's financial health. Unfortunately, while scrupulously making entries in your checkbook will prevent you from overdrawing your checking account, it can't tell you whether you're making money or not. To see why, let's look at how a checkbook record-keeping system works.

Assume it's the middle of the month, and the concrete sub is stripping the forms from a new foundation for a job you've just started. The lumber has been delivered, and you expect the doors and windows to arrive in a week. The total cost of the materials and concrete work is about $26,000, but because everything was purchased on credit, you won't receive the bills for two weeks.

The same day, you receive two checks from clients whose jobs you've just completed, one for $8,000 and one for $4,500. When you add these deposits to the $2,000 balance, you've got $14,500 in your checking account.

If the only financial indicator you have is your checkbook balance, it might

Glossary of Accounting Terms

account: a numbered category that holds records for similar types of transactions

accrual basis: an accounting method that recognizes income at the time it is earned (but before money is collected), and expenses at the time they are incurred (but before debts are paid) (see *cash basis*)

assets: cash, or property and equipment that can be sold for cash

balance sheet: a financial statement showing a company's assets, liabilities, and owner's equity as of a certain date

cash basis: an accounting method that does not recognize revenue until the money owed is actually collected, and does not recognize expenses until debts are actually paid (see *accrual basis*)

chart of accounts: a complete list of accounts, arranged in five sections: assets, liabilities, owner's equity, income, and expenses

cost of sales: see *direct costs*

creditor's equity: see *liabilities*

debits and credits: terms used to indicate increasing or decreasing an account. By convention, debits are always recorded on the left side of a ledger, credits on the right. Debits and credits must always be in balance (see *double-entry*)

direct costs: costs such as materials, labor, and subcontractors that can be assigned to a particular job

double-entry: an accounting method that requires recording each transaction in two or more accounts, with balanced (equal) debits and credits

income statement: a financial statement covering a given period of time, and showing all income and expenses, and the resulting net profit or loss

indirect costs: general operating costs (such as rent, phone service, and office supplies) that cannot be assigned to a particular job

liabilities: the claims of creditors (such as banks) against a company's assets (also called creditor's equity)

net profit: income in excess of all business costs and expenses

overhead: indirect costs included in the selling price (usually allocated as a percentage of direct costs)

owner's equity: the amount of a company's total assets that belong to the owner

profit-and-loss statement: see *income statement*

retained earnings: accumulated business profit that is not distributed to owner, but remains in the business

sales: an account that records income from business operations

appear to be a good time to go out and buy a new truck. The problem, however, is that none of the money in your checking account is yours — you owe it all to someone else. If your business is very small, you might be able to adjust for future bills, because you personally order all of the material for every job. But when you have several jobs going at once, each of which has a foreman who orders materials for his project, it's easy to lose track.

The shortcomings of checkbook accounting are also complicated by payroll withholding taxes, quarterly insurance payments, and other liabilities that accumulate steadily, but are payable at some future date.

Assets, Liabilities, and Equity

The goal of accounting (besides providing tax information) is to determine whether your financial stake in your company, called equity, is increasing or decreasing. The basic formula is:

Assets = Liability + Equity

Assets include cash, plus materials and equipment you own that can be readily sold for cash. Liabilities are all the debts the company owes. Equity is the amount of money left over from company operations after all of the bills have been paid.

Every dollar your company takes in or pays out affects this formula. And like

Chart of Accounts

100-199 Assets (debit to increase)
- 101 Petty Cash
- 102 Cash Account
- 111 Cert. of Deposit
- 115 Payroll Advances
- * 120 Accounts Receivable
- 129 Plan Deposits
- * 131 Prepaid Taxes
- * 134 Prepaid Insurance
- 155 Furniture/Fixtures
- 156 Construction Equip.
- 157 Vehicles
- 181 Accum. Depreciation: Furnitures/Fixtures
- 182 Accum. Depreciation: Construction Equip.
- 183 Accum. Depreciation: Vehicles

200-299 Liabilities (credit to increase)
- * 220 Accounts Payable
- * 231 FICA Payable
- 232 Fed. Income Tax Withheld
- 233 State Income Tax Withheld
- * 234 State Unemployment Tax
- * 235 Workers Comp. Payable
- * 236 Gen. Liability Insurance Payable
- * 238 Fed. Unemployment Tax Payable
- * 241 Accrued Medical Insurance
- * 242 Accrued Employee Payroll Savings
- * 245 State Income Tax Payable
- 251 Note Payable

300-499 Equity (credit to increase)
- * 304 Capital Stock
- * 309 Dividends Paid
- 310 Cumulative Profits
- 320 Retained Earnings

400-499 Income (credit to increase)
- 400 Contract Income – Residential
- 401 Contract Income – Commercial
- 402 Finance Charges
- 405 Design/Plan Fees
- 470 Other Income
- 480 Interest Income
- 490 Discounts Earned

500-799 Expenses (debit to increase)

500-599 (Direct Costs)
- 500 Materials
- 501 Subcontractors
- 510 Trash Removal
- 520 Permits & Fees
- 540 Direct Labor
- 541 Direct Labor – Payroll Taxes
- 542 Direct Labor – Medical Benefits
- 543 Direct Labor – Workers Comp.
- 544 General Liability Insurance
- 550 Vehicle Fuel/Maintenance
- 552 Architectural/Design/Engineering Fees

600-799 (Indirect Costs)
- 605 General Insurance (tools)
- 607 Taxes/Licenses
- 608 Dues/Subscriptions
- 609 Interest
- 610 Education/Training – Employees
- 611 Legal/Accounting Fees
- 612 Utilities
- 613 Telephone
- 614 Rent
- 615 Office Equipment
- 616 Marketing
- 617 Contributions
- 618 Bank Service Charges
- 619 Advertising
- 621 Postage
- 627 Furniture/Fixtures Depreciation
- 638 Equipment Depreciation
- 639 Vehicle Depreciation
- 640 Overhead Labor
- 641 Overhead Payroll Taxes
- 642 Overhead Medical Benefits
- 643 Overhead Workers Comp.
- 650 Tool Repair/Replacement
- 664 Office Repair/Maintenance

700-799 (Administrative Expenses)
- 710 Education/Training – Owner
- 730 Vehicle – Owner
- 740 Owner Salary
- 741 Owner Payroll Taxes
- 742 Owner Payroll Benefits
- 743 Owner Workers Comp.
- 790 State Income Tax Expense

** These accounts are used with accrual basis accounting.*

Figure 1. *All financial transactions are recorded in numbered categories called accounts. The five main groups used by financial reports — assets, liabilities, equities, income, and expenses — can be further subdivided. For example, accounts 500-799 represent expenses, which are organized into three subgroups: direct costs, indirect costs, and administrative expenses. These subgroupings have no effect on the basic accounting formula, but are useful when you want to isolate specific financial information, such as the amount spent on administrative expenses.*

The numbering system has been developed through convention, and varies slightly from company to company. When you set up your chart, leave room between account numbers so you can add accounts as you need them.

any other mathematical equation, whenever one element of this formula increases or decreases, it affects the other two (see "Debits, Credits, and Double-Entry, next page"). The ability to keep track of this constant relationship between assets, liabilities, and equity is the main advantage of using an accounting system instead of a checkbook (see "Accrual vs. Cash Accounting," below). A checkbook balance does not track liabilities (such as money owed subs and suppliers), so it sometimes shows more equity than there really is. On the other hand, because a checkbook tracks only cash, it may show less than actual equity; receivables (such as money owed by clients) are not included.

Income Statement
ABC Construction Company
December 31, 1999

Revenues:		
Sales	$510,000	
Cost of Sales	383,000	
Gross Profit		**$127,000**
Operating Expenses:		
Interest	$2,300	
Marketing	5,000	
General and Admin.	93,100	
Total Operating Expenses:		**$100,400**
Net Profit (or Loss) before taxes:		**$26,600**

Figure 2. ***An income statement (also called a profit/loss statement or "P-and-L") summarizes all revenue and expenses associated with the operation of a construction company. If the "bottom line" is a positive number, the company earned a net profit (more money came in than went out). A negative number indicates a net loss (more debt was incurred than could be covered by revenue).***

Records and Reports

An accounting system is a method of keeping track of financial transactions, which can then be summarized into reports, or financial statements.

Chart of accounts. Whether you keep track manually or on a computer, the first step in establishing an accounting system is to set up numbered categories, or

Accrual vs. Cash Accounting

The accuracy of accounting information depends in part on when amounts are entered, or posted, to accounts. In the early years of my business, I kept my records on a *cash basis.* In other words, I didn't record income until I actually received a check from a customer. Similarly, I didn't record an expense until I paid a supplier or subcontractor.

But cash accounting, like checkbook accounting, doesn't provide for any way to track money you owe but haven't yet paid, or money you have billed for but haven't yet received. If you receive a couple of payments from customers before you receive bills from vendors, cash accounting makes it appear as if you have more money than you really do.

Accrual basis accounting is the most accurate way of knowing where your business stands. This system recognizes income when a job is completed and billed (but before payment is received), and recognizes expenses when a bill or invoice is received (but before it is paid).

Accrual accounting requires several special accounts (marked with an asterisk in the sample chart of accounts, opposite page). For example, *#120 Accounts Receivable,* holds amounts due from customers until payment is actually made. Similarly, *#220 Accounts Payable* holds amounts due to suppliers and subs until the bills are actually paid.

A typical accrual system would treat the purchase of materials — and subsequent payment for them — with balanced debit and credit entries in four accounts:

- When the bill for the materials arrives, #220 Accounts Payable is *credited* (increased), and #500 Materials is *debited* (increased).
- When the bill is paid, #220 Accounts Payable is *debited* (decreased) and #102 Cash is *credited* (decreased).

Accrual accounting used to be a record-keeping chore, but today's "fill-in-the-blanks" accounting software makes it much easier to get accurate, up-to-date financial information. (Accrual accounting may have tax consequences, so check with a CPA before making the switch.)

— *J.P.*

accounts, in which to record all financial transactions. Accounts are organized into five main groups, according to the kind of information they represent — assets, liabilities, equities, income, and expenses — and the whole list is called a chart of accounts (see Figure 1, page 166).

The more complicated your business is, the more accounts you will have. To keep things simple, the chart shown in Figure 1 includes only the accounts that are necessary to keep accurate records for a small construction company. As your company grows, you can add accounts as you need them.

Income statement. Totals from the income and expense accounts all appear on a report called an income statement (Figure 2, previous page). This statement summarizes all construction revenue (usually called sales), and all expenses (cost of sales). For most small construction companies, sales revenue is usually lumped together into one amount. But if you want to keep track of both new construction and remodeling sales, for example, you could list these separately (you would also need to create separate accounts for each type of work).

For a construction company, there are two types of expenses: the costs of construction and the general operating expenses of running a business. Construction costs, or direct costs, include items such as lumber and subcontractors (which can be traced directly to a particular job) as well as other construction-related costs, such as supervisory time and company vehicle expenses.

General operating expenses, called indirect costs or overhead, include administrative costs (such as office supplies and office rent), marketing expenses (such as the cost of an advertising brochure), and financing costs (such as interest on a line of credit).

On an income statement, the sum of cost of sales and expenses is subtracted from revenue, resulting in the "bottom line" — net profit or loss for the time

Debits, Credits, and Double-Entry

In checkbook accounting, only one "account" changes with each transaction: the checkbook balance, or cash account. The amount is either increased or decreased, depending on whether you make a deposit or write a check.

Debits and credits. Double-entry accounting, however, records every transaction in at least two accounts. An entry in one account is offset by a corresponding entry in another account. Accountants refer to these offsetting entries as debits and credits, two terms that are probably responsible for most of the confusion surrounding double-entry accounting. Unfortunately, the way these terms are used is often the exact opposite of their commonsense meaning. Debits and credits can increase or decrease the amount in an account, depending on what type of account it is. For instance, when you deposit money in your checking account, you increase the balance, which common sense tells you is a credit. But cash is an asset account, so it is increased with a debit. Go figure.

The special meaning of these terms has developed by convention, but the important thing to remember is that credits and debits must always be in balance. For example, let's say you purchase $200 worth of materials. Two accounts are affected: Cash is credited (decreased) and Materials is debited (increased):

#102 Cash Account

	debits	credits
ABC Lumber Co.		$200

#500 Materials Account

	debits	credits
Lumber	$200	

The basic accounting formula (Assets = Liabilities + Equity) is set up so that the total of all debit accounts and all credit accounts is the same. In the sample chart of accounts, Liabilities, Equity, and Income are credit balance accounts that are offset by the debit balance Expense accounts (Direct Costs, Indirect Costs, and Administrative Expenses). If the company is making money, the sum of these accounts appears on one side of the accounting equation as a net credit. This offsets Assets — a debit account — on the other side of the equation. — *J.P.*

period covered by the report. You can prepare an income statement as often as you like, but its accuracy depends on how frequently you bring the numbers in the accounts up to date. My accounting information is stored on computer, and my bookkeeper updates all financial transactions daily (including payroll).

I make an appointment to visit with my money every Saturday morning. Why so often? I work hard, and I want to make sure that all my effort is paying off. My income statement helps me gauge my company's performance, and helps me to predict financial disasters before they happen. For example, I once had a couple of less-than-honest employees who decided to enrich themselves at my expense. They were charging clients for extras and pocketing the money. Had I not been watching material and labor costs on my income statement, I might never have found out about their deception.

There's more to an accounting system than I've been able to cover in this section. If you want to find out more about income statements, balance sheets, and financial ratios, I suggest you read the following books:

- *Accounting and Financial Management for Builders* (NAHB Home Builder Press, 1988; 800/223-2665; 83 pages; $25)
- *Managing a Contracting Business* by Harold Squire (Squire and Associates, 1991; 614/451-4860; 185 pages; $31.50)

By Jack Philbin who counts the money earned each week by two companies — Philbin Construction and Remodeling, and Philbin Home Improvement Specialties. Both are located in Orland Park, Ill.

Planning for Growth

Don't let a surge in business take you by surprise: Use last year's sales to predict this year's volume

Last January, I ran a help-wanted ad for a carpenter, and was amazed at the high quality of the applicants. During the interviews, I also discovered that most of these carpenters were applying to only a few companies. This surprised me a little because, even though I didn't yet have a lot of work lined up, I knew I was going to have my biggest year ever. I also knew that if I waited to hire more help until May and June, when I would be swamped with work, the pickings would be slim. The lack of demand for the highly-qualified carpenters I was interviewing could only mean one thing: Other builders in my area didn't yet know that their volume of business was going to be up over last year.

How did I know so early in the year that my volume would be higher? Most owners of small construction companies simply react to growth. Their annual dollar volume steadily increases because they continually take on more work than they can handle. But a rapid increase in dollar volume is the biggest trap a builder can fall into. Unplanned growth works for a while, but eventually it catches up with you.

I would rather manage my company's growth than simply react to market demand. So I use sales data from past years to predict how much future work I can reasonably expect. The advance notice enables me to plan an increase or decrease in my labor force, to redouble or reduce my marketing efforts, and to better manage my subcontractors.

Revenue Ratio

Construction companies grow in many different ways, each of which has its own pitfalls (see "Growing Pains," page 172). But even if a company stays in the same market doing the same type of work at the same price, planning for increased or decreased volume is crucial. If a company's volume of work increases too rapidly, it becomes difficult to hire enough qualified help to maintain quality. More work also means more management time, and unless you plan for increased supervision, your efficiency on the site will suffer. Similarly, if a company's volume decreases unexpectedly, valuable employees may have to be laid off. A sudden drop in sales also leaves little time to design and implement a mar-

Monthly Volume Comparison

	1995 Revenue	%	1996 Revenue	%	1997 Revenue	%	1998 Revenue	%
Jan	$30,000	8	$35,000	8	$45,000	6	$75,000	8
Feb	25,000	7	30,000	7	40,000	5	50,000	5
Mar	20,000	5	25,000	6	70,000	9	65,000	7
Apr	25,000	7	25,000	6	40,000	5	65,000	7
May	25,000	7	25,000	6	65,000	8	95,000	10
Jun	30,000	8	35,000	8	90,000	12	95,000	10
Jul	60,000	16	40,000	9	80,000	10	100,000	10
Aug	50,000	13	45,000	10	95,000	12	110,000	11
Sep	40,000	11	45,000	10	50,000	6	80,000	8
Oct	25,000	7	30,000	7	70,000	9	90,000	9
Nov	20,000	5	45,000	10	55,000	7	85,000	9
Dec	25,000	7	60,000	14	70,000	9	80,000	8
Total	$375,000		$440,000		$770,000		$990,000	

Figure 1. ***The author uses a spreadsheet to compare monthly and annual sales volume. The percentages show what proportion of annual volume occurs in a given month. The historical percentages can be compared with current sales figures to predict annual volume.***

keting plan that will counteract the downturn.

Fortunately, all of these problems can be avoided by keeping track of monthly sales revenues, then calculating the ratio of monthly sales to total sales volume for the year. The dollar amounts will change from year to year, but the ratio is surprisingly constant. That historical ratio can then be used to predict the volume of future work.

I'm busy year-round, but in Massachusetts, where I live and work, winter is the slow season. So I use the months of January through March to plan for the coming summer and fall. I use sales data gathered in the first few months of the year to predict work volume for the other nine months of the building season.

The more historical data you have, the more accurate your predictions will be. I have been using a spreadsheet to keep close track of monthly sales volume for a number of years now (see Figure 1). This enables me to use averages from several years to predict my total sales volume for the coming year. But you can perform the same calculations based only on your total volume for last year. As an example, let's use the amounts from Figure 1 to see how the system works. (All of these calculations can be done by hand, although a computer spreadsheet is faster and reduces errors.)

January 1997. My annual volume jumped from $440,000 in 1996 to $770,000 in 1997 — just the kind of growth spurt that catches many builders unprepared. The biggest increases in monthly volume for 1997 didn't come, however, until June, July, and August. If I had waited until the summer months to find additional carpenters and to line up a second tier of subcontractors, I would have been in serious trouble.

Fortunately, I was able to predict this increase in volume by using a simple formula:

$$\frac{\text{Monthly Volume}}{\text{Annual Volume}} = \text{Percentage of Annual Volume}$$

Using historical data from 1996, the ratio of January volume to annual volume is 8%:

$$\frac{\$35{,}000}{\$440{,}000} = .08\text{, or } 8\%$$

Leads/Sales Comparison														
		Jan	Feb	Mar	Apr	May	Jun	Jul	Aug	Sep	Oct	Nov	Dec	Total
LEADS	1995	8	22	9	18	10	17	12	10	10	20	20	8	164
	1996	17	5	13	14	12	7	11	7	18	14	9	8	135
	1997	6	6	8	13	10	8	6	5	16	8	11	8	105
	1998	8	15	17	12	14	11	13	12	16	14	16	10	158
BIDS	1995	9	10	5	13	8	7	5	7	7	11	15	8	105
	1996	8	3	10	5	8	7	6	8	7	7	8	8	85
	1997	2	3	4	6	8	3	5	4	4	12	9	8	68
	1998	3	4	7	8	7	2	2	5	4	10	3	8	63
SALES	1995	2	1	2	2	5	3	3	2	4	5	4	4	37
	1996	3	1	3	5	5	2	2	2	4	3	1	6	37
	1997	2	1	4	2	6	0	2	2	2	7	7	3	38
	1998	2	1	3	2	4	0	2	4	0	4	3	4	29

Figure 2. *This spreadsheet keeps track of the number of leads received, the number of proposals made from those leads, and the number of contracts, or sales, actually signed each month. The historical figures can then be compared with the current rate of leads, bids, and sales.*

In January of 1997, I used the figures from 1996 to predict total 1997 volume. In other words, I assumed that all things being equal, the ratio of monthly sales to annual sales would be about the same in 1997 as it was in 1996. Since January 1997 sales were $45,000, I plugged this number into the formula to predict total 1997 volume. The equation is rearranged to solve for the unknown — this year's annual volume:

$$\frac{\$45{,}000}{.08} = \$562{,}500$$

So by the end of January 1997, I already had a good indication that my company would do more work than the year before.

February 1997. I performed the same calculations at the end of February, only this time I averaged the dollar amounts and percentages for both January and February:

$$\frac{\$42{,}500 \text{ (Jan.-Feb. '97 Avg.)}}{.075 \text{ (Jan.-Feb. '96 Avg.)}} = \$566{,}667$$

Again, the result confirmed that I would be doing more business this year than last.

March 1997. The same calculation in March was a real eye-opener. Again I used averages, but this time I discovered I was on pace to nearly double my previous year's volume:

$$\frac{\$51{,}667 \text{ (Jan.-Mar. '97 Avg.)}}{.07 \text{ (Jan.-Mar. '96 Avg.)}} = \$738{,}100$$

The revenue ratio can be used by itself to predict annual sales volume. But it's not infallible. The more historical data you have, the more accurate your predictions will be. Instead of using average percentages for two or three months of a single year, for example, you can use averages from several years.

It's possible, however, that heavy sales in the early part of the year may skew the overall numbers. As a check against this kind of anomaly, I also check my historical record of job leads.

Growing Pains

A sudden increase in work volume is the most common problem for growing construction companies. But any kind of change can spell disaster if builders are caught unprepared. If your company is growing in one of the following ways, be sure to plan for the problems you're likely to encounter.

Change in geographic territory. Expanding the area you work in — even working in an unfamiliar part of town — means increased travel time and expenses for your employees and subcontractors. This will affect the job's budget and schedule. An unfamiliar building inspector may give you a hard time on details you thought were standard. And local suppliers may have higher prices and a delivery schedule that differs from what you expected. The same is true of local subcontractors you may have to use.

Also, the farther a job site is from your base of operations, the more difficult it will be to administrate. Communications will take longer and more misunderstandings will occur. You will also be less able to respond quickly to problems both during construction and after the work is complete.

Change in scope of work. An interior remodeler who takes on a room addition, for example, will have to deal with excavators and concrete subs for the first time. New materials and procedures may also require employee training and increased supervision.

Change in job size. On large jobs, payments are spread out over longer periods of time, creating cash-flow problems. The long delay between rough-in and finish also causes scheduling problems for subcontractors. Scheduling is also a problem on smaller jobs. A small delay in material delivery, or the inability to get your own personnel and subcontractors to the site can seriously upset your plans — and your clients.

Change in source of work. A design-build contractor will need to develop a new set of administrative skills the first time out on an architect-designed project. Having to deal with a third party upsets the familiar flow of communicating directly with the owner. Similarly, working for state and local governments often means working with a third party, and introduces a new set of requirements for documentation and inspections. The same is true of insurance work.

Change in type of client. A contractor accustomed to tight budgets may have trouble adjusting to high-end clients, who often have higher expectations and require more service. Your subcontractors may not be accustomed to the standard of quality required on higher-priced jobs.

Likewise, a contractor who does mostly high-end work may have trouble taking on value-priced jobs. Labor costs, for example, may break the budget because employees are accustomed to working to a higher standard.

— *P.F.*

Tracking Leads

I use a lead sheet to track the number of people who call my company about possible projects. The information on the sheet helps me to decide which jobs to pursue, and which are not worth the effort. To make it easy to count leads, as well as to track the number of leads that progress to proposals and finally to sales, I use a preprinted triplicate form. The pink copy is filed in a folder labeled Leads; the yellow copy, in a folder labeled Proposals. When I eventually sign a contract, I file the white copy in a folder labeled Sales.

At the end of each month, I enter the total leads, proposals, and sales into another spreadsheet (Figure 2). I use this data to double-check my revenue ratios. For example, in January of 1997, I received six leads, for which I submitted two bids that led to two sales. Compared with 1996, these numbers were a little low, but the dollar volume was higher. I took this as a sign that my revenue ratio for January 1997 might be predicting a higher annual volume than was warranted. After all, the dollar value of the two contracts I signed in January could simply have been a little higher than usual. If the number of leads I was getting was lower, larger contract amounts might not make up for the difference and my volume might end up lower than predicted.

February's lead figures confirmed, however, that my revenue ratio was probably correct. I took in six leads, sent out three bids, and signed one job — right on target compared with averages for previous years. In March, I took in fewer leads and sent out fewer proposals than in previous years, but I also signed a higher percentage of contracts. These numbers indicated that if the rest of 1997 followed the same pattern, I would indeed do the $738,000 worth of work my revenue ratio predicted.

Working Smart

Why bother to keep track of all these numbers? Accurately predicting annual volume helps me make smart management decisions concerning personnel (both in the field and in the office) and subcontractors. Instead of getting caught short-handed during the summer of 1997, I hired more carpenters and a part-time bookkeeper before the end of April. Not only did I have my pick of high-quality people, but I had plenty of time to train them. The predicted increase in work volume also prompted me to start looking for backup subs in all trades. When the summer crunch came, I already had commitments from subs who would otherwise have been too busy working for other builders to attend to my jobs.

Knowing how much work my company will be doing also helps me manage my marketing budget. In 1990, for example, I used a large part of my budget to buy a booth at a local home show. Of the leads I got at the show, three ended up as signed contracts, and I more than recouped my marketing money. But early in 1997, my leads were strong, and I already knew that my company would almost double the volume of work performed in 1996. There was no reason for me to spend money on the home show.

My lead sheets also tell me where my leads come from. Over the years, I've discovered that 88% of my work comes from past clients and referrals from past clients. As long as the number of leads I get each month falls within historical totals, I know I don't need to explore new markets. Instead, I concentrate my marketing efforts on past clients. The payoff is clear from the sales volume for 1997 in Figure 1. My business has grown in predictable ways, and very little of the time and money I spend marketing, estimating, and selling is wasted.

By Peter Feinmann, owner of Feinmann Remodeling, an Arlington, Mass., design-build company specializing in kitchens and baths.

Time Card Basics

A well-designed time sheet provides a solid foundation for payroll, billing, job-costing, and more

If you're like most builders, you started small — just you and maybe one person to hold the other end of the board. You were friends, you'd worked together for a while, and you were both on the job site every day, all day. It was easy to keep track of things.

When payday rolled around, you'd tally up the hours (identical except for the day you had a dentist appointment) and submit a labor bill to the owner. A "big" job took maybe a month and a half, and you did only one job at a time.

My, how things change.

You got more work, hired more people, and started running more than one job at a time. You put all your workers on the books. In short, you became an employer. And now you find you can't be on every job every day, all day, and when payday rolls around, it's a major event.

Why You Need Time Sheets

A well-designed, thoroughly completed time sheet won't solve your payroll problems — it may, in fact, increase the paperwork slightly — but it can be a great help. It's a part of the business every employer and employee ought to pay close attention to.

The weekly or biweekly record of hours worked provides a crystal-clear record of every employee's performance. It gives you full documentation for federal and state employment records and cost-plus-labor billing, and makes writing payroll a bit easier.

Consider how many times you have come to the end of even a small job and asked your employees how many hours they spent on it, only to find they can't remember what they did last Monday, how long it took, or even where they were working. Guesswork simply won't do, especially on cost-plus work. There

ABC Construction Company
Time Sheet

Name________________________ Pay Period______________

JOB					
Mon					
Tues					
Wed					
Thu					
Fri					
Sat/Sun					
Hrs. by					
JOB					

JOB					
Mon					
Tues					
Wed					
Thu					
Fri					
Sat/Sun					
Hrs. by					
JOB					

21 Excav/Drainage
22 Demolition
23 Perim.Treat.

33 Concrete
44 Masonry
55 Steel

61 Floor system
62 X-Wall system
63 Roof system
64 I-Walls/Ceiling

71 Roof X-Trim
72 Felt/Roofg

73 X-Trim/sidg
74 FG/VB
75 Rigid foam
76 Ridge vent

81 Windows/X-Drs
82 I-Doors
83 Locksets

91 Strapping
92 Drywall
93 Painting

94 Underlay
95 Flooring
96 I-Trim

110 Cabinets
111 Shelves
112 Built-ins
113 Stair/Rail

155 Elect.
166 Plumbing
167 Heating

171 Misc.
172 Scaffold

G=Gopher
CB=Call Back
Cl=Cleanup
P=Punchlist
X=EXTRA*
M=MILEAGE*

S=Supervise
SV=Site Visit
ES=Estimate
D=Design
BK=Books
MTG=Meeting

* Add "X" to number if work is an EXTRA. Explain EXTRA work & MILEAGE on back of sheet.

When job categories are included on a time card, your employees can easily record the time spent on particular tasks. The entry of "5/64" on Monday, for example, indicates that five hours were spent on interior partitions at the Smith job.

are plenty of owners who get a kick out of keeping track of your workers' hours, and taking you to task if your tallies don't match.

The Well-Designed Time Sheet

A well-designed time sheet can provide a wealth of information to help you with scheduling, estimating, change orders, allowance pricing, and personnel-evaluation. The time sheet should be designed to give you the kinds of information you want it to provide. But don't overdo it. Keep in mind the time it will take you to read it, and the time and effort it takes your employees to fill it in.

The time sheet I use (opposite page) may not exactly fit your needs, but will illustrate the principles involved. The size should be convenient. Crew members should be able to carry them in their shirt pockets. (This may seem silly, but your employees won't use a time sheet consistently if they don't carry it.) Mine is letter-size, folds nicely to about 2x4 inches, and files away neatly in a manila folder.

Color makes a difference, too. Something other than white is best to easily distinguish labor records from the other paperwork. I use green, and on those all-too-frequent occasions when someone misplaces a time sheet, it's a lot easier to find.

A space for the employee's name and the dates of the pay period are at the top. I suggest you fill in this part yourself; even the most meticulous employee will forget to, as often as not. The rest of the top half has a list of the days of the week, their dates, and columns for job names and hours worked. This is all you need in order to know who worked where and for how long.

Alphabet Soup

But what if you want to know more? The important thing is to keep it simple. An employee who is skilled at working with wood isn't necessarily good at working with its more refined form — paper. How, then, do you solve the problem of creating a time sheet that is detailed but doesn't require a college education and fine penmanship to complete?

The time sheets I use tell me not only who worked where and for how long, but what they were doing. Before I came up with this, I used to ask the crew to summarize the day's activities. What I got was alphabet soup.

Aside from not being able to read the writing, I found that not everyone categorized the work in the same way. I got things like "Smith job, 8 hrs., framing and vents." Framing what? The roof? Walls? Floors? And what vents? Soffit? Ridge? Gable? Dryer vent?

A good solution is to list job categories and phases. Have them numbered and listed at the bottom of the sheet. A simple number designates a particular activity, and the same number is used by everybody. The list is arranged according to the way a job usually progresses. There are still some areas that overlap, but the bases are covered.

A typical entry — "5/64" — tells me that five hours were spent on interior partitions. The "X" for extras helps me keep track of work that either was priced on allowance or is being done in addition to what was called for in the contract. For instance, "4/110X" means four hours were spent installing cabinets that were priced on allowance.

The last twelve categories, designated by letter, are mainly for me. (I keep a time sheet, too.) They help me keep track of how much time I spend off site, and help me evaluate efficiency and plan for future jobs. How many of us can pinpoint within eight or ten hours how much time is spent cleaning up? And who's doing the cleanup — the lower-wage laborers or the highly paid carpenters?

"Gopher" is another telling item. I think we are all surprised at how much time is spent running to the supplier for materials. With this time sheet, I am alerted to an excess of errand time, and can discuss with my foremen ways to manage the job more efficiently.

Of course, even a well-designed time sheet won't work for you if it isn't properly used. Make sure your workers fill in their time sheets daily. Memory fades quickly when you're engaged in similar activities every day, and all the data in the world won't help a bit if it's incorrect.

Finally, keep a time sheet yourself. For one thing, it sets an example. Also, you might be surprised to discover how you spend your time, and that you might want to use it differently.

—Sal Alfano

Chapter 10

The Art of Delegation

Evolution and Revolution:

Three Stages of Growth for Construction Companies

To successfully "grow" your business, understand the stages, then identify — and avoid — the pitfalls

Builders new to the business imagine that success lies just around the corner. They believe that a few years of hard work, combined with an honest approach and a continuous stream of jobs bid at 10% overhead and 5% profit, will turn their dreams into reality. More experienced builders know, however, that the road to success is full of potholes big enough to sink the company, together with the builder and his or her dreams.

After ten years as a business consultant working exclusively with builders, remodelers, and their subs, I have begun to see patterns common to both successful and unsuccessful companies. A while back, I reread an article from the *Harvard Business Review* called "The Five Stages of Small Business Growth" (May/June 1983), and it inspired me to define the stages of growth for small construction companies. In the process, I identified those patterns and qualities most likely to predict success or failure.

Evolution vs. Revolution

My hypothesis is this: Just as a baby first crawls, then walks, and finally runs, a typical building company passes through three distinct stages of growth. The stages are predictable, and while circumstances may vary from company to company, the problems encountered along the way are of the same type. Success at any stage depends on mastery of critical issues and careful navigation through the danger zones between one stage and the next.

I think of the movement through the stages of growth as a process of *evolution* followed by *revolution*. A company "evolves" as it learns to manage the critical issues of one stage. At first, everything runs more smoothly; efficiency and productivity rise and business improves.

Continued evolution, however, usually propels the company to the next stage. I call this a "revolution," because it is dangerous, terrifying, and often happens suddenly. During a revolution, old systems no longer work as planned, cash flow is always tight, crisis management rules the day, and the company owner works harder with less success.

Luckily, with a little planning and foresight, evolution and revolution can be controlled and predicted. The result is a successful company operating at optimum levels.

BILL ROBINSON

Stage One: One-Man Band

Although hybrids exist, most stage-one construction companies follow a predictable growth path. Stage-one companies usually have only one job in progress at a time, and stage-one owners do it all — bid the job, order the materials, produce the work, pay the bills, and keep the books. Typical stage-one owners work out of a home office and the back of a truck; their hours are long and their vacations infrequent.

To be successful, stage-one companies must overcome the five obstacles that most commonly lead the revolution to stage two:

1. Technical expertise. If you do nothing else to prepare for running your own company, learn as much as you can about your trade and about the proper use of all commonly used tools. Learn to read blueprints and calculate takeoff quantities, and become knowledgeable about contracts and specifications. Watch companies you respect closely to see how they run their job sites and their offices. Evaluate the quality of their work, and begin to track how long it takes you to produce to the same level.

2. Time management. Stage-one owners commonly work 60- to 70-hour weeks, so they must learn to schedule critical tasks for times when they are most alert. Maintain a weekly time card to track how you spend your time. When you decide to hire your first employee, this record will tell you where you need the most help.

Schedule time each week for those tasks you don't enjoy, such as filing or bookkeeping. Don't skip that time — you must understand the basic administrative functions at stage one before you can safely delegate them at stage two. Otherwise, you will have no way to judge your employees' performance.

3. Basic bookkeeping. Owners of successful companies of any size know and understand their numbers. As your company grows, an employee will eventually handle the bookkeeping, but unless you understand the process, you will leave an essential part of your business at the mercy of another. Practice simple cash accounting, balance your checkbook every month, and learn how to read an income statement. Learn the difference between direct costs and overhead, and track them separately.

4. Sales and marketing. Your current clients are the source of a strong referral base. Make only promises you can keep, then keep them — there is no better marketing technique. Be honest, and discuss difficult issues in a forthright and timely manner. Ask for letters of reference, and put them in a presentation folder together with photographs of good examples of your work. Keep a simple list of everyone you've worked for, the type of project, and the lead source. Evaluate what types of projects you do best and most profitably, and what types of clients you prefer to work with. Learn to say "no" to the others.

5. Save money. Spend no dime before its time. Hoard your money, your tools and vehicles, and your time, then evaluate each demand on these resources to determine if it meets your long-term goals.

When the great recession of 1991 hit California, builders who were flush in the '80s couldn't unload their ski boats and jet skis fast enough. Many went under because they failed to preserve their capital. To avoid this fate, put aside a small percentage of each dollar you receive until you have a savings account equal to about 10% of your annual volume. If you plan to grow to stage two, increase cash reserves to about 15%.

Stage-One Pitfalls

If your savings account has grown from profits of well-run jobs, if your phone is still ringing with new and returning clients, and if you still don't have enough time to handle all the demands on you, you're on the way to stage two. But there are still a couple of obstacles that can trip you up.

Underestimating labor productivity. This is the greatest danger between stage one and two. Stage-one builders often estimate employee labor at the same rate of productivity that they themselves work at on site. No matter how experienced the carpenters you hire are, no one will ever approach your speed and efficiency. To allow for this, you must increase labor estimates by 33% to 50%, depending on your circumstances.

Crisis mentality. The overworked stage-one builder never has time enough to plan properly, and runs around constantly putting out fires caused by lack of foresight. Working "under siege" like this results in late and over-budget projects, which can delay moving onward to stage two; worse, it can put you out of business. To break this pattern, set aside a certain part of your week, perhaps Saturday morning, to plan for the next week. Make planning a priority, and never miss a scheduled planning session.

Stage Two: Letting Go

If you perform well in stage one, revolution will propel you to stage two. During stage two, the company office is usually moved out of the owner's home and the company begins to take on more than one job at a time. Stage-two company owners begin to delegate certain

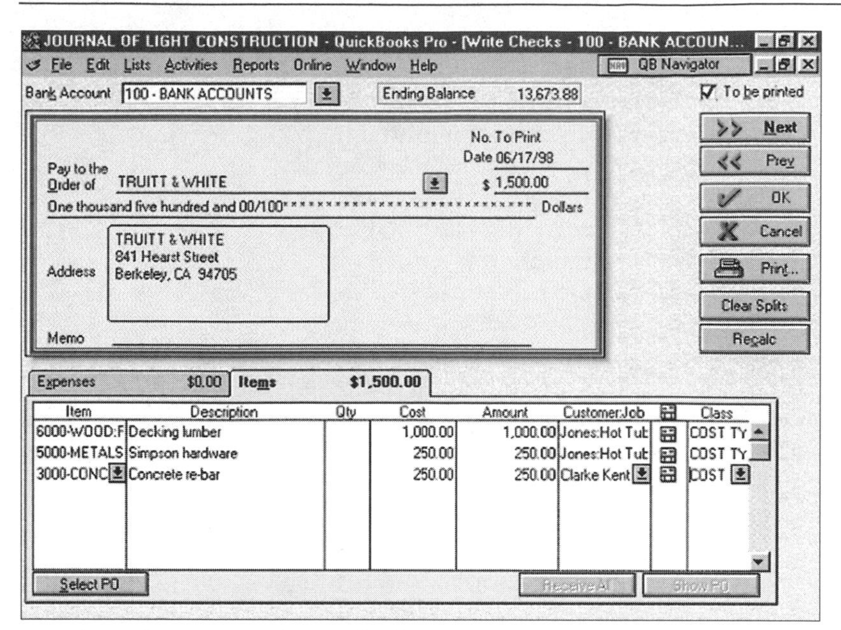

If you're ready to computerize your bookkeeping, simple job-costing and accounting software is a good place to start.

tasks, often hiring a part-time bookkeeper to work in the office and a laborer or helper to work on site. All of this increases both overhead and risk.

For continued success, stage-two builders should focus on the following systems:

1. Computerized job-costing and accounting. Regardless of volume, companies that choose to grow must eventually invest in a computer and computerized bookkeeping system. Simple software, such as QuickBooks Pro, is a good place to start, because it enables the owner to track both accounting and job-cost data. Builders who are comfortable with computers and who intend to grow to stage three might want to invest in a more sophisticated integrated construction accounting and estimating program now, and cut their conversion costs in half.

2. Written job descriptions. The owner who begins to delegate at stage two must decide which work is to be done by employees, what the standard of quality is for that work, how long it takes to do, and when it should be done. This information should be incorporated into written job descriptions appropriate to the functions to be performed, not to the person currently performing them.

3. Sound contracts. As your company grows, risk also increases, especially around common misunderstandings with clients, architects, subs, and employees. Prepare simple, clear contracts for the work you do, and review them with an attorney. Also write simple guidelines for employee hiring, firing, and review, and make them part of the employee file.

4. Standardized estimating. Because a larger company requires a larger volume, estimating must be more efficient. Preparing standard forms is a good first step. These can be as simple as photocopied checklists, so that no phase of work is forgotten; or as sophisticated as integrated computer programs, which itemize the work in great detail. By comparing actual and estimated costs, you can continually refine the accuracy of your labor estimates.

Stage-Two Dangers

By the time a company reaches stage two, profitability is predictable, work is backlogged for a few months, the work force is stable, and the phone is still ringing. Successful evolution at stage two leads to the inevitable revolution and progression to stage three, but greater dangers lie in the transition. As a stage-two company adds employees, overhead goes up; this increases the pressure on the owner to sell and produce more jobs while protecting the bottom line.

Here are some of the greatest obstacles to the natural progression to stage three:

Inefficient delegation. A stage-three company must run like a well-oiled machine. To succeed at stage three, a stage-two owner must be careful to delegate work without duplicating effort. The flow of information must be smooth and efficient.

To ensure that delegated tasks work the way you intend, track each step in the performance of each task. (Flowcharting software makes this easy.) When you have completely defined the task, give the procedure to the person responsible for its completion for a "test drive." After revisions, use this procedure unchanged for at least three months so that an efficient routine develops. (Alternatively, ask the person responsible to define each step in the process, review and revise it yourself, then publish it for testing.)

Low net profit. As their companies grow, many builders imagine that they will be able to make up in volume what they lack in profitability. To be sure, increased volume solves the problem of under-used overhead, but often it creates other, greater problems.

The most important number on the income statement is net profit, not volume. Gross profit margin must be sufficient to cover the increased overhead required by stage-two and stage-three companies, and still leave sufficient net profit to compensate for the greater degree of risk.

Stage Three: Focus on Planning

Stage-three builders delegate all functions, except for a small portion of sales. Typical stage-three builders maintain a large network of job sources and often negotiate the final contract, while employees estimate the job and define the scope of work. An office manager oversees all administrative tasks, while project managers act as liaisons between the estimators and job-site foremen.

To remain successful, stage-three builders should focus on the following:

1. Business plan. At this point in the company's development, planning takes center stage. The organization, heavier with increased overhead, must follow a road map to maintain profitability. Beginning stage-three companies might develop a two-year plan; more sophisticated companies plan five years ahead. A well-conceived business plan defines sources of income, gross profit margin, fixed versus variable overhead, and break-even volume. Such strategies, when defined in a plan, have a better chance of achieving the desired net profit.

2. Financial analysis. After developing a clear understanding of the relationship between gross volume, gross profit margin, net profit, and owner's draw, the stage-three company owner turns to an analysis of the balance sheet. Instead of monitoring the business directly, the owner uses standard ratios and evaluates trends to determine the health of the business.

3. Organizational chart. To maintain a stable work force, successful stage-three companies need a written organizational chart that illustrates the hierarchy of decision-making in the company. The chart serves to promote an understanding of the roles played by each employee as well as a sense of shared commitment.

4. Policy and procedures manual. Policies define the goals in all vital areas of the company; procedures are the steps required to implement any given policy. Written policies ensure that the company's goals and objectives are known and understood by all employees; written procedures define clear steps for meeting policy goals. Stage-three business owners should develop policies and let those responsible for implementing them write the procedures. For example, a policy might state that "cash reserves shall be equal to 10% of projected annual gross volume." The controller would then develop procedures that implement this policy through accounts receivable, accounts payable, and payroll processing.

5. Line of credit. A stage-three business needs a line of credit above and beyond the 10% or 15% liquid cash reserves. This allows the business owner to develop the business by investing in personnel, training, and equipment as strategic planning dictates. In addition, a line of credit enables the company to ride out unforeseen economic downturns. Until the profitability of the company is predictable, however, and actual job costs come within 1% of the estimated costs, lines of credit should not be used to finance additional business growth.

The Final Barriers

The greatest obstacles to the success of a stage-three company are old age and lack of an exit strategy.

Old age. Often, ten or fifteen years of hard work passes before an owner can bask in the fruits of his or her labors. If the owner has failed to put money aside for retirement during his or her 20s and 30s, when "the miracle of compound interest" can work its magic, even a healthy net profit may not accumulate capital quickly enough to provide for retirement at age 60 or 65. It is essential to provide for your future in your youth.

Exit strategy. Busy owners of stage-three companies typically fail to plan for a way to get out of the business. No matter how much he or she loves the work, at some point even the most satisfied company owner looks for relief from the responsibility of managing a large company. The truly successful owner plans for such a possibility well in advance.

Some rely on successful middle managers, whose salaries are tied to company profitability, to run the company while the owner gradually withdraws from management. In other cases, the company can be run by a younger sibling or child. Or, as is the case of some of my farsighted clients, the owners will put enough of the profits of the business into secure investments, such as real estate or mutual funds, that they can live happily on the resulting dividends.

Whichever stage you find your company at currently, future progress and success depends on you as owner. Your vision brought the company into being; your clear and continued attention to the systems necessary for success at each stage will propel the company onward.

By Judith Miller, a construction consultant in Oakland, Calif., who counsels builders on accounting, financial management, computerization, and office procedures.

Hanging Up Your Tool Belt

How to survive the two toughest stages in the growth of your remodeling business

Remodeling companies are like children. They have their own personalities, idiosyncrasies, growing pains, and stages. Just as a toddler's or teenager's behavior is predictable, so too are the stages of your company's growth. Knowing that you're going through a difficult transition — and that it's perfectly normal — helps a little, but getting some advice on how others have gotten through it is even better.

Two very common stages of business growth are (1) when it's time to hang up your tool belt, and (2) when you need to hire a salesperson or production manager. Be aware that these transitions are dangerous; many remodelers end up losing their businesses at just these points.

Stage One: Time To Hang Up the Tool Belt

Realizing it's time to give up swinging a hammer is one of the earliest and most difficult transitions. Let's say you're small; you do about $100,000 to $200,000 of volume a year. You still work a significant number of hours in the field with a tool belt on. But you want out. Your body is beginning to send you the message that it's a limited, not a limitless, resource. You've hit the upper limits of how much work you can sell as well as how much money you can take home, because there are only so many hours in the day. You want to expand and hire others to do the physical part while you supervise and sell. But it's not that easy when you look at the numbers. The biggest barrier is finding the money for your salary once you're no longer working as a carpenter and crew boss.

First you need to assess your strengths and weaknesses in light of the four major focuses of any remodeling company: marketing, sales, production, and management.

Marketing. If the "It's time to hang up my tool belt" scenario fits you, your company has probably needed about $150,000 of work a year to run smoothly. Those jobs haven't been brought in by any organized marketing effort, but rather by referral from one client to the next. Satisfied customers do your marketing for you.

Selling. Since you work diligently (after all, it's your own business and reputation that are at stake), your services are a very good buy for the consumer. You're personable, capable, conscientious. You work from home, which keeps your overhead very low. If you underestimate the labor costs on a job, you simply work longer hours to make up for it. Thus, you haven't needed real selling skills. Between your low price and high praise from former customers, you are very likely to sell 75% of the jobs you price.

Production. Production is your strong point. You are both production supervisor and lead carpenter on your jobs. Since you also bid projects and sell them, you are in on discussions with clients from the beginning. This keeps communications straight.

Business management. This may be your Achilles' heel. You may not know all the local, state, and federal regulations that affect you. Your contracts are simple one-page proposals purchased ready-made, and you carry change orders around in your head. However, success is stalking you. Your good reputation is beginning to pull in more inquiries than you can handle in either sales or production.

Replace Yourself in the Field

You have two options. The first is relatively uncomplicated: you can refuse to grow. The good news is that you can raise your prices, hand pick the very best of the leads, and let the others fall to the wayside. The bad news is that your fortunes depend on your good health and ability to continue doing physically demanding work.

The second option is to ride the growth wave. This will eventually help you to hang up your tool belt, but it raises the stakes and much of what you'll be doing will be risky and unfamiliar. Here are some of the things you'll want to consider, along with their pitfalls:

Step 1. First you'll have to replace yourself in the field. This is probably your first big hiring decision, so take your time. What you're looking for is a skilled lead carpenter. You'll phase yourself out of the field over six months to a year, which will give you a chance to thoroughly train your new hire.

Pitfalls. There are two major errors to avoid here. First, don't hire a lead carpenter who has technical knowledge, but no managerial skills. If you do, you'll be creating a monster. You'll get a carpenter who, instead of being independent, is in constant need of your help. Second, be aware of how hard it can be to turn over the reins to someone else. The art of delegation is a fine one, but you can't be successful in business without learning it. And you might as well learn it with your first major hire.

This means carefully setting goals with your employee and giving him some leeway in achieving them. You have to give your new hire permission to succeed and to fail as well. Since you're doing the training and monitoring the progress, things can't go too awry.

Step 2. As you move out of the field, your salary becomes overhead or part of the cost of sales; when you were still working with your tools it was a direct job cost. In order for the company to carry you in overhead, your volume will have to increase, and this work needs to be done at an adequate markup.

Here's a "for instance." Let's say you hope to do $300,000 in volume. You want to pay yourself $30,000 and end up with a 10% ($30,000) net profit. Your other overhead is very low at 10% ($30,000). Therefore, you need 30% ($90,000) gross profit, and that converts to a 43% markup on your hard costs (in this case, $210,000).

Pitfalls. Again, there are two major pitfalls. First, you may need to sharpen your labor estimating skills. In the past, it was easy enough to work extra hours without pay if your estimate was low. Now you must pay an employee, and that can throw a huge wrench into your financial plans. As a precaution, consider taking a crash course in estimating, buying some manuals, and adding some extra contingency money to your bids

INTERVIEW

Staffing For Growth

To get a first-hand account of what kinds of systems and procedures keep a growing company functioning smoothly, we talked to Kelley Hale, of El Cerrito, Calif. Hale runs a high-end residential remodeling company, which successfully doubled its business volume in 1991 from $600,000 to $1.2 million, and went from five to eleven employees.

JLC: *How fast has your company grown?*
Hale: In January of 1991, we had four major remodeling jobs, worth a total of about $600,000, plus one smaller job worth about $40,000, come in all at once. That meant that we would have to complete our normal year's volume in half a year's time. As I signed the contracts for all these jobs, I realized I was signing commitments to make my company grow.

JLC: *How did you staff all these jobs?*
Hale: I was able to spread the starting dates for the jobs over a five-week period. This gave me time for hiring. We were fortunate to find some really good people, partly, because the economy was slow and there were some good people out of work. We hired two new foremen and made a foreman out of our lead carpenter, who had been working with us for nine years. So, including my original foreman (my first employee, Mike), this gave us four foremen — one for each major job.

JLC: *Hiring the right kind of person to work on a remodeling job isn't easy. What kinds of qualities do you look for?*
Hale: The hard part is finding people who have a good attitude— workers who can convey respect for the owner's belongings and sympathy for the difficulty the owners face when their house is being torn up. I look first for that. If the construction skills are not fully developed, they can come later.

JLC: *That must be hard to interview for.*
Hale: I talk to people for a long time and usually have them back for a second interview to discuss some of the things we miss the first time through. I don't conduct the typical interviewer/ interviewee conversation, since people will respond with what they think you want to hear. Instead we walk around our shop and talk about a new tool or some different types of moldings, or whatever they seem interested in. You can tell if somebody knows what they're talking about — OSB, tools, what have you — and you get them to open up.

I also let people know up front that I'm looking for a long-term commitment. Once people realize you are sincere about that, their attitudes start to change. They see that you are serious.

JLC: *With four or more jobs going, you can't be at any one site for much time. How do you delegate?*
Hale: I'm learning to give the people I hire the space to do the best work they can. Because we've grown so quickly, it's forced me to let go—with good results.

But even the best employees can perform well only in a framework they understand. There is nothing worse than being the foreman on a job and not knowing, for instance, where exactly you are expected to get materials or additional help. So I'm trying to give people some clear procedures and schedules to work with.

JLC: *How do you develop those procedures?*
Hale: Scheduling is an important one, of course, so everyone will know what's expected. We use the Master Builder software package, which allows us to derive our schedule directly from our initial estimate of the job. One copy goes to the foreman and one goes to the owner. We update it as often as we feel is necessary or as the owner requests.

If something starts to fall behind, the foremen and I will figure out why — was this a realistic schedule from the start, or is there a real problem? — and try to fix it.

To order materials, we use purchase orders. To avoid delays, we now have a full-time driver just delivering material and making sure no one needs to run to the store. It's deadly to have to pay a carpenter to run to the lumberyard. So the driver really helps keep the materials flowing efficiently.

The driver also helps serve as a conduit — he's the everyday physical link between the company's different parts. He comes to my office in the morning to pick up messages and a list of purchase orders, such as materials that were not delivered with the main load or special-order items.

The driver has a pager and everybody on the job has that pager number. The driver calls every job at just after 7:00 in the morning to see if that job needs any tools or materials, and he routes himself accordingly. He also shuttles time cards and runs debris to the recycling center and the dump.

If he gets done early, there is always a job that needs a laborer for the remainder of the day. There's never a shortage of that somehow.

The driver is really a very important part of the whole job. It's not a high-paying position, but it is a job with a lot of responsibility.

(continued on next page)

INTERVIEW (continued)

JLC: *Do you have daily meetings with your foremen?*
Hale: Years ago we did that, but it cost too much to pay the people to drive from the office to their jobs after the meetings. So now I meet just once a week with each foreman to go over costs, scheduling, and other details.

We also talk about the customers and how they're coping. It's easy to get wrapped up in the nuts and bolts of construction and ignore your customers. So I encourage my foremen to stay focused on keeping people happy and keeping them informed. I also tell them to keep an eye out for any bad reactions to the progress of the job. That's where the sensitivity to the client comes in. We need to watch for those small shifts in attitude that indicate a customer is growing dissatisfied with the job—that he didn't like what somebody said or the way something looks.

We set up a job phone and a job mailbox at every job so we can always reach each other. This helps move information between me and the site—invoicing, change orders, and that sort of thing. I also developed an index card file to track which tools and which people are on which jobs. Each job has a tabbed section that has cards for each employee and each tool on that job, so that I can see exactly where everything and everybody is.

JLC: *What do you enjoy most about seeing your business grow?*
Hale: Trying to keep four or five jobs going and making sure every client we have is pleased with our work.

I try to talk to every client every day. When I honestly feel that we have pleased those people as much as if we were doing their job only, that makes me feel good and like we really are doing something right. Because without our customers we have no work. They are where it all comes from. I try to pass that on to our employees. I don't pay them, our customers pay them. That is where their livelihood comes from. That is the bottom-line recognition.

until your range of accuracy on labor is within 1% to 3%.

Second, selling jobs at a 43% markup is certainly not as easy as selling jobs where you subsidized labor overruns and marked up perhaps 15% to 20%. You now need some real selling skills. You have to be able to convince the potential buyer that buying from your company is a good decision, that you are reliable, pleasant to work with, and deliver excellent craftsmanship.

Many remodelers have trouble convincing themselves that they are worth the increased charges. But this is the first step to convincing others. In fact, your overhead will continue to go up as a percentage of your sales volume as you get larger in remodeling, so you might as well get used to it now.

Step 3. Because you need to increase your volume, you should start doing some simple marketing like using site signs, sending "thank you" notes for every referral, staying in touch with former clients, printing up fliers and brochures, and doing some home shows.

Pitfalls. Effective marketing — the kind that produces quality leads inexpensively — is a year-round task. If you wait until you need your next job to do this marketing, you'll be pushed into advertising. Advertising produces lower quality leads at a higher cost.

Step 4. As your company grows, office systems, bookkeeping, contracts, and job costing reports all become more crucial. The major difference between a $150,000 company, a $500,000 company, and a $1 million company comes down to increased systemization. This helps others carry out your vision, and allows you to better predict your ability to deliver and achieve your goals.

Pitfalls. Production people like you hate paperwork; real work is done on the job site. Moving from the field to the office can be a difficult adjustment, but the sooner you understand that you make your money in remodeling with a pencil rather than a hammer, the better off you'll be.

Step 5. Communication becomes increasingly important. Where once you sold the job and then delivered it, you now will sell and someone else will produce it.

Pitfalls. Immediately, this requires more complete plans and clearer specifications. Without them, you'll end up spending much of your time straightening out errors and answering questions.

This important transition of leaving field work is usually gradual for the remodeler. Although you can keep your business life fairly simple at this stage, it's crucial that you plan carefully and stay on top of it since each future stage will be more complex and the financial ante will be higher.

This is another fateful moment in the growth of a remodeling business. Let's say that your remodeling company is selling and producing about $500,000 in projects. You wear all three major hats: You're the top (and only) salesperson, the production supervisor, and the administrator. You probably have a part-time bookkeeper or spouse who pitches in to help. But you're still beat. Your week is 65 to 75 hours long. You're late doing everything. Quality is slipping, but not because you don't care. It's because you can't be everywhere and do everything the company needs.

You are ready to hire your first management employee who will take over either production (the actual building) or your selling duties. By now, the experience that you've had hiring and delegating to production employees will be of immense help in learning to shift a major portion of your workload to someone else.

Stage Two: Making a Good Hire

Your new salesperson or production manager should be able to fully take over all sales or production in a $500,000 company. In general, a good, full-line, remodeling salesperson should be able to sell $600,000 of volume, and a good production manager should be able to handle $600,000 to $700,000 of work as a traditional superintendent. If the company uses well-trained lead carpenters who earn bonuses based on job profitability, a sharp production manager should be able to oversee as much as $1.2 million.

Here are some of the steps and precautions that will help get you there:

Step 1. Make sure your new salesperson or production manager is an A+ employee. No remodeling company can survive for very long if either sales or production is crippled by a bad hire.

If possible, look for a remodeler (with strengths in production or sales) who is leaving his own business. Former remodelers have the advantage of understanding the entire business.

Pitfalls. Even if you make the perfect hire, your new employee will still require a lot of training in the way your company does things. This means that for awhile you will be busier than before you hired him. For the first month this training should be very intense. For three months consider that employee probationary; keep up the training and give him lots of feedback. But remember: you probably won't think he's doing the job as well as you did it.

Step 2. Although you're turning over this phase of your job to the new employee, you're not turning over all the control of it. You'll want to monitor his work, and that means much more documentation, which may be a change from the seat-of-the-pants methods you're used to. You didn't have to answer to anyone. But the new employee has to answer to you.

Pitfalls. Taking over part of the boss's job is an unenviable task. Write out a clear job description for your new employee. That will help you clarify just what you are turning over, and provide the new salesperson or production manager with a road map to follow.

Step 3. Do some simple budgeting to assure yourself that you can pay this second management person (you are the first). Will your current markup at your target volume cover your overhead and provide a net profit for your company? If not, you will either have to raise the volume or the markup or both. Either that or you'll have to find a way to reduce costs.

Pitfalls. At this stage it's crucial that you abandon the "I'm only providing a job for myself" business mentality. You owe it to your business and to your employees to make a net profit that you can invest in the future and use to bridge cash shortfalls. Quite simply, you have to replace seat-of-the-pants management with good future planning.

Step 4. You will also need a strategy to develop additional volume. Budget for simple marketing that will generate enough leads to produce the extra work. That marketing needs to continue throughout the year even if you reach your target number of leads. You'll also need to set up simple ways of tracking the marketing. By keeping data on number of leads, source of leads, lead costs, and sales costs you'll be able to budget better and market smarter.

Pitfalls. As your marketing increases the number of leads coming in, it's easy to treat these leads with equal attention. Learn to qualify leads so that your time is spent on the ones that are likely to bring in work.

Step 5. You may remain extremely busy because you are not using your time as efficiently as you could. For two weeks keep a time card of all you do; break it down into 15-minute increments. Then analyze that list and find someone else to do anything that can be done by a person who makes $15 an hour or less. Thus drafting, bookkeeping, running to the lumberyard, typing a contract, etc. should all be farmed out to employees or freelancers.

Pitfalls. This not only requires good delegation skills but may also mean that you have to give up some of the things you've always reserved for yourself because you really like doing them.

Step 6. At $500,000 you'll probably have a number of field employees and a full time bookkeeper/secretary/assistant. Set a goal of no more than one field employee per $100,000 in volume and work to make that output higher every year.

Pitfalls. Production will ultimately be the make-it-or-break-it part of your business. Assuring good client relations and a well-crafted product is ultimately the hardest part of remodeling and should be looked on as the part of the business that all other parts serve. Consider giving your lead carpenters a performance bonus based on how their labor costs match those in the estimate. Create a full loop where everyone, including carpenters, helps to feed data into estimating, and then track those estimates against actual costs.

Step 7. Also plan to invite a computer into your business life. If you are running your business properly, you are producing more and more data on lead production, lead cost, job costs, production output, sales goals, etc. The earlier you computerize, the easier the transition from paper to computer will be.

Pitfalls. Net profit shouldn't go into your pocket (although it's tempting). It should be used as seed money to help your company grow. Switching to computer is an excellent example of spending money and time now — without immediate return — in order to reap later benefits.

When you are inside your company riding the growth wave and trying to cope, the changes can come quickly and seem almost random. But from outside they are predictable and the relationship between them is easily seen.

"Growing" your company is never easy. But if you plan carefully, you'll gain the necessary management experience as the company increases its volume. Each new stage in the life of your company is a challenge that can prepare you for even greater ones down the road.

By Linda W. Case, president of Remodelers Advantage, in Silver Spring, Md.

Working Smarter with Lead Carpenters

Reduce overhead and increase efficiency with this job management system

In a small remodeling company that has just one job going at a time, the owner can keep track of everything. But when the business grows and two or three projects are underway at once, the job of assigning personnel, coordinating subs, and ordering materials for multiple locations becomes more than one person can handle. The owner's time is soon consumed with running from job to job to make certain instructions are being followed, attending all site meetings, and overseeing every decision, no matter how small. Nights and weekends are spent meeting prospective customers and doing estimates; business becomes life, and there's little time left over for personal or family time.

If your typical workweek fits that description, introducing a lead carpenter system into your company could lessen your work load, increase your efficiency, and free up your time. Under this concept, projects are managed from the site by a lead carpenter who organizes the job, schedules and supervises the subs, orders materials, meets with the customer, and performs most of the carpentry work.

Lead Carpenter, Not Foreman

Traditionally, construction companies are organized around carpenters who rotate through a job according to their specialty — foundation forming, framing, finish trim, and so on. In each case, however, the carpenters rely on a foreman or production manager to coordinate the job. This person typically manages three or four jobs simultaneously and does no physical work; instead, he or she is charged with getting materials to the job site, assigning personnel to projects, scheduling subs, and other management tasks.

The lead carpenter system breaks with tradition, placing direct responsibility for job-site management with a working supervisor. For remodeling jobs that exceed $750,000, you may need a full-time, on-site manager; but for most smaller remodeling projects, the cost of having a foreman on site adds unnecessarily to the cost of the job.

I discovered the lead carpenter system when I closed my own contracting business in 1988 and went to work for Hopkins & Porter, a remodeling company in

Lead Carpenter Certification

The National Association of the Remodeling Industry (NARI, 4900 Seminary Rd., Suite 320, Alexandria, VA 22311; 800/966-7601) has developed a certification program for lead carpenters. Applicants must first complete an application, or Qualification Matrix, to show that they have at least five years of continuous work in the remodeling industry, two of which must be as a lead carpenter. The application also includes questions about technical knowledge, community service, and employment background. In addition, applicants must submit two letters of reference from their employer, a NARI Certified Remodeler (CR) or Certified Remodeler Specialist (CRS), or from past clients.

The second part of the certification process requires successful completion of a one-day written examination on a variety of subjects ranging from business management, construction law, and job-site safety to interior finishes, roofing and siding, and mechanical systems. The NARI Certification Board reviews the applicant's exam score and Qualification Matrix before granting certification.

NARI will provide a list of study materials for the exam and will assist applicants in starting or joining a local study group to prepare for the exam. Fees for application materials and the exam are $285 for NARI members and $400 for nonmembers. For annual recertification, CLCs must participate in continuing education and be active in remodeling-industry-related activities.

the Washington, D.C., area. I now work for them as a production manager, but rather than handling the daily operations of three or four projects, I oversee as many as ten lead carpenters, leaving daily responsibilities with them. This section lays out the basic principles of the lead carpenter system. Our company has been fine-tuning the system for 15 years, and — like us — you'll want to tailor the system to your company and personality.

Benefits

The lead carpenter concept introduces a new management style that has many advantages:

Better supervision. Jobs run more smoothly when a lead carpenter handles the day-to-day details. Even the smallest of remodeling projects involves a complex process — there are materials to order, subs to schedule, and helpers to supervise, as well as unforeseen interruptions and delays to work around and unexpected structural problems to investigate. Multiply this by three or four simultaneous jobs, and the number of decisions to be made and problems to be solved can be overwhelming. A lead carpenter, however, can identify and correct problems as they arise, because he or she is on site every day, has a thorough knowledge of the plans, and has the authority to make decisions.

While I was still a lead carpenter, for example, I managed the construction of a two-story addition for a handicapped man who had to be able to move his wheelchair between the old and new building without facing any impediments. When I compared the prints with the actual conditions, I noticed there was a difference in elevations that would have created a problem at the transition where old and new flooring met. I adjusted the framing accordingly, and rechecked the elevations after the oak floor went down. The problem arose suddenly, but because I had the authority to make on-the-spot decisions, I was able to implement a solution without calling my boss to the site.

One man, one job. A lead carpenter concentrates on one job from start to finish. This puts one person on the site every day who understands every aspect of the project, from budget to schedule to choice of finish materials. The lead carpenter isn't distracted, as a company owner would be, by worries about material orders for other jobs, whether it's the Smith or Jones job that needs the gold-plated faucets, or if there's a meeting scheduled across town for another job. Because the lead focuses on the details of one job, there is less chance that something will be forgotten.

I currently oversee multiple jobs as production manager, and it's impossible for me to know all the details of each. Typically, plumbers, electricians, and other subs who are anxious to get started will call me to check on a job's status. I immediately refer them to the lead, who is in a much better position to answer their questions than I am.

Homeowner access. With a lead carpenter on site every day, your customer has immediate access to a company decision-maker. This can save you, the company owner, a lot of unnecessary running around. It's not uncommon, for example, for the homeowner who arrives home after work to review the day's progress and find something that is not being done right. The call usually comes that evening or the next morning at 7:00 a.m. Because you haven't been to the site, you don't know if the complaint is valid, but you promise to come right over. Upon arriving, you find that the carpenter has followed the plan perfectly, but the final product simply didn't look the way the customer expected it to. You've wasted time, and the job has come to a halt while you review the work with the homeowner.

With decision-making authority delegated to the lead carpenter, the homeowner has direct access to the person doing the work and who is in a position to answer questions and speak on your behalf. You'll still have to be involved, but you can eliminate emergency trips and schedule your site visits instead. As production manager at Hopkins & Porter, I meet every two weeks with the homeowner to review job progress and answer homeowner concerns. All communications between meetings, however, go through the lead carpenter.

Motivated employees. When you give lead carpenters decision-making responsibilities, you demonstrate a trust in their judgment that will motivate them to take on more duties. We discovered this benefit at one of our company's monthly staff meetings during a slow period several years ago, when pay raises were out of the question. We were discussing changes in our lead carpenter system, which at the time called for all material orders and sub scheduling to be handled from the office. Our leads realized this arrangement was inefficient, and they volunteered to handle these additional responsibilities themselves. Even though they hadn't been offered more money, they left the meeting feeling they were important to the company.

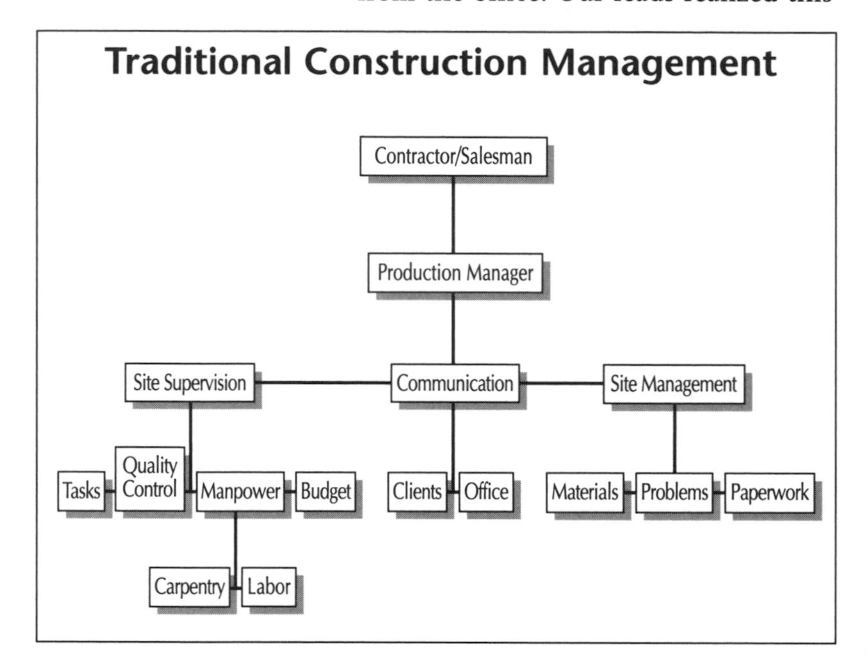

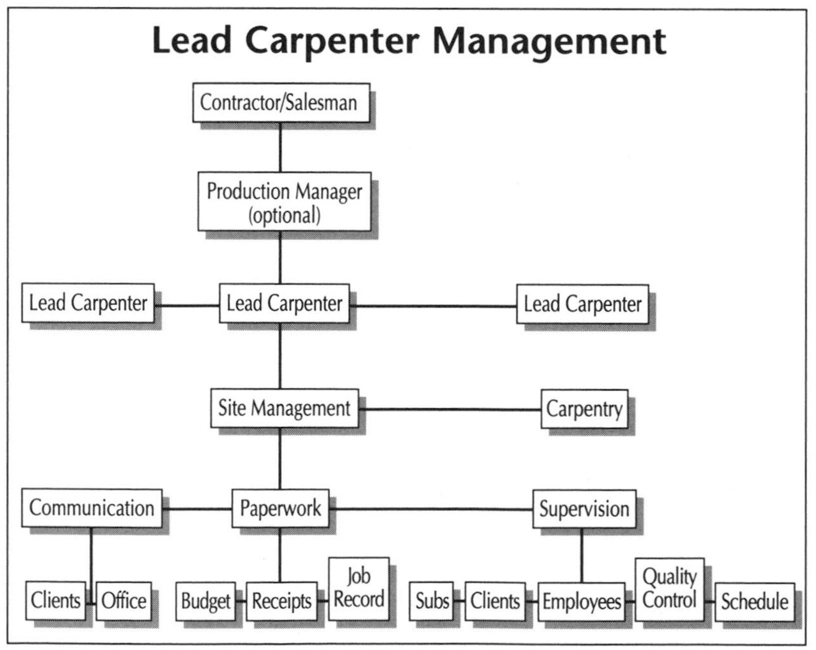

Figure 1. *In traditional construction management (top), the salesman hands off the job to one of several production managers, who coordinates all aspects of the job — labor, materials, schedules, subs, and customer relations — and who typically oversees three or four jobs simultaneously. With the lead carpenter system (above), a single production manager oversees several lead carpenters, each of whom works just one job from start to finish and handles all aspects of project management.*

Free time. Company owners can free up their time by delegating responsibility to the lead carpenter. This allows extra time for business planning; selling and estimating jobs during the day, rather than at night; enjoying more time with your family; or taking a vacation. Conversely, some owners may decide to stay in the field as a lead carpenter and delegate selling and estimating to others. In either case, the company owner has time to pursue other activities, both personal and business-related.

Increased profits. The lead carpenter system improves a company's bottom line, because the lead combines supervision with production. This cuts overhead costs by reducing the number of production managers (see Figure 1). With a traditional construction management scheme, for example, ten jobs would be overseen by three production managers; under the lead carpenter system, the number of production managers can be reduced to one, thereby eliminating two salaried positions.

Recently, a remodeler told me that after implementing the lead carpenter system his profits grew by 15% as a result of the increased efficiency. While you may not achieve the same results, this example shows the potential of this management system.

Drawbacks

The lead carpenter system has some disadvantages, however. For instance, the constant contact between homeowner and lead may develop into a close personal relationship that may cause the lead to forget his allegiance to the company. This could cause the lead to spend too much time on small details or to overlook billable extra work.

Another problem arises when the lead carpenter isn't ready for the added responsibility. He or she quickly becomes overwhelmed, and the efficiencies of the concept are lost.

The same inefficiency occurs if the company owner is not ready to let go of responsibility. Owners who hover over the lead, second-guessing every decision, breed frustration and distrust. This defeats the purpose of the lead carpenter system and sometimes encourages the customer to insist upon talking only with "the boss."

Finally, because the lead carpenter system introduces another person into your company's decision-making process, the chance for miscommunication increases.

The Ideal Lead

It's critical, then, that you find the right candidate for lead carpenter, and that you provide him or her with proper training and support. Finding tradesmen to fill a lead carpenter position who are naturals for the job may be difficult (Figure 2). Some candidates will be good craftsmen but won't understand management; others will be great managers but may lack building expertise. You'll find people who have the potential to strengthen their skills, but you'll have to make a commitment to assist them in developing these talents.

You may find a lead carpenter among your current employees, or you may have to recruit from outside. When you promote from within your company, you have the benefit of placing someone in the lead carpenter position who is familiar with your company's personnel and systems; someone from outside your company may provide new skills that will benefit your company. In most situations, however, promoting from within is a better choice, because you will be familiar with a candidate's work habits.

Here are some qualifications you should look for when hiring a lead carpenter:

Good carpentry skills. Look for a well-rounded tradesperson, not necessarily someone who can cut a perfect miter every time. A lead carpenter will need a solid understanding of the work of subtrades, in order to pass judgment on whether the sub's work is properly installed. Also, a lead will need to understand the normal sequence of remodeling jobs — what trades are scheduled when, how many trips may be necessary for a plumber or an electrician, and so on.

Optimistic attitude. Remodeling work is challenging, and a good lead carpenter

Lead Carpenter Job Description

The Lead Carpenter is the company's on-site construction manager. Lead carpenters are responsible for carrying out the job from start to finish, for coordinating subs, keeping within budget, completing paperwork and job reports, timely code inspections, and representing the company on the job site.

Carpentry: Perform all carpentry work; request help as needed; assign and supervise other carpenters and helpers, including verification of time cards.

Develop and Maintain Project Schedule: Create project flow chart; monitor progress against chart; notify Project Manager and office of schedule problems.

Paperwork: Know and understand all job paperwork, including plans, specifications, and change orders; maintain all job records as required by office.

Material Takeoffs: Prepare final material takeoffs; order materials promptly and accurately; accept and reject materials; confirm quantities shipped (specialty items are ordered by Project Manager).

Schedule and Coordinate Subcontractors: Ensure timely code inspections; confirm proper installation of materials, fixtures, etc.; ensure that subs adhere to company policies regarding safety, cleanliness, alcohol use, and customer relations; approve subcontractor payment.

Change Orders: Carry out change orders prepared by Project Manager or Salesperson; complete no extra work without their authorization.

Job Safety: Promote safe job-site conditions; monitor company and individual equipment for proper safety features, safe electrical cords, etc.

Maintain Clean Work Site: Install dust protection; control mud; contain debris and haul away promptly; leave job broom-clean at day's end.

Protect Client's Property: Enforce hands-off policy of client's belongings; secure and lock job site before leaving for day; store materials in safe place.

Customer Relations: Represent company in its dealings with customers; enforce policy of no loud radios or foul and abusive language.

Job Sign: Install job sign in prominent location.

Figure 2. *A lead carpenter takes on responsibilities beyond those routinely assigned to production carpenters, including scheduling, sub supervision, material orders, change order preparation, and homeowner interaction.*

must be able to roll with the punches. A lead should have a can-do attitude and should not become frustrated easily.

Good people skills. Many different types of personalities come together on a remodeling job, so you'll want someone who gets along well with different types of people. A lead carpenter should be able to handle difficult homeowners, motivate reluctant employees, and calmly deal with building inspectors who complain that something doesn't meet code and must be done over. Ideally, you'll want a lead carpenter who can establish standards and motivate the team to accomplish them.

Good communication skills. Closely linked with good people skills is the ability to express ideas clearly. Your lead should be someone who looks you in the eye when speaking, who lets you finish your sentences, and who has a good technical vocabulary. You'll want a good listener, not someone who monopolizes the conversation.

Team player. The lead carpenter must understand that many people contribute to the success of a project — not just the crew in the field, but office staff too. He or she must understand how the various departments of your company are connected and the reasons behind established procedures.

The successful lead will have a mix of technical and people skills. A lead may be stronger in one area than another, but you should look for a balance. When evaluating a candidate, try to determine whether his or her weaknesses can be strengthened through on-the-job or outside training. Also decide on the degree of commitment you are willing to make to bring this person up to speed.

Finding a Lead Carpenter

The easiest route is to evaluate current employees for performance and suitability as lead carpenters. With a new hire, the challenge is greater and you'll want to be careful in your selection. People with the qualities you are looking for are difficult but not impossible to find. Some of the strongest candidates are business owners who want to give up running their own company, but who want to stay in the construction industry in a position of responsibility.

Hopkins & Porter has had its greatest success recruiting carpenter helpers with the intention of turning them into lead carpenters. Of the helpers we hire, three-quarters develop the skills necessary to move into a lead carpenter position; half of our new hires choose to stay with us, in part because of the advancement opportunities we offer. Along the way, we do annual performance reviews, monitor their job-site behavior, evaluate their communication skills, and get feedback on their supervisory ability from subs. We also pay attention to how quickly they learn our procedures.

Implementation

A good plan is crucial to the successful transfer of management responsibilities from office to field. I was fortunate enough to join a company that had a lead carpenter system in place, but your company can introduce the system by following these guidelines:

Plan ahead. The lead carpenter system is a model, not a monolith. Your company is unique and your plan will need to take into account how your business is organized, the personalities involved, what responsibilities you want to transfer, how coworkers will be affected, and what outside resources are available to implement the system. Also, design a contingency plan, in case the lead carpenter idea doesn't work for you. In developing your plan, include everyone who will be involved in the transition.

Part of the process will include designing a schedule for phasing in the plan. If you load lots of additional responsibilities onto your new leads, they'll burn out quickly. Instead, ease into the situation by gradually increasing the leads' responsibilities. For example, start them off with responsibility for scheduling subs, then add the job of ordering materials; later, add responsibility for approving payments to subs. Allow one or two years to make the transition, and use that time to give the new leads weekly feedback on their progress and provide training to strengthen their weak points.

Solicit input from companies that already employ lead carpenters. Conferences and local trade associations are the best resources for networking. You'll learn how others have tweaked the concept to fit their way of doing business. Also, look into the lead carpenter certification program offered by the National Association of the Remodeling Industry (see "Lead Carpenter Certification," page 188). Individuals interested in becoming a Certified Lead Carpenter (CLC) must complete NARI's background questionnaire and submit letters of reference prior to taking an all-day exam, which tests technical skills and aptitude for project management and customer service.

Training. Without good training, a fledgling lead carpenter system will collapse. As a business owner, you can provide on-the-job training, showing the lead your preferred way of completing procedures, such as how to handle job-site meetings with customers, how to complete change orders, and your way of managing subs. Holding monthly meetings with an assigned topic is another way to introduce new information and promote interaction between field and office staff. Veteran lead carpenters can facilitate these meetings, which should take place during the day with all participants paid for attending.

Take care of business. Most carpenters are good craftspeople, but they have given little thought to the business end of your company. Lead carpenters will have to learn unfamiliar business concepts, like markup, overhead, and profit, and will need to understand how these affect the company's bottom line. You'll need to spend time showing new lead carpenters how to calculate a change order, or explaining why you charge $25 per hour for employees who are paid only $15. And you'll have to convince new leads that all that extra paperwork is necessary.

The hardest part is training leads to think as you do. You'll need to explain, for example, how one carpenter on a job can be more productive than two or three, or what effect regular safety training has on the bottom line, or why sending the best trim carpenter to the lumberyard to pick up a pound of nails is not a wise management decision.

In some ways, lead carpenters will be running mini-businesses, but you'll need to stay involved so that both "businesses" prosper. Include leads in preconstruction meetings, monitor progress weekly, make yourself available to answer questions and lend guidance, and ensure that leads get timely information. Provide leads with job-cost reports (biweekly, at a minimum), and show them how to interpret the reports. Finally, visit the job site regularly, and be sure to compliment the lead on a job done well or offer constructive criticism when he or she doesn't meet your expectations.

The lead carpenter concept not only positions your company for greater efficiency, it also presents an opportunity to review your current systems and make improvements. One of the great benefits of the lead carpenter concept is that there is no definitive "one size fits all." How you adapt the idea to your business will depend upon your personality and those of your employees, as well as your business structure. Properly implemented, the lead carpenter system can work regardless of whether you're a two-person company looking to expand or a big remodeler looking to work more efficiently.

—Tim Faller

You Can't Do It All

Delegating administrative tasks to a capable employee can prevent a host of problems — and free you to do what you do best

When I started my remodeling business 29 years ago, I knew there was more to it than just rounding up some jobs and banging nails. But I have been surprised by the variety of skills I have needed to be successful.

Good people skills, for instance, are as basic to this line of work as the ability to work with tools and wood. You can't sell your business without them, and they're essential to maintaining good relationships with your clients.

But perhaps most important, and most foreign to many contractors, are the administrative abilities necessary to keep the business side running smoothly. People who start businesses are notoriously negligent about tracking the day-to-day administrative tasks such as bookkeeping, correspondence, and filing. Somehow these activities don't seem as productive as making bids or doing the actual remodeling—they distract us and keep us from focusing on the big picture. However, these activities are important and need attention.

Don't Neglect Administration

Every construction business may be divided into three distinct areas: sales and estimating, production, and administration. Even in small companies, no one can do all three. But trying to do it all is probably the most common mistake small contractors make. When one person tries to do all three of these things, all three areas suffer. But it's usually the administrative end that suffers most.

It's easy to underestimate the importance of these administrative tasks. Consider what they actually include: answering the phone, handling mail, typing letters and proposals, filing, verifying and paying invoices, posting verified prices to job cards, placing and verifying purchase orders, billing, handling payroll and taxes, keeping insurance up to date, tracking accounts receivable and accounts payable, and working with the company's attorney, accountant, insurance agent, and banker.

Every construction business must perform these tasks, and in all but the tiniest companies they are a full-time job for at least one person. Neglecting them can cause all sorts of problems: lost sales leads because of unreturned phone calls; credit problems because of late payments to suppliers; overpayments to suppliers because you don't have time to check invoices; inaccurate estimates because of poor cost records; and IRS audits or late payment penalties because of late or sloppy tax work.

Make the Right Hire

Even if you're convinced you need one, hiring an administrator is easy to put off. It's expensive, it's a hassle to train someone, and it's hard to find the right person, someone who understands the construction business. It's also difficult to delegate when you're used to doing it all yourself. But I learned early that neglecting administration is a mistake. You'd never dream of handling production that way.

When I started out, even though I had only four people in the field, I hired a full-time administrative person. That person's salary was added in with the other costs of doing business, such as other salaries, insurance, gas, transportation, and tools. I knew I'd have to sell more to cover that salary, but having an administrative assistant allowed me to concentrate on sales, estimating, and production.

You may have to look hard to find the right person, and when you do, that person should be well paid. You want to hire someone capable and willing to take responsibility for this whole area of your business. You'll probably need to pay more than if you were hiring clerical help. If you aren't sure of the going rate, check with other companies or ask around at a construction trade association meeting.

Define The Job

Before hiring an administrator, you should define that person's duties. The following items should be included:

Phone calls and correspondence. These are your links to the outside world.

The administrator should answer all calls promptly and pleasantly and take good, detailed messages. It's easy to underestimate the advantage of a live voice versus an answering machine, which many people won't talk to. According to some estimates, answering machines scare off as many as 50% of all calls. The administrator should also keep up on correspondence. Prompt, well-written correspondence on attractive letterhead does wonders for your business's image.

Leads. Teach your administrator as much as possible about the business. The more an administrator knows about construction and your company's capabilities and expertise, the better he or she can answer phone inquiries and help you qualify and pursue your leads.

Verifying invoices and purchase orders. Suppliers do make mistakes on invoices and purchase orders. All invoices should be compared against receipts, and everything should be filed promptly and neatly.

Tracking costs. This goes along with verifying invoices. I have my administrator keep my materials price book current. This saves me many phone calls and helps with job costing and estimates down the line.

Bookkeeping. Your accountant may generate your year-end numbers and quarterly taxes, but the administrator should handle the day-to-day bookkeeping duties, such as payables, receivables, payroll, and monthly profit and loss statements. He or she can also stay on top of late receivables.

Scheduling. Since the administrator is in the office all day, he or she makes and verifies appointments with clients.

Working with other professionals. Every business needs its "advisers" — an accountant, an attorney, an insurance agent, and a banker. The administrator can maintain contact with these people and make sure all relevant paperwork, accounts, and insurance coverage are up to date.

Office procedures. This is the rest — the filing, bill paying, processing of time cards, and general paperwork that will otherwise pile up on your desk.

What About Family?

Many contractors hire a family member as the administrative person. This works well for some. But for many, working with a family member causes all kinds of problems, from fights at home to resentment among other employees. If you hire a family member, it's especially important to define their duties and boundaries of responsibility clearly, and make sure you both stick with them.

Do What You Do Best

Hiring an administrator may help your operation run more smoothly and professionally. But its real value is that it allows you to do what you do best: sales, estimating, and production. It also frees you to concentrate on the big picture so that your business can keep growing, and so that you can anticipate and adjust to changes in the business climate. The way I see it, there isn't any way you can afford not to have this kind of help.

By Judson Motsenbocker, owner of Jud Construction in Muncie, Ind., and a frequent speaker on business management for remodelers.

Chapter 11

Scheduling

Planning With Your Schedule

With good scheduling practices, you can manage increased volume and earn greater profits

Scheduling is the key to keeping a building business in order. Good scheduling is especially crucial when you're lucky enough to have more work than you can comfortably handle. Scheduling involves more than planning individual jobs. It also means coordinating multiple jobs of varying size and scope, and with overlapping start and completion times. Obviously, the two activities are closely related and add up to a monumental task. To get started, you must first gather preliminary information.

Boom Or Bust

Preliminary scheduling requires a little crystal-ball gazing to determine what work lies ahead. But predicting the coming building climate is not all guesswork. The trick is to use every resource at your disposal to anticipate the future demand for your services. Start with architects and designers for whom you regularly bid work. Find out what projects they have on the boards and what's ahead. Excavators are another source. Often, owners will talk to an excavator about their upcoming project long before they've decided on a builder. The same is true of real-estate agents and bankers.

Also gauge the demand for repeat business. The owner for whom you built a house last year may want to add a deck or covered porch this year. The key is to find this out early enough to make room in the schedule. Often the best approach is to simply come out and ask your former clients directly. They will likely appreciate your professional attitude.

Small projects can be scheduled in advance for slow times. Or you can split a job into two parts. For example, you can schedule the footings and piers for a deck to be constructed anytime before frost, and save the carpentry for winter when nothing's doing.

In a bust year, you may have to take on a greater number of small projects. In a boom year, you can pick and choose the work more carefully, concentrating on projects that will make the most money with the fewest headaches.

When, How Long, and Who

To schedule successfully, you must answer three questions: What are the start and completion dates? How long will it take to perform the work? Who will be available to do the work?

Start dates. Most customers are only concerned about when you'll be finished. They want the addition done by their daughter's graduation day or some other milestone. But don't fall into the trap of promising a finish date until you can nail down a starting date.

Before you sign a contract with the owner, notify your key subcontractors — excavators, concrete crews, well drillers, roofers — of your best guess for when the job will start. Be up front with them, and let them know that it might be revised. They'll appreciate the help it gives them in their own planning. And they'll be able to tell you if they can meet your schedule.

Owners and architects almost always underestimate the amount of time it will take to draw up the plans and specs, estimate costs, make revisions, and write the contract. Since all of this must be done before you break ground, be realistic when you commit to a start date. If you need two weeks to estimate costs or finish up work in progress, say so, and adjust the starting time accordingly.

Completion dates. When it comes to figuring out how long a specific project is going to take, don't let anyone else's opinions affect your own tried-and-true judgment. Don't consent to the owners' unrealistic timetables; educate them as early as you can. You're better off losing the job than agreeing to an impossible deadline.

When considering calendar-day completion schedules, be sure to allow for delays. Weather will interfere with the work of several key operations — excavation, concrete, and roofing, for example. Two weeks of rain just before your job starts will likely put you just as far behind as two weeks of rain after you start, because the subs you're planning to use will fall behind on the projects they're doing prior to yours.

The same is true for changes in the work. Almost all change orders are written for additional work, which takes additional time. Make sure you allow for this time in your schedule.

Finally, some materials, like windows and doors, require long lead times. If you can't install the siding because you haven't received the windows yet, you're in trouble. Certain other items — light fixtures, plumbing fixtures, and locksets are good examples — are often not chosen until well after the job has begun. If you see a dangerous delay developing because of late orders or slow delivery of key elements, make the appropriate adjustment as early as possible. For instance, you can provide for extensions of time like this in your contracts. But whatever you do, keep your clients informed. They'd much rather hear about a delay sooner than later. Also, if they need to make choices to keep things moving, a little gentle prodding can work wonders.

Labor requirements. You must also determine who is going to do the work. In boom times, you'll need to hire extra help as required, preferably from a pool of people you have hired before. Known degrees of skill and rates of production are important since it is almost impossible to determine how much time an unknown crew will take to complete a given job.

Make sure your long-term employees will be available to supervise the extra help. They will save you time by explaining your normal methods for you, and they'll insure a higher quality, more consistent product. And be sure to tap the extra help as early in the season as possible, before the pool dries up. This will depend, of course, on the kind of season you anticipate.

If it looks like a really busy season ahead, consider subcontracting more parts of the job than usual. If you sub the roofing and drywall, you free up your crew for exterior trim and siding. If you sub the finish work or cabinet installation, you will have more people available to get the next job going.

Task	Date	Personnel
1. Design	9/1	Office
2. Select new entry door	9/1	Office
3. Select new exterior lights	9/1	Office
4. Select paint & stain	9/1	Office
5. Schedule excavator	9/2	Office
6. Schedule electrician	9/2	Office
7. Schedule painter	9/2	Office
8. Order new entry door	9/2	Office
9. Order new exterior lights	9/2	Office
10. Order material delivery	9/2	Office
11. Excavate for piers	9/8	Excavator
12. Place footings and piers	9/8	Crew #1
13. Framing	9/9	Crew #1
14. Lay deck boards	9/11	Crew #1
15. Build bench and railing	9/14	Crew #1
16. Build stair and railing	9/14	Crew #1
17. Break through new doorway	9/16	Crew #2
18. Install new door	9/16	Crew #2
19. Install new exterior lights	9/16	Electrician
20. Trim and punchout	9/17	Crew #2
21. Paint and stain	9/18	Painter
22. Cleanup	9/18	Crew #2

Figure 1. ***This simple schedule breaks down the job into specific tasks, puts them in order by start date, and shows who will perform the work.***

Use A System

Since every client wants to know when their project will be finished, you need a reliable system for predicting progress. Ideally, your system will be easy to establish and maintain, and will incorporate features that allow you to adjust to the inevitable delays.

A good scheduling system accounts for two basic kinds of tasks. Administrative tasks include ordering materials and equipment, selecting products (this often involves helping the owner make choices), and scheduling other tasks, including subcontractor work. Field tasks include all of the work performed in the actual construction of the building: framing, sheathing, siding, trim, and so on.

Each of these broad categories can be broken down into smaller subdivisions, and each builder must decide on the level of detail required. As the detail increases, so does the accuracy of the schedule, but it also becomes increasingly difficult and more time consuming to maintain.

Task List

Let's use a simple example to illustrate how all the parts of the schedule come

Task September	T 1	W 2	T 3	F 4	S 5	S 6	M 7	T 8	W 9	T 10	F 11	S 12	S 13	M 14	T 15	W 16	T 17	F 18	Personnel
1. Design	X																		Office
2. Select new entry door	X																		Office
3. Select new exterior lights	X																		Office
4. Select paint and stain	X																		Office
5. Schedule excavator		X																	Office
6. Schedule electrician		X																	Office
7. Schedule painter		X																	Office
8. Order new entry door		X																	Office
9. Order new exterior lights		X																	Office
10. Order material delivery		X																	Office
11. Dig holes for piers								X											Excavator
12. Place footings and piers								X											Crew #1
13. Framing									X	X									Crew #1
14. Lay deck boards											X			X					Crew #1
15. Build bench and railing														X	X				Crew #1
16. Build stair and railing														X	X				Crew #1
17. Break through new doorway																X			Crew #2
18. Install new door																X			Crew #2
19. Install new exterior lights																X			Electrician
20. Trim and punchout																	X		Sam
21. Paint and stain																		X	Painter
22. Cleanup																		X	Sam

Notes:
11. Send transit to site.
17. Remind Sam to check for buried wires.

Figure 2. *Graphing a schedule makes it easy to read and understand at a glance. This graph shows both start and finish dates, and allows you to track progress by shading each task bar as the work is completed (tasks 1 through 12 are completed).*

together: a small exterior deck with a new door from the existing house. The tasks might break down as follows:

Administrative
- Design
- Schedule excavator
- Schedule material delivery
- Select new entry door
- Order new entry door
- Select new exterior lights
- Order new exterior lights
- Schedule electrician
- Select paint and stain
- Schedule painter

Field
- Excavate for piers
- Place footings and piers
- Framing
- Lay deck boards
- Build bench and railing
- Build stair and railing
- Break through new doorway
- Install new door
- Trim and punchout
- Cleanup
- Install new exterior lights
- Paint and stain

The simplest way to develop this schedule on paper is to first put each task in the proper order, and attach a date to each one. This means reshuffling the original list. You should also note who will perform each task (Figure 1).

This simple listing provides a basic schedule. It shows every task related to the job, when it starts, and who will perform the work. But it leaves a little to be desired. For one thing, it doesn't explain the gaps between dates, or indicate when certain portions of the work will be complete. It's also difficult to see how individual tasks relate to each other.

Seeing Is Believing

A more visual presentation often solves these problems. Using a piece of 1/4-inch graph paper or similarly ruled ledger paper, you can display the same information more graphically and more clearly (Figure 2).

This kind of schedule can be read and understood at a glance. It's now obvious that the gap between 9/2 and 9/8 is the lead time required to schedule the excavator. And the reason "Task 14, Lay deck board" takes four days is because a weekend intervenes. Start and finish dates are shown as well, and you can track progress by shading or coloring each task as it is completed. There's also plenty of room to revise the schedule. If it rains on Wednesday 9/9 and the framing has to be postponed, it's easy to move everything down a notch. Using different colors for revised start and finish dates will help keep things straight. You'll also end up with a clear record of when the job was delayed and how it affected the completion date. You can append notes, footnote style, to the bottom, or write them in alongside the appropriate block.

Many people find it helpful to set up this type of chart on a wall, using movable markers to make changes in the schedule. I use colored 3x5 index cards and push pins, using one color for subs, one for my own crews, and a third color for key dates, such as the completion of framing, plumbing, or rough-in.

Mix And Match

You can combine or modify these methods depending on what you're comfortable with, the size of the project, and the number of jobs you have to schedule in a given period. The basics are a list of tasks, some way to assign them to days of the week, and a simple method of reassigning them as the need arises. A graphically laid out schedule will greatly improve your ability to visualize how the job falls together and to make adjustments before it starts to fall apart.

—Sal Alfano

Simple Scheduling for Remodelers

Two simple charts will help keep employees, subs, and suppliers informed and on track

For years our company has struggled with scheduling our remodeling projects. Not so surprisingly, all jobs seem to take on identities of their own. What works for a bathroom remodel doesn't necessarily work for a bedroom addition. And even "standard" kitchen remodels can be as different as day and night.

Besides, as most of us have discovered the hard way, scheduling a remodel is a little like charming a snake — as soon as you think you've got it made and relax a little, the snake gets restless and bites you. So why spend your valuable time scheduling for a business dominated by Murphy's Law?

Well, as long as your company is doing only a few jobs at a time and you can personally supervise all of them, you can get by without too much structure. But as soon as things get a little more complex, you can no longer supervise every job yourself and you have to begin to delegate management responsibilities.When that happens, a good working schedule that builds out each project on paper becomes a necessity.

This is true in my own business — with a slight wrinkle. I grew up learning the "kick 'em in the butt" system of motivational management. While I was perfecting this technique, however, the management industry switched tracks and began to employ the "pat 'em on the back" method of motivation.

So there I was, completely competent in an outdated motivational skill, and totally frustrated in my vain attempts to master the new technique. Out of necessity, I have developed a scheduling system that allows others (more skilled than me in the new motivational approach

Master Schedule

Ralph's Plumbing Boyd Electric ABC HVAC Valley Drywall **Ace Roofing** Misc. Subs Harvey Lumber Davidson Concrete ***Carpenters*** Painters Laborers	Tuesday 5/9 **Plumbing rough-in** ***Roofing installed*** Electrical rough-in ***Carpentry***	Wednesday 5/10 **Plumbing rough-in** ***Roofing installed*** Electrical rough-in Painters	Thursday 5/11 **Roofing Installed** Electrical rough-in Drywall delivered

Figure 1. *On the Master Schedule, each sub, supplier, and trade is highlighted with a different color (represented here with different type faces). This lets you quickly see who is busy on a given day. If their name and color appear on this calendar, you can consult the Individual Job Schedules for the particulars.*

but less skilled in remodeling) to run our projects smoothly, cover our overhead, and still make a profit.

Getting Started

The best-kept secret in creating a schedule is to keep it simple enough that your office staff will be able to use it to keep your jobs on track.

The second best-kept secret in scheduling is how to use the schedules themselves — they should be right up there on the wall. They also should be in the hands of your subcontractors, and can even be shown to your customers. But I'll get to that in a minute.

The best time to schedule is when it's quiet and there will be few or no interruptions. Write down any questions that arise as you create the schedule, and get the answers later, if possible. Of course, if you have several people capable of scheduling, you may want to employ the think tank method and plan together. The key here is to experiment until you find out what works best. For our company I usually do the rough draft and then call in one or two superintendents to work through it behind me.

Over the years our company has tried many different types of scheduling systems. What we've settled on is a hybrid of PERT (Project Evaluation and Review Technique) and CPM (Critical Path Method), with a healthy dose of SWAG (Sophisticated Wild Guessing) thrown in for good measure. Sounds impressive, but it couldn't be simpler.

First, we make up a master schedule for the entire company. This helps to coordinate all employees and subcontractors, and includes all materials deliveries. Then we create an individual schedule for each job that shows which employees, subs, and suppliers will be on the site each day. Here's how to duplicate what we use.

Cut And Paste

Start with a large desk calendar (pad type), cut it into horizontal strips, and then tape it back together in a single, horizontal line. You'll need as many days as your longest wall will hold for this master calendar, and other different-length calendars for the individual job schedules.

We have a blank page made with several rows of seven squares labeled Monday through Sunday. From this master we can run off as many copies as we need to make up our own calendars. It's also great when we have to add a few days to an individual job schedule.

For both master and individual calendars you'll need a good selection of colored highlighting markers (if you use a computer, this system works well with color graphics) to color-code the different subs, suppliers, and in-house trades on your schedules.

Master schedule. This schedule gives you "the big picture." Once your blank

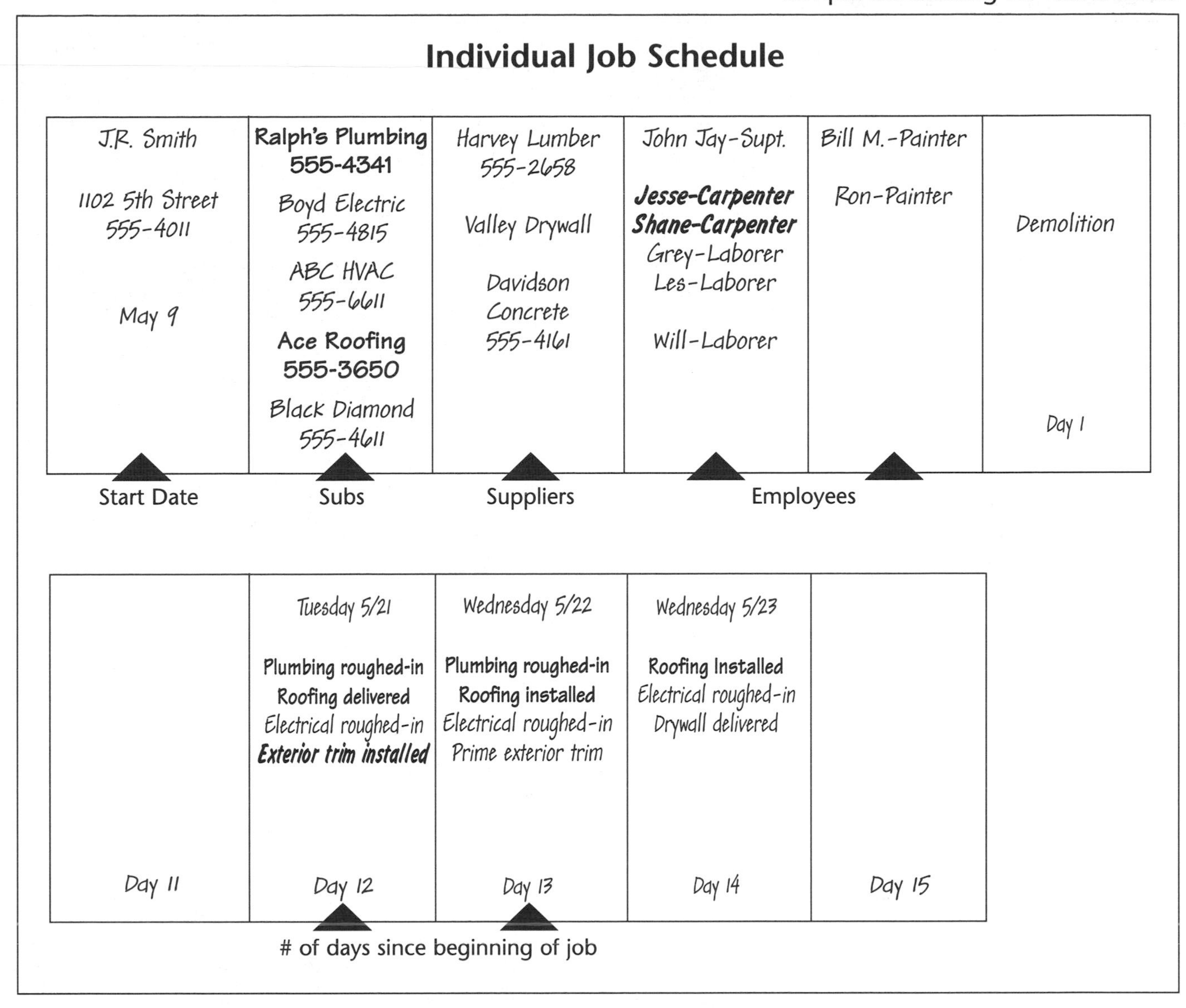

Individual Job Schedule
J.R. Smith
1102 5th Street
555-4011
May 9
Ralph's Plumbing
555-4341
Boyd Electric
555-4815
ABC HVAC
555-6611
Ace Roofing
555-3650
Black Diamond
555-4611
Harvey Lumber
555-2658
Valley Drywall
Davidson
Concrete
555-4161
John Jay-Supt.
Jesse-Carpenter
Shane-Carpenter
Grey-Laborer
Les-Laborer
Will-Laborer
Bill M.-Painter
Ron-Painter
Demolition
Day 1
Start Date
Subs
Suppliers
Employees
Day 11
Tuesday 5/21
Plumbing roughed-in
Roofing delivered
Electrical roughed-in
Exterior trim installed
Day 12
Wednesday 5/22
Plumbing roughed-in
Roofing installed
Electrical roughed-in
Prime exterior trim
Day 13
Wednesday 5/23
Roofing Installed
Electrical roughed-in
Drywall delivered
Day 14
Day 15
# of days since beginning of job

Figure 2. *The first five squares of an Individual Job Schedule contain all names, phone numbers, and employee assignments for that job. Starting with the sixth square, the job is laid out from demolition through cleanup using the same color-coding as the Master Schedule. At the bottom of each square, write the number of days since the beginning of the job. Days 11 through 15 are shown at bottom.*

schedule is all taped together, select a color for holidays and weekends, then fill them in.

Now choose a shade for each major trade and each supplier. You'll also need different colors for each of the different types of work to be done by your company employees (painting, carpentry, etc.) Then, choose one last shade to represent all minor subcontractors.

Now add the date to each square in the appropriate day of the week. The remainder of each square will contain the color-highlighted names of all the subs, suppliers, and employee trades scheduled to work any of the jobs that day. I list my subs and deliveries at the top of each square, and the employee tasks near the bottom (see Figure 1).

Individual job schedules. These are similar to the master schedule, except that their lengths will vary according to the job.

But before you cut your job calendars to precise lengths, let me share a trick with you that works for our company. To allow catch-up time, don't schedule anything for Mondays and only plan for half a day on Fridays. Also, add 15 percent of the total working days scheduled (including Mondays and Fridays) to predict a realistic completion date. However, this new completion date is only for you and your client. If your employees and subcontractors know they have extra time, they'll use it. Work always expands to fill the time allotted for it.

Now that you've got your horizontal calendar ready with weekends and holidays color-coded, you can start filling it in. In the first square, list the job name, job address, job telephone number, and start date (never the completion date) in bold print as shown in Figure 2. In the next square, list the names and telephone numbers of the subcontractors you'll be using on this job. In the third square, do the same with all suppliers, and in the fourth and fifth squares list all employees for that job. Each sub, supplier, and employee trade should be color-coded with the same highlighting marker used on the master calendar. At this point, it is not necessary to fill in the calendar dates; in fact, you shouldn't do so until the construction permits are in hand.

Beginning with the sixth square, lay out the job from permit through punch list and final cleanup. Remember to consult your master schedule to prevent conflicts. Also, account for holidays and vacation days that your clients, key employees, suppliers, and subs will be taking.

Once you've finished with this individual schedule, transfer all sub, supplier, and employee references with their color-coding to the corresponding days on the master schedule (if they are not already listed for another job) to make sure it reflects the sum total activity for each day.

Using Your New Tool

Knowing when to start a job is critical. This is where your master schedule again comes into play. By consulting it, you can give realistic starting dates to your prospective customers. I've found over the years that even the most impatient clients are willing to wait, provided you can show them why. And a schedule can be a very persuasive tool. Why? Very simple. How many remodeling contractors or subcontractors do you personally know who use a scheduling system? My guess is none.

But this kind of scheduling really shines with subs too, particularly the ones that I've encountered. Although very competent, their own scheduling revolves around the age-old principle that the "squeaky wheel gets the grease." That's why we have developed such a "squeaky" system.

First, one of my job superintendents or I call the subcontractors that will work on a specific job (after a client's contract is signed) and fill them in on our schedule. Often we invite them into our office to go over it and make any needed adjustments. (There shouldn't be too many surprises at this stage though, since we already have asked the subcontractor or supplier about their current and upcoming workload at the time they submitted their bids.) They are then given a copy of the new job schedule along with an updated master schedule.

But just in case the subs forget, our office manager/secretary calls one week before each sub's scheduled arrival or supplier's delivery and then again the morning before. This is a precaution against somebody else's "squeaky wheel" getting their attention.

Simply put, a good scheduling system will shape up even the most disorganized company because it forces you to think ahead instead of reacting to the disasters of the moment. And like using a computer, it becomes so much a part of your routine you can't imagine having done business without it.

By Larry Bussey, a remodeling contractor for over 20 years. His company, The Larry Bussey Group, now focuses on the purchase and renovation of older properties.

No-Fault Scheduling

A master list detailing every step of the job can reduce surprises and boost profits

I love some surprises — unexpected snow on Christmas Eve or old college mates calling out of the blue. But surprises on a construction site? No thanks. Construction "unknowns" consume time, energy, and profit. And nothing is more humbling than bringing five subcontractors to a halt after spending a week coercing them to hurry up.

After years of designing and building, my partner and I realized that carpenters are only as good as their tools and general contractors are only as good as their systems. So we got serious about planning.

As my partner Marianne put it, what we needed was "a case of boredom": a scheduling system designed to make our work brainless. We figured the more tasks we could make routine, the less energy we would need to spend remembering the 25¢ decisions that, if forgotten, can stop a $250,000 job.

The Idiot List

To achieve this no-miss scheduling system, we looked to the fundamental teaching technique of breaking a task down into its tiniest and most discrete parts.

We created what we called the idiot list, which included every step in the process: every design decision, every specification needed, every material order, every sub to schedule, every detail to tell our subs, and so on. Distilling the entire contracting process in this way—starting with the first client contact and ending with the champagne toast at the open house—yielded a list of "prompts" for keeping track of the niggling details.

The items, or prompts, are grouped under the appropriate headings, such as design, framing, or electrical. The prompts begin with such flashy verbs as order, call, write, talk to (clients, subs, inspectors), and go to. The list covers nine pages and is about 600 items long.

We've compiled this list into a computerized bookkeeping program called Quicken (Intuit, P.O. Box 3014, Menlo Park, CA 94026; 800/624-8742), a $69.95 program we use for check writing, recordkeeping, budgeting, and financial reporting. We run the program on a Macintosh, but it is also available for IBM-compatible computers.

Although Quicken is not really designed for this type of scheduling function, it's easy to use and gets the job done. Any computerized spreadsheet program, however, would work as well.

You don't have to have a computer to make the idiot list work — it works with pen and pencil too, though you won't be able to sort items easily by categories. But you can put together the crucial checklist and revise it occasionally.

Coding Nitty-Gritty

We had to adapt our bookkeeping program a bit to make it work as a scheduler. Quicken categorizes its "records" (each corresponding to a particular check, deposit, or withdrawal) by several pieces of information (called "fields") such as date, amount, payee, or memo—the usual things you can enter on a check. These fields can also be used to sort or organize the various records. For instance, the program will list all the checks written to a certain supplier or on a certain date.

To use the program for our scheduling, we made each record contain in its "memo" section a single task, such as "Notify drywaller" (see sample list). Along with the task, the record contains a one-letter code indicating what phase of design or construction it is related to (such as X for exterior or N for insulation). Where appropriate, we also include information about what sub to contact or hire, and what larger component or process the task is part of. The "Notify drywaller" prompt, for instance, is one of several items included in the prompt "Insulation Sub Starts."

Finally, items that involve spending or receiving money have a dollar figure attached to them, so that the list doubles as a detailed projection of expenses and billing. This lets you check your pro-

Date	Num	Description	Memo	Category	Clr Amount
9/2	E 870	NOTIFY ELECTRICIAN	verify contract signed		0
			spec smoke detector locate.		0
			spec cable outlet locate.		0
			supply airtight box		0
9/13	E 880	ROUGH ELECTRIC DONE	sched rough inspection	SUB/21	-1,200
			notify insul 3 days		0
			notify drywall 1 week		0
			call for 99: doors/wind/siding		0
			call for 99: rough electric, etc.		0
9/13	890	ORDER FIREPLACE MANTEL	time delay ***		0
9/13	I 900	CALL TOWN - ROUGH INSPECT	electric		0
			plumb		0
9/16	910	NOTIFY AIR SEALER			0
9/16	920	PAY HVAC ROUGH		SUB/20	-1,800
9/16	930	PAY ELECTRIC		SUB/21	-400
9/16	X 940	CLAP 3 WALLS COMPLETE	notify painter to start		0
9/17	N 950	INSULATION SUB STARTS	foam board & acoust seal		0
			foam airtight boxes		0
			foam penetrations		0
			explain winter warm side		0
			sub indoctrination		0
			notify drywaller		0
			order gypsonite		0
			notify int. painter to prime		0
9/17	I 99	INSPECTION - BANK	1 day grace for payment		0
9/17	970	CHECK EXT TRIM			0
9/17	I 99	INSPECTION - BANK ROUGH	1 day grace for payment		0
9/17	P 980	EXT PAINTER STARTS	spot test color for client	MAT/24	-250
9/17	990	CLAP LAST WALL			0
9/17	P 1000	CALL PAINTER TO PRIME	prime uninstalled millwork		0
9/18	I 1010	ECH INSPECTION	sched after insul installed		0
9/18	I 1020	TOWN INSPECTION: INSUL	call town foundation inspec		0
			call 99 driveway/water/sept		0
9/19	I 1030	VERIFY ROUGH INSPECTION	verify cards signed off		0
9/19	1040	PAY DIG-FORM		SUB/03	-2,100
9/19	1050	CHECK SIDING			0
9/19	1060	INCOME: DOOR/WIND/ROOF		SALES	4,500
9/19	1070	INCOME: ROUGH PLUMB/HEAT	chimney/insul	SALES	2,500
9/19	1080	PAY FORMS		SUB/04	-2,200
9/19	1090	DRIVEWAY-PAVE		SUB/04	-1,950
9/19	1100	GET FRONT STEPS		SUB/04	-300
9/20	F 1100	ORDER FINISH MATERIALS	closet shelf? cup or pine		0
			mantels		0
			shelving		0
			special mouldings		0
			door swings		0
			door handle types		0
			casing types		0
			notify int. painter to prime		0

Total 9/2/99 - 9/20/99

Total Inflows 7,000

Total Outflows . . . . -10,200

Net Total . . . . -3,200

The author's 600-item "idiot list" (excerpted above) is written on Quicken and is designed to eliminate surprises. The construction process is broken up into its most basic elements and chronologically organized on the list. Cash flow is also tracked for subs, materials, and progress payments.

jected cash flow at any given point in the construction process.

Making It Work

Compiling this list hasn't been easy, and it's never finished. On the first try, we spent hours visualizing the process from start to finish, hoping to catch as many tasks as we could. It became a game of who could reduce a task to its most basic, critical elements.

Inevitably, we forgot some tasks and had to add them later. For example, one day the electrician asked where we wanted the cable television outlets to be. We didn't know and had to go back to the client, resulting in a time loss. To avoid this in the future, we made an entry in our steno notebook (which we have on hand at all times for this reason) to add the prompt "Ask client for cable TV outlet specs."

In fleshing out these items, it is critical to note and specify the relationships between tasks, trades, and subs. For instance, the cable outlet specs, once obtained, need to be included in the "Notify Electrician" section. This then requires an additional prompt in the design section to enter cable television outlet specs in the "Notify Electrician" list, right after the prompt to ask the client about cable outlet locations.

Vigilance Buys Control

As the list has been refined, it has made the contracting process much smoother for us and for our subs.

Using the list, we have eliminated more than half of our lost days, and have more than doubled our profit margin. Our typical projects are custom homes that cost $100,000 and up to build. Before we developed the list, we often had jobs fall a month or two behind. On a house costing about $150,000, that's nearly $1,000 a week. We were breaking even on most jobs, regardless of size. On some jobs, we made a few bucks, and on some, we lost money. Now we're on time and make sure profits. On our last job, we lost only a few days in a 12-week schedule, and cleared a substantial profit—typical of the improvement we've seen since adopting this system.

Being this well organized shines your image. People in construction are used to things going so-so or even poorly — thus the frequent cries of "Murphy strikes again." But that attitude is demoralizing, and clients don't buy it.

By Doug Immel, owner of Douglas Blake Immel Inc., a design/build, construction management, and energy-consultation company located in Woonsocket, R.I.

Chapter 12

Customer Service

A Customer Service Program That Works

How to keep a close eye on the last project while rushing ahead to the next

The main focus for most young companies is naturally on the next project, rather than on the last. The immediate problem of cash-flow always seems to take priority. That's the basic survival instinct. Because of that, customer-service and warranty-service programs tend to take a back seat. But they are critical to long-term success.

Starting Out

When my company started out four years ago, we had zero starts, zero inventory, zero sales — and substantial personal debt. So we were highly motivated to move ahead. The first thing we had to do was to convince bankers to lend us money, and to get homes built.

So for the first year, the whole focus was on production. Our first sale closing occurred about five months into our first year. That was the first cash we got. It was also our first customer, and our first customer-service problem.

Suddenly, we had two responsibilities instead of one. On the one hand we had the responsibility to the future of the business: designing homes, meeting with clients, negotiating contracts, estimating costs and budgets — tasks I find exciting and challenging. On the other hand, we had a customer saying, "You know I've called three times about that scratch in my floor, and my paint touch up, and I'm not getting the attention I deserve. All you care about is your next sale."

It didn't give me a warm, cozy feeling when I got those phone calls, so I tended to avoid them. I think that's human nature, especially when I had been insulated from these kinds of calls previously.

Not Taking Phone Calls

Early in my career, I had the opportunity to work for a fairly good-sized company with a marvelous warranty-service department. I operated the company's custom-home division and took care of service problems by paying a nominal fee to the warranty-service department. I thought all they did up there was fill out forms, send workers out, get the forms back, and people went away happy.

When I went into business for myself, my perspective changed. Customer calls became a burden. By my second year of business, it reached a point where I didn't take phone calls. Even if I was in, my secretary asked to take a message.

Not that my intentions weren't wonderful. I really wanted all my customers to be happy. I wanted them to be good friends. I wanted them to tell all the world about what a good job we did. But I just didn't have the time. I was going to get to the customer-service problem "tomorrow," if I could just get through the crisis today.

Yet we needed our customers' good will. Like most small builders, we had no organized model-home program. We needed our customers to let us come into their homes with prospective clients to show what kind of work we do. But I wasn't taking care of my new homeowners, so I was on a collision course.

Satisfied Customers Needed

Things got worse until I hit bottom and realized that I had to take time away from day-to-day operations, get organized, and set up a system.

The first step was to send out a letter to our subs and suppliers. It was a statement of our commitment to service and our intention to be Denver's top-quality home builder. This letter also stated that we would require our subs and suppliers to meet certain standards of quality, timeliness, and call-back service. And if they didn't, the letter made clear that we were serious: We would hold checks, and look for new suppliers who wanted to make that kind of commitment to the program.

The letter was not earth-shaking, but it helped me to crystallize my thoughts, and get my subcontractors and suppliers on board with us. The interesting thing I found about taking this step is that when I put my expectations in writing and told everybody what I was going to do, I realized that I had better follow through and do what I said I was going to.

The first six months were pretty rocky. We had a lot of squabbles about whose responsibility a job was, about why the construction manager didn't give a sub the right instructions, and so on. Was it a warranty problem at all? Or was it a walk-through problem that never got fixed and was the construction manager's responsibility?

We had finger pointing. In many cases, subs claimed that we had specified materials that they could not control. Therefore, we should have known better. For example, we gave them a window that was difficult to install square, or a brand of stain or tile grout that didn't perform appropriately.

Administrator Needed

Once we had set up forms, assigned responsibilities, and worked out the kinks in the system, I thought I was home free. Now I could get back to the business of building houses, which is what I enjoyed.

Wrong! The suppliers and subs understood the philosophy, and I had their commitment, but I still had no way to administer the program. I thought the secretary in my office could just send out the service requests to suppliers and subs when we received them from homeowners.

But it didn't work that way. Nobody was there to evaluate the nature of the problem and see which sub it belonged to. Nobody decided whether it was a builder problem or a homeowner-maintenance problem, or not a problem at all.

My problem was partly a financial one. How was I going to find someone in a four-person company to administer the program at that level? I had to find somebody 10 to 20 hours per week, I figured. Through a reference from my interior-trim sub, I located a kind of handyman — an older guy who called himself the House Doctor, and was looking for part-time work. Boy, I thought, that guy's perfect. He could go in, assess the problem, take care of it, clean up any loose ends, and then just send the form back to me. And he could deal with these things before they became big problems.

The House Doctor took care of the little things fine. But he ran into problems when he found something that he couldn't repair himself. For example, a tiny leak in the dishwasher (a manufacturer's defect) had dripped through the bottom of the appliance over a period of months, and down into the oak floor, cupping it all the way across. So he had to get the hardwood floor sub back in. But that required spending time on the phone rounding up people and coordinating things. When he ran into trouble with that, he came back to me with the problem. I was back at square one.

The Flypaper Dilemma

This problem seemed to stick to me like flypaper. I'd take one hand off, and it would stick to the other. So I looked around and found a well-recommended warranty-service guy who had recently been laid off (the Denver market was hurting at the time). I couldn't afford to put him on my payroll, but came up with a solution: We put together a group of four small builders to share the guy.

We set it up on a contract basis on a per-house enrollment fee. Between the four of us, we figured, he could keep busy and make a good income.

Here's how it works: The warranty-service manager takes the report of the problem, calls the sub that's responsible, and asks if he's seen it or if he is familiar with the problem. If not, he goes out personally, and makes a site visit with the homeowner.

After seeing the problem, he decides whether it is in fact a warrantable item, or whether it's a homeowner-maintenance item. If the repair is questionable, but he thinks it will make the customer happy, he is instructed to agree to the work if it will cost less than $100. If it's questionable, and will cost over $100, he says, "I'll have to check with the office on this and get back to you." Within the limits of this one guideline, he's got the field authority to make all necessary decisions. I think that's a key element in the system.

If the service manager finds that there's a subcontractor mistake or something that needs repair, he calls the sub, sets up a time for him to meet with the customer, and sends a confirmation letter to the sub and the homeowner telling them when the appointment will be. Included

The Expectations Game

Bainbridge, Inc., seeks to promote reasonable expectations on the part of their customers, and then to meet them. A key tool in this effort is the Expectations Book, which lists what constitutes warrantable claims, what does not, and how problems will be treated. Below is a brief sampling from the extensive list that is given customers upon signing a sales contract.

CATEGORY: **Sitework**

ITEM: **Excavating and Backfilling**

- **Possible Deficiency:** Settling of ground around foundation, utility trenches, or other filled areas.
- **Construction Standard:** Settling of ground around foundation walls, utility trenches, or other filled areas shall not interfere with water drainage away from the house.
- **Builder Responsibility:** Upon request by the buyer, the builder shall fill settled areas, one time only, during the first year warranty period. The owner shall be responsible for any grass, shrubs, or other landscaping affected by placement of such fill.

CATEGORY: **Concrete**

ITEM: **Expansion and Contraction Joints**

- **Possible Deficiency:** Separation or movement of concrete slabs within the structure at expansion and contraction joints.
- **Construction Standard:** Concrete slabs within the structure are designed to move at expansion and contraction joints.
- **Builder Responsibility:** None.

CATEGORY: **Thermal and Moisture Protection**

ITEM: **Roofing and Siding**

- **Possible Deficiency:** Ice buildup on roof.
- **Construction Standard:** During prolonged cold spells, ice buildup is likely to occur at the eaves of a roof. This condition occurs when snow and ice accumulate and gutters and downspouts freeze up.
- **Builder Responsibility:** The buildup of ice on the roof is a homeowner maintenance item.

CATEGORY: **Mechanical**

ITEM: **Plumbing**

- **Possible Deficiency:** Noisy water pipes.
- **Construction Standard:** There will be noise emitting from the water pipe system, due to the flow of water.
- **Builder Responsibility:** Builder can not remove all noises due to water flow and pipe expansion. However, any "water hammer" is the builder's responsibility.

CATEGORY: **Mechanical** *(cont.)*

ITEM: **Heating**

- **Possible Deficiency:** Inadequate heating.
- **Construction Standard:** Heating system should be capable of producing an inside temperature of 70°F, as measured in the center of each room at a height of 5 feet above the floor, under local outdoor winter design conditions as specified in ASHRAE handbook. Federal, state, or local energy codes shall supersede this standard where such codes have been locally adopted.
- **Builder Responsibility:** Builder shall correct the heating system, as required, to provide the required temperatures. However, the owner shall be responsible for balancing dampers, registers, and other minor adjustments.

CATEGORY: **Doors and Windows**

ITEM: **Wood and Metal Windows**

- **Possible Deficiency:** Malfunction of windows.
- **Construction Standard:** Windows should operate with reasonable ease as designed.
- **Builder Responsibility:** Builder to correct or repair, to provide reasonable ease of operation.

CATEGORY: **Wood and Plastic**

ITEM: **Finish Carpentry (Interior)**

- **Possible Deficiency:** Quality of interior trim workmanship.
- **Construction Standard:** Joints in moldings or joints between moldings and adjacent surfaces should not exceed 1/8 inch in width.
- **Builder Responsibility:** Repair defective joints, as defined. Caulking is acceptable.

CATEGORY: **Finishes**

ITEM: **Gypsum Wallboard**

- **Possible Deficiency:** Defects which appear during first year of warranty such as nail pops, blisters in tape, or other blemishes.
- **Construction Standard:** Slight "imperfections," such as nail pops, seam lines, and cracks not exceeding 1/8 inch in width are common in gypsum wallboard installations, and are considered acceptable.
- **Builder Responsibility:** The builder will repair only cracks exceeding 1/8 inch in width, one time only, during the first year warranty period. Builder is not responsible for color variations in the paint.

in the confirmation letter to the sub is a sign-off sheet for work completed. The sub takes that with him to the home, does the work, and gets it released by the homeowner. Then it goes back to the customer-service man, and finally into my files.

Reasonable Expectations

After ironing out a few wrinkles, everything was working very well except for the grey areas. Our new customer-service manager kept coming back to me with questions: Is this covered? Is this alright? What are we supposed to do about this?

It was a question of expectations. He needed to find out what type of product I intended to deliver to my homeowners, and to convey to them what was a warrantable item. So we put together a full warranty book, which we call the "Expectations Book," and which the customer acknowledges receiving at the time that he or she signs the purchase contract. It describes the warranty coverage itself, and lists each item with a description, a possible deficiency, the standard we expect to meet, and the builder's responsibility to correct it to that standard. It covers many of the components of the home. The package also contains all the warranty-request forms.

In addition, we send out a 30-day letter, a 6-month letter, and an 11-month letter. The 11-month letter tells the owner he has one month left on the one-year warranty. Is there anything he wants us to pay attention to before that expires?

The Best Salesperson

With this program, and personal contact with my customers, I now have almost carte-blanche to go into any home we've ever built. In fact, I have a salesperson on staff who has discovered that the best thing to do is simply walk into a home, introduce the prospective client, and then just shut up. Our customers do the selling. For one thing, the customer's credibility with that potential buyer is a lot better than ours.

So we've found this program to be a very solid benefit. I've got control of a problem that was driving me nuts. My customer-service program generates future business, rather than detracts from it. And finally, I don't have any skeletons in my closet anymore. I can answer any phone call without worrying. And that's a very comforting feeling.

By Ross Robbins, vice-president of Bainbridge, Inc., of Englewood, Colo., which builds about 30 new homes a year.

Service Manuals Make a Good Impression

A service manual that combines maintenance tips with warranty procedures makes for good business and good marketing

Like most remodelers, we're always looking for ways to improve service for our customers, especially after our work is completed. We want our customers to feel free to call us if they have any questions or problems with our work. We also want to maintain our reputation with them since they are a good source of referrals.

With annual sales of about $600,000 and seven employees (including ourselves), our company is not large enough to have a customer service crew. Although we would like to personally call all our past clients to find out how our work is holding up, we don't have the time. Instead, about two years ago, we created a warranty and service manual that encourages customers to get back to us if they are having a problem.

We give out the manual for jobs totaling $5,000 or more. We limit it to this size job since it coincides with the five-year Home Owners Warranty Corp. (HOW) remodeler warranty that we provide.

The manual consists of 14 pages bound in a standard folder that we purchase from a business supply catalog. We use the folder pockets to supply brochures and an application for the HOW program, as well as preaddressed envelopes for customers to return the forms.

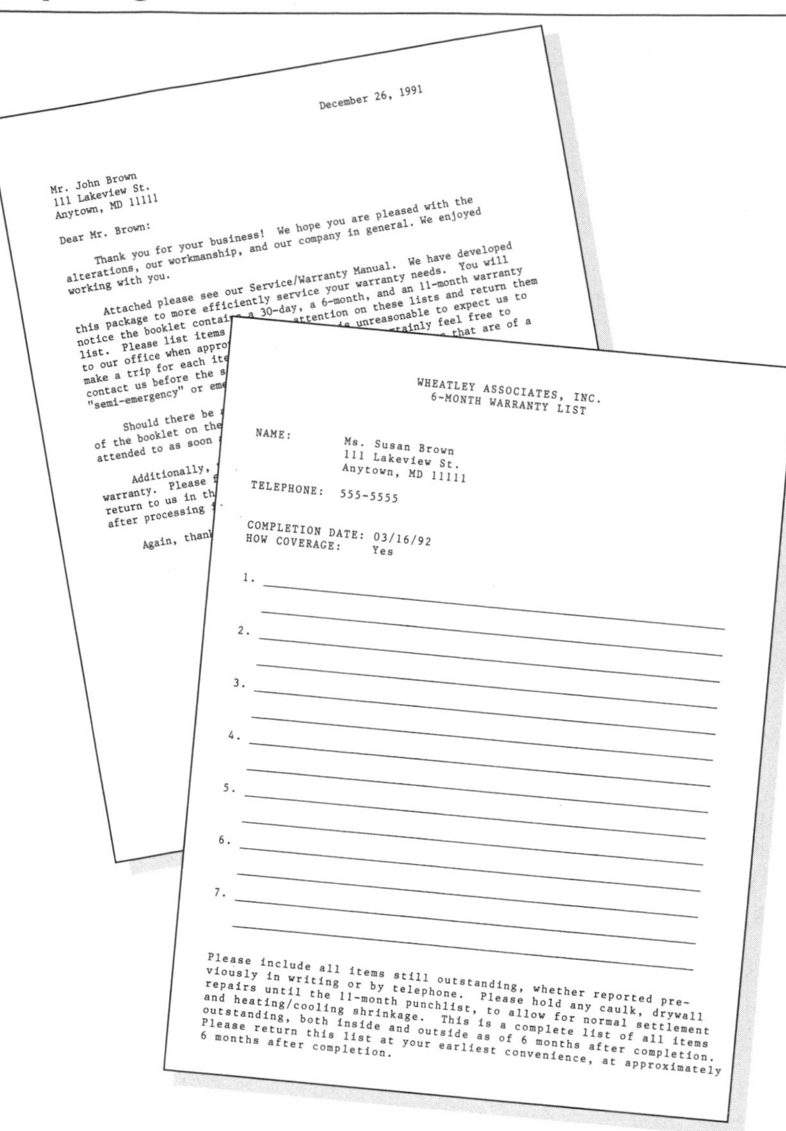

December 26, 1991

Mr. John Brown
111 Lakeview St.
Anytown, MD 11111

Dear Mr. Brown:

Thank you for your business! We hope you are pleased with the alterations, our workmanship, and our company in general. We enjoyed working with you.

Attached please see our Service/Warranty Manual. We have developed this package to more efficiently service your warranty needs. You will notice the booklet contai... a 30-day, a 6-month, and an 11-month warranty list. Please list items ... attention on these lists and return them to our office when appro... is unreasonable to expect us to make a trip for each ite... ...tainly feel free to contact us before the s... ...that are of a "semi-emergency" or eme...

Should there be ... of the booklet on the... attended to as soon ...

Additionally, ... warranty. Please ... return to us in th... after processing ...

Again, thank...

WHEATLEY ASSOCIATES, INC.
6-MONTH WARRANTY LIST

NAME: Ms. Susan Brown
111 Lakeview St.
Anytown, MD 11111

TELEPHONE: 555-5555

COMPLETION DATE: 03/16/92
HOW COVERAGE: Yes

1. ______

2. ______

3. ______

4. ______

5. ______

6. ______

7. ______

Please include all items still outstanding, whether reported previously in writing or by telephone. Please hold any caulk, drywall repairs until the 11-month punchlist, to allow for normal settlement and heating/cooling shrinkage. This is a complete list of all items outstanding, both inside and outside as of 6 months after completion. Please return this list at your earliest convenience, at approximately 6 months after completion.

The manual is divided into four parts: home maintenance tips, emergency procedures, 30-day, 6-month, and 12-month warranty lists, and a record of service calls.

Home maintenance tips. Few people bother to read through the owner manuals for all the products used on a particular job. Doing so would take hours. Yet without proper care, many of the items we have built or installed may not last as long as they should. Also, if problems develop, some customers might blame us. So our manual includes eight pages of maintenance tips to help our clients take better care of their homes, as well as the work we've done.

Our tips cover exterior work, roofing, plumbing, wells and septic systems, hvac, electrical, flooring, windows and doors, bathrooms, and basements. For example, we discourage wallpapering until a year after the job is completed to minimize damage from normal settlement cracks and nail pops, and warn customers that abrasive cleaners will scratch and dull fiberglass and acrylic tubs and showers. We also cover general maintenance items, such as recommending that tree limbs growing on or over a roof be trimmed, or that the water heater be set to the temperature recommended by the plumber or utility company.

Emergency procedures. It seems emergencies always happen after business hours. So we've provided a list of emergency phone numbers where we can be reached, as well as numbers for the electrician, plumber, hvac contractor, and anyone else that was involved in the project. If the listed contractors are unavailable, our clients are instructed to call elsewhere for service. They should pay the bill and then submit it to our office. If we decide the problem is under our warranty, the client will be reimbursed.

Warranty lists. No matter how thorough we are, problems can still develop after we've left the job site. Bathroom fixtures may not function properly, for instance. Normal settlement and the shrinkage caused by lumber drying out are inevitable after the first year and may require caulk and drywall repairs. Screws and knobs may come loose.

As a project nears completion, our superintendent and the clients develop a final quality-control punch list. It is stipulated in the contract that after the items on the list are completed, the client will make the final payment. Any other items found after the list is completed are included on the thirty-day, six-month, and twelve-month warranty lists in the manual. The cost for repairing any items included on these lists is covered by our company's one-year warranty.

The warranty lists not only reassure our customers that problems will be solved, they also keep us from trotting back to past jobs every time a nail pops. We are able to take care of many problems in a single visit. Also, we encourage customers to hold all caulk and drywall repairs until the 12-month list.

Record of service calls. This sheet is intended to help clients track any work that remains. For instance, if something

Wheatley Associates, Inc.

Home Care and Maintenance Information*

Your home represents shelter and financial security. It is important to protect your home by careful maintenance. Please read carefully for there are many important items pertinent to the care of your newly completed project. If you have any questions, regarding any item, please do not hesitate to call.

Exterior:

1.	Fill ruts in stone driveways annually to avoid larger ruts. On blacktop drives do not drive close to the edges. Driveway should be resealed annually.	Spring
2.	Rock salts should not be used on brick, stone or concrete walkways, as this substance will deteriorate these materials. Sand, sawdust or kitty litter are good alternatives.	Winter

Roof:

1.	Clean gutters at a minimum, annually. Some will need to be done monthly so that they can flow freely. It is imperative that the gutters and downspouts be free of leaves before winter sets in.	Fall/Spring
2.	High winds, snow and ice can damage a roof. Check after heavy storms and every spring for water stains in attic and on the overhang.	Periodical

Plumbing:

1.	Before freezing temperatures arrive, you must turn off the exterior hosebibs. The cut-off valve is usually inside the basement directly opposite the hosebib. First turn off the cut-off valve. Then, open the hosebib outside to allow the water to drain. Then, close the hosebib. You must remember to close the hosebib or the cold temperature can run through the pipe and freeze the lines inside.	Fall
2.	Fiberglass and acrylic tub, shower, and whirlpool units should never be cleaned with abrasive cleaners. They will scratch and dull if these cleaners are applied.	Helpful Hint

Heating/Cooling:

1.	Clean or replace heating and air conditioning filters.	Spring/Fall
2.	Heat pump thermostats should be set at a predetermined comfortable setting and left alone. Frequent readjustment of the thermostat is a very inefficient use of the heat pump principle.	Helpful Hint

Flooring:

1.	Even stain resistant grout, used in your ceramic tile and marble areas, will darken with wear. To minimize this occurrence, always change cleaning solution frequently and rinse with clear water.	Periodical
2.	Never use abrasives or steel wool pads on ceramic tile.	Helpful Hint

Windows and Doors:

1.	Vinyl or rubber weather stripping's life can be prolonged by applying petroleum jelly.	Periodical

BASED ON A GUIDE BY THE HOME OWNERS WARRANTY COUNCIL OF MARYLAND

Wheatley Associate's service manual contains eight pages of maintenance tips (excerpts shown above). The tips help the new owners take care of their investment and help reduce callbacks.

is broken during construction and must be reordered, the list serves as a record. It reaffirms to the client that we have not forgotten the item and will attend to it as soon as possible.

Other Benefits

Producing the manual is neither expensive nor time consuming. We use our word processor to customize each page with the homeowner's address and the date the project concluded. We also customize the emergency repair list since we may use different subcontractors depending on the job. We also write a cover letter thanking the customer for their business and encouraging them to contact us if they need assistance.

Ideally, every one of our customers will read the manual and follow all the tips offered. But, we've found that only about 10% of the warranty lists are returned on time. We'd like to believe this is because our work is so good that one year later there are no problems. In reality, it seems that most customers handle the little repairs, such as tightening screws or fixing the caulk, themselves.

The warranty and record of service calls provide another advantage: They create a paper trail that comes in handy in case there are any major problems down the line. We've never had this happen, but there are plenty of remodelers who have wound up in court after clients alleged that some of their work was never completed or that repeated complaints were never answered.

The manual also serves as a selling point. We keep a copy in our portfolio to show potential customers that if they work with us, we will take care of them.

We have learned that differentiating ourselves from the competition is one of the best ways to get more jobs. Our manual tells customers that we are both professional and committed. Many people don't expect remodelers to be either.

By Kathy and Gary Wheatley, owners of Wheatley Associates, a Monkton, Md., remodeling firm specializing in additions, window and door replacements, and light-commercial alterations.

Customer Questionnaire

A simple after-the-job questionnaire can help your company improve its performance and its image

Our company has a motto: Building the Future, Reshaping the Past. The motto, of course, refers to the business of remodeling houses, but it also says something about how this business learns from its customers. When we sent performance questionnaires to our customers, we learned that the best way to build our company's future was to reshape the way we had done things in the past.

Most of our $2 million in business comes from multi-family remodeling, but we continue to remodel many single-family homes, which is how our business got its start. With a simple 11-question form (see questionnaire, opposite) we ask our customers what we do that pleases them and where we can improve. In as long as it took for a brainstorming session, we came up with a form that we can use for all our customers.

The survey form costs no more than paper, ink, and postage. To make it look professional, we print it with our logo. Each survey arrives with a self-addressed, stamped envelope, which is probably why we get about an 85% return. We also offer respondents a company hat or T-shirt, which we promptly send after receiving the completed questionnaire.

Half of our customers respond without any prodding. The other half we may prompt with a phone call, but no more than that—we don't want to annoy anyone, and some people just don't fill out questionnaires.

The Payback

What we get in return is valuable information which we use in two ways:

- *In running our business.* If our customers tell us we're doing something right, we continue to do it. If they tell us we need improvement, we evaluate their concerns and make the necessary changes.
- *In advertising.* We are proud to show that most of our customers rate us

Big River Construction and Remodeling Co., Inc.
372 Rodney Drive, Baton Rouge, LA 70815
Phone: 504/769-9577

A Valuable Evaluation for Big River Construction

1 How did you find out about Big River Construction and Remodeling?

2. If by personal reference, what was it about our company that prompted you to call us?

   Who referred you to us?

3. What are your observations about telephone communications before, during, and after your work?

4. From our first visit to your last construction detail, were our company's representatives courteous, helpful, and knowledgeable?

5. When there were others working on the job (i.e., subcontractors), how do you feel they respected you and your property and how well did they uphold our company's standards?

6. A. How would you rate our company's overall construction performance?
   poor 1 2 3 4 5 6 7 8 9 10 excellent
   B. How would you rate our administrative performance?
   poor 1 2 3 4 5 6 7 8 9 10 excellent
   C. How would you rate our professionalism?
   poor 1 2 3 4 5 6 7 8 9 10 excellent

7. During construction, how did you feel we handled the day-to-day phases of your job?

8. What could our company have done to make your project run more smoothly?

9. Are you happy with your completed project? Yes No

   What, if anything, would you have done differently?

10. How effectively and timely did we handle any problems?

11. May we use you as a telephone reference? Yes No

Please feel free to include any additional comments.

Send Free Gift to: ______________________________

Company: ______________________________

Address: ______________________________

City/State/Zip: ______________________________

Thank you very much for your valuable input.

highly, something the survey lets us measure. We put the figures in our brochures and newspaper ads. We also ask permission, after the survey is completed, to use favorable quotes in our ads. Most people love to see their names in print.

One benefit of a questionnaire is that customers are more comfortable writing their feelings down on paper than expressing them verbally, face to face. That's especially true with homeowners, but even commercial customers tell us more in writing than they do in person. It's this kind of information that helps us make managerial decisions.

The most important change we've made as a result of the surveys is in the way we supervise our subs. We found out that our subs were approaching the owners in our absence to ask questions, and some were not being careful enough about keeping a neat job site. Now we make it very clear before hiring subs that all inquiries go through us, and that we have certain expectations about job-site conduct such as smoking and parking.

Creating Your Own

Creating a questionnaire is relatively simple. To get the necessary detail, however, you should ask questions that encourage your customers to open up. Ask them how they feel about your crews, subs, administrators, and workmanship. Ask for specific examples. Allow enough space between questions for brief answers. Assure them that they are welcome to use the back of the form or other paper if they need more space.

Don't require written answers for every question. A couple of simple yes-or-no questions will quickly gauge the attitude of your customers and help to keep the survey short. Try to keep it to one page.

Make it easy for your customers to evaluate your performance in ways you can really measure. We use a scale of 1 to 10, with 1 rated "poor" and 10 rated "excellent." Our consistently high grades from customers go into our ads. We can say — and prove — that 90% of our customers rate us a perfect 10.

One thing we don't do is ask for job leads. This is not the appropriate place to do that. Customers would perceive it as the real motive of the survey. The questionnaire is the customer's opportunity to speak their piece. Make it just that and you'll leave your customers with your real message—that you are interested in what they have to say. You'll generate lots of goodwill and good referrals.

By Terry Brocious, the former operations director of Big River Construction Co., Inc., in Baton Rouge, La.

Chapter 13

Marketing and Sales

Letting Them Know You're the Best

You do good work. Now take these practical steps to make sure your customers know it.

Doing good work just isn't enough if your goal is to increase the size and range of the business you do. Why not? Because we live in a world of impressions, and how you are perceived has everything to do with the number of customers that will come your way.

Can you imagine a Fortune 500 company —no matter how superior their product — without a marketing department? These giants got where they are because they know their markets and aggressively promote themselves with both old customers and new prospects.

Yet good marketing is even more critical to remodelers. As a service industry, we rely heavily on how customers feel about us. And most of us aren't big enough to grow based solely on reputation, nor do we have the size to sweat out the lean times if we are passively waiting for our next client to call.

But marketing your company doesn't have to mean hiring high-priced consultants or changing the work you do. It does mean becoming more conscious of how others perceive you and making sure that your quality and reliability create a lasting impression.

I spend a lot of time in my nine-year-old design/build remodeling business making sure we do the best work possible, but I put just as much energy into marketing and promotion to make sure that an increasing base of homeowners in our area know about that good work.

First impressions are vital to how you're perceived by clients and prospects. That means ties and jackets for the boss and sales staff, uniforms for the crew, and crisp paint for company vehicles.

The "M" Word

So what is marketing anyway? It's hard to pin down, but here are four things that come to mind:

- Research on what business opportunities exist for your company;
- Knowledge of what consumers want in goods or services and how to approach them for their business;
- Improving your company and its product so that it can deliver what the consumer wants at a price he or she is willing to pay;
- Promotion of your company and its product and services through a range of media.

It's no accident that only one of the four items involves promotion. Promotion is crucial if growth is your goal, but until you've done your market research, most promotion will miss the customers you want most and may even clog your system with unwanted inquiries.

So where do you begin? Try answering the following questions completely and accurately:

- Who are you?
- What is the product or service you sell?
- Who are your customers?
- How do you differ from your competition?

Now boil down your answers to no more than three sentences each. Done? You've just begun your new marketing program. Actually, this little exercise isn't easy if you are being thorough, but if marketing were easy, everyone would do it well, and there'd be no advantages to gain.

Applying a Marketing Approach

I frequently meet people with a good track record in small-job remodeling and a little capital who want to broaden their customer base and build a company that will break the hand-to-mouth cycle. The question for them is how to get started. Here are some of the suggestions I give them.

Analyzing your business. Just because you haven't been promoting your work doesn't mean it isn't a fine base to build on, but first you need to know what value it has. Take a look at your last few years and pay particular attention to the jobs that have produced the best profits and the happiest customers.

Let's say that in the last four years, your 15 most successful jobs were high-end bathrooms. Looking at them more closely, you discover that the customers on these jobs were married couples in that "thirty-something" category. Okay, now it's time to start asking questions that will help you assess the strengths and weaknesses of your company.

Start with those past customers. Tell them that you are planning to expand and need candid answers to help you build a better company. Ask questions that will help reveal what they particularly valued in your relationship with them. Is is workmanship? Or your sense of design when it comes to tilework? Your ability to make them feel taken care of as a customer? Also ask questions about perceived value, what they'd like to have seen handled differently, etc.

But don't stop with your successful jobs. Take the time (and find the courage) to talk to some tough customers too; friends won't report the most important shortcomings you'll need to overcome. And then turn the same questions on your employees, your suppliers, and yourself.

Drawing some conclusions. Some pretty revealing facts will begin to appear as you gather others' impressions. You already know that your most profitable jobs have been master bathrooms for "yuppie" couples, but you may also find out that a lot of your customers mentioned your lead carpenter as being friendly and helpful. And your part-time office person has revealed that over half of the referrals calling in mentioned the tilesetter you use.

Going back over time cards, you discover that you haven't spent much time supervising these jobs, but you did work closely with the customers on the design. And finally, let's assume research shows that your geographic area has a substantial number of two-income professional families who live in homes over 15 years old. And there are enough of these potential customers to support twice your current master-bathroom projects without your taking over more than one percent of that market.

Developing a promotion plan. So you've figured out your strengths, and you know there's a market for what you do well, but how do you get that across to the people who should be dialing your number?

Start with your name. If bathrooms are your speciality, make sure they get mentioned. But to avoid restricting yourself in the future, use *"So-and-So" Remodeling & Design*, and then follow that with "Fine Bathroom Construction" in all your bathroom promotion literature.

You'll also need a logo. Consider arranging with a local technical-school marketing class to pay a prize fee to the student who comes up with the best one. Students should also make suggestions about color schemes for promotional material, but check these with printers, jacket suppliers, sign painters, etc., to make sure your choices won't cost too much or create delays in restocking these items down the road.

Now you can order stationery and forms, business cards for yourself and your employees, door hanger flyers for houses in the neighborhood where you're working, and a simple one-page brochure. Given the market you've defined, tailor all your promotional literature to your upper-middle-class clientele in language and type style. Consider using buzz works like *personal service, expert tile installers*, *friendly*, and *professional*. Graphics should be architectural in nature, with no cute "clip art" or amateur drawings. Above all, keep colors, type styles, language, and presentation consistent.

You might also hire a sign painter to make job-site signs. If you use a material like corrugated plastic, it will keep unit costs low and make the signs easier to discard as soon as they begin to look shabby.

The importance of appearances. Like it or not, your customers (and potential customers) will judge you not on your expertise as a builder, but on the things they are most familiar with; your appearance, their contacts with your employees, how clean your building sites are, etc. Here are a number of things you should consider to make sure you are giving your customers the impression that matches the careful work you do.

If your company truck has accumulated a few years and a few dents, have it repaired and then painted with the company colors, name, and logo. Tell your employees that the truck is now a symbol of the new company image and ask them to take some personal pride in its appearance.

THE SIGN OF
REMODELING
EXCELLENCE
IS IN YOUR NEIGHBORHOOD
The
McAdams
Company
Remodeling • Design • Construction
822-6555

This handout gives the prospective client something to take home from the home show. But it's the personal contact at these shows—and follow-up phone calls— that bring your company to the customer's mind when he or she is ready to act.

Also explain to your field personnel what you are doing to bring in additional business for the company. Talk about the types of jobs you're targeting and explain the customer profile. Make sure that everyone understands that quality and referrals are the lifeblood of the company and give them authority to stop work on *any* job at *any* time if they don't feel that they'll be able to produce top-notch work with the manpower, tools, and materials on hand.

After explaining to your crew the value of appearances to the homeowners, ask your crew to help choose a uniform—something as simple as a T-shirt and cap with the company name embossed on them—for the jobsite. Be prepared to insist, even if it means firing a skilled tradesman who doesn't want to wear "a monkey suit." Appearance and attitude are that critical to your success.

Over the next six months, add personal grooming hints to your regular training program for field employees. Order company jackets to be given to employees who stick with the company six months or more — they can become a kind of status symbol. Key employees should be allowed to buy jackets for family members, or given additional jackets for outstanding performance.

And the boss isn't exempt either. Even if you began your career as a tradesman with a vow never to wear a tie, purchase some dress slacks, dress shirts, sport jackets, and neckties, and wear them. If you do have to work on site, stop at home to shower and put on a tie and coat before visiting current or future clients to discuss business. Sound extreme? It isn't. By dressing like a businessman, you'll be taken as a businessman, and you will set yourself apart from your less professional competition before a word is said.

Putting it to work. Now that you and your company are spruced up, it's time to get out there. Begin by updating your company's mailing list. Gather the names of all former customers, recent prospects, suppliers, subcontractors, and anybody you or your employees know even casually.

Send announcements to the people on this list heralding your name change and your commitment to the master

Company newsletters should be interesting and entertaining. In past issues, the author's remodeling newsletter passed along useful tidbits on design and mortgage money, introduced key employees, advertised new services, announced home show appearances, and even put the word out that the company was looking for a new office manager.

bathroom market. Somewhere in the announcement, ask for referrals by telling these friends that you depend on their help. You should continue to ask for your customers' help every time an opportunity arises, and you should make sure the opportunity arises often.

You should also design a form for taking telephone leads. It should include key questions about the source of the lead, the timing of the customer's construction plans, budget, financing, etc. Have your office help fill out this form for every incoming lead (and don't forget to do it yourself), and then tally these leads monthly.

You may also want to design a form to send to each customer after you've completed their project, asking for their help in improving company service. These report cards are very helpful in fine-tuning project management, a good source for customer testimonials to use in advertising, and often a real boost for everybody's morale.

Some Finishing Touches

The steps I've described so far are a good beginning. You have discovered who your customers are, that they buy on a referral basis, and that the skills and personal handling your company provide are highly regarded. You've begun to build an image for your company that is carefully tailored to that set of criteria, and you've opened communications with your most valuable asset, your established client base.

To date, you've spent a very small amount of money compared to "shotgun" advertising in the newspaper and/or Yellow Pages, and you should begin to see some immediate results if you have correctly interpreted your survey and made wise promotional choices.

But you'll need some additional promotional schemes if you've set rapid growth as a goal. Here are a few resources which have been useful to me in promoting my business.

Home shows. There is no environment quite the same as a home show. We meet most of our nonreferred customers at one of two home shows annually. Since we are a personal service company, we like to meet customers on a personal basis.

Two caveats about home shows: First, these homeowners are seldom ready to do business when they come to the show. Make sure they go home from the show with your literature, but solid, long-term follow-up is critical to being there when their itch to remodel finally becomes irresistible. Also, if you hold a drawing at a home show, make sure it is for your product or service. A drawing for a microwave identifies you as an appliance salesman.

Newsletter. Our company newsletter has kept us in close contact with the people we already know. We keep it news- and people-oriented. The real key for a newsletter is to have it read, so it must entertain and be of value to the reader.

Trade associations. Participate in your local NAHB or NARI affiliate remodeling association. If there is no organized contractor referral system in your area, help start one. Learn to compete with the highest caliber contractors, and you will soon see that there is more quality work available than all of you can do.

Public relations. This is really subject matter for another entire article. Nothing as inexpensive can do as much for your company image — and ultimately your bottom line — as becoming the recognized expert in your field. When you are in print or on the radio or TV, the consumer confers immense credibility on you. If they know how lucky they are to have an important person like you working on their proposal, how many "thinking-it-over" or "waiting-for-another-bid" objections will you have to hear?

Public relations is just plain hard work, like any marketing effort. Get started by entering every contest you can — if the association does not have a contest, start one. The sooner you are an award-winning remodeling company, the better. Send letters to the editors of local newspapers and the columnists who write on home-related subjects. Always respond to a remodeling article with a compliment (this is sometimes difficult to do) followed by some added facts, then volunteer to help in the future.

Local leadership. Get to know the powerful people in your community. Start close by with church and school, then branch out into chambers of commerce or other civic groups. Connections in this power base will help to keep you informed of additional opportunities for public recognition. As you become more successful in your business life, these organizations provide opportunity to "give back" something to society. At the same time, many of those civic leaders will fit *your* customer profile.

Promotion of your company, your product, and your services is a continuous task that should be made a significant part of every work day. Decide to be the best at what you do, and then never stop telling yourself, your employees, and your customers how well you intend to serve each person who hires your firm. Prove it to yourself by making the tough decision to provide warranty service to a difficult customer. Prove it to your staff by praising and promoting those who cater to the customer's wishes, and by sacking the ill-mannered and inconsiderate, regardless of technical skills. Prove it to your customers every day — they are the future of your business.

The ambitious marketing strategies practiced by Madison Avenue seem rather removed from Mrs. Johnson's kitchen remodel, or Mr. Monroe's reroofing project, but using these techniques can help you to stand out from your competition. However intangible qualities like professionalism, reliability, competence, and permanence may seem, consumers will gladly compensate you for the value they add.

By Len McAdams, owner of The McAdams Company, a design/build remodeling firm based in Kirkland, Wash.

Big Bang, Low Bucks Marketing

Adopt these inexpensive marketing techniques to create a steady stream of quality leads

Any successful construction business will become paralyzed without a marketing program. Too many contractors never get started, hiding behind excuses like "I'll begin a marketing program when I have more time" or "I'll start marketing when I have some extra dollars." But when the phone stops ringing, they wish they'd made the effort to attract new customers.

There is no mystique to marketing. The important thing is to control the direction of your marketing so that you can get the maximum benefit from your efforts. To do this, you need to create some tools you can use over and over. You may already have many of these tools, so you'll just need to give them a new twist to make them more powerful.

Our company is a 17-year-old design-build firm with five employees, including me and my wife, Nancy, who does all of our computer work. We're located in a seasonal resort area in New Hampshire of about 350 square miles, and we have targeted our marketing efforts to this area. Fifty percent of the homeowners in our area live out of state, and a lot of our work is completed in the winter months. Most of our marketing tools are designed in-house and are produced at minimal cost. In this section, I'll describe those that have worked best.

What Are You Selling?

Builders and remodelers setting out to create a marketing program should begin by asking the question: "What am I selling?" My answer is that we are selling investment protection. We are protecting the investment of the homeowner who has chosen us for the project.

Too often when builders and remodelers are asked, "What business are you in?" we respond, "I'm a contractor" or "I do building." But we do something far more important: We improve our customer's lifestyle. We are in the business of bringing added enjoyment and comfort to their family. Most important, we're in the business of adding value to their biggest investment, their home. Your marketing efforts must communicate the benefits of doing business with your company and tell your customers how you will protect their investment.

Your goal, then, is to distinguish yourself from competing contractors. You want homeowners in your area to have your company's name on the tip of their tongues, so that when they are ready to build or remodel, the first company that comes to mind is your company.

Marketing tools take time to develop, but those you use repeatedly will help you achieve this goal. Here are the essentials:

Logos. If you don't have a logo, I strongly recommend designing one. It doesn't have to be fancy, maybe a distinctive typeface and layout, as long as it sets you apart from the competition (see Figure 1). Your local print shop is the least expensive place to get help with a

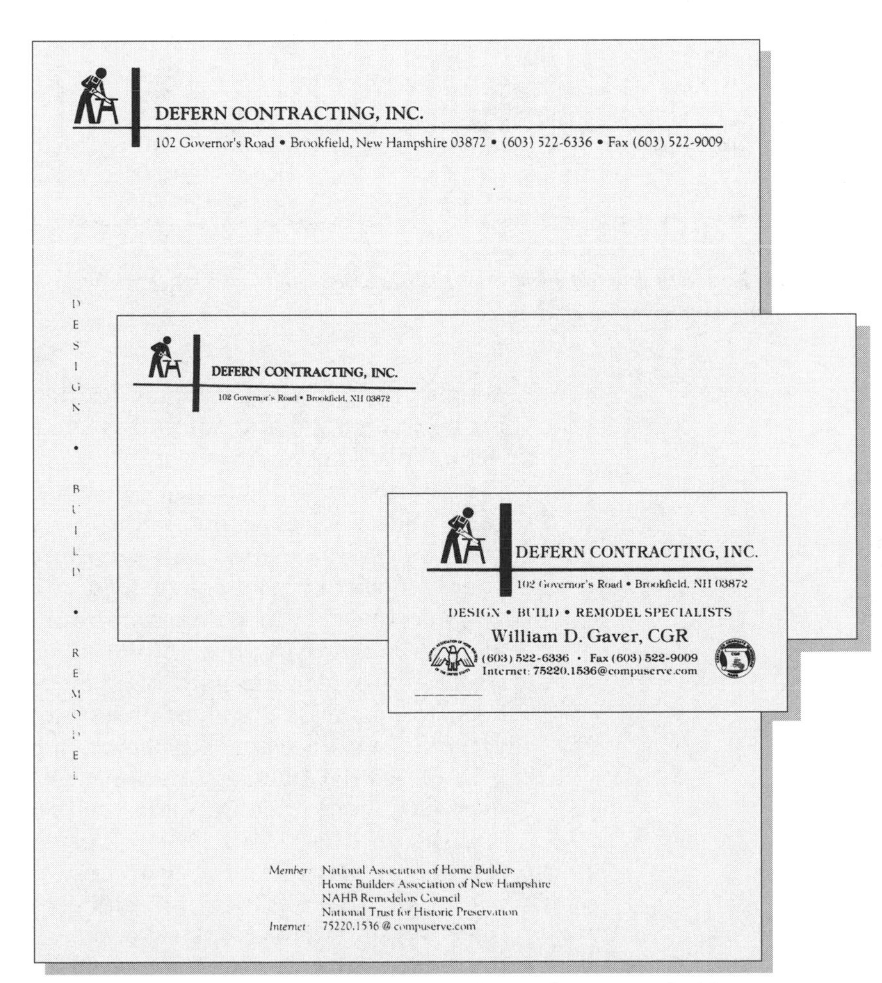

Figure 1. ***Keep your logo simple and don't clutter your business card with extraneous material. Additional information can be printed on your letterhead.***

DEFERN CONTRACTING, INC.
102 Governor's Road
Brookfield, New Hampshire 03872
(603) 522-6336
FAX 522-9009
Internet: 75220.1536@compuserve.com
Internet: defern@worldpath.net

AN OVERVIEW

Defern Contracting, Inc. located in Brookfield, New Hampshire was founded in 1980. Defern specializes in restoration, remodeling, and new construction for both the residential and light commercial markets.

The firm is noted for its full-service and business-like approach to client needs, a staff devoted to exacting standards, the utilization of computer technology for estimating, design, and project control, and foremost -- the application of new and proven building science technology to enhance the comfort and to protect the health of clients and their families, and to provide an efficient and low-maintenance structure. The Defern full-service approach encompasses site evaluation, the execution of conceptual and working drawings with elevations, plus complete specifications and reliable consulting services.

This "one stop" client-centered approach exceeds that of a general contractor. Using state-of-the-art technology, CD-ROM, and the World Wide Web, Defern can share design changes, product images from the nation's leading manufacturers, and a wealth of information to help homeowners explore options and become personally involved in the customization of a home or remodeling project. Defern's construction management services benefit clients by establishing project controls, and ensuring that all financial, quality, safety, start-up, occupancy, and related project demands and objectives are met.

Because of its business-like approach, skilled construction, and exclusive service and warranty program, Defern was selected as one of the top fifty remodeling companies in the United States by **REMODELING** Magazine. As an added dividend for homeowners, Bill Gaver, President of Defern Contracting, Inc. is an active builder-remodeler member of the National Association of Home Builders (NAHB). He is a member of the NAHB Remodelors Council's Board of Trustees, the Home Builders Institute Board of Trustees, and the NAHB Long Range and Strategic Planning Committee. In addition, Defern is the area's only Certified Graduate Remodelor, and earned two Home Builders Association of New Hampshire Sales and Marketing Gold Awards.

Defern Contracting, Inc. and its client-centered approach provides an environment whereby a collaborative effort builds mutual trust, respect and confidence in making a wise financial investment resulting in an improved lifestyle, long term enjoyment, and most of all, satisfied clients.

Figure 2. *An overview statement provides the reader with a quick synopsis of your company. Colored paper catches the eye.*

design, or you can hire a graphic designer for between $200 and $500 to create a logo. Once you've created it, use it on your stationery, job-site signs, business card, Yellow Pages listing, and display ads. You want homeowners to recognize your company by your unique logo.

Overviews. Your company should also have what I call an "overview" statement, explaining how long you've been in business, the types of services you offer, awards won, and membership in professional trade associations. The overview can be brief: Ours is printed on one side of 8½x11-inch colored paper (Figure 2). Distribute your overview statement to Chamber of Commerce members, Rotarians, bankers, and realtors, and send it to potential customers. We update ours two or three times a year.

Brochures. A company brochure can be an effective way to introduce your business and services. In it, you can summarize your services and illustrate them with drawings or photos of completed jobs. Nancy laid out our brochure using CAD, a word processor, and a rendering from our designer (Figure 3). She produced a camera-ready original, and the print shop charged us 15¢ per copy (including folding) for a run of 350. We distribute it as we do our overview statement, and it also is an important component of our initial meeting with homeowners.

Initial Contact

Homeowners are interested in your reputation. They'll want to know about your financial stability, whether you have experience doing the type of project they have in mind, and the scope of services you offer, both prior to the start of the project and after completion. They'll also want third-party endorsements. Used effectively, this information can set your company apart from your competitors.

The presentation. Your presentation begins with the first phone call to your office.

Ask the caller about his project, how he learned about your company, who referred him to you, how soon he would like to start, and whether he is getting other bids. At Defern Contracting, we collect this information on a Sales Lead sheet (Figure 4, page 228).

Set up an appointment to meet with the prospective customer and follow up with a letter confirming the time and location. In the letter, express your interest in the project and reiterate your experience working on similar jobs. We also include a flyer listing emergency phone numbers, plus our business card, brochure, and overview statement.

Be punctual for the first meeting. Remember, you have less than three minutes to establish rapport with Mr. or Mrs. Homeowner. Everything that happens in those first three minutes will determine whether you're going to develop a relationship of mutual trust. What you say and how you conduct yourself is very important, because the homeowner is looking for a builder or remodeler with whom he or she feels comfortable.

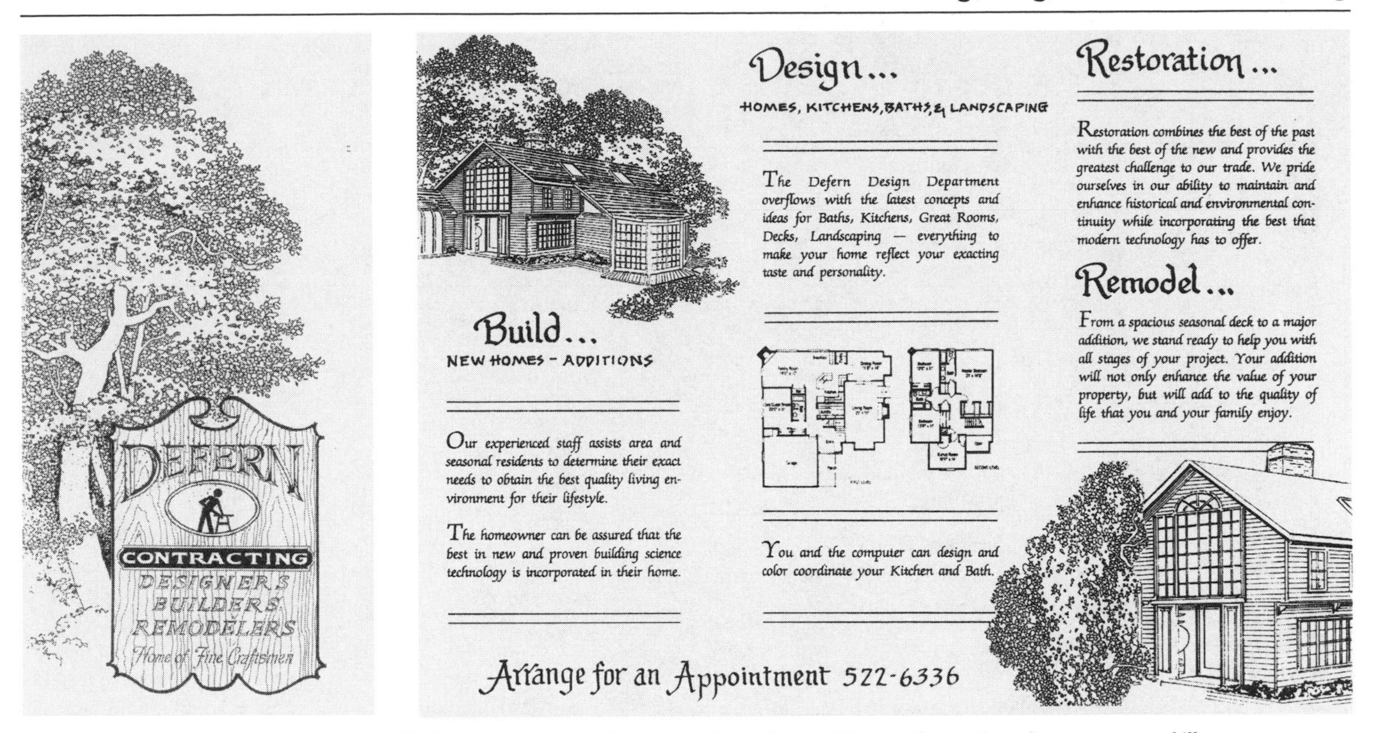

Figure 3. ***A brochure conveys a "picture" of your company, using text and simple graphics or photos that showcase your skills.***

Homeowners are interested in describing to you the scope of work they have in mind, some of their ideas and dreams. They're depending on you to help fulfill those hopes and expectations. Listen carefully and offer suggestions based upon your experience. Build their confidence in you.

Presentation package. The real moment of truth for customers comes when they weigh the contents of your "package." That information packet will determine whether you're going to be the remodeler or builder of choice. It contains tools you already have (many of which your competitors have, too, but don't use), such as copies of your contract, certificate of insurance, change order, warranty, and sample specifications. We keep ours in a three-ring binder along with before and after photos of our jobs.

Take 15 to 20 minutes to walk prospective clients through your agreement. Show them where you quote your price, give allowances, specify inclusions and exclusions, and set the start and completion dates. Likewise, review your warranty, point out the detailed specifications, and if you'll be supplying plans, show them a set of drawings you've done.

After explaining the contents of your package, leave the homeowner alone to review it while you take measurements and scope out the job. This builds trust: They look at your material at their own pace and you get to browse the job unaccompanied. Before you leave, ask if they have questions. We tell prospects that we will get back to them in one week with a quote, and we always do. This immediately sets us apart from our competition and never fails to elicit a positive response.

Follow up. When you return to the office, write a letter telling the prospect how much you've enjoyed meeting them, reviewing briefly the services provided by your company, and reminding them of your experience doing similar projects. Confirm that you will call ahead to schedule a meeting to present your quote.

After the Job

After you've completed the job and it's gone well, what's next? Your marketing efforts don't stop when you've gotten your last payment or when the prospective customer has chosen another contractor. Your goal is to build name recognition by keeping yourself and your company on their lips. You want them to refer you to others, and you want to build their next project. We keep a 10-year list of customers; 5 years for prospects. Here are some inexpensive ways we keep these relationships alive.

Sales Lead

Date of appt./Day of week/Time ________ Salesperson ________
Client ________
Spouse's name ________ Lead rec'd by ________
Mailing address ________ Date ________
Town, State, Zip ________
Home phone ________
FAX ________ Office phone ________

1. How did you hear about Defern? ________
2. Describe the project (size/type/purpose) ________
3. What is your time frame or target date? ________
4. How long have you lived at this address? ________
5. How long have you been planning this project?
   3 months______ 6 months______ year______ longer______
6. Are you planning to get other proposals?
   Yes______ No______ How many______
7. Have you ever had remodeling or new construction done before?
   Yes______ No______ If yes, when?______ What________
   Who ________
8. Additional comments: ________
9. Directions to project: ________

Sales Leads 1999

	Total number	Percentage
Referral	17	23.6
Former Client	13	18.1
Realtor	5.	6.9
Bluehill	4	5.6
Personal contact	4	5.6
Homeowner Seminar	4	5.6
Reputation	4	5.6
News Story	4	5.6
Architect	2	2.7
Chamber of Commerce	4	5.6
Accountant	2	2.7
Welcome Wagon	2	2.7
Supplier	2	2.7
HBA of New Hampshire	1	1.4
Miscellaneous	4	5.6

Figure 4. *The author uses a lead sheet (left) to collect the same kind of information from every prospective client. At year end, he reviews a summary of lead sources (above) and adjusts his marketing strategy accordingly.*

Customer satisfaction survey. We send out a follow-up questionnaire with a self-addressed stamped envelope about two weeks after we have completed a job. We ask the customer to tell us what they thought of our company, to make suggestions for improving our performance, and to describe any changes they would make in the design. The survey demonstrates to the customer that we have a formalized follow-up program and helps continue our relationship with them. It becomes an educational tool for us in identifying our strengths and those areas needing improvement. Additionally, we share the survey results with our lead carpenters and subs; this encourages teamwork among our workers and subs, which ultimately allows us to provide better service.

Inspections. As we hand off our warranty, we always tell the homeowners that we'll come back in a year to take care of any small details that need attention. This may include adjusting a door or installing a missing screen (we build the cost of the follow-up inspection into the original quote). This kind of service shows professionalism, plus it's a great way to maintain contact with past clients.

Keep in touch. Every day we make a phone call to two or three previous clients. We may tell them about a local event that might interest them, or perhaps we'll call to congratulate them on a newspaper report that their son or daughter has graduated from school. Similarly, after a particularly heavy rain-storm, we'll call to ask how the new roof held up.

For seasonal customers, who may live as far away as Arizona or Florida, we call in the off-season to keep them abreast of the work we're doing on their summer home or to update them on the condition of the cottage they've asked us to check while they're away. It's a real confidence builder for them to hear from their contractor in distant New Hampshire.

Cards. Many remodelers send out thank-yous and Christmas cards (and you should, too), but don't be afraid to try something different. In late January, for example, we send out our "January letter." This arrives after the hubbub of the holidays has subsided so it's more likely to get the reader's attention. In it, we wish their families success and health in the coming year, but we also remind them of our services. The most important part of the message, however, is in the last sentence: "In closing, we want to express our appreciation for the many leads you have given us, and we look forward to your continued support." Many of the people who get this letter haven't provided any leads, but this simple statement gets them to think about us in conjunction with someone who might use our services.

Invitations to company events. I can't emphasize enough how strong this is as a marketing tool. We always have a Christmas party at our house and invite our employees, subcontractors, suppliers, and the customers we have served over the last two years. About 70 people attend, and our cost averages $7 per person. The party will build team players, and those subs, suppliers, and customers expand your sales force. They'll go home and talk about your company with everyone they meet. The more people you have on your bandwagon working for you, the stronger your company is going to be.

The DEFERN DIFFERENCE

Published by: Defern Contracting, Inc., 102 Governor's Road, Brookfield, NH 03872 (603) 522-6336

Volume 3, Issue 1; February 1996

All Hale the Vernal Equinox

Put a red circle around March 20th on your calender, set your alarm for 3:04 A.M. EST!

Believe it or not, ready or not -- Spring will be here before we know it. And, who among us is not ready for that first balmy breeze, and, yes, even that first **BLACK FLY!**

While we in New England have "suffered" at the hands of Mother Nature this winter, we once again have been blessed and not had to weather the hardships of most of the rest of the country. Yes, even those of you who bask in the warmth of the southern climes have had a taste or two of "Old Man Winter's handiwork".

All of which makes Spring that much more welcome, and enjoyable.

CENSUS UPDATE

Newborn girls still outnumber newborn boys in the Defern family of staff and team members coupled with clients, but Alan and Sue Harding welcome a new grandson, and the Gavers are enjoying a new grandson as well.

Score: Girls - 9 Boys - 2

Stay Out of the Gutter

While we discourage homeowners from considering standard gutter/downspout systems for their homes, there are a number of new products on the market that are engineered to eliminate gutter cleaning resulting from leaves, pine needles and debris build-up.

If you are interested in knowing more about these systems, please call the Defern Office for literature.

EXPANDED OPTIONS FOR HOMEOWNERS

Following numerous requests, Defern Contracting, Inc. has formalized and expanded that which has been a part of Defern for many years -- providing consultation and expert guidance through the challenging, confusing, and time-consuming process of planning a new home, the remodeling, and/or improvement of an existing home.

Learning the whole "menu" of planning and constructing an addition, remodeling an existing home, or building a new home tailored to ones' individual and family needs can be an anxiety-ridden experience.

Defern's detailed approach focuses on the client's lifestyle, defined budget parameters, and the buildability of a plan. Increasing the homeowner's confidence in material and product selection coupled with rapid feedback and information of materials, products, costs and construction estimates aids the homeowner in developing a realistic budget to meet investment requirements.

Working together as a team, Defern and the homeowner can develop and implement the best course of action to achieve the best investment value. Whether a "turn-key" project, phased, or Assisted Do-It-Yourself, the homeowner can take full advantage of the best the industry has to offer.

The Information Highway Has a Brookfield Exit!

Defern has for some time offered computer assisted design. Now, state-of-the-art technology, CD-ROM, and the World Wide Web allow Defern to share product images from the nation's leading manufacturers. Viewing color photos of actual products superimposed on a client's proposed home makes the complete design concept come to life in just a few minutes.

Planning a project -- call to see it come to life.

Figure 5. *Newsletters are an inexpensive way to get people to talk about your company. Provide a mix of local news, helpful hints, and recent accomplishments.*

Press releases. Press releases promote third-party credibility. There are four weekly newspapers in our area, and every season we send out a press release to each. The fall release might cover tips homeowners can use to prepare for winter; the spring release might talk about designing a sunroom. The ideas and content for these releases come from articles we've read or from our own experience. In addition, we send releases after speaking at a Rotary luncheon, having an article published, or attending a conference. Press releases help establish you as an expert; newspapers now call me asking for an article.

Newsletters. Newsletters are an excellent way to stay in touch with former and prospective customers, as well as with subs, vendors, and real estate agents. And they don't have to be expensive. Nancy composes our quarterly newsletter, The Defern Difference, on a word processor in two days. It's a single 8½x11 sheet printed on both sides (Figure 5); printing costs run 10¢ each for 500 copies, plus first-class postage.

Content for your newsletter is readily available: You can showcase an employee, include articles such as "What to look for when choosing a contractor," or write about a new business in your area (we once reviewed a restaurant that opened in a restored 1950s diner). The most popular feature of our newsletter is the recipe column. In keeping with the season, we include one of Nancy's recipes — an apple pie recipe in the fall, for example, and vegetable dishes in the summer. You can also team up with a local business to offer a discount on their products or services; we recently included a 10% off coupon for an ice cream shop. The purpose of the newsletter is to get people to respond to it; in doing so, the reader is more likely to remember your company.

Whichever low-cost marketing ideas you embrace — and there are many more — remember that your goal is to keep your name in front of as many people as possible who are in a position to use your services.

What Works, What Doesn't?

Finally, take a look at the sources of your leads. Knowing where your jobs are coming from will help you spend your marketing time and money more wisely by enabling you to target the best prospects. This will increase the exposure of your company, bringing you more leads and more jobs. As the number and quality of your leads increase, so will your profits.

Every January, we sit down and review the previous year. In the upper right corner of the the lead sheets that we filled out when our customers first called we make notes telling whether we got the job, the type of job, and the dollar amount. We take all the lead sheets for the year, count the number of leads and jobs, and separate them by type and dollar amount. This data tells us what kinds of jobs we're doing and the annual dollar volume of each category. We also monitor lead sources.

We then use this information about our jobs to refine our marketing plan. For example, we do one or two whole-house renovations a year for out-of-state homeowners, which keeps our crew busy during the winter months. So, every year we concentrate some of our marketing energy on finding jobs that will carry us through the winter. In your own business, you'll discover that some marketing efforts work better than others. You may learn, too, that certain types of marketing attract less profitable jobs, so you can change the direction of your marketing to attract more profitable jobs. By fine-tuning your efforts, you can strengthen your marketing program and get a greater return on your investment.

By Bill Gaver, who with his wife, Nancy, runs Defern Contracting, a design-build company in Brookfield, N.H.

Market Research For Small-Volume Builders

You can profit from the same marketing information big builders use if you're persistent and know where to look

Whether you like it or not, if you're a small-volume spec builder, you face a marketing challenge in today's economy. While the new buyer pool shrinks and the existing owners age, the big guys just seem to keep getting bigger ("...they have more consultants than I have employees"). How does a small-volume builder compete in a market that is more and more dependent on sophisticated strategies for targeting and pleasing the buyer?

The answer is plain, old sweat-of-the-brow homework. It doesn't take a lot of money, but it does take time and some knowledge of how to get there from here.

Asking The Questions

The first challenge is to really know your marketplace. Here are ten questions that will test your knowledge:

1. How many new homes (in the product type you build) were sold and closed in the last year in your specific market area?
2. What was the monthly sales rate for the builders and/or projects of those homes?
3. How many existing homes in each product type and price range were sold in your marketplace last year?
4. What is the projected annual demand for new housing by product type and price range in your marketplace for the next 12 months? For the next 24 months?
5. Does your marketplace have enough qualified buyers to adequately absorb your proposed product and that of your competitors?
6. Can you accurately identify the predominant age groups and average household incomes of the new home buyers in your marketplace?
7. Do you know the current exterior elevation design and color preferences of

the anticipated buyers of your new or proposed projects?

8. Do you know which current floor plan layouts and room configurations are preferred by the buyers in your projects' price range?
9. What standard features or amenities do the buyers for your product really want and expect?
10. Do you know the average retail price per square foot of your three top competitors' projects?

If you cannot correctly answer at least eight of these questions, you may end up making development decisions about your project and marketplace that lead you down the well-trodden path to failure. But don't give up hope. The answers you need can be found—without spending a lot of money — by asking the right people the right questions.

Getting The Answers

First, identify your specific market area by outlining its boundaries on a map. Note the location of each new home or development within that market area that represents direct competition. Pick normally slow traffic days to visit each project and walk each model that's available for viewing. Develop your own *competitive analysis form* where you note square footages, room configurations, elevation design, standard and optional features, base pricing per home and any lot premiums assigned.

Sales info. Spend time with sales agents or brokers discussing the floor plans that buyers favor and the standard features that generate the most favorable comments. Ask for general buyer profiles for the overall project and for each plan or house sold. Ask the sales agent what floor plan or plans he or she would like to see the builder offer if the builder already doesn't, and why. Ask how many of each type of plan they've sold. Remember that your approach and attitude will probably determine how helpful the sales agent will be and how much valuable information you will get.

If you don't have much luck in approaching the sales agent and builder, contact your local title company. They should be able to provide you with the number of closings recorded for each competitive project. The only information they'll need is an assessor's parcel number, which is readily available from local and county governments. Your title company should be able to give you a specific address, lot number and recorded sales price for each unit sold. Just take this data, drive around the project, and note which plans have been sold.

Still another source is your real estate broker. Typically he or she will be a member of the local multiple listing service (MLS). Have your broker run an MLS competitive analysis of your competitor's projects. The MLS report should give you all the essential information you need, including how many days each home was on the market.

From these three sources you should be able to determine the answers to Questions #1 and #2. The answer to Question #3, on resale activity, also lies with your real estate broker and his connection with the local real estate board/multiple listing service.

An analysis of prices and size trends can tell you what demands aren't being satisfied by new home development. Also, a specific area with strong resale home activity that brings equity to sellers often indicates a good move-up market for buyers — particularly if the area has excellent schools.

Demand and its profile. For marketplace depth, contact government agencies that forecast population growth and new job growth for your area. Take the forecasted growth for the next one- to two-year period and divide that figure by the average household size for the area to determine *housing unit demand.* Household make-up estimates can also be obtained from governmental sources or data retrieval firms.

To "qualify" that demand depth, and quantify it by age and household income level, you can again turn to retrieval firms. For $100 to $200, they can provide you with demographic printouts for specific market areas. In larger metropolitan areas, there are also private or quasi-governmental agencies such as chambers of commerce or trade development associations that have most of the essential demographic information you'll need. Just ask.

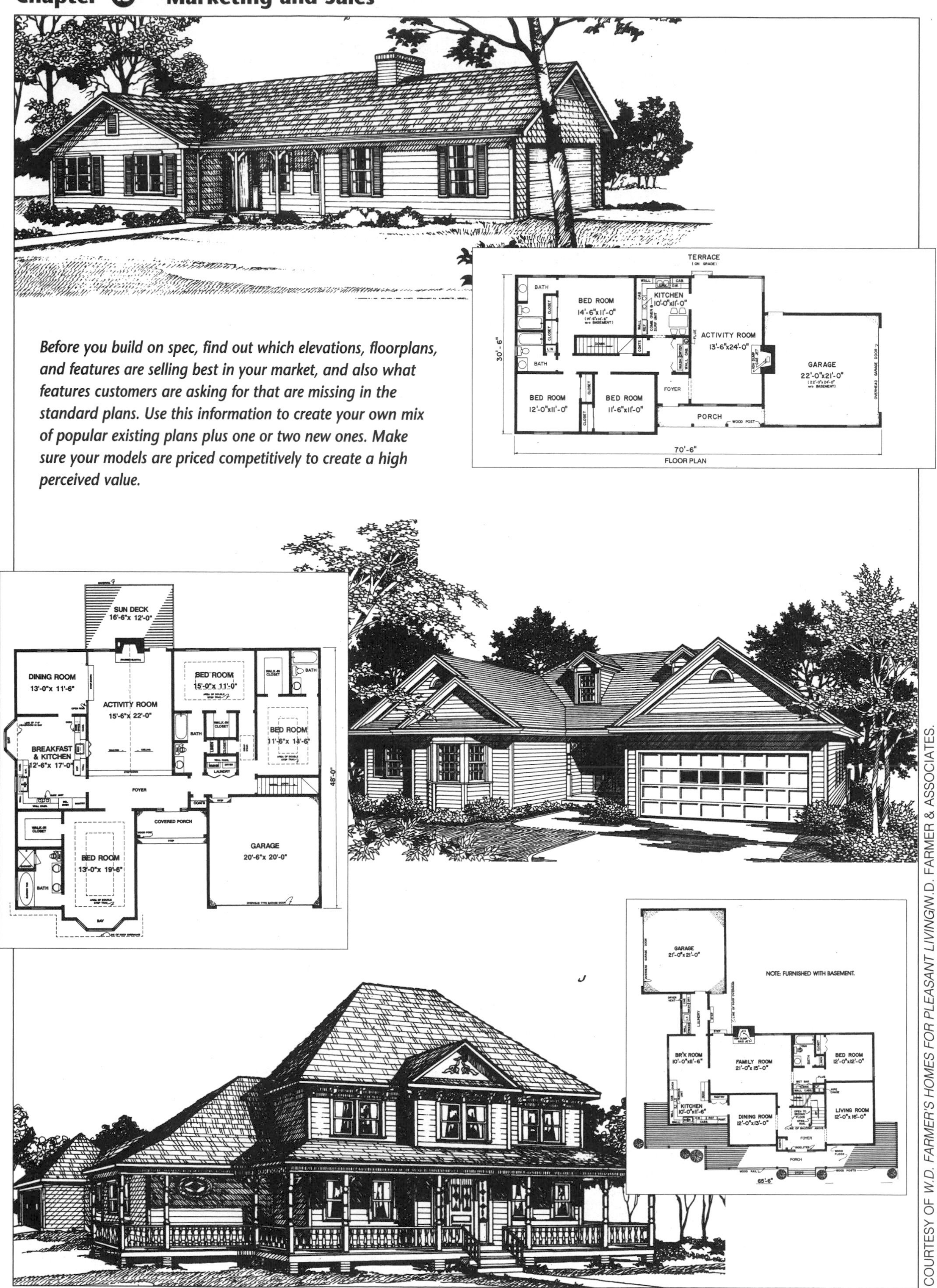

Before you build on spec, find out which elevations, floorplans, and features are selling best in your market, and also what features customers are asking for that are missing in the standard plans. Use this information to create your own mix of popular existing plans plus one or two new ones. Make sure your models are priced competitively to create a high perceived value.

COURTESY OF *W.D. FARMER'S HOMES FOR PLEASANT LIVING*/W.D. FARMER & ASSOCIATES.

The right package. To determine exterior elevation design and color preferences for your anticipated buyers, again use your in-field survey of primary competitors. Unless an existing project is selling rapidly because of pricing advantage or a superior location, those projects with higher sales rates generally have the elevation designs and exterior colors that are preferred by most buyers. You can also contact local paint stores to ask what exterior colors are most in demand.

Now for what I consider the key for the small volume builder: offering a better product. The main components are offering the right floor plan designs, including the standard features expected by the buyers, and correctly pricing the product to create *perceived value.*

Go back to the information you compiled from surveying your competitors and talking to their sales representatives. Those on-site salespeople normally tell you what their buyers love in terms of plans and features, as well as what buyers have been asking for that the standard plans don't have. This is an excellent starting point for determining your product design and floor plan mix (as well as pricing structure). Next, check with your local building department and take a look at what future competing projects will be offering in their floor plan mix. Remember, once a builder has submitted his plans for review and approval, they become public documents that you have a right to view.

After looking at existing and future projects offered by your competitors, you may find one or two plans that buyers have been asking for but that aren't being offered. However, don't end up "reinventing the wheel;" if there are several existing floor plans that are selling faster than others, make sure to include them in your mix. Buyer preference trends take at least 18 months to change, so a competitively priced mix of popular existing plans with one or two new ones should be well received once built.

Other Information Sources

In-field research is not the only answer to your product determination needs. You must also *read* and *attend* anything that even remotely addresses these subjects.

Magazines and newsletters that cover buyer profiles and preferences are often excellent sources. Magazines such as *Builder* and *Professional Builder* have numerous articles every year — from market researchers, product development specialists, and architects — which discuss both existing and future housing trends. And these publications are also filled with analyses of the marketing approach used in successful projects. Look for projects from your area that have been written up, then go to school on their product lines, floor plans, and buyer profiles.

Seminars and courses that deal with housing market trends can also be very helpful. This is particularly true if these seminars and courses feature industry professionals or experts on your local market.

You will also want to attend regional and national industry conventions such as the builders' show that NAHB sponsors. From their extensive menu of seminars, choose programs dealing with buyer product and feature preferences, new product design concepts, and how to conduct your own research or analysis. If there are experts from your local market featured, so much the better.

Another excellent source of help at industry gatherings is "workshop programs." These usually allow attendees to sit down and informally discuss special situations or problems dealing with research, product design, marketing strategies, advertising, etc. They often feature prominent names in these respective fields. In a limited sense, you're getting the expensive consultants the big guys are *paying for.*

Still, there is no easy way to predict demand for any given market area or buyer profile. However, if you use some of these suggestions, you should know more about your market area and buyer profiles than most of your competition. Although it's a shopworn and hackneyed dictum, knowledge is power, particularly in gaining a competitive advantage in your market.

By John Schleimer, president of Market Directions, Inc., a Sacramento, Calif., firm specializing in market research, product development, and master marketing programs.

Selecting Quality Customers: The Art of Prequalification

Sales lead sheets can help to prequalify customers over the phone, saving time and money

During the first few years in business, most small remodeling companies take on every job that comes their way. But time is an expensive commodity in the construction business, and can't be wasted chasing down leads that never amount to anything.

Our solution is to prequalify prospective customers before spending a lot of time pursuing the work. By the time we return a customer's call, we already know the lead is strong so we don't feel we're wasting our time. Our prequalification process also gets callers to commit to more than simply making a phone call — they must also provide a certain amount of information. Sometimes their unwillingness to do that is enough to make us think twice before following the lead.

Using a Lead Sheet

When we first started our business, we used a standard phone message pad that only had room to take down the caller's name, phone number, and a brief description — like "second-floor bath" or "wraparound deck" — of the work they wanted done. All of the messages went to Tim, the company owner and its only salesman, who followed up every call. At first it was easy, but the more successful we became as a company, the harder it got. When the number of calls we were getting topped 150 per year, Tim couldn't keep up, and he had to be more selective. But he had no means of deciding which call to return first. Strong leads that should have been at the top of the pile often ended up near the bottom. And weak leads — sometimes ones that shouldn't have been pursued at all — were right on top.

We first heard about using a lead sheet to prequalify customers in an educational seminar for remodelers. We used a preprinted form for a while, but we soon realized that we needed to tailor the form to our business. We developed the Sales Lead sheet we use now over a period of several years (Figure 1). On the front side, we record the basic information about the caller; on the back is a point system we use to prioritize the lead. The main purpose of the form is to make sure that we put the limited time and resources we have to good use by following up only strong leads, and letting the others go.

We've deliberately kept the Sales Lead sheet simple. An early version had a series of boxes you could check off, but it took more time to find the appropriate box than it did to just take notes. Our current sheet is more free-form. We store our Sales Lead sheet as a file on our word processor so we can change it easily. We've toyed with the idea of having the form printed on two-part carbonless paper, but for now we just make photocopies.

We keep lead sheets near all of the phones in the office, and we always use the form when answering a call from a prospective customer. Debbie and Linda answer the phone most of the time, but if they're not at their desks, everyone in the office has been trained on how to use the lead sheet to field a call.

By the Numbers

We designed a point system to help us prioritize our leads. From our records of past jobs, we determined that there were two main indicators that a lead was more likely to result in a contract for the work: the type of work the caller wanted done, and how they came to call our company. Under "Type of Project" on the back of the Sales Lead sheet, the order and point value assigned to each entry is in descending order based on several factors, including overall job profitability, ease of construction, and our work preferences. In practice, there isn't much difference between types of work that are just two points apart. The important differences are between types of work at the top of the list and those at the bottom; when we're busy, we pick from the top of the list and avoid the bottom.

One exception is when a past customer or a strong referral wants work done that we consider to be low priority. That's

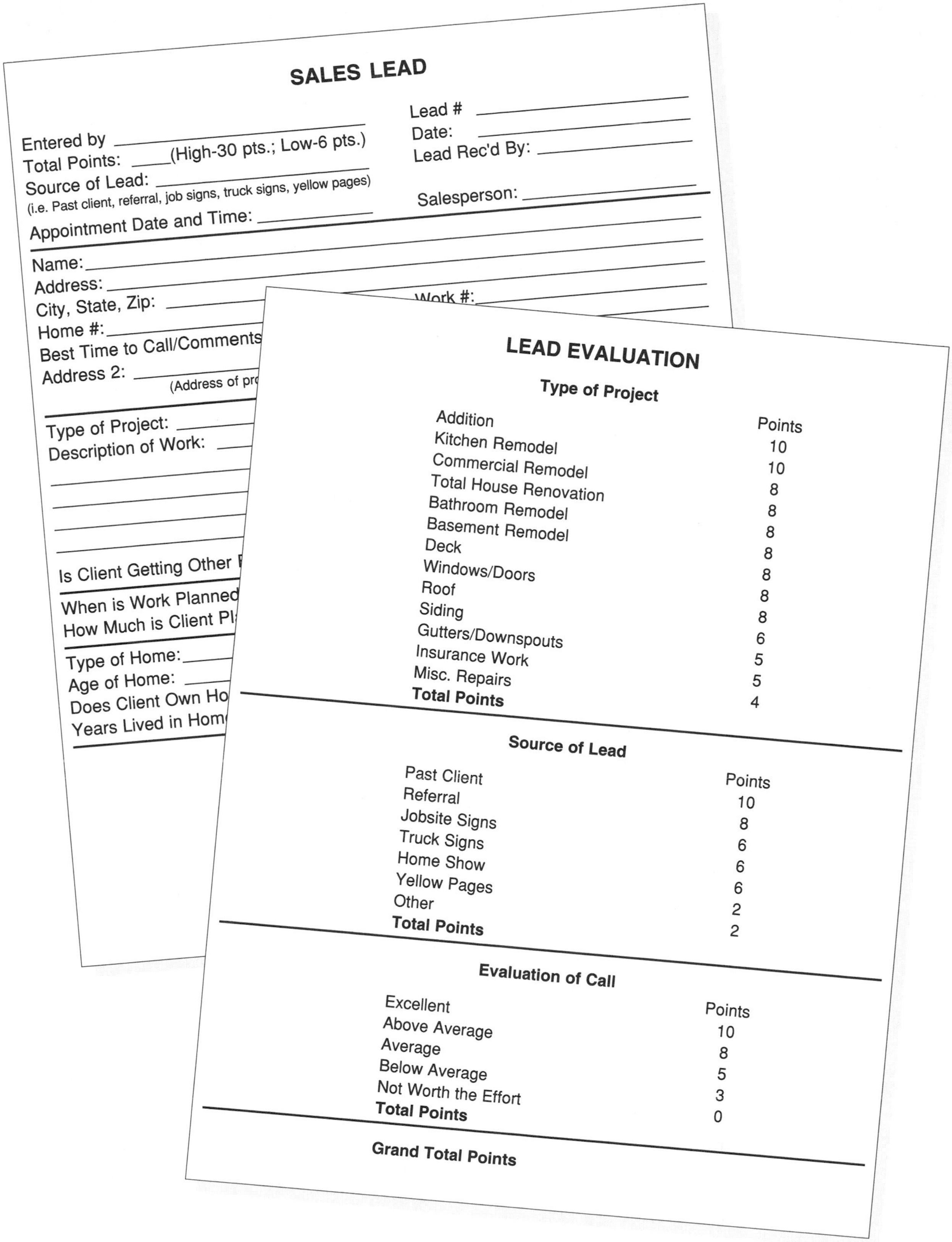

SALES LEAD

Entered by ______
Total Points: ____(High-30 pts.; Low-6 pts.)
Source of Lead: ______
(i.e. Past client, referral, job signs, truck signs, yellow pages)
Appointment Date and Time: ______

Lead # ______
Date: ______
Lead Rec'd By: ______
Salesperson: ______

Name: ______
Address: ______
City, State, Zip: ______
Work #: ______
Home #: ______
Best Time to Call/Comments
Address 2: ______
(Address of pr

Type of Project: ______
Description of Work: ______

Is Client Getting Other P
When is Work Planned
How Much is Client Pl
Type of Home: ______
Age of Home: ______
Does Client Own Ho
Years Lived in Hom

LEAD EVALUATION

Type of Project

Addition
Kitchen Remodel
Commercial Remodel
Total House Renovation
Bathroom Remodel
Basement Remodel
Deck
Windows/Doors
Roof
Siding
Gutters/Downspouts
Insurance Work
Misc. Repairs
Total Points

Points
10
10
8
8
8
8
8
8
8
6
5
5
4

Source of Lead

Past Client
Referral
Jobsite Signs
Truck Signs
Home Show
Yellow Pages
Other
Total Points

Points
10
8
6
6
6
2
2

Evaluation of Call

Excellent
Above Average
Average
Below Average
Not Worth the Effort
Total Points

Points
10
8
5
3
0

Grand Total Points

Figure 1. *The front of the Sales Lead sheet is useful for gathering information from every prospective customer who calls. In the Lead Evaluation section on the back, points are assigned based on the strength of the lead in several categories.*

November 10, 1999

David Smith
45 Main Street
Wadsworth, Ohio

Dear David:

Thank you for calling Tim Englert Construction, Inc. with your remodeling needs. Unfortunately, we have been unable to respond to your request in a timely fashion, and must therefore decline to quote on your remodeling project at this time. We apologize for any inconvenience this may have caused.

Sincerely,

TIM ENGLERT CONSTRUCTION, INC.

November 10, 1999

Julie Jones
123 Main Street
Wadsworth, Ohio

Dear Julie:

Thank you for calling Tim Englert Construction, Inc., with your remodeling needs. Unfortunately, we have been unable to respond to your request in a timely fashion, and must therefore decline to quote on your remodeling project at this time. However, if your project schedule has changed and you are still interested in obtaining an estimate from our company, please contact our office at 336-2770 or 864-3637 to further discuss your project. We apologize for any inconvenience this may have caused.

Sincerely,

TIM ENGLERT CONSTRUCTION, INC.

Figure 2. *All leads who don't receive a follow-up call are sent a form letter. The letter at top politely declines the work; the other leaves the door open for future follow-up. Both letters put the ball in the customer's court: If they call a second time, chances are they're serious about having the authors' company do the project.*

where the second category, "Source of Lead," is helpful. A strong lead source greatly increases the chances that we'll actually do the work, so we've assigned points to the various types of callers depending on how they heard about our company. Historically, past clients and personal referrals are our strongest leads; Yellow Pages callers are our weakest.

First impressions. The final section of the point system, called "Evaluation of Call," assigns a value to the general impression left by the caller on the person who took the call. It's an attempt to quantify the subjective element of screening leads. Debbie has been fielding calls for a long time, so she has a feel for whether or not we should put more time into follow-up. She uses the information recorded on the front of the form, plus her overall impression of the caller, to assign a value. For example, if the caller is very frank and open about seeking other bidders and about discussing the budget, Debbie might interpret that as a sincere interest in hiring our company. On the other hand, if a caller immediately asks how much a job will cost without first talking about the project, that's a red flag signaling a lead that would probably not result in a contract. Other factors, such as the urgency for the work to be done and the extent to which the caller has worked to seek financing, to name a few, also enter into the evaluation.

Red flags. We can try to eliminate some leads during the first call. For example, we don't do new construction, basement waterproofing, detached garages, or concrete driveways, so we turn down that type of work immediately.

One sign of a weak lead is an inadequate budget. If a caller doesn't have enough money for the project they describe, we usually don't pursue the work.

We don't spend a lot of time on shoppers, either. We have found that most callers who get our name from the Yellow Pages are "tire-kickers" who are usually calling half a dozen or more builders. Chances are usually slight that we'll get the work. The same is true of callers who ask for prices during the first call. We usually won't quote a price over the phone (small jobs, like gutter replacements, are an exception), and people who ask for pricing are usually just shopping.

Following the Lead

The process we follow is simple. When someone calls, we fill out the front side of the lead sheet, getting as much information as we can. As soon as the caller hangs up, Debbie immediately reviews the information while it's still fresh in her mind, and assigns a point value in each of the three sections on the back of the lead sheet. She then transfers the total to the front page (in the top left corner) and hand delivers the sheet to Tim. If Tim's not at his desk, the form goes into his "In" box with a prominent note to attract his attention.

When Tim first looks at the form, he checks the "Total Points," reads Debbie's comments, and looks on the front of the sheet for any information concerning the budget, schedule, other bidders, and so on. A strong lead is usually in the range of 25 points, but during this quick screening, a low point total doesn't automatically rule a job out. For example, a past client who calls to schedule miscellaneous repairs and who doesn't need an estimate would get a total of 24 points — 4 points for "Type of Work," plus 10 each for "Source of Lead" and "Evaluation of Call." Even though this total is slightly lower than the average strong lead, this is a job we would want to follow up right away.

The opposite is also true. We may get a call for a kitchen remodel (10 points) from someone referred to us by a past client (8 points), and who Debbie feels is an excellent prospect (10 points). But the total of 28 points doesn't guarantee that we'll pursue the job. If, for instance, the house is located outside the geographic area in which we feel we can comfortably operate, we may decide not to pursue the work.

Point totals are also cumulative: A deck (8 points) and a roof replacement (8 points) would total 16 points under "Type of Work." We add the points together because the quantity of work we'll be bidding on is greater. If the caller is also a referral (8 points) who has already taken a loan and is talking only to one other company (10 points), the total would be 34 — a very strong lead.

Tim takes all of this into consideration when deciding which leads to follow up. If a lead is obviously strong, he'll put it at the top of his list and make the call immediately. We discuss more marginal leads at a weekly sales meeting, during which we debate the pros and cons of each lead, and give more weight to our subjective opinions about the likelihood of getting the work. From this discussion, Tim can decide which jobs are worth the time and effort of a follow-up call.

The final step is the follow-up call itself. Tim often talks for 20 minutes or more before deciding to make an appointment to visit the site and do an estimate. If the lead doesn't pan out, Tim generally declines the work during the follow-up call.

Dead Leads

Before we used the point system, rejected leads were dropped: We simply never called back. But we soon realized that it would be a better marketing practice to stay on the good side of everyone who calls. So now we send one of two form letters to everyone whose call we have decided not to return (Figure 2). The first letter goes to callers who we decide are merely shopping. The letter politely declines the job in a way that says "Thanks for calling, but we're not interested."

The second letter tries to keep the lead alive in cases in which we want to pursue the work, but for which we don't have room in our schedule at the moment. The letter leaves the door open for future follow-up.

Both letters accomplish two things. First, the letters are consistent with good marketing practices, because everyone who calls gets a reply. Second, the letters put the ball back in the caller's court. If a prospective customer wants to discuss the job further, they'll call back — and we'll know they're serious about using our company, without having put a lot of time and effort into follow-up.

How well does our prequalification system work? This year, we'll get about 450 calls from prospective customers. If we followed up on all of them, we'd hardly have time to do anything else. Instead, our bid ratio is about 50%: In other words, we submit estimates on about half of the calls we get. Of the callers to whom we submit bids, about half will contract with us for the work. It's a lot easier to follow-up more than 200 calls per year when you know you'll get half the jobs.

By Tim and Linda Englert and Debbie Land. The Englerts own and operate Tim Englert Construction Inc. in Wadsworth, Ohio. Debbie Land is the company's office manager.

Sales for People Who Don't Like Selling

Use these tried-and-true techniques to land more jobs and spend less time selling

Sales. The very word conjures up images of a vacuum cleaner salesman coming up the sidewalk in wingtips. Contractors who dislike wearing the salesman's hat (along with the wingtips) often rely on word-of-mouth referrals to keep the jobs coming in. But no matter what you call it, calling on potential customers makes you a salesperson.

In many ways, selling is like a building project. Successful building or remodeling projects start with a set of plans. By following the plans carefully, you achieve your goal: a quality job and a satisfied customer. Selling is no different. You start with a sales plan, and follow it step by step until you achieve your goal: new business.

Qualifying the Lead

The first step in effective sales is weeding out the "suspects" from the "prospects." You've got to concentrate your efforts on people who actually want to do business. It's surprising how many sales appointments are spent with the wrong people present or wasted on "window shoppers." You (or your office help) need to do a little phone work before you schedule an appointment.

Nail down the time frame. Ask your phone prospect when they actually plan to do the work. Don't be rude, but excuse yourself unless they're planning the work for the immediate future. In selling, the last person in the door usually gets the job, so any time spent in preparation for a job two years from now will almost certainly be wasted.

Scheduling the appointment. Make sure everyone has allowed enough time for your appointment. If your presentation takes two hours, then make sure the client or clients will be available for at least that length of time. If they are serious about the job, they'll be happy to set aside a block of time for you. This is a good way to test the water before going further, and it will weed out the suspects.

Make sure everyone is present. Never schedule an appointment unless all the decision makers will be present: both the husband and wife, the entire church board, and so on. Otherwise, you'll be relying on someone else to sell your product to the absent decision makers. This is one of the biggest mistakes made in sales, and one of the easiest to avoid.

Older clients. Always find out if older folks have adult children or other relatives who will be part of the purchasing decision, and make sure all are present at any sales meeting. If you doubt the importance of this issue, think about your own parents and how you would react if you thought they were being taken advantage of by a salesperson.

Setting Sales Goals

Once you've qualified the prospect and scheduled your first sales call, you need to set a goal for the sales meeting. Different products and services have different "sales cycles" — the length of time between the first meeting and actually doing business. Replacement windows and roofing, for example, can and should be sold in one call. A room addition, however, might take a couple of meetings, and a custom home might take months of intense design and selling effort. No matter what the length of the sales cycle, you need to establish a goal for what each sales call will produce.

Your first goal is to get the prospect out of the marketplace as quickly as possible. If your potential customer becomes significantly involved with another company while waiting for you to "get back to them," you're a goner. This means always going to an appointment with the idea of getting some type of commitment from the prospect.

While it's not reasonable (or appropriate) to expect someone to commit to a custom home the first time they meet you, it is reasonable to expect a commitment for the next meeting, and possibly a refundable deposit for design services. In the sales world, these little commitments are called "closes," and they should all lead to the big close — a signed contract with your company. A good way to keep your prospects dealing with you and not your competition is to develop a system that can provide pricing and other information on the spot.

Your First Call

The days of a fast sales pitch are over. Today, the salesperson has to be a trusted adviser, an expert in his or her field. That doesn't mean that a planned sales call is no longer needed; in fact, just the opposite is true. Everything you do and say should be a planned event, and should be written out, memorized, and practiced. The better prepared you are, the easier it will be for you to deal with events that could undo your entire effort (an unusual question or an intervening friend, for example).

Classic sales training emphasizes five basic steps for sales calls:
- Warm-up, or approach
- Questioning or investigation
- Presentation
- Close
- Follow-up

The Approach

The approach involves getting comfortable with your prospect. First impressions are hard to undo, so always be on your best behavior. Some sales courses insist that you shower the prospect with "sincere compliments" and other gimmicks to gain trust quickly. I've found the best approach is to sincerely thank your prospect for taking the time to see you. People are very busy today, and their time is important to them.

An emotional issue. People make purchases primarily for emotional reasons, then justify their decision later with facts. This law of human nature almost never changes. If you think selling is a matter of going to someone's house and spouting off for an hour about how great your product or service is compared with the competition's, you're missing the boat. Before you present facts and figures, you need to develop the emotional issues that will persuade your prospect to do business with your company.

No one buys a room addition because they want a room. What people want is more comfort or a nicer place for their kids to play. A new furnace doesn't just give them heat, it gives them peace of mind by providing good health and safety for their family. Vinyl siding is more than just siding, it's prestige in the neighborhood and pride in ownership. By focusing on the emotional issues, your prospects will talk themselves into doing business with you — if you let them.

Investigate and Interview

The interview can and should take place while you're measuring and poking around. While you're getting the physical facts you need to do the job, you will also be getting the emotional facts you need from your prospect. Conduct the interview in a conversational tone, and ask about the prospect's personal interests, family, and so forth. Your prospects will feel much more comfortable and you'll develop a sense of trust and credibility in their eyes.

Advice On Price

- **Never reveal your prices until you're sure the prospect is ready to do business.** Once you reveal the price, any value you've added to the job will be forgotten; warranty and service won't mean a thing once you're out the door. Chances are your prices will wind up in the hands of your competition and become a tool used to sell against you. Instead of leaving written estimates, I provide prospective customers with a professionally printed "17 Reasons Why" sheet that outlines the advantages of working with our company, along with an 8x10 photo of our staff.
- **Compare apples to oranges.** Make it difficult to compare your price to the competition's by adding extra value to the package. Offering better warranties or extended service agreements are two that I like. Also, try to feature products that no one else makes available.
- **Always sell value, not price.** Find creative ways to point out that the low price is seldom the best deal. I like to compare long-term costs of ownership that include not only the selling price, but also the yearly maintenance and energy costs.
- **Use equivalent monthly costs.** A $30 "monthly investment" is a lot easier to swallow than a purchase of several thousand dollars. Compare the daily investment to something easy to give up, like a cup of coffee.
- **Work from a price book.** Work from a standardized price book whenever possible, and structure your prices so you have a little room to offer discounts for cash payment or senior citizen eligibility, for instance. Documented pricing is a lot more credible than making prices up as you go along.

— J.S.

Loose Lips Sink Ships

The hardest thing for salespeople to do is stop talking. They can't wait to tell a prospect what a great job they can do, and will often interrupt with their own thoughts and ideas the minute a prospect starts to speak. Here are some guidelines to follow as you interview your prospect:

- Let your prospect talk twice as much as you. Keep time mentally to make sure you are not dominating the conversation.
- Never cut off your prospect. After you ask a question, allow them to talk until they are done.
- When asked a question, mentally count to three before responding. Prospects want to feel that their questions are being taken seriously.
- Always have a blank pad of paper handy and take lots of notes. You'll talk less when you're taking notes.
- Avoid discussing controversial subjects. An off-hand remark about politics or religion can cost you a sale.
- Never use foul language or tell off-color jokes.

— J.S.

A big mistake I used to make in sales was not involving the customer. I used to wander around by myself measuring and writing while the prospect waited in the kitchen. Having the prospect help you as you measure or sketch is an ideal way to keep them involved and offers you an opportunity to keep painting those vivid emotional pictures. You should also ask questions that will help discover the buried pipe in the wall or the hot water heater that vents into the attic.

The interview and investigation phase offers salespeople many opportunities to close in small ways. Having your prospect answer certain types of questions will establish a "yes" momentum that will help set the stage for doing business with you. "Won't it be great to look out your new window at the sunset?" "Would you like us to repair this door when we do the rest of the job?" Other questions invite the prospect to make decisions as if they had already committed to the job: "Do you think the gray or the brown shingles would look better?" "Would you rather we use the side door or the garage?" These are all referred to as secondary closes.

Handling Objections

During the interview and investigation, your prospect may question or raise objections to what you are doing and saying. Don't make the mistake of interpreting objections as some kind of personal insult. Objections should be viewed as an opportunity to continue selling.

For example, suppose a prospect says: "We don't think your company is big enough to handle this job." To respond to this type of objection, you should repeat the objection, acknowledge that it's a good question, and then give an example of someone else who had the same concern: "That's a good point, Mrs. Brown; I'd be saying the same thing if I were in your shoes. Mr. and Mrs. Jones had the same concerns, but then were very pleased with the job we did for them...."

Always agree that the question is a good one and provide reasonable proof that there is nothing to worry about. The most common objection encountered is the price. You'll never eliminate this objection, but you can learn how to respond to it (see "Advice on Price," previous page).

The Sales Presentation

The sales presentation is arguably the most important phase of the sales process. But no matter how strong your sales presentation is, it alone will not convince a potential customer to choose your company. The actual presentation should only be done when you are fairly certain the prospect is ready to make a decision in your favor. At this point in the sales process, you're now providing evidence to support the decision. The real purpose of the presentation is to provide the facts necessary to confirm the buying decision and to obtain a commitment from the customer.

A Presentation Book

Most presentations today are assembled in the form of a book and include company history, testimonials, product literature, photographs of jobs and customers, and warranty information. The following guidelines will help you prepare your presentation book:

Include "hands-on" items. Prospects need to stay involved during a sales call. Having something in their hands — photographs, product literature, and warranty cards — helps relieve tension.

Use the right photographs. Every single picture you carry should have people in it. I personally think the "people" content of the picture is a lot more important that the project content, although obviously your photos should pertain to what you're trying to sell.

All testimonials are not created equal. Testimonials are valuable sales tools, but don't stop there. Try to get testimonial letters, along with a photograph, from people who work for the same company as your prospect, or go to the same church.

The Close

A presentation should be simple and direct, and you should always ask for the business. It has been estimated that more than 80% of sales calls end with no one asking for business. This doesn't mean you have to apply high-pressure sales techniques. People have been hassled by salesmen for several thousand years and will absolutely resent pressure from you. But you shouldn't end the presentation until you have asked for the business; if you don't, there's almost no hope that you'll get it.

If, after asking for the business, the prospects say they need to "think it over," try to uncover any underlying objections. It's surprising how often you can close a sale by clearing up a final point or two. If they still need time to think, set up another appointment to "work out the final details," and thank them for their time. The fact that they're willing to meet again means you're still in the running.

There are a couple of other items to keep in mind during the presentation. Never assume that someone referred to you by a past customer is automatically a buyer. In these situations, you should always give your entire presentation. Cutting your presentation short will cost you business.

On the other hand, know when to quit. You can talk yourself right out of the work by not being aware of subtle clues. If your prospect asks, "How soon can you start?" or offers some other buying clue such as a noticeable change in body language, ask for the business, and be prepared to pull out your agreement and start writing.

Always Follow Up

Even if you failed to land the job, follow up on your sales visit with a phone call thanking your prospects for their time. If the job later goes sour, they may very well tell others that they should have gone with your company. But if you successfully sell the job, the follow-up list is a little longer.

Send a small gift immediately after the sales closing. On a recent sales call, the customer had a four-year-old son who kept walking away with my tape measure. A day or two after closing the sale, I delivered a tape measure to the customer's son.

Take photos as the job progresses (don't forget to include people in the photos), and send copies to your customer.

Make sure your company provides all that was promised to the client. I hand out referral certificates when I write the sales agreement, and after the job is complete (and the customer is satisfied), I ask them to fill out the certificate.

Cultivate goodwill by occasionally calling the customer or sending a holiday card. This requires scheduling discipline, but keeps your name fresh in the client's mind.

You don't have to enjoy sales to recognize the important role it plays in your business. And if you truly dislike the sales process, that's all the more reason to be an effective salesperson. Remember, the more effective you are at sales, the less time you'll spend selling.

By Joseph Stoddard, a Certified Professional Building Designer and former home builder from Elkland, Pa., and assistant editor at The Journal of Light Construction.

Using Previous Clients To Win New Ones

Don't hesitate to ask former clients for testimonial letters. They're the most effective marketing tools you have.

How do you convince new clients that your company is the one to go with? One approach is a presentation book full of beautiful photographs detailing your handiwork. Such a book can be helpful; but more important, I've discovered, are the words of satisfied clients. Their descriptions of your company and your work carry a lot more weight with your prospective clients than any claims you can make about yourself.

Like many contractors, you probably give your prospective clients a list of names and phone numbers of people you've worked for in the past, but they don't often call more than one or two. And who knows what kind of mood your old customers will be in when they're called?

Enter the testimonial letter or, better yet, a batch of testimonial letters. As a design/build contractor, I hit on this idea while trying to develop a brochure to inform prospective clients about my company. I decided that a brochure becomes outdated quickly and has room for only a few excerpted testimonials, like the ones we've all seen in magazines. "This company did a great job for us! — J. L., Turlock, Calif." or "Couldn't have done without your fabulous advice! — L.P., Greenacre, Ontario." Convincing? Sure, about as believable as a left-handed spirit level.

Excerpts Are Limited

At first, I devised a testimonial summary — similar to excerpts, but with the full name, city, and state of each client. A client list with about 50 names and phone numbers, including those quoted, accompanied the summarized testimonials so that prospective clients could call for verification or clarification. I knew it would help to use real names of real clients to tell our story. But would the excerpts do a good enough job of communicating to prospective clients the capabilities of our company?

Even this type of testimonial excerpt, however, has a limited appeal, a sort of staged appearance. To the skeptic, it raises more questions than it answers. Prospects wonder what the rest of the letter said. What about the screw-ups? How were they handled?

I followed up with prospective clients to find out how reading the excerpts affected them. Let's just say I was underwhelmed by their responses. So, on impulse, I grabbed copies of the complete, original letters and gave these to the next five prospects along with the sheet of excerpts. When I checked back with them, I was pleasantly surprised to find that all five preferred the original letters, and recommended that I abandon the excerpts. I took their advice.

Using the Original Letters

Here's how we currently use these letters in our company. We copy each one and staple together a packet of about 25. We arrange them in chronological order with the most recent on top. Then we send a packet to each prospective client, along with a business card, a list of about 50 client references (names, phone numbers, city, type of project), and a note confirming their appointment to visit our showroom.

When asked if they received the material we sent them, many of our prospects volunteer that they not only received it but read every letter. It makes me wonder if there isn't a Dear Abby syndrome, something in all of us that makes us enjoy reading other people's mail. In any event, the response continues to be very positive.

These letters are a natural way for your clients to say thank you for a job well done. But it isn't easy or cheap to produce and deliver them. Doris, our office manager, says postage to send the letters is now approaching $1.44 per packet, and this doesn't include the cost of the manila envelope, copy paper, and her time. So much for this idea being less costly than a brochure. The results, however, are worth it.

Dear Larry,

Home remodeling can be one of the most painful experiences anyone can go through. The dislocation, the disruption, the dirt, the anxiety, the uncertainty, the cost, etc., can throw any family into turmoil. But Federal Building Company made it as painless as possible. We believe this was due to your professional approach to project planning. From the very beginning, you sat down with us and outlined the entire scope of the project. There were never any surprises. Everything was clearly spelled out in writing. At all times, we knew where we stood with the project costs, which is critical when dealing with a big home remodeling job. Scheduling was also carefully planned, and schedules were adhered to. This also helps reduce owner anxiety.

Of particular importance were the hard-working, courteous workmen on the job. They paid special attention to our needs and welcomed our questions and input. Perhaps most importantly, they cleaned up after themselves every day and kept the job site as neat as possible.

As the job progressed to the finish work, we were impressed by the attention to detail. If we noticed an imperfection, no matter how small, you unquestioningly went back and corrected it. This may be the most important aspect of the job and an area where client and contractor can run into difficulty. There are many horror stories where the contractor refused to fix something, feeling it was done well enough. Or cases where the item is fixed, but the client is made to feel that he/she was being too fussy. This was never the case with Federal. The outcome was a beautiful home with all the details attended to and only warm and respectful feelings for the contractor.

Mark and I would wholeheartedly recommend Federal to any of our friends who wished to do a home remodel. Again, the most important component that you bring to the job is your professionalism. Everything is clearly spelled out, there are no surprises, and the work is done to the highest standards. Friends who have used other contractors cannot claim that they have received the same high level of service.

Again, thank you for a job well done, and done on time. Hopefully, we'll be here for a long time, enjoying the space you created for us. But should we ever need another remodel, we will come straight to you.

Good luck in the future and many thanks.

Sincerely,

Mark & Betty

CLIENTS TELL OUR STORY BEST

"Everyone on your staff was a complete professional, a real craftsman, and an absolute pleasure to be around. I brag about how easy this remodeling job was... the way Federal Building Co. performs is... exceptional... the quality team every homeowner should have the pleasure of working with...

ilton / Castro Valley

Federal restored our faith in contractors; thanks for a great design and execution.

a Archie / Kensington

Your quality craftsmanship, attention to detail, and sound approach to project management all coincided to make our dream a reality... I selected you because the approach you took, managing the work from cradle to completion is the best approach... You remained in budget, on schedule and worked to keep our home as clean and comfortable as possible.

da Permaul / Oakland

I wanted a 'WOW' kitchen and with Federal Building Co.'s help I got it. ...and I love my 'new' living room, dining room and entry.

leigh Redus / Montclair

...a job WELL DONE! ...final result surpasses our expectations... completed on schedule and within contract budget... workmanship is superb... cleanliness maintained was remarkable.

& Artenzio DiOrio / Montclair

What a pleasure... professional approach all the way from design to completion. This bathroom is fabulous!

/ Berkeley

...most amazing of all, the project—which included a family room addition and kitchen remodeling, was finished ahead of schedule and stayed on budget!

d Walkley / Lafayette

The kitchen is perfect... comparing notes with friends... I realize that I was very fortunate to have chosen Federal as our contractor. Many thanks for a well done job. Your crew are professionals... the product is a fine testimonial to your firm.

thur Weil / Piedmont

Scheduling was carefully planned and adhered to... hardworking and courteous workmen... cleaned up after themselves every day... we were impressed by the attention to detail... wholeheartedly recommend Federal... the most important component that you bring to the job is your professionalism.

impson / Piedmont

We not only appreciate the design and quality of your work on our new kitchen and bath, but also your dedication and follow-up to see we remained satisfied.

enschau / Berkeley

The true measure of a contractor... Federal responded to our desires and created the perfect kitchen for our home.

ncy Bauer / Montclair

Our new walk-in shower and whirlpool bath dramatically transformed our master bedroom suite... great design and execution."

License No. 285785 — *Jim & Jane Trimble / Piedmont*

Even a lengthy excerpt is no substitute for a complete copy of the original testimonial letter.

In Their Own Words

There is a distinct value in quantity here: Up to a point, the more testimonials the better. How do you amass enough testimonial letters to create the desired impression? The first step is to do a fabulous job for your clients. As designers/builders, we include a lot of detail on the plans so that misunderstandings are rare. It's easier to do the most pleasing work the first time. When problems do arise and client satisfaction is at issue, we have what I call a "rubber spine." That is, we bend over backwards in our desire to please.

It's also important to tell your prospects how many testimonial letters you have received from your clients since you started collecting them as a marketing tool. Explain that you and your crew will be working very hard to please them, and will be checking with them during the course of construction to see how your company is doing.

There is nothing wrong with telling your client before, during, and after construction that their testimonial letter will be an important marketing tool, and that you are counting on their help. Most people will be delighted to assist you in this way. A contractor friend of mine even goes so far as to coach clients to use certain phrases that he wants to see in their letters. I think it's better to let people use their own words, and to encourage them to "let it all hang out."

Prospective clients want and deserve to hear the truth about you. If you make mistakes on the project, your clients might be afraid to write a letter for fear of expressing some negative information. Don't let this stop them. Encourage them to tell it like it is. Your prospects will appreciate reading the letters all the more and will really learn about your "rubber spine." It's better advertising than any words you could say.

Recently, we received two letters from the same client. One was nicely typewritten because she thought it would be used as a testimonial. The other was handwritten and, while it was complimentary overall, it covered the parts of the job that she thought could have been handled better. Even though we had gone over her constructive criticisms during and after the job, it was good for everyone in our company to reflect on her letters. We now include both letters in the packet we send to prospective clients. What an effect. Showing all the letters we get goes a lot further in establishing our credibility than the fanciest showroom, the most polished presentation, or a few handpicked or excerpted testimonials.

By Larry Hayden, president of Federal Building Company, a design/build firm in Oakland, Calif. He is also the co-owner of Damage Control Mediation Service, which resolves construction disputes.

When Sales Hype Becomes A Warranty

If you're not careful, your marketing statements could be construed as an enforceable guarantee of workmanship

Good builders of new homes are often proud of their work and zealous of their reputations. Frequently, when marketing their services to a new home buyer, they are tempted to treat the purchase and sales contract as a marketing tool. Statements in their purchase and sales contracts which promise that the new home will be "a first class dwelling with first class materials" or constructed "in a workmanlike fashion" may be construed by courts as creating express warranties. These statements have more than a marketing impact — they can create legally enforceable guarantees of workmanship that will survive, under the terms of most purchase and sales contracts and under state and federal law, for at least some time after the closing.

Where There's Smoke...

The case law surrounding express warranties can be confusing. One of the primary distinctions that courts typically make is whether the statement — and express warranties can be created verbally as well as in writing — was one that a purchaser could justifiably rely upon as a guarantee of the builder's performance. "Is it merely sales talk and puffery — or is it an express warranty?" courts will ask. If the statement is the former, the buyer will not be able to recover — at least not on a theory of breach of express warranty.

But the distinction is not very clear. In a case where the builder's sales brochure had stated that the builder had a "good reputation," that it "had been building homes for 35 years," and that "all homes were good homes," the court held that the purchaser was not entitled to recover from the builder on a breach of express warranty theory. (*Shapiro v. Kornicks*, 124 N.E.2d 175, Ohio, 1955.) Contrast that case with one in which the builder told the purchaser that an uncompleted house would be "completed right," that he "took pride in his homes," and that he "watched every detail." In that case, the court held that the purchaser could recover on the express representation of the builder.

Don't Go It Alone

Sound conflicting? The warranty question is one area where it does not pay for the builder to negotiate the purchase and sales contract without legal assistance. Without guidance it's easy to be pressured by the buyer's lawyer into giving his client "a little comfort" or assurance that the building won't fall down next year, the brickwork won't crack, the basement won't be filled with water next spring, or the roof won't leak.

Moreover, builders in many states have to worry about warranties that courts in those states — either because of state statutes or judge-made law — *imply* in construction contracts, regardless of what the builder expressly warrants. Typically, the warranty implied is that the builder warrants that the new home is habitable and/or that it is constructed in a good and workmanlike manner or using reasonable construction methods. Implied warranty cases and statutes run against the grain of the familiar "caveat emptor"—or "buyer beware" rule that courts have traditionally applied in the context of a real-estate purchase.

Because jurisdictions are divided on whether an implied warranty of habitability is recognized, it's particularly important to get competent legal advice during the contract negotiation stage. In addition, some states permit limitations, under particular circumstances, of implied and express warranties. It's important for the builder to know which warranties he can limit and how he can limit them legally under his state's laws. In some cases, the federal Magnuson-Moss Act, a consumer warranty statute with complicated requirements regarding warranty and service contract programs, may set limits on how warranties are limited or disclaimed with respect to certain personal property classified under the Act as "consumer products."

Avoid Making Problems

From a risk management point of view, knowing something about the law of express warranties — and particularly the unexpected ways in which they can be created — may prove very useful to the builder in managing his everyday sales and marketing efforts. Unlike implied warranties, which the courts or the legislatures impose, the creation of express warranties is, with proper education of the builder's sales and marketing staff, almost entirely within the builder's control.

The basic rule is a common-sense one: If there's a chance that the project as delivered won't conform to a statement or representation made in advance about it, the statement or representation shouldn't be made. It's important to keep in mind that "statements" and "representations" can be other than oral or written. Models, plans, specifications, and other graphic or visual depictions are representations creating express warranties, the breach of which will create liability. (*Wheaton Park, Inc. v. Lombardi*, 149 A.2d 422, D.D.C., 1959.) Sales and marketing personnel should be educated so that they avoid using pictorial images in sales brochures or other graphic depictions that "set the mood" but may ultimately be misleading to purchasers. For instance, if your project is located in a resort town on the ocean, but the project is situated three or four miles from the beach, it may be misleading to present photographs of swimming and sailing in a brochure without a statement that the project is located three or four miles from the beach.

Builders may create express warranties unexpectedly where, in an effort to define what it is they have contracted to build or deliver, they attach a set of plans and specifications to the purchase and sales contract and agree to build in accordance with those plans and specifications. In such circumstances, courts have held that such plans and specifications create an express warranty that the building is *properly* constructed according to them. (*Lipson v. Southgate Park Corp.*, 189 N.E.2d 191, 1963.) In Connecticut, if a builder contracts to deliver a certificate of occupancy at the closing, that promise creates an express warranty that the building will be constructed in a workmanlike fashion and according to accepted building practices. (*Maier v. Arsenault*, 100 A.2d 403, 1953.)

In summary, builders would do well to consider all possible forms of representation as capable of creating express warranties, and to think carefully about their chances of living up to the promises they make.

By Reina A. Calderon, Esq., vice president and general counsel of Calderon Energy Company of Bowling Green, Inc., in Bowling Green, Ohio.

Chapter 14

Design/Build

Design/Build Remodeling: One Company's Approach

With a unified approach you can offer design creativity while keeping costs under control

A number of years ago, we realized that in order to thrive in the very competitive "Gold Coast" region of Connecticut, we needed to do something different. Because we had already established a reputation for service and quality, it made sense for us to build on that. We felt that a design/build approach would expand our services to the customer, and offer us a way to provide flexibility, while controlling quality and expenses. Since then, we have grown from a small, family-run business to a $1 million-plus company. We've also learned a great deal about the benefits (and difficulties) of this approach. Among other things, it requires new billing, scheduling, and management procedures.

How We Got Started

Before we incorporated, we had a great deal of involvement with architects. They knew the design of a job inside and out — that's why we hired them. But they often seemed unable to have a job completed on time and within budget. Generally, they had little idea of the true cost of the project until they bid everything out. And often they created innovative designs that turned out to be impractical to build and in need of expensive, budget-busting modifications. As builders, we would catch all the customer's heat, while we waited for the architect to come survey the situation and find a remedy. This would often take days, much to the frustration of the homeowners and ourselves.

In addition, whether practical or not, blueprints and designs can be misinterpreted. The architect designs his plans to be read one way, while the customer may have something else in mind. Meanwhile the remodeler may interpret the plans yet another way and builds as such.

Our decision to offer design services and avoid these problems led me to take courses in architectural design, drafting, and interior design at local colleges.

Slowly, we incorporated what I was learning in many of our smaller assignments, such as porches, dormers, and great rooms. I would consult with my instructors, many of whom were licensed architects, who would review my drawings and suggest modifications. Eventually, I didn't have to depend on my instructors' critiques anymore and we were on our way to becoming design/builders.

At first, I combined design responsibilities with production. My brother, Gregory, who is a tremendous help in evaluating the practical application of a design, became the production supervisor. As a family-run business, this worked well.

But as our company matured and grew larger, so did our responsibilities. We found it necessary to delegate duties to other professionals outside the family circle. Again, because of our emphasis on service and quality, it was very important for us to recruit someone who really cared about home remodeling as an art form. Most young graduates of design and architecture schools concentrate on landing a position with a firm that has many commercial and industrial concerns. But we were lucky to find a young and creative architect interested in applying his talent to the area of home remodeling. At this point, we had truly made the transition to a design/build firm.

How It Works

Although every customer is different, and some are more interested in the design while others are more interested in cost, we generally proceed as follows:

Our first step is to meet with a customer. Here we function less as remodelers or designers and more as interpreters. During this "feeling-out" stage we listen very closely to the clients as they talk about the things most important to them— their home and family. In this consultation we learn about the family's personality, habits, and lifestyle. We also find out if the potential clients are a potential heartache to us.

Often the clients will come equipped with magazine clippings to give us an

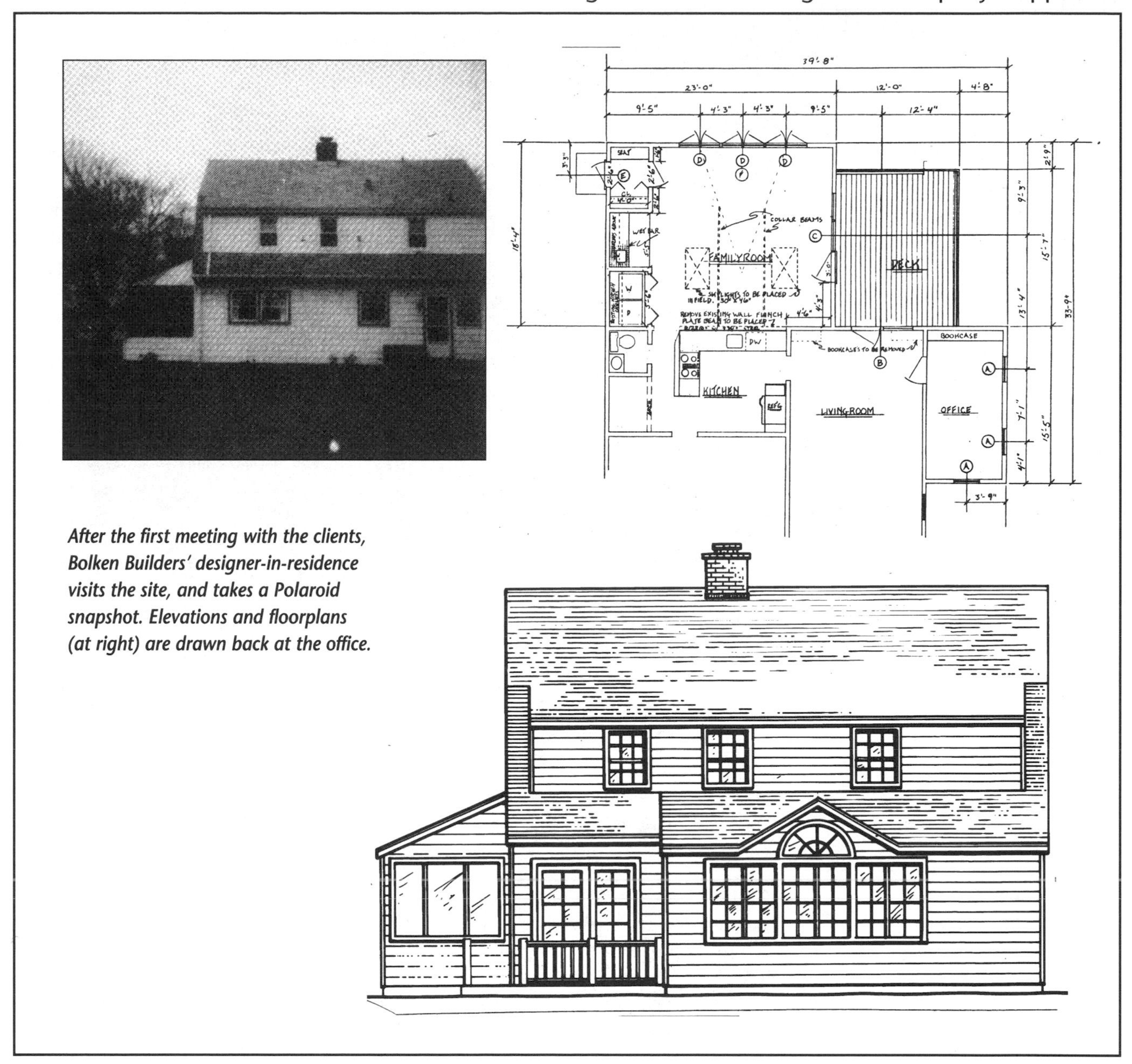

After the first meeting with the clients, Bolken Builders' designer-in-residence visits the site, and takes a Polaroid snapshot. Elevations and floorplans (at right) are drawn back at the office.

idea of what they want. Clients' requests can be pretty zany. We had one client who requested that the skylight in a new addition be located so that the moonlight would reflect on a certain spot. The fact that the moon isn't always in the same place didn't seem to matter — until the job was done and the moon wasn't in the right place that week. We ended up moving the skylight.

But generally we try to steer the customers toward reasonable expectations. We supply them with our in-house design booklet, "How To Get The Most Out Of Remodeling Your House," which includes checklists and suggestions to help them formalize their ideas. We also have the customers complete a questionnaire (see Figure 1) to help them clarify their objectives. It covers everything from roofing, flooring, and window treatments to some personal questions regarding room traffic.

After the consultation we prepare a "ballpark" estimate of the project and a preliminary cost of the plans themselves. Once we get a verbal go-ahead to draw up plans, our architectural designer visits the site and takes a number of photos. He also records detailed measurements of the structure and the area to be remodeled.

We then work up preliminary plans — sometimes producing two to three differ-

Bolken Builders Design and Planning Guide

What type of project(s) are you thinking about

- ___ Kitchen
- ___ Bathroom
- ___ Addition
- ___ Master bedroom suite
- ___ Sunroom/Greenhouse
- ___ Second-story addition
- ___ Familyroom
- ___ Interior renovation
- ___ Replacement window(s)
- ___ Repacement door(s)
- ___ Skylight(s)
- ___ Other ________

Does the owner have a plot plan ________

Septic ____ City sewer ____ Well ____ City water ____

How many bathrooms ____ How many bedrooms ____

Aproximate dimensions of addition ________

Can the existing heating system handle the increased demand ________

What type of heat: Existing ____ Desired ____

Do any services need relocating ____ Size of electric panel ____

Window manufacturer ____ Window area, large or small ____

Window material: Wood ____ Alum ____ Clad ____ Vinyl Clad ____

Window type: Casement ____ Double-hung ____ Sliding ____ Circle top ____ Bay ____

Flooring: Wood ____ Tile ____ No-Wax ____ Ken-tile ____ Carpeting ____ Other ____

If tile: Ceramic ____ Marble ____ Other ____ Size(s) ____

Area: Floor ____ Wall ____ Shower area ____ Whirlpool surround ____

Door(s): French ____ Slider ____ Patio ____ Single ____ Other ____

Access from what room(s) ____ Open to outside,deck, patio, balcony ____

Skylight(s): Fixed ____ Venting ____ Motorized ____ In what room(s) ____

Ceiling: Cathedral ____ Tray ____ Flat ____ Beamed ____ High ceiling ____

Lighting: Recessed ____ Wall-mounted ____ Track ____ Ceiling fan(s) ____ Other ____

Figure 1. *Early on, a remodeler should clarify the clients' objectives. Bolken Builders uses a form that covers items such as window treatments, flooring, and roofing, as well as lighting and decorative elements.*

DESIGN/BUILD PROPOSAL
Design Phase Only

Bolken Builders, Inc.

Page ____ of ____

Date ____ 19 ____

We herewith submit Design/Build proposal at the sole request and order of:

NAME ADDRESS, CITY, STATE & ZIP CODE		Home Phone
		Office Phone
		Office Phone

hereinafter referred to as owner, for plans and specifications of projected work to be performed according to the following terms:

1. Contractor agrees to provide working plans and specifications for Company's own use in constructing proposed ________ (Type of Project) at ________ (Job Address)
2. Plans to consist of ☐ Foundation Plan ☐ Floor Plan(s) ☐ Elevations ☐ Section ☐ Perspective ☐ Other ________
3. Proposed budget range for construction of the above under the presently understood scope is $ ________ to $ ________, inclusive of ________ (Major items included)

   Major items not included: ________
4. If the scope of either the proposed construction work or design phase work is changed after the signing of this agreement, the design fee will be changed and the above proposed construction budget range will be void.

   Any alteration or deviation from above terms involving extra costs will be executed only upon written order from owner or his authorized agent and will become an extra charge over the below agreed amount. No statement, arrangement or understanding, expressed or implied not contained herein will be recognized.

   The plans and specifications described in this proposal are intended for construction by this company and no liability or responsibility is assumed for construction by any other company using these plans and specifications. Said plans and specifications become the sole property of the owner upon full payment of the below agreed amount.

   We propose to furnish the above complete in accordance with the above terms for the sum of ________ dollars ($ ________). Payment to be made in full upon acceptance of this agreement.

You, the buyer, may cancel this transaction at any time prior to midnight of the third business day after the date of this transaction. See the attached notice of cancellation form for an explanation of this right.

Contractor's Acceptance

Design work to be started on or before ________ 19 ____

and be substantially completed on or before ________ 19 ____ assuming present scope of work.

Company Representative ________ Lic No.

Accepted By Contractor ________ Lic. No.

This proposal may be withdrawn if not accepted within ____ days.

Owner's Acceptance

The foregoing terms, specifications and conditions are satisfactory and are hereby agreed to. You are authorized to do the work as specified and payment will be made as outlined above. The owner upon signing this agreement represents and warrants that he is the owner of the aforesaid premises and that he has read this agreement.

Owner ________ Date

Owner ________ Date

Figure 2. *The design/build proposal makes very clear what kinds of plans the customers can expect: foundation, floor, elevation, perspective, and sections if necessary. It also provides a budget range for the proposed project.*

ent design alternatives, which we present to the clients. If they like what they see, we go over the specifics involved in our design/build proposal (see Figure 2). The proposal makes clear to the clients what they will be receiving: foundation plans, floorplans, elevations, structural sections, and detailed schematics if necessary. Kitchens and bathrooms often require such detail. The proposal will also provide a budget range for the construction based on these plans.

It is at this point that we ask for full payment for the design aspect of the remodeling. We also aim for a complete understanding of the clients' goals. This is a time for keen listening, for the clients' feedback at this point will be instrumental in generating a set of plans that should satisfy their objectives. Since no actual construction has taken place yet, careful attention to the clients' message can eliminate costly delays and mistakes. Listen hard and ask the right questions. If we plan to use any nonstandard materials that might affect the total cost (but increase the quality), now is the time to explain why. Hopefully the clients will understand and approve.

After a couple of weeks, usually after some additional phone consultation with the clients, we produce final plans and drawings that incorporate their suggestions. We then present these to the clients. If they are happy with the presentation, this is the final rendering. There are times, however, when additional fine-tuning may be needed. Again, time and patience are the operative watchwords here. We try to avoid thinking of customer satisfaction in terms of just one job or this one client we are working with. We're working on the best form of marketing there is — the satisfied customers' testimonial.

Once the clients sign off on the plans we get into the production phase of the project.

Billing For Design

Unlike architects, we don't charge a fee based on a percentage of the estimated final project. Our fee structure is based on the project's complexity. Some remodeling projects are very simple to design, and we feel these should be priced accordingly.

Although all clients have the option of taking the design out to bid (once they have paid for the design), about 85 percent of our design customers have us do the remodeling. We find that the willingness to pay a design fee is evidence of a serious commitment to the project. The fee also takes care of those who would have us design for free and walk away to another builder who might build more cheaply. However, we do refund the design fee upon the first scheduled payment for the actual construction of the project.

Benefits of Design/Build

A full-fledged design/build team can provide the clients with virtually all the services generally accorded to an architect during the design phase, such as developing the outlines, schematics, preliminary drawings, and blueprints.

There are several immediate benefits that a design/build team has over a separate architect and contractor:

- ***Control.*** A design/build team supervises the whole remodeling job. Hiring, scheduling, and interacting with a horde of subcontractors is almost always left to the builder or remodeler, rather than the designer. Over the years, we've learned which subcontractors we can trust to turn out various phases of the remodeling project on time, on budget, and on a consistent basis.
- ***Quality.*** As builders, we are on-site from design to finish — to ensure adherence to plans, codes, and quality workmanship in construction.
- ***Flexibility.*** Design/builders don't seem to get in the type of bureaucratic logjams that the "traditional" approach to high-end home remodeling often results in. The design/builder can alter plans during construction without having to consult another professional, thereby avoiding added downtime.
- ***Savings.*** Additional architectural consultations also cost money. But even if additional consultations are not required, architectural fees can eat up a remodeling budget. Fees for architects here in Fairfield County vary from 8% to 15% of building costs, but can be higher. Our design process is billed at a much lower rate — usually less than 5%. If the design fee is refunded, as it is for most of our clients, the cost of the design process is covered under overhead.

"Disadvantages" of Design/Build

Perhaps the hardest part of being a design/builder in the remodeling field is that the approach is unfamiliar to most consumers. Generally, consumer magazines play down the clear advantages of the design/build approach and treat the designs offered by a design/builder as pedestrian. If the design/build service is not understood by the customer, he will not pay for it. So the biggest challenge is educating the consumer about the design/build idea.

A secondary problem lies in the standards that we have set for ourselves. As design/builders, we have more than just our reputation for quality workmanship at stake, we now have to maintain a standard for design excellence as well.

Without a doubt, every remodeling project is an opportunity to improve the existing home. A good design will carefully harmonize an addition with the original house and create a well-proportioned and hopefully, better-looking house.

Therefore, we like to discourage clients from cutting corners for the sake of economics when the result detracts from the house architecturally. A poorly designed addition is never a wise investment and should always be avoided.

We believe that the design/build approach, an approach that harkens back to the long-gone days of the "Master Builder," is a viable solution for most remodeling projects. But the burden of proof lies with the design/builder whose challenge is to design and build in ways that enhance the home — most families' largest investment.

By Matthew DeTroy, president and director of Bolken Builders, a design/build team in Fairfield County, Conn.

Design Fees for Remodelers

To avoid long hours without pay, ask for a design retainer after presenting rough drawings and a ballpark estimate

There is nothing more frustrating to a design/build remodeling contractor than spending 15 or 20 hours with potential clients — coaxing budget information from them, suggesting approaches and products, developing drawings, and generally holding their hands as we're expected to do — only to be told "Sorry, but my husband and I have decided to build a new house instead," or "We've decided to have Contractor B do the work you drew up because his price is $1,100 less." All you can do is smile weakly and suppress the impulse to say, "Lady, I'd have given you $500 two weeks ago to know this."

New Approach

In the last few years, I have been using a system that eliminates some of this risk. It's helped me sign nearly 80% of the clients I work with on a design, and pays me for part or all of the time I've put in on the other 20%.

Here's how it works. Once I've spent just enough time with potential clients to get an idea of their budget and the changes they want made, I prepare rough drawings and a ballpark estimate (I guarantee that it will be within 10% of the eventual price). Based on this, I ask them for a retainer of three hundred to several thousand dollars so I can proceed with a detailed estimate and a full set of plans and specs. The retainer is applied to the final draw of the construction contract if I end up doing the work, but it stays in my pocket if they drop the project or go elsewhere.

The beauty of this approach is that in presenting myself as a professional, I get treated like one, right from the start. It also puts me in control of the process. I was a remodeler for quite a while before I realized how important it is to be in control. My business life was built around what others asked of me. If the clients wanted the estimate a certain way, I gave it to them. If they wanted to see hard-to-find finish materials early in the planning process, I delivered. I gave them anything I thought would inspire their confidence, including detailed, original plans that I spent hours on. Sound familiar? When all this time leads to a signed contract, it's worth it. But when you see the plans that you sweated over and never got a dime for being built by another contractor, it feels a lot different.

Initial Contact

The first step in using this approach is to carefully qualify your leads on the phone. A lot of remodelers respond to almost any inquiry by making an appointment with the caller. But it's important to realize that you're committing a minimum of ten hours of your time in sketching, estimating, drive time, and subsequent appointments by doing that. Spending between 10 and 30 minutes on the phone asking the right questions can save you that time if the caller just isn't ready, is working with an unrealistic budget, or is just shopping. I also use this initial contact to explain how our company handles design/build and our policy on retainer fees.

Assuming that this "lead" is a good one, I set an appointment time that allows me at least one to two hours with the clients. If you have a showroom you might want to make the initial appointment there, but I prefer the job site. I think people feel more comfortable talking about their personal habits and budget expectations (information you have to get in order to produce a good design) on their own turf. Also, it's a lot easier to talk about changes when you're standing in the "before" picture and can measure for fixtures, appliances, etc.

At this first meeting, I walk through the house with the clients looking at the scope of work. Much of this visit is spent listening to what the clients need and want. I keep careful notes and update them if new decisions are made in the course of the appointment. I also keep a running total in my head of approximate costs. This helps me to ensure that the clients' budget matches what the work will really cost. If I see things getting out of hand, I'll let them know a ballpark figure right away so I don't have to hit them with what amounts to a huge letdown later on.

You really can't proceed effectively without a clear notion of what the clients can afford. With some clients, I find it most effective to ask outright "What is your budget?" But with others, you have to probe more cautiously. Some clients hear these questions as "How much do you think this project is going to cost?" Since my clients are typically 30% to 40% under when it comes to guessing what things will cost, it's important not to mistake their "estimate" for their budget. Try to walk away with as clear an understanding of their real budget as possible.

Once I've felt the situation out and explained design/build again, I tell the clients that I will need to take some measurements before I leave. I then set up a second appointment to approve the sketches and budget on which I will base the final estimate. I schedule this appointment on the spot, and write it down in my book with the clients watching. I try to keep the time fairly short between these two meetings, although I have to give myself enough time to squeeze in the rough estimate and drawings—about four to six hours of work—along with all the other demands of my schedule.

If the house is vacant, I arrange to come back when I can check things out without interruptions. Otherwise I do the measuring during my first appointment. I use a checklist to jog my memory. A combination of photos and graph paper help me record the details. Some of the key locations and measurements I take are:

- Height of floor from grade
- Slope of grade away from house
- Style, size, and location of existing windows, including height above floor
- Style, size, and location of existing doors
- Ceiling height
- Size and location of radiators/ducts
- Location of main electrical service/sub panels
- Existing roof pitch/covering
- Width and type of siding
- Location of existing water lines and sewer
- Location of heating/cooling systems and possible tie-in points
- Location of possible obstacles such as gas, electric meters, hose bibs, well, septic, etc.

Two other things I keep an eye out for that can trip you up later are code violations on the existing house, and how local zoning requirements affect both these and the proposed changes.

Ballpark Estimate and Drawings

The size of the job affects how long you need for a preliminary estimate, but most estimates take me three to four hours. This is only a "ballpark" figure in the sense that the scope of the work is not yet precisely defined. However, I use accurate labor and material rates on the preliminary plan and do an actual takeoff. Where quantities are not precisely known, I round off high.

For subs, I use figures based on going rates. That's usually close enough. For example, in my area, it costs between $100 and $125 to relocate an hvac opening; $350 to $450 to paint walls, ceiling, trim in an average room; an electrical service upgrade runs $900 to $1,200. I typically use the higher of the two prices to cover the "I forgots," and then add my markup.

In fact, I tell my clients, "With a ballpark estimate, I would rather give you a high number to work down from than give you a lower one and keep adding to

Remodeler John Cargill, on the right, discusses design options with two potential clients. After he produces rough drawings and a ballpark estimate, he asks for a retainer before progressing with a full set of plans and detailed estimate.

Cargill Design/Remodel
John R. Cargill IV
Certified General Contractor

We hereby express our interest in pursuing a project at the above address. In consideration of that interest we engage Cargill Remodeling to define and clarify a project consistent with our design requests and budget expectations.

We understand that a designer in the office of Cargill Remodeling will produce a floor plan, preliminary specifications, and a budget range.

The development fee will be applied towards a construction contract, and should we elect not to proceed, the fee is nonrefundable.

Project: ______________________

Target budget: ______________________

John R. Cargill IV

Date: ______________________

Development fee: ______________________

Special note: Because the development fee does not reflect the full cost associated with the definition of the project, all sketches and specifications shall be retained by Cargill Remodeling.

The author uses this preliminary contract to collect a retainer fee that covers his costs in developing finished drawings, specs, and prices.

it." They appreciate this. When you add on to the price or say that something will be extra, clients get the feeling that there's no cap, and they get anxious.

Drawings

Although I try not to spend more than two or three hours on sketches at this stage, I also don't want to leave too much to the imagination. First, I work up a 1/4-inch scaled drawing of the existing floor plan with stuff that I know will be torn out drawn a bit lighter. With this drawing taped to the drafting table, I roll out 12-inch tracing paper over the scaled floor plan. Using a soft-lead 7mm pencil and scale rule, I do quick, free-hand "sketches" of the new work. When I see a dead end, I just roll out more paper, and start again until I get it right.

Once you have the basics sketched on tracing paper, you have to make a judgment call about how much further you want to go at this stage. I've shown clients everything from the bare bones tracing paper sketch to neatly drawn, color renditions. Time, client temperament, and a sense of how much more this plan will have to evolve before the clients are satisfied will help you decide what to present.

Second Appointment

For this appointment you have to take off your design hat and put on your sales hat (hat changing comes naturally to small contractors). First, I present the sketches and ballpark estimate, explaining that this is a custom plan fitted to their budget, needs, and desires. I listen and watch carefully when I'm presenting the drawings. Clients don't necessarily speak up if the design isn't what they had imagined, or if they haven't been clear about their budget with me and the one I'm presenting is too high. If I sense they're uncomfortable, I remind them that there is flexibility at this point and get right into exploring alternatives with them. Often the clients do more designing than we give them credit for.

On most of my jobs, I can make the necessary adjustments to the rough sketches and the ballpark estimate with the clients at this second appointment. And in most cases, they are pleased with what I've presented and have developed some trust in me.

The next step is to ask for the retainer. I explain again that they are paying for my time as a professional to develop a complete set of plans and a price that is within their budget, and that the money will be applied to the final payment if they proceed with construction. I also give them an idea of how I arrived at the ballpark estimate. This reassures them that I have done my homework, and that the final price will be within 10% of the ballpark estimate (if it's not, I return the retainer to them).

I don't have a set retainer amount. It depends upon the clients and the work. The larger your company appears to the clients, and the more established you are, the easier it is to ask for a substantial retainer—$1,000 to $2,000. However, starting out with a small retainer—$300 or so—is less risky, and it's better than none at all.

The contract that spells out the retainer is just one page (see sample contract, previous page) and is quite simple. I remind the clients that this isn't the construction contract, but just a go-ahead for me to develop a full set of plans and specs, and an estimate. Then we read through it together.

Once they've signed, I go right ahead with developing the final estimate and plans. It's important to remember that you don't have the job yet. That's also the reason for not leaving the budget or sketches behind, which the retainer contract makes clear.

Sound simple? Applying new approaches to your business is never easy. But this is one that works for companies of almost any size. I started using it when my volume was just $131,000 annually (I should do $325,000 this year), but I picked it up from a firm that does over $3 million.

Like any new business approach, you should check with your attorney to be sure that state laws allow you to collect a retainer for design work. And you should remember that this method isn't foolproof. Asking for a retainer can run a client off to one of your competitors who doesn't require a retainer. But the few times this has happened, I've wondered whether I'm losing a qualified client or a price-shopper who just wanted to pick my brain.

You can also get a retainer, put in all the work, and still lose the client. Even if you receive $1,000 retainer, "your" client may go with a competitor who is willing to come in $1,500 below your price in order to keep his guys working. That's a $500 savings for the clients even after forfeiting the retainer. But I find it doesn't happen very often. And when it does, there's not much you can say but "that's life."

By John R. Cargill IV, owner of Cargill Design/Remodel in Columbus, Ga., since 1980.

Contracts for Design/Build

For best results, use a contract that makes builder and architect partners, not adversaries

One autumn, a few years back, our construction company was nearing completion of a substantial new addition and renovation when we ran into a problem. The architect had specified a light fixture we thought inappropriate, and it occupied a highly noticeable spot in the new addition. This posed a dilemma for us, since we work frequently and well with the architect, and we were on great terms with the homeowner. We did not want to insult either of them, nor did we wish to buy the fixture, put it up, and then take it down again, especially since it was an expensive, nonreturnable, special-order fixture.

Builders often find themselves in this position. The architect has made a questionable call, and the builder is left with the decision of how to handle it. Unfortunately, a builder in this position is often tempted to play the hero and tell the owners about the architect's mistake, and how he, the builder, will fix it. This approach usually advances the builder's standing at the expense of the architect. At best, you may sacrifice a good source of future job leads. At worst, you may get sucked into a raging whirlpool of litigation.

We wanted neither. So the light fixture went up, the owner blanched, the light fixture came down, and it was replaced. It now sits in storage at our expense. At the time this seemed to be a small price to pay to preserve our relationships with the architect and the owner. But in retrospect, what we needed was better communication with the architect. Then we might have felt freer to question the architect's decision without fear of reprisal, and the light fixture could have stayed in its dark, dusty corner at the electrical supply house.

In an effort to improve our service to customers in situations like this, I set out to explore ways builders and architects could better work together. I began by examining the basis for the traditional architect/ builder alliance, and I interviewed a number of architects to get their input on the best way to structure a relationship. The result — a team approach — is founded largely on trust and communication. But since trust is a nebulous entity in a court of law, the team approach also provides a clear-cut method for handling disputes and resolving differences.

Traditional Contract

The architect has traditionally been the owner's representative, often taking full control of the construction itself. The contract architects have used is AIA Document A201, "General Conditions of the Contract for Construction." This document is based on the principle of inclusion — that is, include everything you think could ever happen in any construction project. It is long, complex, and certain to scare the hell out of any owner wanting to build a 2,500-square-foot custom colonial. But more importantly, it is written by AIA lawyers to favor the architect, often at the expense of the builder.

A201 puts the architect in control of everything and makes the contractor an adversary to be controlled. For example, Clause 3.18.1 under "Indemnification" states that the contractor shall indemnify the owner, architect, and their agents from any damages caused by the construction to the extent that the damage was caused by negligence of the contractor or subcontractors, "regardless of whether or not such claim, damage, loss, or expense is caused in part by a party indemnified hereunder." In other words, the architect is indemnified — that is, protected from liability — even if he is partly responsible for the problem.

Another example of the document granting unfair protection to the architect at the builder's expense is under "Execution, Correlation, and Intent." Item 1.2.3 ends with the statement: "Performance by the Contractor shall be required only to the extent consistent with the Contract Documents and reasonably inferable from them as being necessary to produce the intended results." This last clause could be interpreted to mean "if the architect left anything out, it is the contractor's responsibility to include it." This not only makes it difficult to bid jobs tightly, but puts an undue burden on the contractor.

Architect Mollie Moran, of Bourgeois-Moran and Associates in Dedham, Mass., points out that the contracts the AIA uses, as well as the training architects go through and the AIA specs, all put the architect and builder in an adversarial relationship. As a matter of practice, owners are led to believe they need a representative to act as bulldog and make the builder tow the line. This connotes a lack of respect for the builder as a professional, and puts the architect in the police business rather than in the consulting and design business he or she should be in. Moran and other architects I interviewed feel this archaic attitude must be replaced with a spirit of cooperation.

Recipe for a Team Approach

The architects I spoke with emphasized several important ingredients in the recipe for a team approach.

Early builder involvement. Most architects agreed that the earlier the builder is involved, the better. The builder is the one member of the team who is best able to provide accurate cost estimates.

Peter Thomas of Lincoln Architects in Lincoln, Mass., for example, has made this policy part of his regular business procedure. Rather than opening a project up to bid, Thomas likes to bring a good builder on at the very beginning of a project to get an early estimate based on a preliminary design. This assures him that his design is within the realm of the budget, and keeps him from having to do extensive changes during the expensive working drawing stage. The more complex the design, the more valuable is the early involvement of the builder. Thomas strongly advises the owners that they'll get the best deal by negotiating a price with one builder selected at the beginning of the project.

Without early builder involvement, a project can easily go awry before it ever gets out the door. Last winter, for example, our company bid on a project alongside two other builders. The bids all came in within 5% of each other, and approximately 50% above the budget the owner gave the architect. One problem was that the architect specified numerous flitchplates. He had little understanding of the costs he was running up for the owner. We submitted the bid with LVL beams as an option, with a corresponding reduction in price of almost $4,000. This was a small part of the project, but it's characteristic of the problem. Had we been involved early on, both the owner and the architect would have benefited.

Realistic expectations. According to architect Dave Glassman of Glassman Associates in Needham, Mass., setting realistic expectations is the architect's number one job. The architect should hold the owners' hands and explain the likely track the new construction or renovation will take.

For example, to be responsible, an architect should say, "We will take every precaution to minimize dust and give you back your kitchen quickly. But to be truthful, there will be dust and your routine will be interfered with, so please expect it. This is, after all, a major renovation project." Contrast this statement with an architect telling his client that he will stay on top of the builder and ensure that there will be no dust and only minimal disruption of daily routines.

Glassman believes these overly high expectations set the builder up for failure. Getting the owner to face reality as early as possible makes the rest of the process much smoother.

Mutual respect. Any type of team approach will depend heavily on the support each party can offer the others. The architect must take the opportunity to praise the builder to the owners, and the builder must do the same for the architect.

Think about it from the owner's standpoint. When are the owners more likely to feel confident that they are getting the best job possible? When the architect and builder support each other and communicate problems in an unbiased and constructive manner? Or when the architect and builder are locked in the all-too-familiar pattern of mutual blame and finger-pointing?

But while most architects will agree in theory that trust is of paramount importance, different architects have different ideas about how this trust is achieved. Not all the architects I interviewed were ready to advocate an equal relationship with a builder, especially regarding the issue of money.

The Money Issue

In the traditional model, the architect is the owner's advocate when it comes to money. In a team approach, the architect functions more as an adviser to recommend initial disbursement schedules, percentage of completion, and retainage.

Glassman sees the architect's role as a facilitator in these matters. In this capacity, he thinks the architect must balance the builder's need for sufficient cash flow with the owner's need for a level of comfort about money paid out. He stressed, however, that he is an adviser; the money decision rests with the owner, and ultimately this is the builder's concern.

To handle this, our company always presents a fair disbursement schedule up front with our contract. This ensures that our need for a reliable cash flow is met. We are much more sensitive than any of the other parties involved about who has to get paid how much and when.

An architect has a much different perspective, and his "advice," however casual, might not square with a builder's. Glassman, for example, feels the last 5% to 10% of the project is the most difficult, and he always recommends a modest (5% to 10%) retainage to the owner on those items where it is appropriate. I feel strongly, however, that retainage is often perceived by the owners as money for the taking if they can come up with enough complaints about the construction. It creates a monster out of an otherwise perfectly reasonable client. People hate to think they are giving up something they don't have to. I would never agree to more than 5% retainage, and then only very reluctantly as a last resort and only if we are working with an architect we know and trust.

Team Structure

The desirability of an architect/ builder/ owner team came through loud and clear from all the architects I interviewed. They all recommended this as a necessary condition for a successful, enjoyable project. However, not everyone agreed on the actual structure of this team.

The team approach can take many forms. A team can be a loose association, or it can be a builder with an architect on staff, or vice versa. It can also be a partnership between builder and architect.

In its simplest form, a team can be defined by a simple understanding between a builder and an architect to work together when necessary. Whenever either secures a client who also needs the other's services, that person agrees to call the other in. In this case, contracts for the architect and the builder will be with the owner, and will be separate from each other.

Our company is very comfortable with the simplicity of this approach. It brings the team together when there is a need, without prolonging the relationship after the need has been satisfied.

A more formal partnership, on the other hand, is an easier sell to the owner. You can offer one-stop shopping every step of the way. However, as the survivor of a couple of partnerships, I urge caution. Don't become a partner without weighing the pros and cons. These relationships are extremely hard to sustain. If you do intend to join a partnership, make sure it is a relationship built on the true needs of all parties involved. This need should be spelled out in a formal agreement that clearly defines shared responsibilities and benefits.

Fair Documents

Above all, make sure you understand the project documents you sign. Ideally, you should make a point to write any contract you sign, but because we aren't all lawyers, this isn't always possible. You may have to find a friendly contract written elsewhere.

Another AIA document, A191, "Standard Form of Agreements Between Owner and Design/Builder," is a good place to begin. This document governs the relationship between the owner and a single party contracting to both design and build the house. The agreement is written in two parts: The first is for the preliminary design and budgeting phase, the second for the final design and construction phase. In many cases this contract is far more appropriate for a team approach to design and construction than any other document; A191 is easier to read and less detailed. And while every contract tends to favor whoever writes it, in this case the favoritism also works for the builder, since the builder and architect are virtually indistinguishable.

A191 is best suited to a team that exists as a single business entity — a builder and architect that have a formal partnership. If you are not part of such a partnership, you may still want to use this document as a basis for your contract with the owner. You contract with the owner for your services, and the architect contracts for his services. Hire a lawyer who is knowledgeable in construction law to walk through the document with you, omitting items relating to design, unless your firm actually does the design as well.

By using A191, you are not a party to a contract with an architect, and consequently, you are not submitting yourself to the architect's formal control of the project. You and the architect work together to satisfy the owner's need, but each is responsible for his own work, and is legally answerable to the owner, who controls the purse strings.

The owner may request that the architect help interpret the degree of completion you claim on your disbursement request. You probably cannot escape this. It is the owner's right to do so. However, you have not agreed that the architect is a party to your contract, so his control is only in influencing the owner, which, if you have a good team, should not cause problems.

At the very least, make sure your contract includes an arbitration clause, so you have a clear-cut method for resolving differences without resorting to full-blown litigation. Arbitration may be painful at times, but it will almost always prove cheaper than going to court. An arbitration clause generally says that each party agrees to be bound by the findings of an arbitration hearing, alleviating the need for a judge or jury. A more detailed version of this clause appears in both AIA documents mentioned above.

By Calvin Goldsmith, a former contractor and present business manager of Tornesello Construction Company in Bedford, Mass.

The Perils of Design/Build

The move from building or remodeling to design/build is a natural progression. Most contractors don't hesitate to add a finished basement or a deck to a customer's prepared plans. Similarly, few hesitate to design a remodeled bath or small kitchen. From there, the next step may be designing a major addition or even a whole house from scratch. Such growth may proceed smoothly and seem natural, but there are many pitfalls that a contractor would be wise to consider.

When does a builder or remodeler who does a little design work become a "designer"? Can a builder/designer legally advertise design services? Can a designer who is not an architect get insurance against "errors and omissions" in design? And can he charge separately for design services?

While these questions are central to the livelihood of the design/builder, few have clear answers. The laws governing design vary greatly from state to state. In some states, builders who advertise and perform design services are on solid legal ground; in others they are technically breaking the law and are subject to criminal penalties. But even in the stricter states, the laws are generally unenforced. The issue does get raised in civil cases over insurance payments or contract disputes, but even here the guidelines are ambiguous.

So those who venture into design/build may face considerable risks, and those who don't may be losing out competitively. What's a reasonable course of action for the small contractor to follow?

Contractors who make the leap into design/build face an array of legal obstacles in many states

State Laws on the Practice of Architecture

Every state has its own laws defining the practice of architecture, which spell out who may do what. Some of these laws are actively enforced and others are not, so it's important to determine if your area enforces them. Your state builders association can be a good source of information.

Most states define "architecture" quite broadly, including everything from structural design through supervision of construction contracts, as well as the design of additions and other remodeling. Some include "aesthetic" design, environmental analysis, or "utilization of space." Literally interpreted, many of these laws would apply to interior decorating, siding on a garage, or installing a closet rod.

Typically, the laws allow only licensed architects to provide these services. Builders who violate these laws are subject to criminal penalties. In Pennsylvania, for example, if you prepare preliminary sketches or floor plans, you're subject to a maximum sentence of up to 30 days in prison and a $500 fine.

Fortunately, many of the laws are limited in scope. For example, 32 states exempt design of single-family residences from the architectural licensing requirement. Some of the laws are limited to larger structures, or ones intended for public use.

But many design laws are not so limited and, if enforced, would severely restrict the rights of nonarchitects to design. To a large extent, these broad-based statutes are ignored by builders, architects, and law enforcement officials. This puts the burden on the builder to decide whether he wants to take a chance by assuming, like everyone else in the business, that he need not pay attention to the strict language of the law.

If you're thinking of getting a friendly architect to put his seal on your plans, the lawmakers have thought of that, too.

It's specifically banned by many state laws, and in most states architects are subject to disciplinary action or penalties if they place their seal on any plan not prepared by them or under their direct supervision.

While legislative activity and legal challenges have heated up a bit in the current building slump, there is little interest in "policing" the architectural state laws. This is certainly true here in Pennsylvania, which has some of the nation's strictest architectural statutes. So if the laws are largely ignored by those who are charged with enforcing them, what difference do they make?

The main way these laws come into play is in civil suits, most commonly in contract disputes. For example, let's say you're having trouble getting the last check, and you sue your client for the contract price. If he hires an aggressive lawyer, he might claim that your contract is unenforceable because it is illegal. In fact, agreements to violate the law, such as practicing "architecture" without a license, are usually not considered valid in court.

You, in turn, might argue that everybody ignores the law regulating design services, so the contract wasn't really illegal. Such cases can go either way depending on the specific state laws, contract language, and judge's interpretation.

Design Insurance

Another way the law could come back to haunt you is if your building were to suffer a structural failure resulting in personal injury or property damage. If that happened, your first phone call would likely be to your insurance agent, not to your lawyer.

Does your insurance cover your design services, and does it make any difference whether the services were technically illegal (because you're not a licensed architect)? None of the insurance agents we contacted in researching this article were able to answer this one definitively.

In some cases, they said, the insurance company would simply pay; in others, the answer would come only from a court after a lawsuit was brought against the insurance company. At issue is whether the "general liability" coverage most builders carry will cover the "professional liability" incurred by a design error. Most builders' policies do not specifically *exclude* such professional liability. But they don't specifically include it either.

For example, let's suppose a structural failure was caused purely by the design, not by any error in construction — for instance, a main beam was undersized and caused damage. Your first resort is your general liability insurance, which protects you against ordinary "negligence." This covers any mistakes you make in your construction of a building (or any claims in a lawsuit that you made mistakes, even if you say you didn't).

But most insurance companies will tell you that your policy was not intended to cover "professional liability" or "malpractice" — such as design errors. They didn't add in that risk when they figured up your premium, since few insurance companies recognize that most builders and remodelers do design work.

When such cases have been litigated, courts have generally ruled against the insurance company, unless professional liability was specifically excluded from coverage. The courts have argued that an insurance company should know enough to clearly state what its policy does and doesn't cover.

A few policies do clearly exclude professional liability. But many policy forms don't mention it at all. If you write your agent a letter asking about this, his answer will probably be that you are not covered for design liability, since it is not the insurance company's intent to provide that. At best, the agent might admit that a court would probably rule in your favor since there is no exclusion in the policy for design services.

If you want to buy insurance that will definitely cover your design services, your insurer might sell you an "errors and omissions" policy similar to the policies that architects have. More likely, you'd need to shop around for a company willing to underwrite such a policy. Your premiums may be higher and your limits lower than for a licensed engineer or architect, who often pay well in excess of $10,000 per year. The best strategy may be to purchase insurance through a trade association such as the American Institute of Building Designers.

Associations For Designers

The American Institute of Building Design (AIBD) is a nationally recognized association of building designers. It was formed in California in 1950, is active in 46 states, and has over 900 members. Most of the members specialize in custom residential and small commercial projects. According to its literature, "it is the responsibility of the association to encourage members to comply with state statutes and to design their projects within the guidelines as set forth by prevailing building codes and engineering practices."

AIBD accepts members based on field experience and the ability to produce professional plans. It offers its members many services, including access to professional liability insurance, and an exam that can qualify them as Certified Professional Building Designers. For more information, contact AIBD at 800/366-2423.

Other organizations that offer training and certification for designers include the American Society of Interior Designers (ASID), 608 Massachusetts Ave., NE, Washington, DC 20002-6006; 202/546-3480; and the National Kitchen & Bath Association (NKBA), 687 Willow Grove St., Hackettstown, NJ 07840; 908/852-0033. ASID's program focuses on building interiors and NKBA's program focuses on kitchen and bath design.

— C.H. & T.A.

Minimize Your Risk

Depending on your state laws, the design/build picture may appear pretty grim. Despite the lack of clear answers, however, there are ways to minimize your risk if you live in a state with restrictive laws.

The first and easiest strategy is to avoid the appearance of practicing architecture. If you advertise design services, don't use the word "architectural" or anything like it. Many state laws specifically bar use of the terms "architect" or "architectural" by nonlicensed persons describing their services. In fact, in 1991 the state architectural board in New Jersey attempted to ban the use of the word "design" by a remodeling contractor.

Second, it is best to state clearly that your design services are offered only in conjunction with your building services — that is, you are not offering to design anything unless you'll also be the builder. Some courts have decided that the licensing regulations don't apply to a designer who also builds the projects. Also, your design activities are less likely to come under legal challenge if you're the builder on the job.

When you're pricing the project, don't charge separately for "design." Instead, you could charge an hourly rate for "preconstruction services," or find some other way to get paid for your time. If the client is willing to sign a contract for the job before the detailed plans are drawn up, you could schedule periodic payments based on percentages of completion — which would include the "preconstruction" phase.

Sometimes your plans may find their way into the hands of another builder, exposing you to potential liability. Let's say a couple, who signed a contract and proceeded through the "preconstruction" phase with your company, decided to spend their money on divorce lawyers instead of building a house. They later resolved their differences, and decided to build the house after all — in another state. You can't keep them from taking the plans; after all, they've paid you and the plans belong to them. To guard against such situations, you should put a rubber stamp on all your plans stating that they are intended only for your use as the builder. This won't necessarily protect you from all risk, but it will help and the cost is low.

If the project is large enough, consider bringing in a licensed engineer or architect to "supervise" your design work, and put his seal on the plans. This may comply with your state licensing law, and would also give you a stronger position if an unhappy client sues you for problems with the design. It's interesting to note that many state laws don't address the fact that many professional engineers, who are not licensed architects, are performing work that falls within the definition of "architecture."

Safety Not the Issue

Arguments against builders having the right to offer design/build services often

Rating The States

In this chart, each state has been listed in one of three categories according to how restrictive the state's statutes are regarding the design of single-family residences. The chart is intended only as a general guideline for builders and designers. For more detailed information, contact the NAHB Remodelors Council (800-368-5242) or the American Institute of Building Design (800-366-2423).

Very Few Restrictions		Some Restrictions	Many Restrictions
Alabama	Nebraska	California	Hawaii
Alaska	New Hampshire	Connecticut	Maine
Arizona	North Carolina	Delware	Nevada
Arkansas	Oklahoma	Idaho	New Jersey
Colorado	Oregon	Indiana	New York
Florida	Rhode Island	Michigan	North Dakota
Georgia	South Carolina	New Mexico	Pennsylvania
Illinois	South Dakota	Ohio	Tennessee
Iowa	Pennsylvania	Utah	
Kansas	Tennessee		
Kentucky	Texas		
Louisiana	Vermont		
Maryland	Virginia		
Massachusetts	Washington		
Missouri	West Virginia		
Minnesota	Wisconsin		
Mississippi	Wyoming		
Montana			

contend that the state architectural laws are in place to ensure public safety.

In most locales, however, plans are reviewed for code compliance before the building department issues a building permit. Many municipalities retain engineers to perform this review, and it's the building inspector's job to see that new buildings comply with a code that was written with the public safety in mind. For most single-family residences, it would seem that this procedure is adequate with regard to safety. For a structurally complex custom home, review by an engineer for structural soundness would certainly do the job.

Furthermore, virtually every state, with the possible exceptions of Hawaii and Tennessee, lets an individual design his own home, which could later be offered for sale. If public safety were really at issue, would the law permit this?

Look Before You Leap

As your building or remodeling business grows and you take on more design work, keep in mind the problems you may face. If you perform only enough design work to avoid misunderstandings with your customer, you may have little to worry about. If, on the other hand, you're considering an active design/build operation, you may be headed for some surprises.

While the intent of this article is to help alert builders to the risks of offering design services, it's important to note that it is not meant to be a legal guide. Contact an attorney before you make any final decisions.

Do your homework and know where you stand before you decide on a new venture. At least you'll know where the pitfalls are, and that can be a big help in keeping you out of them.

By Carl Hagstrom and Toby Anderson. Hagstrom is a design/builder in Montrose, Pa., and a contributing editor at The Journal of Light Construction. *Anderson is a retired lawyer, turned writer, also in Montrose.*

Copyright Basics for Design/Build

Before tweaking — or even *using* — that set of plans, know what constitutes copyright infringement

If you bill yourself as a "design-build" company, you're probably asked not only to design new houses from the ground up, but also to make modifications to plans customers bring into your office. These "stock" house plans often need tweaking to comply with your local code — changing the foundation type, making the stairs longer, or moving the garage doors off the street. You may also see lots of pages torn out of plan books, with customers asking you to incorporate this or that detail from one plan into another. You might even be asked to draw up a set of plans from scratch based on a photograph or floor plan a customer has clipped out of a magazine.

In all of these scenarios, you might be breaking the copyright laws intended to protect you and other designers from those who would steal the unique features you've worked hard to provide for your clients. Copyright law is complicated, so it's important to have a basic understanding of how it works, both to stay out of trouble and to make it work to your advantage.

The Law, Then and Now

It has always been illegal to copy any printed work without permission, be it a magazine article, a book, or a house plan. Until recently, however, the copyright law didn't consider the constructed version of a house plan to be a copy, so there was nothing to stop a builder from purchasing a plan and building as many houses as he or she wanted from that one plan. In addition, since the constructed project wasn't protected by copyright, it was also okay to "measure and observe" an existing building and whip up a new set of plans from notes, sketches, and photographs taken at the site.

On December 1, 1990, the copyright laws got much tougher regarding architectural design. Today, the constructed building, called the "Architectural Work," can be copyrighted as well as the physical plans. If someone is caught building multiple projects, or copying or incorporating someone else's design ideas without permission, the penalty is more than a slap on the wrist. In North Carolina, a professional building designer was recently awarded $60,000 from a builder who illegally built six versions of a single-use plan he had purchased. Similar awards are now commonplace throughout the United States.

Copyright infringement usually falls into one of four categories. Here's how to deal with each one.

Reuse Without Permission

When you buy a house plan or contract with a designer, you should assume that all you are buying is the right to use the plans for a single project. Of course, like all contracts the terms can be negotiated, and there is nothing wrong with selling a plan for multiple uses — or even selling the design outright — as long as all parties agree to the terms. If a client brings you a plan, it's up to you to confirm that they have the right to distribute and build it. Likewise, if you're selling the client design services, make sure they understand what you will and won't allow them to do with the finished product. Some designers are now handling the reuse issue by licensing the design for construction (see "Sample License Agreement"). A license agreement lets you spell out exactly what can and can't be done with the plans. All notices must be in writing, and ideally should be on each sheet of the drawings.

> **Sample License Agreement**
>
> The original purchaser of this plan, # ___, is granted a limited non-exclusive and non-transferable license to build one and only one home using this plan. Use of this plan to build more than one home is prohibited. The plan may not be reproduced or transferred without the express written permission of the copyright owner. The plan may be modified for code compliance only to secure a building permit for one project. Said modifications become the property of the copyright owner. Any other modifications require the express written permission of the copyright owner.

Unauthorized Modification

Only a design's "copyright owner" has the right to grant permission to modify it. Just because your customers bought a copy of a plan does not mean they can legally have you or anyone make changes to it. Some plan companies will sell "reproducible" copies for that pur-

Before modifying a so-called "reproducible" plan, check for a stamp like this one in colored ink. If the stamp is black or missing, the plan is probably an illegal copy.

pose, but beware: You need to verify that the copy presented to you is legit. It's easy enough to take a reproducible drawing to Kinko's and make a full-sized copy. Normally, the original will bear a stamp in colored ink (see sample stamp). If that stamp is in black ink when you get the drawing, there's a good chance you're working with an illegal copy.

Ignorance is no excuse. If you modify something without permission from the copyright owner, you can still be sued, regardless where you got it from. The best policy is to always contact the designer and get permission, in writing, before making any changes.

On the flip side, if you provide plans for someone, you should clearly spell out what they can and can't modify. Many designers allow builders to make code modifications, but draw the line at changes that could affect the look of the project. You should put the "can's and can'ts" on a sheet attached to the plans, and make references on each individual sheet. Better still, include a license agreement in your design contract and spell out the terms there.

Copying a Plan from a Plan Book or Copying an Existing Home

Homes designed and built prior to the 1990 copyright change can probably be recreated by "measurement and observation," with little, if anything, the author of the original drawings can do about it. Anything newer than 1990, however, is still the intellectual property of the original designer. You don't have to copy the blueprints to get in trouble: Starting from a page in a plan book, which is probably derived from the original work, is just as bad.

A fundamental principle of copyright is that an author may not copyright ideas contained in a work, just the expression of those ideas. This principle precludes protection for common, generic themes in architecture or design. What it means to you is this: If your clients see something they like in a plan book, instead of clipping it, have them describe it to you. "A colonial house with two side wings and a fancy front door and a kitchen in the back" is generic and open to your interpretation; tracing over the picture in the plan book is not.

Buildings Built from Preliminary Plans

Because a constructed building is now considered a "copy," if you build from a preliminary plan or conceptual design, you are stealing the intellectual work of the copyright owner. If you are the designer and don't want your plans peddled to other builders, the best defense is to plaster the drawings with "Not for construction" disclaimers and the like, and exclude their use in your design contract with the client. Communication is critical. Many times people don't understand that you're producing something that they can't take elsewhere.

Sample Copyright Notice

Copyright © 1998 by David A. Designer: These plans are protected under the Federal Copyright Laws. The original purchaser of this plan is authorized to construct one and only one home using this plan. Modification or reuse of this plan is prohibited without the express written permission of the designer.

Register Your Work

As of March 1, 1989, it is no longer necessary to place written notice of copyright on an original work, but it is still a good idea to do so. A notice makes the end user aware that you're serious about protecting your copyright, and helps establish the date of creation or publication. The notice must contain three elements: the statutory symbol (©) or the word "Copyright," the date of creation or first publication, and the copyright owner's name (see "Sample Copyright Notice"). The author and the copyright owner don't necessarily have to be the same person.

In addition, the 1990 law permits you to register both the "architectural plans" (the drawings) and the "architectural work" (the design). Registering both requires two separate applications and fees ($20 each). Designs produced prior to 1990 can still be registered, but as "architectural plans" only.

Why register? Unregistered designs are technically protected, but you won't be able to file suit in court until you formally register the work in question. Filing before infringement occurs, or within 90 days of publication in a plan book, entitles the copyright owner to additional damages that would not be awarded otherwise, including statutory minimum damages and attorney's fees. Without prior registration, legal fees alone would likely cancel any net gain from a win in court.

Everything you need to register your copyright is available from the Federal Copyright office in Washington, D.C. (202/707-9100); ask for form VA. Forms can also be downloaded from the Web (www.loc.gov/copyright/forms/).

By Georgia Toney Lesley, and David E. Bennett, J.D. Lesley is a professional building designer based in Summerville, S.C., and the national copyright committee chairperson for the American Institute of Building Design. Bennett is a partner in the firm of Rhodes, Coats, and Bennett in Raleigh, N.C., who is registered to practice before the United States Patent and Trademark Office. His manual, Copyright Basics for Home Designers and Builders, *is available from AIBD (800/366-2423).*

Chapter 15

Risk Management

How To Buy Construction Insurance

A guide to purchasing workers comp and general liability policies

Most builders buy general liability and workers comp insurance from the same company. While there is no reason to change this strategy, the rapid increase in workers comp rates has changed the way insurers sell construction insurance, and the way builders shop for it.

Worker's Comp Markets

There are still two primary markets for workers comp insurance: the voluntary market, and the assigned risk pool. In the voluntary market, insurers can decide whether to underwrite policies based on the track record of each construction company that applies. Insurers have no choice, however, when it comes to the assigned risk pool. Builders in this category are either engaged in dangerous work, such as blasting or mining, or have a poor claims record. No builder in the assigned risk pool can be denied insurance.

Years ago, rates were the same for companies in both the voluntary market and the assigned risk pool. The major difference was that voluntary market policies offered several different plans to spread out premium payments, while assigned risk premiums had to be paid up front. Today, policies in both markets use payment plans, but assigned risk pool premiums are higher than those in the voluntary market.

Losses are also handled differently, depending on which market the policy is written for. Insurers must cover all losses from the policies they write for the voluntary market. That's why they insure only companies with a good track record. Losses in the assigned risk pool, however, are spread among all insurers who sell policies in the voluntary market. This protects a single insurer from having to bear the full cost of the individual high-risk policies it writes.

Even so, the assigned risk pool runs a deficit. In many cases, assigned risk losses account for as much as 20% of premiums charged for policies in the voluntary market. The reaction of insurance companies has been to reduce the number of workers comp policies they write and to charge higher premiums for them.

ARAP. Unfortunately, the higher premiums caused by the assigned risk deficit raises workers comp premiums for everybody, even builders in the voluntary market who have good claims records. A new program called the Assigned Risk Adjustment Program (ARAP) aims to make the assigned risk pool self-supporting by charging higher premiums to builders with poor claims records. Under ARAP, builders with an experience modification rating higher than 1.0, and who meet other criteria (such as consistently high premium costs) will receive an ARAP charge on top of their regular assigned risk premiums (actual criteria vary from state to state). This can result in premiums that can be twice the normal rate. While ARAP is relatively new (about half the states have it now), the National Council of Compensation Insurers (NCCI) is trying to institute ARAP in all states.

How does ARAP affect the way builders buy insurance? Obviously, the most important factor is to find an insurance carrier who will write your workers comp insurance in the voluntary market. For new carpentry contractors with no track record, this may be difficult. That's because construction traditionally has some of the highest claims rates, and insurance companies are gun-shy about newcomers. The best strategy is to shop around. If you can't find a voluntary market policy, find the best deal you can for an assigned risk policy. Then use safety policies and employee education to keep your claims low, and shop around again next year. After two or three years with a clean record, chances are good you'll find an insurer in the voluntary market to write your policy.

General Liability

In most cases, workers comp insurance determines the buying strategy, and general liability insurance is of less concern. There are exceptions, however. Some contractors (roofers and blasting contractors, for example) are in higher risk classes, so their workers comp insurance is always written in the assigned risk pool. This leaves only general liability insurance to dicker over.

Buying general liability insurance is not as difficult as it used to be. Broad form coverage, which used to be optional, is now standard for most policies. In a broad form policy, a general contractor's liability insurance covers claims caused by the work of subcontractors. This is important "fine print," however, so it's still worth asking your agent if your policy includes broad form coverage.

In fact, it's always smart to ask questions when buying insurance. Ask your agent questions about how your liability policy actually works. Did you know, for instance, that even a broad form policy does not cover defects in workmanship, regardless of whether the work is done by a subcontractor or by your own employees? For example, if a plumber installing a new shower head gives his wrench one turn too many and breaks off the shower head, damage to the fitting he was working on is not covered. On the other hand, the policy probably does cover damage to the tub when the shower head falls and chips the finish. Similarly, if your employees install a new roof and it leaks, your liability insurance will not pay to repair the roof because that is your work product. Insurance will, however, pay to repair drywall and wallpaper damaged because of the leak.

Policy limits. Also ask about policy limits when buying general liability insurance. A typical one-man outfit should buy limits of $500,000/$1 million (per-occurrence/aggregate). Higher limits are available for most trades, but contractors engaged in dangerous work (such as roofing, blasting, and installing gas lines) will pay higher premiums for higher limits. A jump to $1 million/ $2 million, for instance, might increase premiums by 15%. The good news is that you can increase your policy limits for a particular job at very little extra cost. When the job is over, simply reduce the limits back to normal levels.

Builder's risk. Many large damage claims, such as collapse or fire, are covered by a standard homeowner's policy. A building that is still under construction, however, should be protected with a builder's risk policy. In addition to covering the structure itself, builder's risk insurance also protects against loss by theft or disaster of materials stored on site (such as windows) that have not yet been incorporated into the building. Make sure the policy limits cover the value of the work you are doing. Most contractors prefer to buy the policy themselves, because in the event of a claim, the person who owns the policy is the person who gets the check. The next best thing is to purchase a policy jointly with your client, so that any claims checks require signatures from both parties.

Inland marine. I also recommend insuring your tools with an inland marine policy. This type of insurance will cover your tools wherever they are: on site, in your truck, or stored in your shop. Watch out for a "locked vehicle warranty," however, which doesn't protect tools stolen from an unlocked vehicle. This shouldn't make too much difference, however, since most builders use common sense and lock up their trucks if there is any danger of theft.

Likewise, you should use common sense even if your insurance policy doesn't have such a stipulation. If you store tools on a wide-open site, your policy may cover the loss — but only the first time. The insurer will probably refuse to write a second policy, and other companies will not look favorably on this type of claim.

The same is true of the other construction insurance you purchase. Insurance coverage is not an excuse to be careless. Your policies may cover your losses the first time something goes wrong, but every strike against your record makes insurers less likely to renew your policy. A poor claims record also tends to increase your premiums. Buying the proper insurance is a good first step, but using common sense is the only sure way to keep costs down and maintain a clean track record.

By Peter Hood, owner of The Noyle Johnson Insurance Agency, with four offices in the central Vermont area.

Buying Disability Insurance

You *can* find good coverage at an affordable cost—if you understand the options

According to statistics from the National Safety Council, the average American is five times more likely to be disabled in an accident than to die prematurely. Despite these odds, most of my contractor clients who have life insurance policies balk at buying disability insurance. One reason is that disability insurance seems to be very expensive. But there are several different types of coverage, and these can often be combined in ways that provide good protection at a reasonable cost.

Two Types of Coverage

Contractors need to consider two main types of disability insurance: income and overhead expense. (A third type, called buyout insurance, provides one partner with the funds needed to purchase an injured partner's interest in the company. Premiums are very high, however, and few small companies buy this type of coverage.)

Income insurance. If you get injured and can't work, your income may decline or dry up altogether, but you will continue to incur personal expenses. Disability income insurance can supply the money you will need to pay your bills until you can return to work. (This type of insurance covers non-occupational injuries only; if you get injured at work, you're covered by workers comp.)

The monthly benefit payment depends strictly on your income. (Premiums are set by other factors, such as waiting period and benefit period, which I'll discuss later.) Most companies will pay benefits equal to about 60% of your gross monthly income as determined from your tax returns.

Some newer disability income policies pay benefits equal to the percentage of income actually lost. Typically, such "partial disability" benefit plans are attached as a rider to a standard income policy. The premiums are very low, but are paid in addition to the standard premium.

Business overhead expense insurance. When you are injured, your company will continue to incur certain regular expenses, such as rent and utility bills. If you don't continue to make these payments, *you* may survive your injury, but your company won't.

Business overhead expense insurance will pay for certain cost-of-doing-business expenses for as long as you are unable to work. The amount varies, depending on what your actual overhead expenses are at the time you buy the insurance. To receive payments, you will have to submit actual bills. Remember, only fixed expenses are covered; costs for materials or subcontractors do not qualify.

Group policies. In addition to individual disability policies, group plans are also available — and at much lower premiums. In a group plan, the terms of the policy are the same for everyone, although the premiums and payments

Table A.
Disability Income
(annual premiums based on a 45-year-old male)

Waiting Period	Benefit Period				
	15 months	30 months	60 months	Age 65	Life
30 Days	$1,592	$2,047	$3,025	$4,770	$5,913
60 Days	1,024	1,403	2,118	3,233	4,419
90 Days	658	951	1,498	2,335	3,465
180 Days	519	914	1,252	1,975	3,100
365 Days	478	651	1,114	1,766	2,906
430 Days	—	596	947	1,545	2,651

Disability income policies commonly carry a 90-day waiting period, and benefits continue to age 65. But the savings on annual premiums can be substantial for different options.

may vary for different salary levels.

One disadvantage is that policy options that make group insurance more affordable may leave you with less coverage than you'd like to have. Fortunately, you can supplement the group policy with an individual policy for yourself that makes up the difference between the coverage you want and the coverage provided by the group plan. Individual employees can also buy supplemental policies and increase their protection at their own expense.

Premium Options

If you shop for just the coverage you really need, you can put together a disability insurance package that's affordable and provides adequate protection.

For both types of disability insurance, you can reduce costs by extending the waiting period (the amount of time you can wait before payments begin) and by shortening the benefit period (the length of time benefits are paid).

Waiting period. Insurance premiums are lower the longer you can wait before payments begin. Most people can wait at least 30 days before receiving income payments. Most contractors can also extend the waiting period for overhead expense reimbursements. This is especially true if your company can continue to complete and bill for jobs while you're injured.

Benefit period. The longer the policy pays benefits, the higher the premiums. Most companies no longer offer lifetime payments on income policies, and those that do charge high premiums for them. Premiums drop significantly, however, if disability income payments stop when you reach age 65, when you become eligible for social security.

Choosing a reasonable benefit period can save even more money on business overhead expense insurance. The more your company depends on you, however, the shorter the benefit period you need to buy, because if you're out of commission for too long, chances are your business won't survive.

Mix and match. Different waiting periods and benefit periods can dramatically affect annual premiums. For example, in the disability income sample in Table A, increasing the waiting period from 30 days to 60 days reduces annual premiums for disability income insurance by 25% for a lifetime benefit period. Longer waiting periods and shorter benefit periods yield even lower premiums. The same is true of the premium example for business overhead expense insurance in Table B (above).

Table B.
Business Overhead Expense
(annual premiums based on a 45-year-old male)

Waiting Period	Benefit Period		
	12 months	18 months	24 months
30 Days	$1,314	$1,425	$1,889
60 Days	886	1,027	1,314
90 Days	607	725	942

Benefit periods are typically limited to 24 months, by which time most companies are either out of business or under new management.

But buying the cheapest — or the most expensive — policy isn't always the best course. Instead, try to match the coverage to your particular circumstances. For example, suppose your company usually has a couple of good-sized jobs going, and that you normally supervise the work. If you get injured, your short-term need is for someone to come in to supervise those jobs to completion. This could be covered by a disability income policy with a short waiting period.

But you can delay the waiting period for any business overhead insurance, because the payments your clients make for the completed work will cover fixed expenses for six months or more. If no new work has been sold by then, the business overhead reimbursements will kick in and will keep the balls in the air long enough for you to recover.

The most important point to keep in mind is that disability insurance, like other types of insurance, can be tailored to suit your company and your personal financial circumstances. Before you buy a policy, analyze your situation and make sure you don't end up paying for more coverage than you need.

—Peter Hood

Am I Covered?

The wording and coverages of liability policies vary. Make sure you understand yours before you need to make a claim.

Unfortunately, many contractors don't check their liability insurance coverage until there is an injury or property damage on the job. When the contractor does contact his insurer, he is often surprised to find he's not covered. In this era of high jury awards for personal injuries, lack of coverage could mean the end of a good contracting business. So it's important to understand the basics of your liability coverage. Let's start by looking at the standard coverage available, using three basic questions as a framework:

- Who caused the injury or damage?
- How did the injury or damage happen?
- Who or what was injured or damaged?

Standard Coverage

The standard liability policy states that it will: "pay on behalf of the insured all sums which the insured shall become legally obligated to pay because of bodily injury or physical damage to which this insurance applies, caused by an occurrence." What does this actually mean? By using our three questions, we can make sense of this insurance language.

Who Caused the Injury?

The policy states that it will pay those sums that "the insured shall become legally obligated to pay." The key terms here are "the insured" and "legally obligated to pay." The term "insured" is defined in the policy. The "insured" includes you, the contractor buying the policy, who is known as the "named insured." If the contractor is an individual, the term "named insured" covers the contractor and perhaps a spouse. If the policy is bought by a contracting partnership, the policy will cover the partnership itself and perhaps the directors or officers of the corporation. The term "insured" also includes employees who are performing certain acts for you, such as operating your equipment.

The policy states it will pay for those sums that the insured is "legally obligated to pay." Under agency law, an employer is generally liable for the acts of an employee who is acting within the scope of his employment. Consequently, you may be legally obligated to pay for those injuries and damages caused by your employees while the employees are working on the job. The policy would cover these injuries or damages. However, an employer is usually not obligated to pay for the acts of an independent contractor. Consequently, the liability policy would not generally cover injury or damage caused by an independent contractor working on your job.

If you want to have the actions of additional parties covered under your policy, you need to have these parties named as insured on the policy. This type of coverage is available and is called "extended coverage."

How Did the Injury Or Damage Happen?

The policy states that it will cover "an occurrence." Simply put, an "occurrence" is an accident. An accident is an unintended, sudden, unexpected event.

All liability policies exclude coverage of "intentional damages or injury," a term carefully defined by law. The definition of intentional damage or injury goes beyond the intention to perform an action which subsequently happened to cause an injury or damage. It means, rather, that one not only intended to perform an act but that the action was also intended to cause injury or damage, or was substantially certain to cause injury or damage. Thus, if your employee intentionally drops a board on someone's head or drops a board from a second story window knowing that it is pretty certain that the board will strike someone below, the action is "intentional" and the results will not be covered by the policy. In contrast, if the employee stacks boards on the second story, anticipating that the stack is stable, and a board slips from the pile and strikes a passerby, the injury would probably be covered.

The policy will also state that it excludes certain types of events. These items are found in the "exclusions" section of the policy. There are four common exclusions that are of particular interest to the contractor:

Collapse hazard. The policy generally excludes the "collapse hazard." This exclusion means that there is no coverage for structural property damage or the collapse of or structural injury to a building or structure if (1) the damage is caused by you or your employees and (2) the damage is caused by the grading of land, excavating, burrowing, filling, backfilling, tunneling, pile driving, coffer dam work, or caisson work, or the moving, shoring, underpinning, raising or demolition of any building or structure, or the removal or rebuilding of a structural support. Incidental coverage is available for the "collapse hazard."

Underground property damage hazard. Policies also generally exclude the "underground property damage hazard." The policy thus does not cover property damage to wires, conduits, pipes, mains, sewers, tanks, tunnels, or any similar structure that is located beneath the surface of the ground or water if (1) it is caused by you or your employees and (2) is caused by and occurs during the use of mechanical equipment for the purpose of grading land, paving, excavating, drilling, burrowing, filling, backfilling, or pile driving. Coverage for this type of damage is available through incidental coverage.

Completed operations hazard. Policies also generally exclude the "completed operations hazard." Under this exclusion, there is no coverage for bodily injury or property damage that occurs on the construction site after construction has been completed or abandoned. Construction is deemed completed when one of the following events occur:

- When all operations to be performed under your contract have been completed;
- When all operations that you are to perform on the site have been completed;
- When the portion of the site on which the injury or damage occurs has been turned over to the owner or user and that portion of the site is being used for its intended purpose.

Even if further service, maintenance or warranty work is required on the site, the project will still be deemed to be completed for coverage purposes.

Violation of law. Policies also usually do not cover those injuries or damages arising from violations of statutes or ordinances, such as OSHA or state safety codes.

Who or What Was Injured or Damaged?

Most liability policies do not cover injuries to your employees if the injuries are covered by workers compensation. Thus, if your employee falls or is injured by another employee, the liability coverage usually does not extend to those injuries.

In addition, your own property is usually not covered by the liability policy. Property or equipment that you are renting, using, borrowing, or is in your care, custody, or control is also excluded. Many things can be under your care, custody, or control. For example, if you have exclusive access to a building and damage occurs to that building, you may not be covered by liability insurance. Items that are not in your control, like tools of employees that you cannot borrow except with express permission, will be covered. It is important that you have adequate property or equipment insurance to cover the excluded items.

The liability policy usually does not cover damage or injury occurring during the use, loading or unloading, operation, ownership, and maintenance of your on-road vehicles, like automobiles or trucks. Your vehicles include those that you own, operate, or rent. The exclusion is so broad that injuries to an independent contractor occurring during the loading or unloading of your vehicles may not be covered. The on-road vehicle exclusion does not apply to vehicles parked on the site if the vehicles are owned by your employees or third parties, and the vehicles are not being used in the course of construction.

Conclusion

The wording and coverages of liability policies vary. Using this guide can help you understand your coverage, but you should read your policy carefully. And if you are uncertain as to what is covered under your liability policy, discuss the policy with your insurance agent.

By Patricia A. Ayars, Esq., an attorney with Perlstein & Ayars of Glastonbury, Conn.

Fighting Workers Comp And Winning

To avoid overpayment, keep good records and learn how to accurately calculate workers comp premiums

As a small contractor, it's important that I accurately predict my expenses. I can do that now. But I used to have one expense that was about as predictable as the weather: workers compensation.

Like many contractors, I get audited every year by my insurance carrier. The auditor used to go through my books, prepare the audit, have me sign it, and a few weeks later I would be surprised with a bill larger than anticipated. Often the unexpected charges were premiums charged against wages paid to subcontractors whom I couldn't show were insured, and who were therefore considered by my insurer to be risks under my policy. I tried to learn the rules so that I'd know how to avoid these charges (or so I'd at least know which subs I was going to end up covering); but no matter how much I tried to learn about the system, I couldn't predict my charges.

Both my insurance agent and my carrier told me it was simple. (I work in New York State, but most of the basics in this article apply in most states.) All I had to do, they said, was multiply my uninsured payroll (employees and uninsured subcontractors) by the rates set by the rating board for each trade, and I would have my liability. They also advised me to keep it safe and simple — use only subs that carry their own workers comp, and get documentation to show it. That way, they said, I would be liable only for my own employees.

I tried to do this, but still ended up with unexpectedly high bills. Usually they would be $500 or $600 higher than expected. Though I hated writing the check, I would figure it was an amount I could live with. I figured I couldn't afford the time to haggle over these charges with the insurance company, especially since it seemed I would lose anyway.

After my 1990 compensation audit, however, I was given a bill for around $3,700 in unpaid premiums. I was expecting a bill for $600. With $3,100 at stake, I decided to take the time to haggle. It ended up taking nine months, but I got all but $600 of the bill erased.

Running Down the Facts

I started with a number of phone calls to my agent, my carrier, the state compensation board, the state insurance rating board, and the state office of consumer affairs. I told them I suspected I was being charged for covering people I shouldn't really be charged for, and tried to get them to clarify the rules for me. They all proved better at referring me elsewhere than answering my questions.

Things didn't start moving until I hired a lawyer. Suddenly the various bureaucracies involved seemed to take me more seriously: Here was someone who wasn't going to go away. A lot of the workers comp regulations are gray, and I suspect what often decides an inquiry is how big a fuss you are willing to make.

Of course, the lawyer was more experienced in querying those involved in the dispute about the critical issues. He was able to put his finger on the regulations and rules that were being overlooked or misinterpreted by my carrier, and which were resulting in my overcharges. Specifically, he found that:

- I was incorrectly charged $900 for covering the employees of an uninsured, but incorporated, plumbing and hvac sub I often used. Under New York State law, incorporated companies are required to carry their own comp insurance, and other companies cannot be charged for it.
- I was incorrectly charged $1,600 for covering subs who had no employees — a mason, a drywall taper, a trim carpenter, and a painter, all of whom I use often, but who also work for others and who are independent contractors. New York law does not require that I provide comp insurance for such sole proprietors who have no employees.
- I was incorrectly charged another $400 for charges relating to work done on a shop I was building on my own prop-

erty. Apparently, a complicated interplay of insurance law, at least in New York, has it that a contractor does not have to pay workers comp for work on a property he owns — presumably other insurance already covers it.

- Finally, when these overcharges were corrected, I was relieved of another $150 or so that was basically service charges connected with the other overcharges.

Getting over $3,000 in charges canceled improved my mood. What made me feel even better was having a firm grip on the rules involved and why I had been overcharged, so that I could prevent these overcharges from happening again.

It Pays to Know Your Stuff

I now keep my books on labor and sub charges very carefully, tracking the charges for which I am truly liable. This, and knowing the areas where I have been overcharged before, helps tremendously when the auditor comes around for his yearly visit. Dealing with this audit visit properly, I believe, is a key to preventing future problems.

When my auditor comes around, I show him both my own payroll records and the ledger on which all my chargeable subcontractor payments are listed. This ledger does not include sole proprietors working alone, and it does not include subs for whom I have proof of insurance. It does show what part of each payment is for labor, so that material costs don't get included in the basis for my charges.

The auditor then compiles the chargeable wages straight from this ledger and my payroll. He might also flip through my checkbook to check the payments there against the ledger. Anything that doesn't match, we hash over. So far, with my better recordkeeping and knowledge of the rules, I've won all my small disputes. I've had two audits since the year I was overcharged, and haven't had any further problems.

What if the auditor does find a problem? If he disagrees with my listed chargeable wages, I'll tell him, "Fine" — he can turn in his audit to the carrier, but I won't sign it. Here I'm gambling a bit on how the audit game works: My auditor works piecework, and, I'm guessing, doesn't get paid for a completed audit unless I sign it. My persistence and confidence in my numbers, I like to think, has made it clear to the auditor he won't leave with my signature unless I totally agree with the audit. I think this may be one reason he's been willing to take my objections into account.

Doing Your Homework

To deal with auditors with this sort of confidence, of course, you have to be on top of your numbers and have everything well-documented, so that if the auditor questions something, you can show him why you're right. This means having the documentation and financial records to back yourself up.

Substantiate those subs. If you don't

SET TAB STOPS AT ARROWS

CERTIFICATE OF INSURANCE

ISSUE DATE (MM/DD/YY)

PRODUCER
Acme Insurance Agency
P.O. Box 1000
Burlington, VT 05402

THIS CERTIFICATE IS ISSUED AS A MATTER OF INFORMATION ONLY AND CONFERS NO RIGHTS UPON THE CERTIFICATE HOLDER. THIS CERTIFICATE DOES NOT AMEND, EXTEND OR ALTER THE COVERAGE AFFORDED BY THE POLICIES BELOW.

INSURED
Rocky's Drilling & Blasting
P.O. Box 1000
Burlington, VT 05402

COMPANIES AFFORDING COVERAGE

COMPANY LETTER	
A	Ace Insurance Company
B	
C	
D	Ace Insurance Company
E	

COVERAGES

THIS IS TO CERTIFY THAT POLICIES OF INSURANCE LISTED BELOW HAVE BEEN ISSUED TO THE INSURED NAMED ABOVE FOR THE POLICY PERIOD INDICATED. NOTWITHSTANDING ANY REQUIREMENT, TERM OR CONDITION OF ANY CONTRACT OR OTHER DOCUMENT WITH RESPECT TO WHICH THIS CERTIFICATE MAY BE ISSUED OR MAY PERTAIN, THE INSURANCE AFFORDED BY THE POLICIES DESCRIBED HEREIN IS SUBJECT TO ALL THE TERMS, EXCLUSIONS, AND CONDITIONS OF SUCH POLICIES.

CO LTR	TYPE OF INSURANCE	POLICY NUMBER	POLICY EFFECTIVE DATE (MM/DD/YY)	POLICY EXPIRATION DATE (MM/DD/YY)	LIABILITY LIMITS IN THOUSANDS	EACH OCCURRENCE	AGGREGATE
A	GENERAL LIABILITY COMPREHENSIVE FORM X PREMISES/OPERATIONS X UNDERGROUND EXPLOSION & COLLAPSE HAZARD X PRODUCTS/COMPLETED OPERATIONS X CONTRACTUAL X INDEPENDENT CONTRACTORS X BROAD FORM PROPERTY DAMAGE X PERSONAL INJURY X	L1M0111011	1/1/99	1/1/99	BODILY INJURY	$	$
					PROPERTY DAMAGE	$	$
					BI & PD COMBINED	$ 100	$ 100
					PERSONAL INJURY		$
	AUTOMOBILE LIABILITY ANY AUTO ALL OWNED AUTOS (PRIV. PASS.) ALL OWNED AUTOS (OTHER THAN PRIV. PASS.) HIRED AUTOS NON-OWNED AUTOS GARAGE LIABILITY				BODILY INJURY (PER PERSON)	$	
					BODILY INJURY (PER ACCIDENT)	$	
					PROPERTY DAMAGE	$	
					BI & PD COMBINED	$	
	EXCESS LIABILITY UMBRELLA FORM OTHER THAN UMBRELLA FORM				BI & PD COMBINED	$	$
D	WORKERS' COMPENSATION AND EMPLOYERS' LIABILITY	M2N1222122	1/1/99	1/1/99	STATUTORY	$ 100 (EACH ACCIDENT) $ 500 (DISEASE-POLICY LIMIT) $ 100 (DISEASE-EACH EMPLOYEE)	
	OTHER						

DESCRIPTION OF OPERATIONS/LOCATIONS/VEHICLES/SPECIAL ITEMS

CERTIFICATE HOLDER
Tri-State Construction
123 Meadow St.
Pleasantville, VT 22222

CANCELLATION
SHOULD ANY OF THE ABOVE DESCRIBED POLICIES BE CANCELLED BEFORE THE EXPIRATION DATE THEREOF, THE ISSUING COMPANY WILL ENDEAVOR TO MAIL 30 DAYS WRITTEN NOTICE TO THE CERTIFICATE HOLDER NAMED TO THE LEFT, BUT FAILURE TO MAIL SUCH NOTICE SHALL IMPOSE NO OBLIGATION OR LIABILITY OF ANY KIND UPON THE COMPANY, ITS AGENTS OR REPRESENTATIVES.

AUTHORIZED REPRESENTATIVE

Subs with employees should provide you with certificates of workers comp insurance. Otherwise, you risk paying higher rates to cover the sub.

want to have a sub's wages included in the chargeable wages, you need to be able to show either that the sub carries workers comp insurance, or that he or she is an independent contractor who works alone.

For subs with employees, this means getting copies of their certificates of workers comp insurance. I won't contract with or pay a sub unless I have a current copy of his certificate, or unless his price and/or work is so good I'm willing to carry him for the length of the job in question.

For subs working alone, your problem will be proving that a) they are working alone, and b) they are truly independent contractors and not employees. Establishing these conditions with absolute certainty is often difficult, but there are a few crucial pieces of documentation that will usually convince your auditor. One is a certificate of general liability insurance showing the sub either has a "dba" (doing business as) or is incorporated. If he's incorporated, then he is an employee of his own company and must, by law, carry his own compensation policy.

Another way to show that a sub is independent is by doing business only under individual contracts for each job, which describe the work to be done and a payment schedule. It helps if subs use their own tools, set their own hours, and are self-directed. According to the New York compensation board, it also helps your case if your subs supply their own materials.

I also make sure to get my bills from subs broken down into labor and materials; I won't pay a sub's bill unless it's itemized like this.

All this has paid off. I've saved thousands of dollars. And I now know how to predict my charges and avoid being overcharged, so I can set aside the right amount of money before the bill comes at the end of the year.

Many contractors are overpaying. Most auditors know little about what to look for. Your best protection is to understand the rules, and thus your own liability, and impress upon the auditor and your carrier that you won't agree to anything more than the proper charges.

If that doesn't work, call your lawyer. For about $400, mine saved me thousands.

By Richard Cooley, a general contractor in Schenectady, N.Y.

Chapter 16

Conflict Resolution

The Business of Lawsuits

Even if you win, you can lose, unless you carefully evaluate a lawsuit as a business proposition

Lawsuits are often initiated or fully defended in court because the participants have strong feelings about justice. Unfortunately, finding someone "guilty" or "not guilty" does not prove someone "right" or "wrong." Forget the romantic notions you learned from the movies about how the legal system works.

Let's Make a Deal

The most cost-effective result you can get from the litigation process has nothing to do with "justice" in any absolute sense, just as a good deal on a new truck doesn't require buying the "best" truck. You pass up the Mercedes-Benz and buy a Chevy or Ford because it's more efficient and there are other things you can do with the money you save. In a lawsuit, your money "buys" the resolution of a dispute and the best result is still the one that's most cost-effective. Spending $10,000 in legal fees for a negotiated settlement of $50,000 is better than spending $40,000 in fees to win a $75,000 judgment in court.

Forget revenge. Considering the bad feelings created by the exchange of threats and insults, it's not surprising that many otherwise rational business owners treat a lawsuit as a means for revenge. But as with any business transaction, when the goal is revenge, the result is a bad deal. A lawsuit sets the price of a resolution to a dispute according to the odds of winning or losing. To refuse to pay the market price or to insist on more than the market price in order to get revenge makes no sense.

Know Your Costs

The most important thing your lawyer can do for you is provide the information you need to decide which alternative is more cost-effective: going to trial or settling out of court.

Written predictions. A lawyer should be able to give you periodic written estimates of both the cost and the likelihood of success of going to trial. Far from a sign of distrust, putting this information in writing protects you and your lawyer from later confusion about who said what and when.

Strategy. An experienced lawyer should be able to break down the litigation process into phases and to articulate in advance a strategy for each phase. Again, you should ask for a written estimate of the approximate cost for each phase and each strategy.

Poker Anyone?

Many business owners believe that settlements are always defeats, but nothing could be farther from the truth. Settlements are business deals that should be evaluated in terms of the available alternatives and their relative costs and risks.

A trial is a gamble. In the construction business, nothing is a sure thing. Regardless of your market share, the skill and loyalty of your employees, and the reliability of your suppliers, things can and do go wrong. The same is true of a trial. No matter how talented or self-confident your lawyer is or how many of your friends believe you are "in the right," going to trial is always a gamble. Key witnesses may die, move away, or forget what happened. Even if you tell the truth and your opponent lies, the jury may not believe you because of the way you look, dress, or talk. Remember also that judges, like other people, make mistakes, and that the law is often unclear. If it were simple, thousands of lawyers wouldn't be arguing about it.

Delays are expensive. A wait of several years until trial is common in many locations. This means you will pay or be paid in inflated dollars, which, if you had them now, could be invested in your business. There's also a chance you won't be paid at all. I remember a case where the plaintiff rejected a settlement offer of $75,000 in favor of going to trial to recover the full claim of $100,000. The delay was only six months, but it was long enough for the defendant to go out of business, leaving the plaintiff with nothing.

Hidden costs. Finally, litigation diverts time and energy from other aspects of your business. You need to supply information and make decisions throughout the process, and the confrontational aspects often drain your emotional

Case Study: An Unsettling Matter

Two weeks after submitting a final bill for $17,500, representing 5% retainage on a new $350,000 house he has just completed, a builder gets a call from the owner. He is told that nail pops and cracks in the wallboard have begun to appear in two first-floor rooms.

At the house, the builder explains to the owners that new houses experience normal settling in the first year. He tells them that his warranty covers these repairs, but that it's best to wait and then make all repairs at once. If he fixes the problems now, he doesn't want to be called back in five months to redo them when they recur. The owners explain that it's "very important" to make the repairs now because they have a number of dinner parties planned and it will embarrass them if their friends see these cosmetic problems. "Whatever you want," the builder replies. He comes the next week and makes the cosmetic repairs.

A few weeks later the problems recur, as predicted, and the owners want the builder to come back again. The builder reminds the owners of his policy and the outstanding retainage. The owners maintain that they thought the original repairs were done as a "favor." They never insisted he come back at all; they remember saying only that it was "very important."

Over the next few weeks, the discussions deteriorate rapidly. The builder feels that he is being punished for being right about the recurring problems and doesn't think he should be expected to do more free work. Feeling frustrated, he puts a lien on the house. The owner, angry now, and feeling that the builder is refusing to stand behind his work, files a lawsuit. When the builder gets the summons, he sends it to his lawyer, telling him to "take these people to court" to get the $17,500 retainage. The lawyer files a counterclaim.

Things quiet down for six months while lawyers for both sides photograph the house and take depositions from both parties. The owners get an estimate from another contractor of $18,000 to repair the damage. He says that he thinks the house is settling more than usual because one corner of the foundation is built on inadequate fill. The builder thinks this price is high and that he could do the repairs for $12,000.

June – September Expenses	
Repair costs:	$400
Legal fees:	$650

In March, the court sets an August trial date. In May, the builder hires a soils expert to testify that settling in the first six months is normal. He doesn't determine the quality of the fill because the builder doesn't want to pay for the heavy equipment and testing procedures. In July, the builder's lawyer orders copies of all of the depositions, prepares the builder and the soils expert for direct testimony, and prepares his cross-examination of the owners and their new contractor.

October – March Expenses	
Legal fees, incl. depositions	$6,150
Photographs:	$350

As the trial date approaches, the builder asks his lawyer what the outcome is likely to be. The lawyer says he has a 50-50 chance. The conversation between the builder and owner is not disputed, but it's ambiguous as to what each side meant by what they said. The testimony from the two experts could be a wash, and in the absence of clear-cut guidelines, the judge may rule in favor of the side who evokes the most sympathy.

April – July Expenses	
Legal fees:	$3,000
Soils expert:	$1,550

Settlement discussions continue until the eleventh hour. Not trusting the builder to do the work, the owners hire the second contractor to begin the repairs.

Finally, fourteen months after the original problems arose, the builder agrees to settle for $9,000 — 50% of the repair cost. His total investment is $22,100: out-of-pocket expenses of $11,700, including the settlement, and legal fees of $10,400.

August Expenses	
Settlement:	$9,000
Legal fees:	$1,000

Total Expenses	
Total Out-of-pocket:	$11,300
Total Legal Fees:	$10,800
Total Cost:	$22,100

Had he made the repairs himself a year earlier and split the costs with the owner, his total costs would have been $7,050. And he may even have gotten a referral.

— *H.K.*

energy. This is as much a "cost" as legal fees or a settlement payment.

Settling Out of Court

It's a cinch to determine which cases should be settled: They should *all* be settled, *provided the price is right.* What you and your lawyer need to determine is whether a settlement is a rational business alternative to the cost, risks, and rewards of going to trial, and what negotiating tactics you can use to persuade the other party to make a more favorable settlement offer. This analysis is one of the main functions your lawyer should perform and should take place during discovery (the period of time leading up to trial when information is exchanged between parties).

Lawsuits are usually initiated after talks break down. But far from signaling the end of negotiations, a lawsuit actually propels negotiations forward, for several reasons.

Pay to play. Talk is cheap until a lawsuit is filed. After that, the process gets more expensive the longer the parties disagree. This has the effect of putting a penalty on refusing to take the negotiation seriously.

No exit. When you negotiate in the face of a lawsuit, there is no way out except to settle or go to court. Without the lawsuit, the parties can ignore each other indefinitely.

Actions speak louder than words. Once a lawsuit is initiated, the parties no longer talk directly to each other. Instead, they speak through their lawyers, who are paid to appear self-confident and to say "no." It quickly becomes apparent that a lawyer cannot simply talk the other side into a good deal. Consequently, what the parties do is more important than what they say. For example, if you offer to settle for 80% of a claim shortly after a case is filed against you, nothing your lawyer says will ever persuade your opponent that you seriously believe you have a good chance of winning. The timing and amount of the offer will overpower whatever is said when conveying it.

Changing the odds. All of the tools used in negotiating a lawsuit are actions, not words. For instance, you can find new witnesses, or make a motion to exclude critical evidence or for "summary judgment" (which asks the judge to resolve disputed questions of law prior to trial). The overall strategy is to alter one or more of the elements that determine your opponent's settlement position. When the odds of winning change, negotiating positions almost always change, too.

Each of these actions, however, costs money to pursue. As with any business decision, the cost of a particular action must be weighed against the likelihood that it will significantly change the other side's perception of its chances of winning or losing.

Strategies For Negotiation

No one wants to leave anything on the table. Effective negotiating strategies help you to "shake the tree" to make sure that everything that's there has fallen out. There are several important rules you can follow.

Don't get mad, except on purpose. Some lawyers coach their clients in deliberately staged displays of anger with the idea of convincing the other side that they're dealing with an irrational person. But even if you can pull it off, there's no guarantee it will have the desired effect. Anger is almost always a liability because it impairs good judgment and prevents you and your opponent from making rational decisions. If you must display your anger, make it brief and then walk away. A prolonged display may deteriorate into an exchange of insults that will hurt your case.

Don't make an offer that is too low or demand a settlement that is too high. For example, if you and your lawyer determine that, as a defendant, there is a 30% to 40% chance of winning the case, your final settlement offer should be in the range of 60% to 70% of the claim. You may offer slightly less to test the other side's resolve or information, but if you offer only 5% or 10%, you run the risk of your offer being viewed as "not in the ball park."

Don't negotiate against yourself. When you reach a stalemate — because of an unrealistic offer, for example — it's important not to "sweeten" the offer until the other side has countered with a meaningful compromise. By increasing the amount of your offer (or decreasing the amount of your demand) without any movement from the other side, you are making a gesture that will always be viewed as a form of weakness.

Don't make your best offer first. Some people think that offering their real "bottom line" and threatening not to budge will shorten the costly negotiating process. But this works only if the other side believes the threat and does not test it by "shaking the tree." If they don't believe you (and they usually don't), the process goes on and both sides still incur the costs they wanted to avoid. More importantly, the party who gave its best offer first will almost always change that offer if the other side comes close. Giving your best price too early also prevents you from shaking the tree.

Don't sell your case. Many business owners want their lawyers to trumpet the strengths of their case and catalog their opponent's weaknesses. This is probably because the technique is so similar to how most businesses sell products and services. But in litigation, you often don't want to educate the other side.

Force your opponent to spend money. Like you, your opponent is spending money for attorney's fees that they would rather spend on something else. Increasing the investment reduces the return, which diminishes the desire to go forward.

Litigation almost always disrupts a person's business and personal life. A deposition, for example, can really inconvenience someone, and it's worth considering its disruptive effect on your opponent when planning your strategy.

Divide and conquer. Nothing makes a client more willing to give up than losing confidence in their lawyer. If you can frustrate the other lawyer's strategy through motions or delay, your opponent will begin to doubt the reliability of his lawyer's judgment and predictions.

Similarly, your lawyer can work behind the scenes to make the other side's lawyer think that his or her client has not told the whole story. This decreases the lawyer's motivation to give optimistic predictions which, in turn, may encourage your opponent to settle.

Doing nothing is sometimes the best strategy. Not responding to a settlement proposal is a dramatic way of stating that it is not acceptable.

By Henry Krasnow, a partner with Butler, Rubin, Saltarelli, Boyd & Krasnow of Chicago, Ill. Krasnow specializes in business law problems.

Don't Sue, Arbitrate!

Arbitration is somewhat faster and less expensive than going to court. But you must understand the rules if you hope to get satisfaction.

Construction projects begin with contractual agreements and too often, these days, end in courtroom disputes. In the past ten to fifteen years the number of such disputes has multiplied many times over.

The arbitration system was designed to handle this increased load, and to more quickly settle construction disagreements. This method of third-party intervention offers several advantages. It can be less formal, less expensive, and less time-consuming than the court system. For example, in some large cities it can take seven to ten years just to get into court. This extended wait can cause you to lose at the bank even if you win when you finally get to the courtroom. Arbitration, on the other hand, can take as little as a few months. But before you can make it work for you, you must know the rules.

The rules, in this case, are the Construction Industry Arbitration Rules, which are available in pamphlet form from the American Arbitration Association (140 West 51st St., New York, NY 10020-1203; 212/484-4000). They have been simplified so the reading is not tedious and it is well worth your time to read them.

It's always better to settle your dispute amicably if possible; but if you must use arbitration, the following tips should help you.

American
Arbitration
Association
CONSTRUCTION
INDUSTRY
ARBITRATION
RULES
REVISED RULES AND FEES
FOR CASES FILED
ON OR AFTER MAY 1, 1992

The Arbitration Clause

First, check your contract document for an arbitration clause. AIA documents and other industry-standard contracts contain these, but don't assume the provision has been included. Many owners, or their agents, will use these standard contracts, but stack the odds in their favor by adding or subtracting pertinent clauses. (This advice applies not only to arbitration clauses, but also to other important contract clauses such as liquidated damages and interest-bearing clauses).

Make certain you understand the entire arbitration clause, including *all* of its terms and their implications. Consult your attorney about unfamiliar language. You may be in a hurry to sign the contract and begin working, but take the time *before* signing to fully understand how your disputes will be settled if they do occur. No one likes to begin a relationship with a discussion about future arguments. But, it's much easier to lay the ground rules in the beginning when the association is still rosy.

Filing The Claim

When filing your claim, answer, or counter claim for arbitration, provide as many details as possible and identify any unusual, industry-specific details that could influence your case. For example, an owner may be unhappy with material you used on the job. Provide any product literature, photographs, or other evidence indicating that the item you used is standard and recommended by the industry for the job.

A detailed claim serves a dual purpose: first, it satisfies the technical requirement of sufficiently notifying the other party of your position (Rule 7) and second, it provides the AAA Regional office with an adequate background of the case so that an appropriate list of arbitrators can be selected.

While contractors can competently speak the language of their trades, the climate of the industry today forces them to learn the legal language and communicate in these terms as well.

How well you document the day-to-day events of the job will often be the pivotal point in your case. Develop standard procedures to document change orders, payments, deliveries, etc. If events occur that spell future conflicts, document them well: for example, with photographs, measurements, detailed notes. This paperwork is just as important to the job as are your tools and equipment.

Contractors often feel that they can best represent themselves because of their expertise in the field. But you should consider consulting a lawyer to at least draw up your claim. This will help you to understand the type of information the arbitrators will be looking for. The claim should not be verbose, just clear and concise. Remember, always stick to the facts.

Discuss Your List

After filing your claim, the Regional Arbitration Director will provide you with a list of potential arbitrators. When you receive it, call the Director and discuss the list. You need to find out the rationale for each candidate (usually 10 to 15 possible arbitrators are chosen from a list of from 500 to 2,500 names). The answer you get can give you valuable insight into how a third party viewed your case. It will also demonstrate whether you provided enough information for a third party to understand the principle issues of your claim.

The Arbitrator

From the list you receive, you will choose three to four names. Consider your choices carefully. Although your first reaction might be to choose a panel composed entirely of industry-related individuals, consider having a lawyer on the panel. All arbitrators, whether lawyers or laypeople, are trying to reach an equitable agreement. If your case will be heard by more than one arbitrator, an attorney/panelist can provide guidance and direction for the lay panelist. He can also be helpful in conducting the hearings. You may want to avoid choosing panelists within your trade. They tend to be less sympathetic to your predicament than a business owner in another trade who has perhaps been in your shoes in a similar suit. In general, your competitors will tend to judge your work more harshly.

The list of three to four names you choose will be compared to the opposing party's list. If you've both chosen a particular person, that person will arbitrate your case. If no names coincide, the Regional Director will then choose an arbitrator you'll both have to live with. Usually, only one arbitrator is chosen, but if the case appears complex, the Director may choose more than one.

Cost

The arbitration system is not free. When deciding the issue of payments, you may want to waive the "one-free-day" rule and pay a little extra. A few extra hundred dollars can be money well spent to get the most knowledgeable and intelligent arbitrator(s).

Generally, the person filing the claim is required to make a deposit if the case looks like it will get complicated and run on. In any case, when judgement is finalized, fees are usually split 50/50. But don't assume, be certain to check out the arbitration clause in your contract. It may specify a different method, and you don't want to get caught holding the bag because you failed to read the fine print in the arbitration clause.

One way to keep costs down is to keep the process simple. Although some people go to great expense by renting fancy boardrooms, and catering fancy lunches, you needn't do that. The rationale for arbitration is to avoid courtroom expense. It doesn't make sense to substitute other types of expenditures. Simple cases can even be held at the job site.

Prearbitration

The prearbitration conference is the first opportunity you will have to present your case to your arbitrator(s). Yet, if your arbitrator has not scheduled this conference, request that he does so. You will need to prepare an outline of your case to present at this meeting. Construct it as carefully as you did your initial claim. A written copy is not required, but it makes an impressive added touch. It will also relieve the arbitrator(s) of burdensome note-taking.

During this session you will discuss and agree on issues such as the guidelines for "discovery," which is how each party may get information from the other. Remember, volunteering information is a far more effective tactic than appearing to try to hide it. You will also set the times, dates, and locations of the hearings. The best plan is to use a low-cost central location. Simple cases can be decided in a day, but it is wise to schedule more days than you will need; it is always easier to cancel a hearing than to add extra dates. Although you should avoid several back-to-back sessions that will tire out your arbitrator, the Arbitration Association prefers that you schedule all hearings within a five-day period.

Once your dispute has reached the point of arbitration, you will have become acutely aware of the importance of documentation. All of the facts and information concerning the case will, at this point, be included in a claims/defense book. Your success or failure can ultimately hinge on whether this book is complete and contains the necessary paperwork to support your claims. Keep the need for this information in mind when you begin working on a contracted job. It will take time and effort to maintain this degree of paperwork, but think of it as an investment in legal insurance. Contracting parties never begin their relationship with the expectation of future conflicts. But later, when the honeymoon is over, they often wish they had started out with a clearer perspective.

By Perry Safran and Carolyn Annis. Safran is a North Carolina construction attorney, and he and Annis are associated with Proof Management consultants of Richmond, Va.

Mediation: Peaceful Solutions to Client Disputes

A third-party mediator can help you keep small conflicts from growing into major lawsuits

Building and remodeling breed strong emotions, and strong emotions breed disputes. As consultant Linda Case says in her remodeling seminars, "There will come a time in every remodeling project when the client will be very, very angry with you."

Construction disputes may be inevitable. But if you plan for conflict, rather than hope to avoid it, it can strengthen rather than threaten the owner-contractor relationship. Mediation is perhaps the best way to plan for conflict, by providing an amicable way to resolve it. Unfortunately, few contractors know how mediation works and what it offers.

Maintaining Focus

Mediation means asking a neutral third party to intervene between two conflicting parties to help them settle a dispute. The mediator does not dictate the solution; he or she simply helps the two parties find a mutually agreeable settlement.

As a nonconfrontational, voluntary means to resolve a dispute, mediation offers great advantages over arbitration or court. The mediator improves communication, keeps things focused, and helps the owner and contractor address the root questions of why there is a dispute and how it can be settled. This helps them avoid getting sidetracked into other disputes and constantly raising the stakes, as so often happens when lawyers run the show in the arenas of arbitration and court. In mediation, it is the two parties, not a third party, who control things.

Perhaps most importantly, mediation is the only dispute-resolution method that requires a mutually satisfactory result. And it works: According to the American Arbitration Association, 90% of all cases submitted to mediation are successfully resolved.

The beauty of the mediation process is that both sides receive positive affir-

Mediator Larry Hayden, at center, helps client and contractor hash things out with minimal cost and distress. The mediator can only suggest solutions, not dictate them. Nevertheless, 90% of mediated cases end with both parties agreeing on a settlement.

mation of the results. Without the neutral mediator, almost any resolution will leave one party feeling victorious and the other itching to get even. This residual negative feeling causes subsequent disputes to get off track and moves the parties in the direction of lawyers.

Excising The Cancer

If you intervene early with something like skin cancer, it's an in-and-out office procedure. But if you wait, it may require major surgery or even kill you. Disputes are the same: Intervene early and you can be in and out quickly. But if you wait, you may end up in arbitration or court.

We feel that arbitration and litigation are surgical solutions for disputes that have been too long ignored. To operate requires two or more lawyers, their paralegals, investigators and experts, three arbitrators or a judge, etc. It also means long delays, hours of painful hearings, and incredible expense. The process leaves personal scars and can bankrupt a business.

Of course, some situations do require the use of lawyers and a judge or arbitrators. *But these are exceptions.* In our opinion, you make a big mistake when you take any construction dispute to arbitration or court without first going to mediation. Construction disputes are too complex to settle efficiently in court. Going through the rules of evidence in court or the battle of expert witnesses in arbitration is at best a zero-sum game. But if you intervene early with mediation, you can address the gut issues and resolve the dispute quickly and to everyone's satisfaction.

Our personal experience suggests that 95% of disputes involve honest people who believe their opponents are crazy, malicious, stupid, or all of the above. It is these unreasonable assumptions that some lawyers prey on, and on which they base their approach.

In reality, all contractors want a profit and a referral out of every project. Every homeowner wants the job done well with minimum hassle and no legal entanglements. Contractors and owners frustrated with their inability to communicate often go to arbitration or court hoping to make things right again, only to be disappointed. In doing so, they lose any chance of getting what they originally wanted, which is a fair settlement that leaves everyone satisfied, if not exactly happy. Mediation, on the other hand, because it requires a mutually satisfactory result, offers a way to resolve a dispute and probably even maintain a positive relationship afterward.

Two Approaches

To get an idea of the difference between a mediated dispute and one that goes to arbitration, consider the following two cases that we handled. In one case, Larry Hayden served as one of three arbitrators, in the other he acted as sole mediator. In both cases, the amount in controversy at the outset was $7,000. The names and some of the facts have been changed for the usual reasons.

The arbitration approach. In one case, a contractor named Bill asked Larry to arbitrate a case that had been pending 18 months. The client was upset because of some problems with the stucco finish. Bill had proposed ways to fix the problem, but was frustrated because the client would not give him a final punch list so he could finish the job and deliver the final bill, which was for $7,000. Bill wanted a written punch list, because he feared he would have to go back repeatedly to fix an ever-increasing list of problems he felt he wasn't responsible for, or that he would be asked to meet unrealistic expectations.

For months, Bill and his attorney had been unsuccessfully trying to get the homeowner into arbitration. So Bill finally decided to exercise his arbitration clause. He knew he had made mistakes on the job, but he thought arbitration would settle things quickly and fairly and get the irrational homeowner off his back.

Unfortunately, once arbitration papers were served, the homeowner counterclaimed for $158,000. (The original contract was for $135,000.) Once the client received his summons to arbitration, he contacted a lawyer, who recommended that he have an engineer "expert witness" look the place over. The engineer drafted a long list of code violations and work that didn't precisely meet the specs. Suddenly Bill, instead of

Getting To Mediation: Some Essential Tools

Mediation is a tool, much as a hammer or a change order is, but you need to know how to use it—how to actually get a client into mediation. To do so, we recommend that you incorporate two elements in the way you do business: a Mediation Clause in your contract, and a Mediation Agreement that allows you to set aside disputes during the course of construction (if their size doesn't warrant mediation at the time they occur, but you want to keep the job moving) so that they can be mediated later.

Mediation Clause

The parties to this construction agreement establish this dispute resolution section to resolve any misunderstanding, concern, dispute, or question about this agreement and/or the related construction work, in a prompt, efficient, and cost-effective framework.

Mediation: In the event either party desires an independent, neutral third party to act as a mediator, they may call any independent mediator or mediation organization mutually acceptable to both parties to request a nonbinding, confidential mediation.

Mediation Agreement

This Agreement Is Between:

Contractor:____________

____________ Owner ____________

____________ Owner ____________

Contractor and Owner hereby appoint Damage Control Mediation Service as mediator of their dispute. Both parties have read, understood, and agree to be bound by the Mediation Rules appearing on page 2 of this document.

The Issues To Be Resolved Are As Follows:

____

Contractor: ____________ Owner ____________

Owner ____________

By ____________ Date:____________

Mediation Fee Deposited: $________

—1—

Put It in Writing: Mediation Contract Language

Although the Mediation Clause shown here draws on 57 combined years of legal, business, and construction experience, it may not be appropriate for your construction contract. For example, we have intentionally omitted an "attorney's fee" provision—a common provision stating that the loser has to pay attorney's fees resulting from any disputes. We feel that requiring each side to pay its own legal and arbitration costs encourages mediation of disputes. Others might rather have the "protection." You should check with your attorney before including these clauses in your own contract.

You may also want to include a standard arbitration clause, such as that supplied by the American Arbitration Association, specifying that any disputes not settled by mediation will be submitted to binding arbitration.

seeking a final $7,000 payment, was fighting for the life of his company.

So what happened? The arbitrators had a prehearing to gather basic information and then made a site visit. At the visit, the homeowner's engineer expert pointed out construction defects and code violations ad nauseum.

At the arbitration hearing itself, the contractor, being the plaintiff, went first. He presented his case in about half an hour. The homeowner's rebuttal took eight hours, during which he cited documents filling four 3-inch binders.

After many hours of debate, the arbitrators awarded $40,000 to the homeowner, with each side to bear its own attorney fees and half of the arbitration costs. For the homeowner, these fees added up to $34,000, leaving a net award of $6,000. The contractor, meanwhile, is today pursuing his subcontractors and his own insurance company for approximately one third to one half of the $40,000 award against him.

Who won here? Clearly, the lawyers,

Agreeing to Disagree: The Mediation Agreement

The mediation agreement is a form that can be used to begin the mediation process. It also lets you "sign up" for mediation but set aside until later any small disputes that are not worth the cost to mediate right away. While this may seem like procrastination, it is actually much better than "settling" a disagreement unsatisfactorily and causing resentment that can sabotage the relationship. This is usually the result when even a minor dispute is settled unsatisfactorily; at least one party will feel like a loser and want to "get even" later on, so that even a minor problem can later assume epic proportions. When each party gets validation from a neutral third party that they have reached a fair settlement, this resentment doesn't crop up.

The mediation agreement does not in itself settle disputes; it merely lists the things on which you agree to disagree. This keeps the project moving forward while setting up an amicable way to settle things at the end. It also gets everyone thinking mediation from the beginning.

The mediation agreement shown here is one used by our mediation company, Damage Control Mediation Service. Other agreements could appoint predetermined mediators (as does this one) or specify that the parties could later choose a mediator together.

— *L. H. & H. S.*

Mediation Agreement

NONBINDING MEDIATION RULES

1. Nature of Mediation

Damage Control Mediation Service (DCMS) is the mediator appointed by
the parties to facilitate negotiations between them. Mediation is an agree-
ment-reaching process in which DCMS assists the parties in reaching an agreement in an informed manner. DCMS has no power to decide disputed issues.
(This is not binding arbitration.) DCMS acts solely as a facilitator between parties who choose to preserve their relationship. DCMS may communicate separately with an individual party, but DCMS shall remain impartial and shall not
champion the interest of either party.

The objective of this mediation is to assist each party in quickly and inexpensively reaching their own best agreement. DCMS has an equal obligation
to work on behalf of each party. DCMS will not give legal advice.

2. Absolute Confidentiality

DCMS and the parties shall conduct the mediation as a strictly confidential
exchange of information including records, reports, statements, or other documents. None of the statements made, opinions expressed, admissions of
responsibility, agreements to pay, and/or unsigned mediated agreements are
admissible in any subsequent dispute-resolution process. The parties shall sign
a state law-required confidentiality agreement which will establish confidentiality of this document and all other communications related to this mediation.

DCMS shall not be called to testify concerning this mediation or to provide
any materials in any other dispute resolution process. The mediation process is
a settlement negotiation that is intended to result in a signed agreement.

3. Fee Schedule

a. Filing/administration (nonrefundable) . . . .$100.00 ($50 per party)
b. Mediation sessions (per hour/per party) . .$100.00 (per party per hour)

When the parties execute their Agreement to Nonbinding Mediation, on
the reverse hereof, they shall each send a deposit of $250.00 to cover
filing/administration, and the first two hours of mediation. If the mediation is
completed in less than two hours, a pro rata refund of the initial deposit shall
be returned to the parties. After completion of the first two hours of mediation, DCMS and the parties will estimate the remaining time to complete the
process. The parties shall deposit the estimated fee with DCMS at that time
subject to a pro rata adjustment at the conclusion of the mediation.

—2—

the expert witnesses, and the arbitrators, who were all paid fees and costs.

The mediated approach. Once again, the amount in dispute in our second case was $7,000. At issue was the cost of shoring up foundation diggings when unseasonably heavy rains threatened to collapse them. The contractor felt justified in asking for the money because in California, where this took place, it wasn't reasonable to expect rainfall at that time of year. However, the owner didn't feel he should have to pay for it.

The parties met with Larry for a total of three and a half hours. It was understood that nothing said would be used anywhere else, and that the mediator could not be called as a witness by either party in any subsequent litigation if the parties couldn't reach an agreement.

The parties met together in joint sessions, and then each met with Larry in private. Discussions focused on the diggings and on the key point that emerged during the mediation — the time factor involved. The contract had called for the job to be completed by a certain date so that a special event could be held at the home. The contractor felt "under the gun" to get the job done on time, and so spent the $7,000 to keep things moving. The contractor never felt he had the option to stop the project to save the money. As it turned out, the owner felt the contractor should have given him the option of slowing the job to save the money; but he never told the contractor that, so the contractor did what he had to do to stick to the schedule.

When these misunderstandings came out, the two sides began to see what had happened and moved toward a mutual understanding. Subsequent joint sessions showed that a resolution was possible. They finally settled, agreeing that the client would pay the contractor $5,000. The mediation cost each side $350.

Conclusion

The homeowner hires the contractor to make an intangible idea—a new house or remodel—a three-dimensional reality. Often, the reality fails to meet expectations. Disputes arise. The smart contractor anticipates these and uses them as constructively as possible. Mediation, used as a tool in the construction project, is the state of the art when it comes to dealing with disputes. If successful, it can actually turn a dispute into a referral.

By contractor Larry Hayden and attorney Herb Schwartz, co-owners of Damage Control Mediation Service in Oakland, California, specializing in construction disputes.

How to Prepare for Small Claims

You don't need a lawyer, just a well-documented presentation, to win your case in small claims court

Consider this scenario: you're a successful floor finisher and have just completed a project that consisted of sanding and resurfacing a client's dining room floor. You've made the floor gleam, packed up your equipment, and even finished the job on schedule. But when you request payment the client expresses dissatisfaction. Portions of the floor were gouged, he says, and the surface appears to have bubble spots. The client refuses to pay the bill, which — labor and materials included — you've set at $575. How can you collect payment without hiring a lawyer? By taking the matter to small claims court.

Quite often, a small contractor is in the position of seeking relatively small monetary damages from a client, supplier, or co-worker. Rather than requiring such cases to go through the civil docket court procedures, which can be a long and expensive undertaking, most states have an informal process that allows the average lay person (often without aid of an attorney) to pursue legal action to resolve such claims. This avenue of relief is small claims court.

Keeping Things Simple

While states vary in their precise filing requirements and court procedures for small claims court, these guidelines and rules are generally designed to keep things simple. All states, for instance, have monetary limits beyond which cases can't be heard in small claims court; in Connecticut, for example, the maximum is $2,500, while in Virginia it's $1,000. And most small claims courts encourage the parties to represent themselves. Thus, both plaintiff and defendant must be strong advocates for their own interests.

For the sake of brevity, this section will follow the small claims procedure for the state of Connecticut. To familiarize yourself with your state's procedures, call the small claims court there; court officials are usually quite helpful and willing to provide any information you need.

How to Succeed in Small Claims

The most basic directive for success in small claims court is to be prepared at all stages of the process. This means collecting and organizing all the relevant evidence and testimony you can. It also means knowing what's expected of you in court. If you adhere to the following basic steps and prepare yourself well, you stand a good chance of winning.

The first step is to determine which court has jurisdiction over the location in which the incident occurred. Contact the small claims court there and discuss your claim with the clerk to make sure, first of all, that the dispute can be handled through small claims. Find out the monetary limits for damages sought, and have the clerk send you any information you'll need to file a claim. Filing a claim will probably involve submitting a "letter of intent" and a claim form with the court, which will then deliver those documents to the defendant.

Once the letter of intent and claim form have been sent to the defendant and a court date has been set, organize your court presentation, beginning with any evidence you've accumulated. Evidence might include copies of work orders, correspondence, requests for payment, canceled checks, or photographs. Photographs work particularly well to graphically support a claim.

You should also try to find witnesses who can support your claim. If a witness can't attend the court proceeding, ask the witness to write a letter stating his or her testimony so that you can read it in court. (Check the court rules on this; some courts may not allow testimony from persons not present.) Be sure you know what the witness's testimony will be before entering the courtroom.

At the actual presentation, be brief and to the point. A judge will hear your case. The plaintiff — the person seeking damages — will be heard first, followed by the defendant. If you're the plaintiff, usually the judge will simply want you to describe (and document with your supporting evidence) what happened. Referring to an outline will help things go smoothly. Also, have your documents neatly organized in chronological order to facilitate review by you, the defendant, and the judge. Neat organization will get your story across more clearly and effectively. Always give the opposing party the opportunity to ask questions, and respond in a professional manner. It is to both parties' benefit to follow court procedures and to not speak out of turn.

Finally, make sure your documentation includes something — such as estimates, supply bills, or work orders — to corroborate the amount of damages you are claiming, and be prepared to explain why you are requesting this amount.

If You Are a Defendant

If you're a defendant, the guidelines above still apply. You respond to notices from the court as requested. If you fail to contest a claim within the specified time, for example, a judgment may be rendered in favor of the plaintiff. Judgment may also be made against you if you respond that you are contesting the claim but do not attend the hearing.

Prepare your version of events so you can explain it at the hearing. Be organized and bring whatever documentation you can. During the plaintiff's presentation, write down questions and make note of where the testimony may be contradicted. Following the plaintiff's presentation, you will have the opportunity to present and document your side of the story and to question any witnesses.

Judgment

Once the judge has reviewed all the submitted evidence and testimony, he or she will render a judgment. In certain cases, the judgment may be delivered at the court proceedings; in others, the parties will be notified through the mail a short time afterward.

Small claims court isn't perfect. But it does provide a relatively simple and effective way to settle the sort of small legal disputes that occasionally pester contractors. Use it judiciously and you'll have a fair chance of getting justice.

By Lorie McCollum-Lombard who works in the real-estate research department at Fleet Bank, N.A., in Hartford, Conn.

Chapter 17

Diversification

Diversification and the Small Builder

You can put your building talents to use in many ways—from home inspection to real estate management. But you need to find the right mix for profits and peace of mind.

I'm a principal in a small, well-diversified building company in Seattle, Wash. When my partner and I established our business in 1976, our sole purpose was to purchase, improve, and resell or rent single family residences within the city limits of Seattle. Our goal was simply to acquire enough rental property to provide ourselves with sufficient income to enjoy our "golden years" (you know—when we turned 40). We have since diversified into several related fields including property management, construction management, custom home building, design/ build, marketing real estate partnerships, home inspections, bookkeeping for small companies in related fields, and consulting for other contractors and subcontractors.

Obviously, some of these endeavors have fared better than others and what follows is my experience in the various fields. We have kept the ones that worked for us, and thrown out the ones that didn't. Our successes and failures have been strictly a function of our personalities and strengths and I would encourage other builders to try any and all diversification opportunities that present themselves, even though they may have failed for our company.

Some of the areas we have explored have been natural extensions of our original business, whereas some have been things that we just wanted to try. But we have done them all with an eye towards simplicity of structure and operation. What we have never wanted was a top-heavy organization fueled by its subsidiary parts in a never-ending quest to pay for all the additional overhead.

My partner and I excel at sales and at developing long-term relationships. As a result, we have been particularly interested in businesses that depend heavily on these. We leave the mundane (but all-important) daily business operations to our general manager and staff.

Delving Into Real Estate

When we started our business, we were buying, rehabbing, and reselling or renting single-family homes. As the market tightened, we sold our inventory of rental homes and bought several larger buildings for rehab. Some of these we kept for rental income and long-term gain, some we sold on contract to produce interest income, and some we sold for cash to produce working capital. This end of our business is shaped by income tax issues and our long-term retirement goals.

A natural extension of this business was offering partnership opportunities to other investors. As the General Partner, we would acquire an interest in the building without using any of our own capital. We would also charge a management fee to the Partnership for managing the building.

It is surprisingly easy to come by investors for real-estate opportunities. We have never advertised for investors, but we have often been approached by people who know what type of work we do. These people include past clients, friends, employees and many professional people we have met through our years of business.

Most people recognize the value of investing in real estate but don't want the hassle of maintaining and managing buildings. I'm one of those people myself, but I also love looking for property, working deals, and selling partnerships. Fortunately, my partner doesn't mind showing rental units, and our secretary does quite well in collecting the rents.

Our rental buildings are small, mixed-use or apartment buildings. Although smaller buildings probably take more time to manage (percentage-wise), they are easier to keep full and are much more liquid than larger complexes. We have found our best opportunities in the more marginal (affordable) type of apartments than in the higher-and lower-end units. Middle-income tenants just seem better at paying their rent on time.

Most of our mixed-use buildings are in neighborhood business districts. They typically have one to four street-level

Before

After

Spec remodeling has paid off for both the contractor and the investors who put up all the cash (in return for 50% of the profits upon resale). This Seattle bungalow was transformed into a two-story contemporary and yielded these figures:

Purchase	$58,000
Rehab	55,000
Sales price	157,000
Sales cost	11,920
Net profit	32,080
50% to investor	16,040

= 29% return on investor's money

commercial spaces with apartments above. We spend a lot of time looking for buildings that are underutilized and undermanaged. The best ones are buildings where we can lease the commercial space to tenants who have money to spend on improving the space.

As we gained experience managing our own buildings, it was natural to begin managing rental properties for other owners. For 10% of the gross, we show apartments and collect the rent. If the tenants have problems, they call our office (they generally don't even know who the owner is). All advertising and maintenance costs are additional. Basically, we relieve the owner of all the headaches of owning rental property and provide a bookkeeping service. Depending on the owner's needs, we can pay underlying mortgages, taxes and insurance, or simply subtract our fee and send the proceeds to the owner. Additionally, we give the owner a monthly financial statement and a year-end profit and loss statement on their building.

Reluctant Remodelers

Since the housing market was exploding during the early years of our business, we were able to successfully market our rehabbed single-family units ourselves. With the aid of our site signs and advertising, our name became synonymous with quality remodeling work. Our first diversification opportunity presented itself when we somewhat reluctantly began accepting remodeling contract work. I say reluctantly because I still don't quite know how I ended up doing so much contract work and making so little money at it. But since our speculative business was extremely profitable, we were able to make many families happy by unintentionally subsidizing their remodeling projects.

It wasn't until we got out of single-family remodeling that I realized how poor this end of our business really was. Not having been active in my local homebuilders association, I was busy reinventing the wheel on pricing and markups. My accounting system would not give me the information I needed to accurately assign overhead costs related to the contracting side of my business, as opposed to the speculative side. So it was quite a shock when I finally realized how much this business was costing me. With that knowledge in hand, I quickly raised our prices — and our construction gross dropped from $450,000 to $80,000 in one year's time.

But at least I made money on that $80,000.

Now I knew how to make money in the contracting business, but unfortunately the contractors I was bidding against still didn't. So I was consistently 20%, 30%, even 50% over the competition. As a result, we lost most jobs that we bid on. But by this time, we were a lot smarter than when we had started out, and we had joined the local chapter of the National Association of Home Builders. Our membership gave us access to educational opportunities that we hadn't known even existed. Through the local chapter's Remodelors Council I had the pleasure of meeting many remodeling contractors in my area. It amazed me how open and friendly these contractors were and how willing most were to answer our questions.

My best educational opportunity came when I started attending the annual NAHB show. Participating in seminars and roundtable sessions brought me the friendship of remodeling contractors from across the country. These people have been my best resources for making my remodeling division a profitable venture.

Design/Build

Since I couldn't get a job at my price through the competitive bid process, we diversified into design/build remodeling. Every time I met someone who was into design/build I would grill him on how he did it and what his experiences were. It took several years to get good at it but now it comprises 95% of our residential work. We still do some bidding for a few select architectural firms, but we always find out who our competition is so we don't waste our time when there is no chance we will get the project.

There are a multitude of advantages to design/build, not the least of which is control. When a customer hires you to both design and build a project, you are the undisputed expert and the project usually just rolls along smoothly.

Another advantage is that you are getting paid to do the budget. When you bid on someone else's design, you have less than a 50% chance of getting the job, depending on how many bidders there are and whether the project even gets built. With design/build, you have a 100% chance of getting the job.

But the best part of design/build is that you can quit competing on price and begin selling value. I personally find it extremely rewarding to take a family's dreams and work through the design process to give them the project they want at a price they can afford — and at a price that I can make a fair profit on.

Design/build also seems less prone to lawsuits. This is probably because both you and the client have a chance to get to know each other before your crew moves in with them. And it's far easier to walk away from a project with a difficult client during the design stage than when it's half completed.

Tenant Improvements

We have also enjoyed tremendous success in the field of tenant improvements in retail stores and offices. Back in the days when I couldn't get any bid residential work, I started calling on building managers and architects looking for office and retail improvements. Here was a field in which I could be extremely competitive since I was at the smaller end of the scale in company size. The repeat business is also fantastic. Since most retailers upgrade their stores about every five years, you can enjoy a relatively stable work load by developing a good list of commercial clients.

Custom Home Nightmares

And then there's custom home building. The opportunity to build someone a custom home is something most of us don't want to pass up, probably because it satisfies our egos. I have built half a dozen homes, generally for people who didn't have the money to pay for them.

Actually, the biggest problem in custom homes is that the owner generally does not pay the architect enough to provide a complete set of drawings and specifications to accurately price the job from the site work to the towel bars. Since I don't want to hire a house designer, how can I build custom homes without the benefit of complete plans and specifications, yet still make money on them? Enter the concept of construction management. We will build your home at cost plus a predetermined fee. My one experience in this had a court date of July 1988.

This particular owner dragged me out to a subdivision and took me through a model home he liked. The house was priced at $150,000. Could I build him one like it with a "little better quality" for the same price if he furnished the lot? No problem, I stupidly replied. He started in on his drawings, we both looked at several lots, and finally he purchased one in a relatively complete development of $200,000 homes. We received several generations of drawings and by the time the actual building had started, the construction budget had grown to $190,000. The lot cost $50,000 so we were now in the $240,000 range, definitely at the top end of this particular subdivision.

While the foundation was being poured, I was trying to get the finish package together. We were having a difficult time specifying what was going into this house, so I went on a Sunday drive with the owners to see several examples of what they would like. By the end of the day I was very quietly sitting in the backseat thinking "How am I ever going to get out of this one?" All the homes they had shown me were in the $400,000-plus range and I knew we were in big trouble. While they were busy chattering about swim spas in the basement, I was trying to figure out how we were going to build this home without any lumber so we could use the framing budget for the interior finishes.

These people were anything but novices. The husband was a mortgage broker whom I had known for years and had done some business with. His wife was a real estate appraiser.

The following day I met with the husband and explained my fears of the cost overruns involved. He immediately recognized the concerns, but the house was his dream home — his response was: "Let's do our best on the budget and just build it." In order to save money, we would just set the fiberglass swim spa in the basement and he would hook it up in a couple of years when he could afford the dehumidification system required.

Of course when the hvac man arrived, it was only an additional $10,000 to install the system — so the owner decided to go ahead and do it. I reminded him of our tight budget but since the owner was paying all bills directly, I gave in and figured he knew what he was getting into.

To make a long story short, I think the house finally cost the owner a total of somewhere around $350,000. Who ultimately absorbed which costs was in the hands of the lawyers.

Profitable Partnerships

Over the past couple of years, we have begun to do some speculative projects in partnership with private parties. Because of the low interest rate banks are currently paying on CDs, we have found many people interested in financing the acquisition and rehabilitation of existing homes for resale.

The concept is simple. The investor puts up the cash, and we put up the expertise. To keep the acquisition costs low, we buy the homes on real-estate contracts with short-term cashouts. We retain 10% of the gross construction cost as an offset to our overhead for doing the project, and split the net proceeds 50/50. The investor is protected because he holds title to the property; we are protected through the lien provisions of our state law. The hard part is finding a property that has the potential for the return we expect. There has to be substantial profit in it or it simply isn't worth doing. We have found them, however. Over a typical six-month period, our investors have enjoyed returns of 14% to 60% on their money.

This system works well for both parties, but gets bogged down if you are borrowing money from a bank. The additional fees and interest charged by the bank make many of these projects strictly marginal.

Home Inspection

Over the years, some of our past clients have asked us to look at homes they were thinking of buying. For a nominal fee, we would go out and look over their prospective purchases. As these calls increased, we decided to formalize the business and actually started marketing home inspections. Because of the liability risk, we decided early on to keep this business small enough so that only the partners handled the actual inspections. We already earn our attorney a pretty good living so we didn't need the risk exposure of a hired inspector signing off on a crawlspace without actually inspecting it.

This said, I think home inspections are an excellent opportunity for the owner of a small company to generate some additional income without having to add to his overhead. If you run a company that does not require your constant presence on job sites, you could begin marketing for home inspections and create a nice little cash cow with just a little better organization of your day. The fees for home inspections seem to be very market sensitive so you would need to do a survey to find what the going rate is. In our area it averages about $200. Our housing market is relatively stable right now, so it is fairly easy to schedule the inspections to meet our needs. Our early marketing efforts were directed towards real-estate agents and we spent a lot of Sundays at open houses meeting them.

Direct your efforts at the top agents in your community and you can keep yourself busy during a recession. The best agents continue to sell year in and year out, just like the best remodelers continue to work right through the downturns in the economy.

There's Always Consulting

Over the years many subcontractors have asked for my advice and expertise on business management. I offered to help some of the people that I knew and particularly liked, but quickly found I had to start charging for my time. So another natural diversification was to do business consulting on a fee basis. Surprisingly enough, not only were people willing to pay me, they were much more likely to follow my advice than when I was advising them for free.

I have consistently found that the building industry is made up of expert craftspeople who are lousy businesspeople. To be successful does not mean running a million dollar business. It means making a profit. Far too many of us have absolutely no handle on the costs of doing business and can only afford our Porsches and Mercedes because we have such dynamic cash flow. When that flow is turned off, we suddenly find we can't make last month's payments with this month's retainers. The biggest hurdle I have is convincing contractors that it is not the gross dollar amount done yearly that makes their business successful.

As our business became fully computerized, we decided to turn our office into a profit center and started marketing bookkeeping services to other small companies. Although we do some retail shops, we concentrate on small subcontractor companies where the owners want to spend their time on activities other than bookkeeping. Of course this is also a natural extension of my consulting practice. Our contractor clients easily pay our fees through their increased profitability.

Over the years our business goals and strategies have changed and some years we emphasize some areas of our business more than others. The general economy, our hired expertise, and the partners' personal goals all play a part as we plan our future business strategies. We retain our ultimate goal (enjoying our golden years) but the road there is ever changing. Ours is a well-diversified company—which is ideal for us. Others, however, find it better to do just one thing and do it extremely well. We find it best to do many things, throwing out the unprofitable ones along the way, and retaining the profitable ones that interest us. Because of our diversification, our work load is extremely stable and we find that we are well-equipped to ride out the economy's ups and downs.

As I said in the beginning, our successes and failures are strictly a function of our personalities and strengths, and each person has to determine what works best for him.

By Chuck Moriarty, a former chairman of NAHB's Remodelors Council, and president of Moriarty & Matzen, a Seattle-based general contracting firm specializing in residential and commercial remodeling.

Interview:

Spec Remodeling Strategies: Tips from a Pro

Smart buying, frugal rehab, steady rentals, and timely selling add up to a good living

Over two decades, spec remodeler Larry Dworin has mastered the art of buying fixer-uppers to rent and resell. He's has also authored two Craftsman books, *Profits in Buying and Renovating Homes* and *Renovating and Restyling Vintage Homes*. During a phone interview and site visit, Dworin shared the secrets of successful spec rehab.

Getting Started

JLC: *How did you get into this business?*

Dworin: Back in the 1970s, when I was about 25, I wanted a nice house, but I couldn't afford anything that was in good condition. So I fixed up an old house and when I sold it, I wound up making $10,000 for $500 worth of fix-up. That was a year's pay back then for what was really just a few weeks' work. So I said, "I think I'll keep on doing this." Not every project has been that profitable, but I'm making from 20% to 30% — and up into the hundreds-of-percent for the houses I hold on to.

JLC: *What's the basic concept of your business?*

Dworin: Mostly I look for run-down houses that have a lot of appreciation potential. They've got to be in good neighborhoods, and they have to look a lot worse than they really are. I want to do as little work as possible, because everything I do comes out of my profit. On the other hand, if they didn't need any work, I wouldn't be able to get them cheap.

After I fix the houses up, I usually rent them rather than sell them right away, for two reasons. First, I try to buy in neighborhoods where the property values are appreciating, so the longer I hold them the more they are worth. Secondly, holding the houses has tax advantages. If you hold the property for a year or more, your income from selling it is taxed as capital gains instead of earned income, and the tax rate is lower.

Also, you can deduct depreciation on the houses on paper over 29 years, even if the value is really going up, not down. Combined with my own personal deduction for the mortgage on my own house and so on, that is enough to shelter $40,000 or $50,000. Some years I pay no income tax at all. Of course, I have a lawyer and an accountant who advise me. You wouldn't want to go into a situation like this on your own.

JLC: *You mentioned mortgages. Do you borrow money to buy your houses?*

Dworin: I prefer to pay cash. If I have money from the sale of a house, sometimes I'll turn around and buy another one. Good handyman specials turn up at irregular intervals and you have to grab them whenever you can.

But it's easier to borrow money to buy an existing house than to build a new one. With a construction loan for a new house, banks are afraid you might not finish the project. But an existing house,

Another Fine Mess

I recently dropped in on Larry Dworin at a property in his own neighborhood that he had purchased for $65,000. The rehab was well into the demolition phase. "This isn't really a 'before' picture," he said. "This is a 'during' picture. It looks even worse now than it did when I bought it." On a tour of the grounds, Dworin ticked off the property's assets and liabilities:

Location, location, location. Surrounded by fields and woods on a quiet country road, the one-acre lot with barn has a very pleasant setting. The area's becoming popular with career people who commute to nearby Detroit, Mich., and property values are on the rise. "Just down the road, someone's building a $350,000 house," says Dworin. "This house will never be worth that much, but it will be a way for someone with less to spend to get into a nice area."

Foundation. The turn-of-the-century stone foundation needs just a little patching, says Dworin. The concrete slab is recent, and underfloor drainage keeps the basement dry. "I think someone lived down here during the '60s," Dworin comments, pointing to psychedelic graffiti on the wall. It's typical of the cosmetic problems that scare buyers away, enabling Dworin to buy houses like this for much less than they're worth. A little drywall and paint will take care of the eyesore.

Structure. The entire house was rebuilt in the 1940s after a fire. The framing met code at the time and is still in good shape. A roof leak several years ago was patched, but water damage to plaster was never fixed. Dworin plans to drywall over the stained plaster, and leave the roof alone.

Space and amenities. At 1,400 square feet, there's plenty of room for a small family. A downstairs bedroom could serve as an office or den, and two reasonably large upstairs bedrooms need only drywall and new windows. Dworin has already converted a tiny

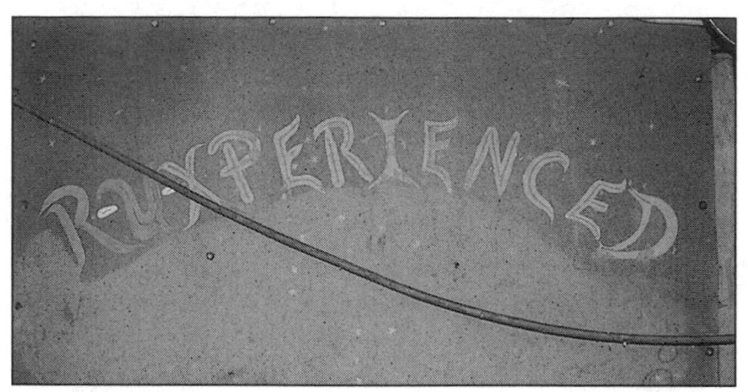

Graffiti from a former tenant turns off most buyers and drives down the property's price. Removing it is a cheap improvement.

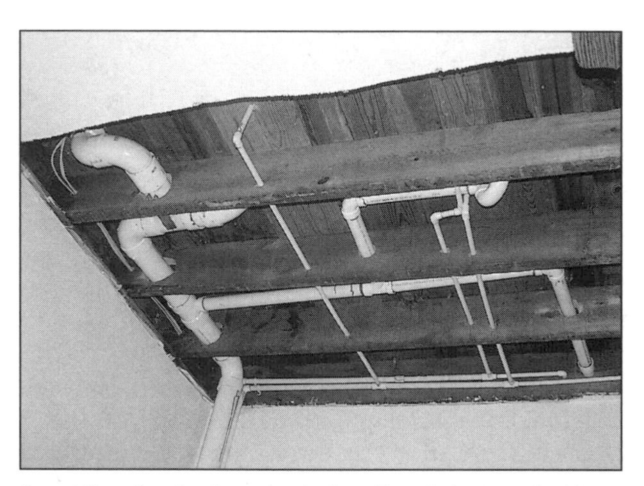

Sound floor framing is exposed where Dworin has roughed in new plumbing for the upstairs bath. A planned closet will support the joists he has drilled through.

is good collateral: Even if you don't fix it up, it won't be worth less than when you bought it. When I first started out, I was borrowing the money for my own house. That's a good way to start: Even without a good credit history, you can usually borrow money to buy your own home.

JLC: *How many houses do you have in the cycle at one time?*

Dworin: Right now I own six houses, plus one I'm working on. Eight rental properties is a better number, because six don't provide quite enough rental income. But when I have too many rental properties, I spend too much time on maintenance. A little while ago I was up to 14 rental houses, and I was spending all my time fixing things for the tenants. I couldn't get any remodeling work done.

Occasionally, I'll buy more than one house at a time if they're super deals that aren't going to be around later. But I only actually work on one at a time, because I have to finish up and get them rented. I once remodeled three houses at the same time. Three mortgage payments and no rent coming in — that can kill you.

fourth bedroom upstairs into a large bathroom, taking the house from a tight four-bedroom, one-bath plan to a more modern and spacious three-bedroom, two-bath edition. The downstairs bath, inconvenient as the house's only bathroom, will now be an attractive extra.

A narrow doorway into the staircase was too small. "The people living here told me they had to bring furniture in through an upstairs window," says Dworin. "My tenants aren't going to want that." To solve the problem, Dworin has cut out a bigger opening at the bottom of the stairs.

Exterior. Removing 1950s-era mineral siding revealed the original wood siding, still in good shape despite flaking paint. The porches look terrible but are still sound, says Dworin. "I'll spruce up the outside for now, recast the cement stairs, then improve the porches over several years while I'm renting the place out."

Plaster in this room was applied too thin and has stains from an earlier roof leak. New drywall is a simple fix.

Profitability

In all, Dworin expects to spend about $7,500 fixing up a property he bought for $65,000. When he's done, he'll have a rental unit he "could sell in a week if I offered it for $99,900," he predicts. "A $27,000 profit isn't bad for four months of work, but I think I'll hold it for a few years and try to sell for $130,000 or $150,000."

In the meantime, he says, he'll rent the house for about $800 a month. The rent typically amounts to about a 7% annual return on his investment, says Dworin — roughly what a Treasury bond might pay, but not much compared to the stock market. Most of his annual gains, he explains, come from appreciation of the property value. "Combining the rent and the appreciation, we look for about a 25% annual return on investment,"says Dworin.

The key is patience and timing. "You have to be careful," notes Dworin. "Sometimes, a property will stay flat for several years, and you'll get tired of waiting and sell it. Then, of course, it goes up 30% the next year."

— *T.C.*

Once a tiny fourth bedroom, this room is now a large bath with a big window, part of a spacious new second floor layout.

Working Alone

JLC: *I know you do most of the work yourself. Did you start out with a background in the building trades?*

Dworin: Just what I learned in high school shop class. Over the years, I've learned things a little at a time — plumbing, electrical, and so on. Most of it is pretty straightforward stuff. The really difficult part of those trades is the commercial work. To an electrician, houses are easy.

JLC: *Don't you need licenses for plumbing or electrical work?*

Dworin: That depends on the locality. In my area, you can do any work on houses you own, and technically, I'm the homeowner. But I did a house once where the building department was very strict about owners doing work, and they wouldn't let me do anything at all. I couldn't even touch a tool. I generally stay out of those areas, because it's more expensive to do the work that way.

JLC: *Do you ever hire employees? With a four-man crew, you might be able to knock out six of these jobs in a season.*

Dworin: Yes, and I've done that. I've had up to four employees at times. But I can't always find six jobs in a season. Sometimes I don't find any for a while. Then I lay people off and they get other jobs, and by the time I do find something they're not interested anymore.

Anyway, there are a lot of advantages to working alone. For one thing, you don't have to deal with tax withholding and paperwork. Also, I find that if you have three or four people, you're not necessarily tripling or quadrupling your output. I used to waste a lot of time on organizational stuff, just trying to keep all these guys working.

JLC: *What about subs? When would you call an electrician or a plumber?*
Dworin: Anything to do with the utility companies I might hire an electrician for. Sometimes the utility company doesn't want to deal with non-electricians for things like service drops and meters. Generally I'll do the panel myself, unless there's no way to turn the power off, and I don't want to deal with it.

I'll hire a plumber for anything that requires excavation. I don't really want to dig up the main sewer line or make alterations to septic systems. I don't have a backhoe or a bulldozer.

I also hire out anything to do with cement, other than real small things. I'll do a service walk, but not driveways and sidewalks. It's just too heavy, and you need a crew to get the cement in and finished before it sets up. I try to avoid those jobs. Cement flatwork doesn't add much value to the house anyway. A homeowner will never come out and say, "What a lovely sidewalk. I really like this." They'd much rather have a bigger bathroom. But on some houses, the city says we have to put a new sidewalk in, and that's it. Those are just expenses, and they're to be avoided unless it's a really profitable job.

I do all of the flooring, drywall, tile, and finish carpentry myself. Both my wife and I paint, too.

Sizing Up Properties

JLC: *It seems as if any skilled remodeler could make a living the way you do.*
Dworin: The thing that's hard is the real estate part — picking the house out. You've got to be real sure that this is just the right house. It should be such a bargain you can't believe it, so that you say, "Why isn't anybody else buying this?"

The perfect property is one that is all overgrown so you can hardly even see the house, with mountains of trash all over the place. This drives off all the other buyers. Inside, I like to see falling plaster, more trash, peeling paint, real ugly colors — one of my favorites is 1970s shag carpet with dirt ground into it.

So most other buyers take one look and say, "Get me out of here, I don't care how cheap it is, I don't even want to look at it." But if you look the house over, you often discover that the superficial problems are all that's wrong with it. Houses like this sell for 30%, 40%, 50% below market because they are so ugly. But you clean up the yard, get rid of the trash, put up new drywall, get some new carpet, and you're done.

JLC: *Does anybody help you find the property?*
Dworin: A good real estate agent can help a lot. Ask them, "What areas are really moving up? What's desirable? Can you tell me about some older areas that might have fixer-uppers, neighborhoods that people are moving into?" The first area they suggest might not be perfect for you, but it will give you a place to start.

Then check it out yourself. Drive around the neighborhood on a Sunday afternoon when they have open houses, just to see what you get for the money. If you see a house for $100,000, okay, that is what you can get for $100,000 in that neighborhood. Then if you see one that is similar but is a mess and is only $50,000, you know you're looking at a bargain.

JLC: *What are some red flags that would tell you that you don't want a certain house?*
Dworin: The foremost concern is the location. You don't want a bad neighborhood. Even in a desirable neighborhood, you don't want to be next to commercial operations, like gas stations, noisy bars, or party stores that throw trash in your backyard. If your house is right next to something like that, it will

always be cheaper than others even just a few houses away.

JLC: *What else should you watch out for?*
Dworin: Major foundation problems. I will deal with minor problems, like one little section that needs some tuck pointing, but if the house is going to have to be lifted up and a new foundation put under it, you're looking at a minimum $10,000 cost. This house better be a super deal before I'm going to approach anything like that. Usually it won't be, because the houses are generally priced on how they look, and buyers don't know what foundations are supposed to look like.

As for other problems, it's not so much any one thing as a combination of things that start adding up. Say the house has a bad roof; okay, I'll fix the roof. But if it also needs to be replumbed and rewired, and the floors are sagging, and, and, and — at some point, it isn't worth doing.

Another caution is houses that are too small and can't be expanded reasonably. Sometimes they look big on the outside, but the layout's bad and there's no practical way to fix it on a reasonable budget. You might as well just tear it down and start over.

JLC: *Would you ever do a room addition to add space?*
Dworin: So far, I have never built a room addition from the ground up. But I do a lot of conversions — turn attics and garages into rooms — because that can be done a lot cheaper. I would add a room if that was the only thing the house really needed. But usually, these houses are not just small, they have poor layouts, they're cramped, and the kitchens and bathrooms are ugly. When you add it all up, there's no profit left. Even with an addition, it's still going to have a rotten layout.

JLC: *What about major systems, like rewiring or upgrading the water supply?*
Dworin: I inspect the wiring and if it needs a lot of work, that lowers the price I'll offer. But rewiring isn't that hard. A couple thousand dollars will usually cover it.

A lot of my houses are on wells, and I always have the water tested before I buy. If the groundwater's polluted, I won't buy the house. I've never had a problem with city water.

I've had a problem with the waste line, though. One time, the drain to the street was crushed after I'd been renting the house for two years, and that was expensive to replace. That's just one of the risks you take.

JLC: *What about energy upgrades — insulation, better windows, a new furnace?*
Dworin: My customers never ask about it. People care about kitchens, bathrooms, space — not insulation. I put insulation into spaces that are easy to reach if the wall happens to be open anyway. I also blow insulation into attics, because that's cheap and easy.

I fix windows if they're rotting out. Nice windows I repair, ugly windows I replace, but not for energy reasons. For energy efficiency, I put on storm windows. That's cheaper than a new window and just about as good.

I replace furnaces if they're broken or really inefficient, like the old octopus furnaces from the thirties. They put out a lot of heat, but the fuel bills are astronomical. Anything from the 60s or later, though, I usually keep if it's working.

JLC: *What about porches?*
Dworin: Porches are a lot easier to fix than people think. A porch is a simple structure — no wiring or plumbing running through it, just simple framing. Even if the porch is sagging badly, usually the only problem is wood that's rotten where it contacts the ground. So I jack the porch up, put a concrete pad in if possible, replace anything rotten with pressure-treated wood, and paint the whole thing. It's a huge improvement for just a little work. If the floorboards are too soft to save, I replace them with pressure-treated plywood and paint it.

Reported by Ted Cushman, a carpenter and photojournalist who lives and works in South Bend, Ind.

Profiting From Insurance Work

In the insurance game, thorough estimates, clear contracts, and production efficiency add up to profits

Last year, our area was hit with its worst hailstorm in 100 years, damaging residential and commercial buildings to the tune of more than $35 million. Overnight, the storm created hundreds of potential customers who needed a contractor to repair the damage. We are a quality remodeling company with a good reputation.

We normally look down our noses at insurance work, because the insurance companies often require the customer to submit two or three estimates for the work to be done but usually approve the estimate with the lowest price regardless of the contractor's reputation or the customer's preferences. Since it's our policy not get involved at all if a prospective customer is looking for the lowest possible quote, insurance work has never been part of our marketing plan.

Soon after the storm, however, our phone started ringing with calls from past customers who wanted us to fix the hail damage to their houses. I finally called my own insurance agent (I had to talk to him anyway, because my house had been hit, too). "Jim," I said, "we're avoiding all this insurance work because there's usually no money in it, but my phone is ringing off the hook. How can we do this work, satisfy our customers, satisfy the insurance companies, and still make a reasonable profit?"

In a disaster situation, my agent told me, the "low estimate" format is not the way most insurance companies choose to go. Local offices are swamped with claims, and they want to get them settled quickly. Instead of requiring the insured to round up several estimates, they send an adjuster to each claimant's house to estimate the repair cost. The adjusters work from their own estimating manuals and cost databases, with established standard rates for nearly every kind of replacement and repair. Once the repair estimate is done by the adjuster, any legal contractor who can do the job at that price can have the work. When I heard this, I decided to look at a few repair jobs and see if my company could make money on them.

Fudge by the Square Foot

On the first few jobs I estimated, I quickly learned that the adjusters' estimates were running low when it came to the actual scope of damage. There were a lot of square-footage and linear-footage mistakes — curiously, almost always in favor of the insurance company.

Time after time, I'd sit with a customer and start calculating the extent of damage to the home. "Your house is so many feet long, so many feet wide, 2-foot overhangs, 1-foot gable extension, 6/12 pitch roof" (hit a few keys on the calculator) "the roof area of your house is 2,240 square feet. The insurance company estimate only has 1,960 square feet. I wonder which part of the roof they don't want me to fix?" And the client would say, "Well, they said this was to replace the whole roof."

Siding was just like roofing: Take a two-story house with hail damage to the west side. I figured the surface area at 756 square feet. The adjuster had allowed only 672 square feet. On the phone with the adjuster, the conversation would go something like this:

Me: "We both agree that only the west side of the house got hit. You show 672 square feet of siding to be removed and 740 (640 + 10% for waste) square feet to be installed."

Him: "Right, 42 feet long, 16 feet high."

Me: "Where do you get 16 feet? That's a two-story house."

Him: "Right, 8 feet per story."

Me: "Wait a minute. You're forgetting the height of the floor joists and subfloor. Those outside walls are more like 18 feet high, not 16 feet.

Him: "Oh yeah. That's right. Let's call it 18 feet. Change the allowable amount from 672 square feet removed and 740 square feet installed to 756 square feet removed and 832 square feet installed."

Beyond the obvious goofs, there was a whole raft of little (or not so little) extras that routinely did not make it onto the adjusters' estimates. For instance, with hip roofs there's a much greater standard waste factor than applies to a gable roof because of the angular trimming at both ends of each course. Although that adjustment is printed in black and white in the insurance company adjusters' manuals, they often didn't include it. The same held true for second-story and steep-pitch adjustment factors, the removal and replacement of shutters, electrical fixtures, utility service lines, dumpsters, and on and on. They'd forget to mention it, but if you knew to ask for it you got it.

Advocating for the Customer

Most of my clients' homeowner insurance policies entitled them to full replacement of what was lost or damaged. As their contractor, I saw it as my professional responsibility to use what I knew about estimating construction to make sure that they got full and complete compensation for what was damaged by the storm.

Once I had figured out what was going on with most of the adjusters' estimates, I knew how to lock in the sale of most of these insurance jobs on the first call. Right up front, I would show the potential customer several original adjusters' estimates from other homes in their neighborhood, and then the revised estimates for the same homes done by me and approved by the insurance companies. I told every customer: "I will go over your estimate with a fine-tooth comb and make sure they've included everything, and I will take the responsibility to get the revised estimate approved by the insurance company. Then we'll do the job for just what they will pay — no more and no less. If that is acceptable to you, we can go forward from here; if it's not, we politely decline to look at the job."

Once I had shown the potential customer a couple of the other original and revised estimates, they would just hand me their insurance folder and say, "Go for it!"

Over the course of more than 30 jobs (and counting), our average customer had the original estimate increased by over 50%. One job went from $7,000 to $27,000, and there were others just like it.

Firing Up the Computer

With such a volume of calls coming in, I could not spend hours of every day on the phone haggling with adjusters. I decided to make my first shot count. I have been using computerized spreadsheets and 3-D CAD to do my estimates for a couple of years, and it was now time to put the crank to it.

The first step was to get the unit-pricing information I had from the first three or four insurance adjusters' worksheets into the computer. As soon as I put together that database for my estimating spreadsheet, I had a good idea what the allowable rates were for about 90% of the work that needs doing on a hail-damaged house. Just by inputting the unit amount of the damaged areas, I could whip out a fully detailed and itemized estimate on any house in half an hour.

After that was set up and running, I developed a standard proposal form that only needed minor modifications from customer to customer. Once the estimate was ready, I could complete and print a

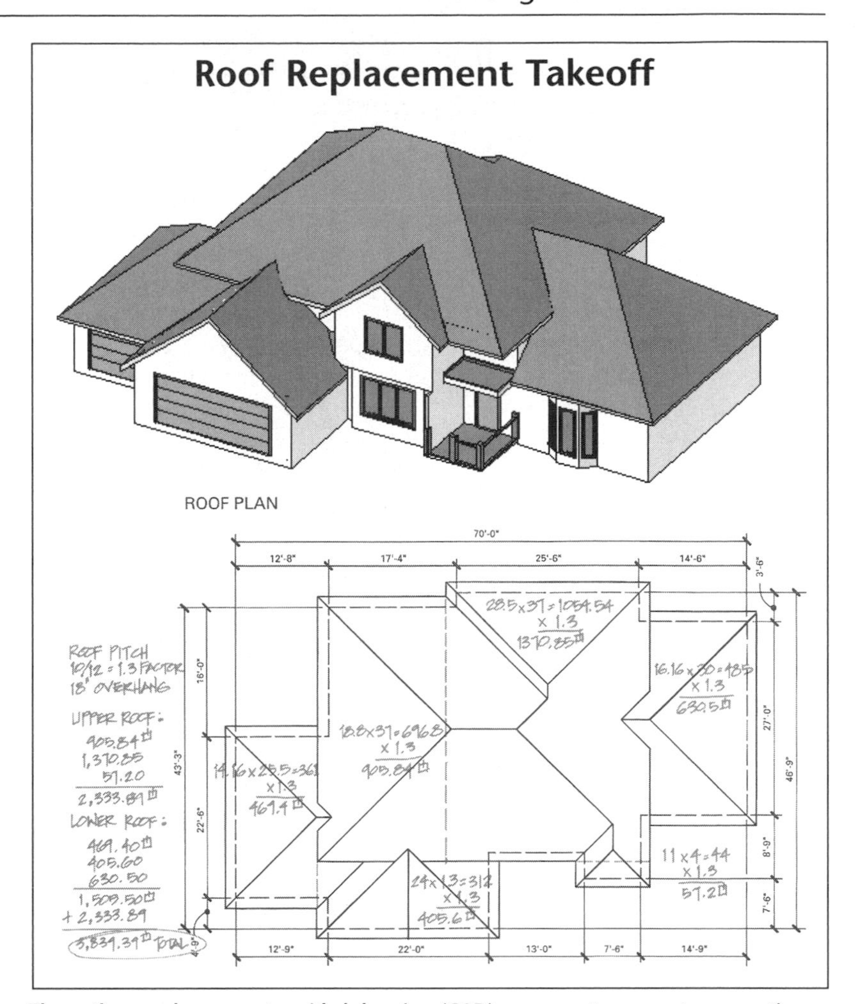

The author used a computer-aided drawing (CAD) program to generate supporting documentation for his careful estimates. First- and second-story roof areas were shown in a plan view, with square-footage calculations noted (above). The author also provided a three-dimensional computer drawing of each house (top).

Takeoff Comparison

Allowed Repair Costs*		Adjuster's Takeoff		Author's Takeoff	
Item	**Allowance**	**Quantity**	**Cost****	**Quantity**	**Cost**
Remove Shingles	$.40/sq. ft.	3,130 sq. ft.	$1,252.00	3,838 sq. ft. [1]	$1,535
Replace Shingles	$1.05/sq. ft.	3,600 sq. ft.	$3,780.00	4,261 sq. ft. [2]	$4,474
Allowance for Hip Roof	$.23/sq. ft.	not noted	-0-	4,261 sq. ft. [3]	$973
Steep-Pitch Allowance	$.15/sq. ft.	3,600	$540.00	4,261 sq. ft.	$639
Second-Story Allowance	$.15/sq. ft.	not noted	-0-	2,334 sq. ft. [3]	$350
Remove/Replace (R&R) Drip-Edge	$.78/linear foot	not noted	-0-	50 linear feet [4]	$39
R&R Power Vents	$100.00 ea.	1 ea.	$100.00	1 ea.	$100
R&R Pod Vents	$27.23 ea.	4 ea.	$108.92	4 ea.	$109
R&R Aluminum Fascia	$2.27/linear foot	42 linear feet	$95.34	42 linear feet	$95
R&R Gutters and Downspouts	$3.42/linear foot	76 linear feet	$259.92	302 linear feet [5]	$1,033
R&R Wall Lights and Fixtures	$83.24 ea.	1 ea.	$83.24	1 ea.	$83
R&R Window Skins	$80.00 ea.	not noted	-0-	11 ea. [6]	$880
R&R 9'x7' Garage Door	$552.42 ea.	1 ea.	$558.01	1 ea.	$552
R&R 9'x16' Garage Door	$760.35 ea.	1 ea.	$760.35	1 ea.	$760
Paint 9'x7' Garage Door	$46.43 ea.	not noted	-0-	1 ea. [7]	$46
Paint 9'x16' Garage Door	$63.04 ea.	not noted	-0-	1 ea. [7]	$63
Paint 9'x7' Garage Door Trim	$25.76 ea.	not noted	-0-	1 ea. [7]	$26
Paint 9'x16' Garage Door Trim	$33.58 ea.	not noted	-0-	1 ea. [7]	$34
Fill and Paint Garage Head Trim	$95.00 ea.	1 ea.	$95.00	1 ea.	$95
MISCELLANEOUS					
Medium Dumpster	$200.00 ea.	not noted	-0-	1 ea. [8]	$200
SUBTOTAL			$8,702.78		$12,087
Contractor's Overhead	10%	not noted	-0-	1 ea. [9]	$1,209
Contractor's Profit	10%	not noted	-0-	1 ea. [9]	$1,209
		Total	$8,702.78	**Total**	$14,505

***from insurance adjuster's estimating guide** ****undepreciated**

[1] The author's estimate of shingle area is higher than the adjuster's because the adjuster did not account for roof overhangs.

[2] The amount of shingles to be replaced is greater than the amount to be removed because the author has applied a waste factor to account for shingle off-cuts. The waste factor used by the author was lower than that applied by the adjuster — the author could have increased his estimate.

[3] The author has applied adjustment factors for material waste on hip roofs and added labor cost for second-story work on a portion of the building. These "adders" are allowed in the insurance company's estimating manual, but were not applied by the adjuster.

[4] Damage to the drip-edge was not evident from the ground, but the author noticed it when he climbed on the roof. Insurance adjusters do not always bother to get on the roof.

[5] Damage to the gutters on the downwind side of the roof could not be seen from the ground because it was caused by hail striking the inside of the gutters from above. Adjuster did not mention this damage, but the author noticed it during his rooftop inspection.

[6] Damage to the metal cladding of windows was only noticeable if you looked closely. The adjuster didn't; the author did.

[7] Adjuster did not include the cost of painting the new garage doors.

[8] Adjuster did not include the cost of a dumpster. "You only get it if you know to ask for it," says the author.

[9] A 10% charge for overhead and a 10% allowance for profit are key to the author's ability to do insurance work at a profit. This cost is allowed whenever a single contractor's work involves three or more different trades, but adjusters' estimates seldom mention it.

proposal in less than 15 minutes.

While at the customer's house on the first call, if we agreed that I would do the work, I would hand-sketch the perimeter floor plan with measurements, noting which areas and items were damaged. Back at the office, I would work the sketch into my 3-D CAD program and generate the perimeter plan of the house. I would print out the affected elevations to exact 1/8-inch scale, and I would do a three-dimensional full overview from the side the storm came in on. On those images I would do the actual calculations for the square and linear footages, noting every item — every vent cover, light fixture, shutter, screen, the whole nine yards. This took one or two hours, depending on the size of the house and how many sides were affected.

Then I would fax all of these documents to the insurance adjuster with a standard cover letter: "Dear So and So, I have examined the such-and-such house at such-and-such a location. There are some differences between my figures and yours. Please review my estimate, and if you disagree, I would be glad to speak with you over the phone or meet with you at this location to double-check these figures. If you agree with my figures, please write 'approved as submitted,' sign and date the proposal, and fax back to me."

Nearly every proposal came back with "approved as submitted." Those that did not were usually settled with a five-minute phone call, and on only two of them did I actually have to go out for a reinspection.

I'm sure my computerized estimates, drawings, and proposals were the key factors in getting the response I got. Doing them by hand would have been much less effective and much more time consuming.

Careful Contracts

Even after the proposal had been approved by the insurance company, the work did not always go according to plan. In one case, my guys called me from a job saying, "Dave, there's two layers of shingles on this roof — we're going to need some additional money to take off the second layer of roofing." I called up the adjuster and told him we needed to revise the estimate.

This time I got an adjuster with whom I hadn't dealt before, and he handed me the line: "Don't you have a signed contract with the customer to remove and replace the entire roof?" — implying that I was locked into a contract, and that he didn't care if there were two layers of roofing there or not. He figured it was my problem now.

Well, I didn't fool around. I said (expletives deleted), "Listen, I have an agreement to remove one layer of roofing and put on 2,200 square feet of shingles — nothing more, nothing less. He said, "How do you think you are going to get off just one layer of shingles?" I said, "I don't know, but I'll tell you this, my customer deserves better treatment than this from his insurance company." Thirty seconds later I had the customer on the phone and told him what the insurance company's position was. Fifteen minutes later I got a call from the regional manager for the insurance company, offering to help us figure out how much extra money we would need.

The key to handling those occasional disagreements was to have a proposal that specified every item to a specific unit. If the estimate showed 1,200 square feet of siding to be removed, the proposal stated "we will remove up to 1,200 square feet of siding." I never made the specification by stating the "entire side" or "all of the damaged area." If additional damage was found or additional work was required, there was never any question about whether it was or was not included.

Making Money

When we first looked at this market, the hardest thing to adjust to was the dollar amounts the insurance companies allowed per specified unit for the repairs. They were well below the unit-price numbers in most standard remodeling estimating manuals or programs.

Take vinyl siding, for instance. Walt Stoeppleworth's *1996 HomeTech Remodeling and Renovation Cost Estimator* gives a figure of $3.08 per square foot for materials and installation of 8-inch double-4 vinyl siding (with a 50% markup included). The insurance companies were only allowing $2.28 per square foot for materials and installation, with 10%

overhead and 10% profit included. Logic and a little quick math would seem to indicate that at $2.28 we would barely break even. Even so, when we calculated the gross profit margin on our first storm job, it was about the same as we make on a typical room addition. Frankly, we're still surprised we did so well.

There are two primary factors that made these jobs as profitable for us as they turned out to be. First of all, we took the jobs as the general contractor. If you cover three of the trades, the insurance company deems you a general contractor and allows you an additional 10% for overhead and an additional 10% for profit. Siding and roofing, for instance, are two different trades; gutters and downspouts are another. Windows are another trade, broken lamps and electrical fixtures are still another, and so on. We needed that 20%, so our standard proposal clearly stated that the only way we'd take the job was if we worked as the general contractor.

The other factor was the economy of scale and repetition. Our efficiency in siding and roofing jumped dramatically when compared with a typical remodeling job, where the unit amounts are typically smaller and set-up and wrap-up times are a much larger percentage of the total labor time. Exterior replacement and repair work is almost like new construction.

For ordinary remodeling work, we take all our hard costs and multiply by 1.55, so we're working with a gross profit margin of about 35% (a little low for our size, but we get by).

We ended the year with 27 storm damage jobs completed at gross profit margins at least as good as our average remodeling job, and we did it at pricing levels that would have scared us to death to even think about as full-line remodeling contractors.

Marketing Magic

While we were learning the ins and outs of insurance repair work, we were developing some very happy customers. We had not only gotten them more than they had expected from their insurance companies, but it was obvious that we were doing good work and we were not cutting any corners. At staff meetings, in the coffee shop, after church, or at parties, when the talk turned to the hailstorm damage, our customers couldn't wait to brag about how well we'd done for them. The next day the phone would start ringing at my office again — another two or three insurance jobs!

In addition, I was amazed by the number of people who turned to me and said, "Well, listen, we've been thinking about a remodeling project for years, and while you're here you might just as well have a look." Over the course of the summer, I picked up a half-dozen kitchen and room addition jobs that way. One storm damage customer who saw me visiting the site asked me about doing a 16x28-foot room addition. I listened to his wish list for the room, looked at the area where he wanted the addition and told him it would probably cost $45,000 plus or minus 10%. He said, "Okay, can you start as soon as you finish the storm damage?" Two days later we signed the contract and I got the deposit.

The Competition

The storm that hit our area in northern Indiana pulled in roofing companies from as far away as Texas and Colorado. A lot of strange companies turned up in town, and horror stories of substandard work with illegal labor were being told everywhere.

One out-of-state roofing company even purchased rights to use the name of a local roofing firm, but the crews were all from out of state. They didn't do bad work, but it wasn't great, either — and they sure won't be around next year if there's a problem.

It was actually quite easy to turn that kind of lowball competition to our advantage. I could tell all my customers that the work would be done by the same local people that always do our work — and that we would be around next year and the year after if there was any problem. The anxiety my clients were feeling about their damaged house was turned into relief and confidence.

By Dave Bowyer, a designer and sales manager for Peacock & Co., a South Bend, Ind., remodeling firm.

No Job Too Small

Rather than turning down small jobs, learn to make them profitable

For most remodelers, small jobs are a nuisance. While everyone defines a small job differently, something simple like replacing drywall after a roof leak, patching around a toilet, or replacing rotten deck joists still means two or three trips to the supplier, half a day wasted while the mud dries or the tile sets, and rounding up a sub or two who are willing to do a few hours worth of work.

Then there's all that overhead for a job that may yield only a few dollars in profit. For most companies, scheduling, billing, and contractual procedures are the same whether the job is worth $100 or $100,000. Yet on a small job, passing along that overhead to the customer may put you out of the bidding competition.

Here are two contractors who have found a way to make small jobs profitable. Their approaches are different in many ways. For instance, one emphasizes the quality of the people he hires to perform small jobs, while the other uses these jobs as a training ground for new employees.

But despite the differences, they have at least three things in common:

- *Each has created a separate division with streamlined scheduling and billing practices designed to cut the overhead on small jobs.*
- *Both add in liberal markups to their small jobs. This means they can't compete with the guy who operates from the back of his pickup. But the companies are providing professional service with guaranteed workmanship and fast delivery. They figure that's worth the extra cost.*
- *And finally, they have both changed their attitudes toward small jobs. No longer are these jobs a bother. Instead they are a productive, profitable part of the business.*

Call The Handyman

By Tom Swartz

About thirteen years ago, we set a new company policy: no more small jobs. A look at our books for 1986 showed that of the 1,500 jobs completed that year, fewer than 300 earned 80% of our profits. The remaining 1,200-plus jobs were small ones, netting less than $2,000 each. But each one passed through the sales, production, and accounting departments, requiring the same kind of paperwork as the $100,000 additions. They were eating us up in overhead.

Often these jobs were even more troublesome than the big jobs. Scheduling was a hassle. It meant pulling our crews from the big projects to attend to the little ones. If we were busy, the small jobs had to wait, often for weeks, resulting in customer complaints. To top it all off, we were spending a fortune to bill all these people for jobs costing as little as $50.

Everyone agreed that the company's policy to turn down small jobs was a good one. Yet despite our intentions, month after month the small jobs kept appearing on our records. Our company has been around for more than 70 years and has built up a strong and loyal client base. We found it impossible to say no when these people asked us to come and hang a storm door, repair a roof leak, or even get a squirrel out of an attic. It was time to change our objective from eliminating the small jobs to finding a way to make them profitable.

Introducing the Handyman Service

With great fanfare, we introduced our Handyman Service in early 1988. We rented four booths at the local home show and parked one of our newly painted handyman vans right in the middle of the space. No one could miss the big, shiny, orange truck. We started getting calls the next day.

Our system for handling the calls is simple. Our receptionist first asks the caller exactly what type of service is needed. In many cases, people respond to our Handyman Service advertising by asking us to do larger jobs like additions or decks. These calls are routed to the sales department.

We define small jobs as those that can be completed by one person in a day or

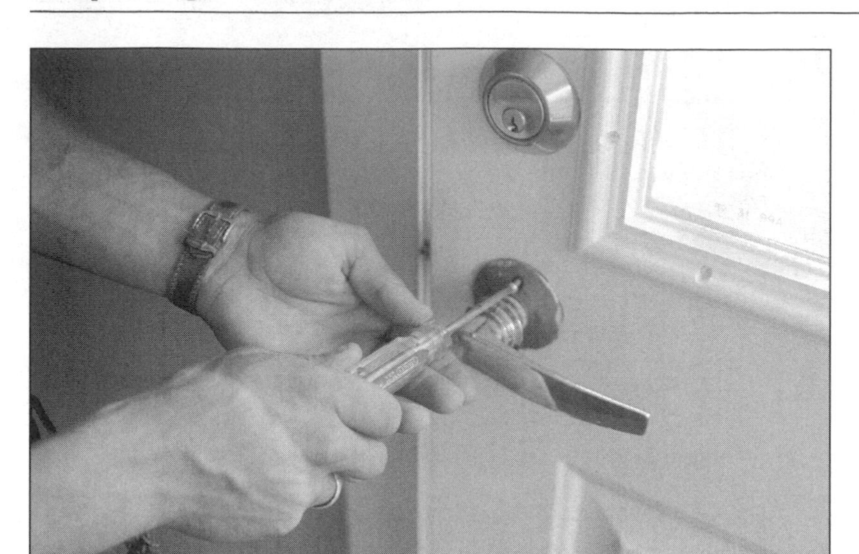

Condo associations provide a steady source of small jobs, such as this lockset replacement.

two. We don't attempt to classify them by dollar volume. (The customer may be asking us to hang a door, but the price of the door could range from $100 to more than $1,000).

If the job is meant for the Handyman Service, the receptionist gets the ball rolling by taking all the information required for scheduling and billing. We've designed a simple, four-part form that we call the handyman ticket. This acts as invoice, work order, receipt of payment, and control copy. If you have ever had a service call on an appliance, you'll recognize the system.

Rough estimates are usually easy to provide since all service jobs are based on time and materials. The receptionist will tell the customer our basic charges, roughly how long the job will take, and what materials might be involved. The handyman will provide a final estimate to the customer before starting the work.

We charge $50, plus materials, for a service call which lasts less than an hour. Calls lasting more than an hour are billed at $32.50 per hour, plus materials. These prices may be considered high by some remodelers in our area. But we've found that most of our customers will pay them because they know we'll get the job done right and on schedule.

We've also developed a price list that includes about 200 standard items, such as cutting off a door, fixing roof leaks, and patching plaster. If the customer is looking for one of these services, the receptionist simply quotes the price from the most recent list.

The customer is then informed that upon completion of the job, the handyman will accept Master Card, Visa, a check, or cash. Thus the administrative expenses of billing and collecting are eliminated. We've found that 90% of our handyman jobs are collected before leaving the job site. The additional 10% are usually commercial jobs where payment policies vary.

Scheduling

After the receptionist takes the information, the form is given to our production supervisor, who passes it on to one of our four handymen. The handyman is then responsible for calling the customer and setting up a time to take a look at the job and provide a final estimate. Our goal is to get back to the customer and have the job completed within a week of the initial call. In some cases, a roof leak for instance, we try to get there within a day or two.

It is up to our handymen to give the final estimate, do the work, turn over the invoice, and collect the money. The handymen are educated about our pricing policies, including markups and overhead. They recognize that a minimum gross margin of 50% (achieved by marking up materials and labor by 100%) is necessary to cover the costs of the Handyman Service. They keep all they need to provide an estimate in the truck, including a copy of our price list, a schedule of basic material costs, and job contracts.

Once the handyman has taken a look at the job, he goes back to the truck, figures the price, and writes up a contract that's presented immediately. The customer must sign it and put down 50% on the spot. The handyman then schedules the job. We've found that we close on about 80% of the jobs we estimate this way.

The handyman gives the office the control copy of the handyman ticket so that we can track the jobs. Within 30 days of completion, the handyman receives a commission on each job that achieves the targeted gross margin. This has proven to be a good incentive to

J.J. SWARTZ CO.
GENERAL CONTRACTORS
2120 N. OAKLAND AVE
DECATUR, ILL.
62526
TELEPHONE
877-2611
AREA CODE 217
HOME BUILDING & REMODELING

INVOICE

Name: Joseph Green Date: 3/30/99

Address: 11 Walnut St.
Anytown, UT 11111

Phone #: 222-3333 Job #: H/123

Work #: 222-4444

Work to be completed:
Replace existing rear storm door with wood combo (style #1). Salvage and reinstall latch and closer. Add new weatherstrip. (Owner will paint.)

Amount due for above work $285.00

Additional Work Completed:
DOOR CLOSER MISSING PARTS — INSTALLED NEW ONE.

Special Instructions:

Labor: Hrs. Rate

Material: 1 EA. DOOR CLOSER $12.75

TOTAL DUE $297.75

METHOD OF PAYMENT:
X Check ___ Master Card ___ Visa

Acct. # ___ Expiration Date ___

Authorized Signature ___

To hold down small-job overhead, this simple, four-part form serves as an invoice, work order, receipt, and control form.

schedule more effectively and charge customers correctly.

Profile of a Handyman

Our handymen are different from the typical carpenter. For one thing, all of them have a lot of experience. Two of the four have had their own companies so they know how the business works. They also know how to sell our company and our services. Most importantly, they know how to deal with people. Not everyone can cope with customers peering over their shoulders while they work.

The handymen are probably more independent than other members of our field crew. They have to be good at setting their own schedules and working alone. Now and then, if the handyman end of the business is slow, they'll work with the other field staff on bigger jobs. But for the most part, the handymen are in and out of the office only long enough to pick up their work orders.

Making the Division Work

The Handyman Service has been part of our company for three years now. We still do as many small jobs as we used to, but every year we've gotten a little smarter, and these jobs are now earning higher profits. In 1990 we did about 2,000 jobs, generating $3 million in sales companywide. The Handyman Service earned about $600,000 of this.

There are other benefits from providing this kind of service. Our customers are happy. They know they can turn to us for any type of job, from building a crate to shipping a giant cactus across the country (yes, it's true), to redesigning the entire downstairs of their home. At the same time, our Handyman Service has generated lots of referrals for bigger jobs.

By Tom Swartz, president of J.J. Swartz Company, a 77-year-old remodeling firm with offices in Decatur and Bloomington, Ill.

A Niche for Small Jobs

By Jim Walter

Like many remodeling firms, we got our start doing small jobs. And we quickly learned that you don't prosper on small jobs alone. Gradually, as our business grew, we turned our attention to larger, more profitable jobs like room additions and whole house remodeling. These now make up about 80% of our annual sales. But after 12 years in business, the small jobs still play an important role in our company.

In 1990 we did about 500 jobs, generating about $750,000 in sales. Of these, 480 were small jobs, grossing about $150,000. We have a full-time staff of 14 with two part-time employees. All of us, from the most experienced to the new hires, do small jobs now and then.

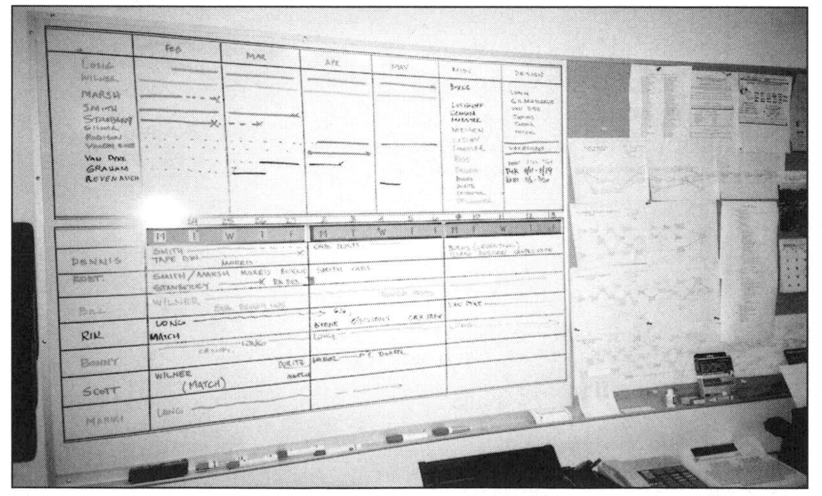

The author completed 480 small jobs last year and 20 large ones. All are tracked in bins and on the erasable schedule board shown above. The goal is to complete small jobs within a week of the initial call.

Small Jobs, Big Perks

While many remodeling firms consider small jobs more work than they're worth, we've found that they offer several advantages. First, none of our crew needs to worry about getting laid off: There's always plenty of small jobs to provide us with a steady source of work. These jobs provide constant income that gets us through the slow times.

Also, we like the scheduling flexibility that small jobs give us. A two-day job fits neatly into the schedule when, for example, you're waiting for the electrician to finish the rough-in on an addition. At the same time, that flexibility lets us use the whole crew if we need to get a roof torn off and a second-story addition roughed in. Nothing pleases a customer more than the sight of a big crew working together to get a job done quickly.

Small jobs are also a good source of referrals. We usually pick up at least two referrals on every job we do (we ask for them). Many of these may not pan out, but those that do help us to expand our customer base.

Finally, small jobs are a service to our customers. They appreciate the fact that we show up on schedule and do a good job. And we give them a price up front and stick to it. That creates goodwill, which means more jobs down the line.

Managing the Small Jobs

Most of our small jobs come from two sources: condominium associations, and a local home center for which we do product installations. In the case of the associations, we're familiar with the projects, usually small repairs and maintenance, and we know right away what the job will entail. And since the home center reimburses us a fixed amount for each installation, all we have to do is schedule the work. This enables our production manager, Tom Walter, to estimate and schedule most of our small jobs right over the phone, thus cutting out overhead costs and increasing profit.

About 15% of our small jobs come from past customers or other sources. In these cases, the work is more of a service. We typically spend more time on these jobs since we take a look at the work before providing an estimate.

We've created a separate division that we call the Service Department to handle small jobs. Our goal in that department is to strip away as much overhead as possible. We define small jobs as anything under $10,000, but the majority fall in the under-$1,000 range. These jobs, as a rule, don't require subs and rarely need more than one or two workers to complete them. Except for the jobs assigned by the home center, all our estimating is based on time and materials.

We charge a higher markup on small jobs than on bigger jobs since costs on small jobs can be disproportionate to profits, especially if things don't go smoothly. You can easily eat up the profits on something like hanging a storm door if you accidentally get the wrong size door.

Our fee is $30 per hour with a one-hour minimum per job. Labor is marked up 100% and materials by 20%, yielding an average profit margin of about 40% per job. On almost all small jobs, labor is the larger share of the cost.

We have a unit-pricing system which we update constantly. This gives us standard prices on things like reroofing (usually $75 per square, depending on pitch), siding replacement, ceramic tile installation, and drywall. We track our job costing and do all our billing on a computer.

We use a simple, standard work order that Tom fills out while talking on the phone to the customer. If Tom needs to see the job to give an estimate (if it's not on our unit price list, for instance), he drives to the site, meets with the customer, and mails out or delivers an estimate the next day. He typically collects a deposit of 20%.

Scheduling

We try to get to all the small jobs as quickly as possible, usually within a week of the initial call. In fact, it's one of our biggest selling points and something we're known for in this community. But scheduling can be tricky, especially when the weather isn't cooperating or one of the jobs takes longer than expected.

Once again, Tom is in the hot seat. He keeps an erasable board in his office with the names of all our employees and a roughed-in monthly schedule. When one of our crew members is between jobs or waiting for subs to get his work done, Tom greets him in the morning with a pile of small-job work orders. Tom has already made the appointments, so our person just has to show up and do the work.

It's a system that works well most of the time. But when there are problems, Tom will call the clients and reschedule. Then he'll contact our crew members and make some quick reassignments, often giving out work order information over the phone.

Who Does the Work

The best way we've found to train new employees is in the Service Department. They gain all kinds of technical experience in a wide variety of trades, and they get used to dealing with customers. It's also a quick and easy way to see where their abilities and weaknesses lie. Because the jobs are small, feedback from the customer is immediate.

Small jobs give our crew members a chance to do something different, to take a break from their everyday work. We don't provide bonuses on these jobs, since we've never come up with a fair method for quantifying them. But for the most part, our employees enjoy the change of pace and the responsibility of seeing a job through from start to finish.

By Jim Walter, co-owner of Lakeview Lumber & Construction, Inc., in Lake Barrington, Ill., a full-service remodeling company that specializes in second-story additions and other small-repair and light-commercial jobs.

Authors' Contributions

Sal Alfano is a former builder from East Calais, Vt., and the editor of *The Journal of Light Construction.*

Norman Allaby is the owner of Coppermine Construction in Bethel, Conn.

Toby Anderson is a retired lawyer, turned writer, from Montrose, Pa.

Carolyn Annis works with Proof Management Consultants of Richmond, Va.

Patricia A. Ayars is an attorney with Perlstein & Ayars of Glastonbury, Conn.

Denise David Baer is co-owner of Restore-N-More, a remodeling and restoration company in Lancaster, Pa.

Paul Barbahen is a partner in the law firm of O'Brien and Barbahen, in Chicago, Ill., which specializes in construction law.

David E. Bennett is a partner in the firm of Rhodes, Coats, and Bennett in Raleigh, N.C., and is registered to practice before the United States Patent and Trademark Office.

Rob Boram is owner of Rob Boram Construction, a remodeling company in Wellsburg, W.Va.

Dave Bowyer is a designer and sales manager for Peacock & Co., a South Bend, Ind., remodeling firm.

Terry Brocious is the former operations director of Big River Construction, Inc., in Baton Rouge, La.

Larry Bussey is a remodeling contractor whose company, The Larry Bussey Group, focuses on the purchase and renovation of older properties.

Reina A. Calderon is vice-president of and general counsel at Calderon Energy Company of Bowling Green, Inc., located in Bowling Green, Ohio.

John Cargill, IV, is owner of Cargill Design/ Remodel in Columbus, Ga.

Linda Case is president of Remodelers Advantage, Inc., in Silver Spring, Md.

Michael Chapman is president of Michael Chapman Homes in Santa Fe, N.M.

Lynn Comeskey is a remodeling contractor whose firm, Mac & Lou Construction, is based in Palo Alto, Calif.

Richard Cooley is a general contractor in Schenectady, N.Y.

Robert Criner is president of Criner Construction Company, Inc., of Yorktown, Va.

Ted Cushman is a carpenter and photojournalist who lives and works in South Bend, Ind.

Michael Davis is the owner of Framing Square Construction in Albuquerque, N.M.

Clayton DeKorne is a former builder and former editor at *The Journal of Light Construction.*

Matthew DeTroy is president and director of Bolken Builders, a design/build team in Fairfield County, Conn.

Paul Eldrenkamp is president of Byggmeister Associates, Inc., in Newton, Mass.

Tim and *Linda Englert* own and operate Tim Englert Construction in Wadsworth, Ohio.

Timothy Faller is a production manager at Hopkins & Porter Construction, in Potomac, Md.

Peter Feinmann is owner of Feinmann Remodeling, an Arlington, Mass., design/build company specializing in kitchens and baths.

Howard Ferree is the co-owner of Halco Construction, Inc., in Greenville, N.C.

Bill Gaver, with his wife Nancy, runs Defern Contracting, a design/build company in Brookfield, N.H.

Jeffrey G. Gilmore is a lawyer with the firm of Wickwire, Gavin & Gibbs, specializing in construction and public-contract law.

Calvin Goldsmith is a former contractor and present business manager of Tornesello Construction Company in Bedford, Mass.

Carl Hagstrom is a design/builder in Montrose, Pa., and a contributing editor at *The Journal of Light Construction.*

Bob Hanbury is a partner in House of Hanbury, a remodeling firm in Newington, Conn.

Devon Hartman is a partner in Hartman-Baldwin, a design/build firm in Claremont, Calif.

Larry Hayden is president of Federal Building Company, a design/build firm in Oakland, Calif., and the co-owner of Damage Control Mediation Service, which resolves construction disputes.

Peter Hood is owner of The Noyle Johnson Insurance Agency, with four offices in the central Vermont area.

Doug Immel is owner of Douglas Blake Immel Inc., a design/build, construction management, and energy-consultation company located in Woonsocket, R.I.

Martin King is president of Martin Churchill Associates, Inc. in Arlington, Va.

Henry Krasnow is a partner with Butler, Rubin, Saltarelli, Boyd & Krasnow of Chicago, Ill., specializing in business law problems.

Debbie Land is the office manager for Tim Englert Construction in Wadsworth, Ohio.

Georgia Toney Lesley is a professional building designer based in Summerville, S.C., and the national copyright committee chairperson for the American Institute of Building Design.

Richard Lind is a builder in the Wellesley, Mass., area, and a longtime member of the Builders Association of Greater Boston.

Michael C. Loulakis is a lawyer with the firm of Wickwire, Gavin & Gibbs, specializing in construction and public-contract law.

Len McAdams is the owner of The McAdams Company, a design/build remodeling firm based in Kirkland, Wash.

Lorie McCollum-Lombard works in the real-estate research department at Fleet Bank, N.A., in Hartford, Conn.

Judith Miller is a construction consultant in Oakland, Calif., who counsels builders on accounting, financial management, computerization, and office procedures.

Chuck Moriarty is a former chairman of NAHB's Remodelors Council, and president of Moriarty & Matzen, a Seattle-based general contracting firm.

Judson Motsenbocker is owner of Jud Construction in Muncie, Ind., and a frequent speaker on business management for remodelers.

Cheryl Norris operates Order Out of Chaos, a Washington, D.C., consulting business specializing in office organization.

Thomas O'Brien is a partner in the law firm of O'Brien and Barbahen, in Chicago, Ill., which specializes in construction law.

Jack Philbin is the owner of Philbin Construction and Remodeling and Philbin Home Improvement Specialties, located in Orland Park, Ill.

Art Prindle is a contractor based in East Palo Alto, Calif.

Gary Ransone is a general contractor and a practicing attorney specializing in construction law near Santa Cruz, Calif.

Ross Robbins is vice-president of Bainbridge, Inc., of Englewood, Colo., which builds about 30 new homes a year.

Perry Safran is a North Carolina construction attorney associated with Proof Management Consultants of Richmond, Va.

John Schleimer is president of Market Directions, Inc., a Sacramento, Calif., firm specializing in market research, product development, and master marketing programs.

Herb Schwartz is an attorney and the co-owner of Damage Control Mediation Service in Oakland, Calif., specializing in construction disputes.

Scot Simpson is the owner of SS Framing in Edmonds, Wash.

Joseph Stoddard is a Certified Professional Building Designer, a former home builder from Elkand, Pa., and an assistant editor at *The Journal of Light Construction.*

Walter W. Stoeppelwerth is a founder of HomeTech, Inc., a remodeling and home-inspection consulting firm in Bethesda, Md.

Quenda Behler Story is a partner with her husband in a remodeling company in Okemos, Mich., a member of the National Association of Women in Construction, and has practiced and taught law for 23 years.

Tom Swartz is president of J.J. Swartz Company, in Decatur and Bloomington, Ill.

John Sylvestre is owner of Sylvestre Construction, a design/build firm based in Minneapolis, Minn.

Jim Walter is co-owner of Lakeview Lumber & Construction, Inc., in Lake Barrington, Ill., a full-service remodeling company that specializes in second-story additions and other small-repair and light-commercial jobs.

M.M. (Mike) Weiss, Jr., is president of Weiss & Co., Inc., a design/build remodeling firm in Carmel, Ind., and national chairman of the NAHB's Certified Graduate Remodelers Board of Governers.

Kathy and *Gary Wheatley* are the owners of Wheatley Associates, a Monkton, Md., remodeling firm specializing in additions and light commercial alterations.

Index

E

T

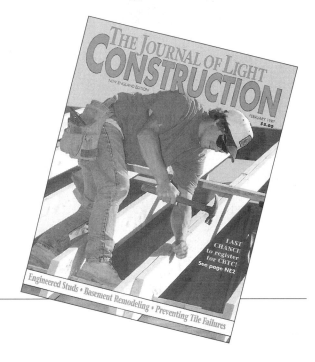

The Lead Carpenter Handbook

This powerful management system will let you grow your company and your profits without sacrificing quality or personalized service to your customers. Based on his extensive field experience, author Tim Faller tells you everything you need to know to recruit and train lead carpenters to take full responsibility for job-site management, and to implement this system in your remodeling or custom building company. *The Lead Carpenter Handbook* includes detailed case studies, numerous real-life examples, and field-tested forms and checklists you can copy and use.

196 pages, 7x10, softcover

#TLF98: $29.95

The Lead Carpenter Training Audiobook

Based on Tim Faller's best-selling *Lead Carpenter Handbook* and popular training workshop, this set of four 90-minute audiotapes gives you everything you need to know about implementing the Lead Carpenter System in your company.

Managers will learn how to hire and train lead carpenters, what responsibilities to give them, and how to troubleshoot problems that arise. Lead carpenters will learn strategies for scheduling, cost control, people management, and managing job-site paperwork.

Also included is a 24-page workbook with all the charts, outlines and forms needed to successfully implement the LCS in your company.

THE LEAD CARPENTER TRAINING AUDIOBOOK
BY TIMOTHY FALLER
FOUR 90-MINUTE AUDIO CASSETTES, PLUS A 24-PAGE HANDBOOK!
LISTEN AND LEARN TO A LIVE PRESENTATION!
LEARN AS YOU GO...
A Journal of Light Construction Audiobook

Four 90 minute audiocassettes with 24 page workbook

#TLA99: $79.95

Lead Carpenter Handbook *and* Audiobook Set

#TLC99: $99.95

(800) 859-3669 • www.jlconline.com/bookstore

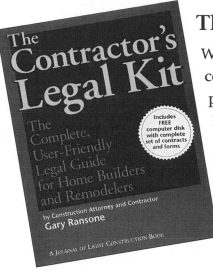